An African American in South Africa

Ralph J. Bunche

An
African
American
in
South
Africa

OHIO UNIVERSITY PRESS ▬▬ ATHENS

ШJ? WITWATERSRAND UNIVERSITY PRESS ▬▬ JOHANNESBURG

THE TRAVEL NOTES OF

Ralph J. Bunche

28 September 1937–1 January 1938

Edited by

Robert R. Edgar

98 97 96 95 94 93 92   7 6 5 4 3 2 1

Ohio University Press books are printed on acid free paper ∞

Library of Congress Cataloging-in-Publication Data

Bunche, Ralph J. (Ralph Johnson), 1904–1971.
    An African American in South Africa : the travel notes of Ralph J.
Bunche, 28 September 1937–1 January 1938 / edited by Robert R.
Edgar.
        p.   cm.
    Includes bibliographical references and index.
    ISBN 0–8214–1021–0
    1. Blacks—South Africa—Social life and customs.   2. Blacks—
South Africa—Social conditions.   3. Bunche, Ralph J. (Ralph
Johnson), 1904–1971—Journeys—South Africa.   I. Edgar, Robert R.
II.   Title.
DT1058.B53B86   1992
916.804′54—dc20   92–6621
                                                                                CIP

Published in the Republic of South Africa
by Witwatersrand University Press,
1 Jan Smuts Avenue, Johannesburg 2001, South Africa
ISBN 1–86814–217–5

To an African in America

Leteane Monatsi

Contents

Johannesburg I

159

Pretoria

229

Johannesburg II

243

Bloemfontein

256

Durban

287

ILLUSTRATIONS

Photographs

Durban

Maps

Preface and Acknowledgements

Ralph J. Bunche was embedded in my subconscious long before I began work on this editing project. In the early 1970s, I spent many hours as a graduate student at the University of California at Los Angeles contemplating his bust at Bunche Hall; then, as a teacher at Howard University, I learned about his contributions to the Political Science Department and his activist politics. But it was not until the 1980s that I began looking more deeply into Bunche's life as a result of coming across his South African research notes.

Even then, I would never have followed through on this project without the backing and assistance of a number of friends and colleagues. At a very early stage, when I had doubts about the merits of editing the Bunche notes, I received encouragement from Belinda Bozzoli, Charles van Onselen, Colin Bundy, and Phil Bonner.

Then, as I began researching Bunche's notes, I had to devote considerable time to annotating the hundreds of major and minor details that are mentioned in them. This meant drawing on resources from libraries and archives in South Africa, the United States, and Great Britain as well as calling on numerous contacts, who have tracked down obscure bits of information. I have been taken off on all sorts of detours, but it has been a rewarding experience and I have had engaging exchanges with dozens of correspondents. Individuals who helped me include: Ray Alexander, David Anthony, Chris Ballantine, Charles Ballard, Hilda Bernstein, Phil Bonner, S. Bourquin, Helen Bradford, Luli Callinicos, Jim Campbell, W. Carr, John Comaroff, David Coplan, Anna Cunningham, Elizabeth Eldredge, Bill Freund, Gail Gerhart, Jane Gool, Michael Green, Albert Grundlingh, Louis Grundlingh, Catherine Higgs, Phella Hirschson, Isabel Hofmeyr, Shamil Jeppie, Tom Karis, Hilda Kuper, Paul La Hausse, Shula Marks, Don M'timkulu, Andrew Manson, Fatima Meer, Connie Minchin, Peter Molotsi, Colin Murray, Bill Nasson, Andre Odendaal, Vishnu Padayachee, Howard Phillips, Robert Shell, Jack Simons, and Maureen Swan. David Ambrose, Baruch Hirson, Edgar Maurice, and Christopher Saunders have been especially helpful in answering repeated inquiries along the way.

I thank the staffs of the following institutions, who supplied me with information from their collections: Church of the Province of South Africa archive at Witwatersrand University; the Johannesburg Public Library; the State Library, Pretoria; the South African Library, Cape Town; the Cape Argus Library, Cape Town; the Killie Campbell Library, Durban; the Cory Library, Grahamstown; the Moorland-Spingarn Library, Howard University; and the Library of Congress, Washington, D.C.

The following persons and libraries have also assisted with photographs from their collections: Moorland-Spingarn Research Library, Howard University (1, 2); Cape Town Library, Cape Town, South Africa (5, 8–12, 16, 21, 31–32, 34–35, 44, 51–52, 54–56); Jack and Ray Simons (7); Jane Gool (53); Ralph Bunche Papers, University of California at Los Angeles Manuscripts Collection (3, 4, 6, 13, 15, 17–20, 22–30, 33, 36–43, 45–50, 57–62). I thank the University of California at Los Angeles for waiving their fee for reproducing Bunche's personal photographs.[1]

I had the good fortune of interviewing or corresponding with individuals who met Bunche on his 1937 trip: Jack Simons, Ray Alexander, Isaac Schapera, Edwin Mofutsanyana, and Don M'timkulu. Sometimes, their meetings with Bunche were fleeting, but they all added interesting bits of information.

An important find for my research were several personal diaries that Bunche kept from late 1936 through 1938. The 1937 diary contained important information on Bunche's preparation for his trip in London as well as notes on his daily schedule in South Africa. The diaries were held in Bunche's home and did not become available until after the death of his widow, Ruth, in 1988. I would like to thank Bunche's daughter Joan, who graciously allowed me to use the diaries, as well as Ben Rivlin of the Ralph Bunche Institute in New York, who arranged for me to look at them.

I am indebted to a group of friends and colleagues who have pored over my introduction and annotations and offered numerous suggestions and corrections. These are David Anthony, David Dean, John Hope Franklin, George Fredrickson, Baruch Hirson, David Hoffman, Helen Hopps, Clifford Muse, Nell Painter, Ben Rivlin, and Christopher Saunders. Although I am tempted to introduce collective guilt to scholarly ventures, I have to take full responsibility for any errors that have made their way into this manuscript.

Throughout this venture, I have enjoyed the full support of Howard University's African Studies Department, the Graduate School of Arts and Sciences, and Office of the Vice President for Academic Affairs. They were generous with several grants for typing and travel. Joanne Jackson was helpful in typing up Bunche's research notes. I would also like to thank Bob Furnish for his meticulous copy-editing.

Finally, and for no particular reason, I would like to mention the following people: Edward Fobo, who likes to see his name in print; Leteane, who always starts my day with a smile; and an anonymous colleague who warned me that I would be drummed out of the profession if I titled this book *An American in Parys*.

1. Bunche's photographs were taken with a camera borrowed from Essie Robeson. Bunche's collection at UCLA also includes four twenty-minute reels of film taken on the trip. They focus largely on East Africa and are titled "Random Glimpses of Native Life in South and East Africa," "Male and Female Circumcision Rites among the Kikuyu of Kenya," and "Safari Views." The fourth, on East Africa and Southeast Africa, is untitled. For an examination of Bunche's films, see George Potamianos, "Visions of a Dying Africa: Ralph J. Bunche and His Second African Journey, 1936–1938," (unpublished seminar paper, University of Southern California, 1989).

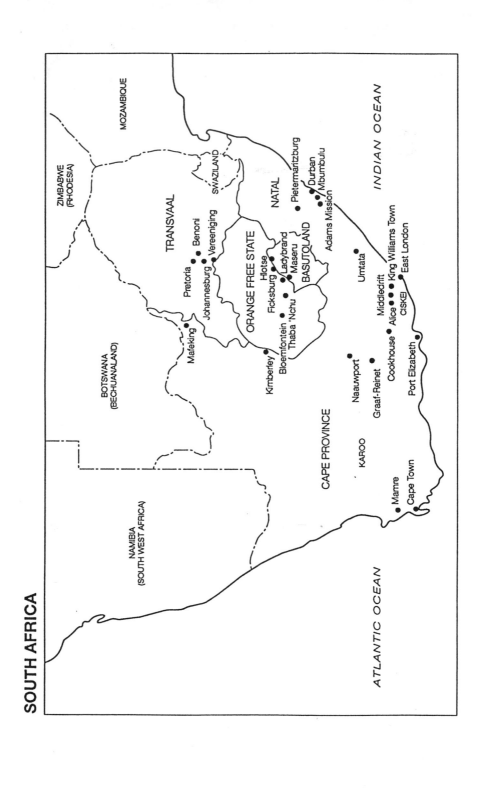

SOUTH AFRICA

South Africa is an entire [emphasis in original] *country ridden by race prejudice—unlike U.S. in that there is absolutely no escape at all for black and colored people. (Ralph Bunche Research Notes, 9 December 1937.)*

Prologue

I

Some years ago, while reading Brian Bunting's biography of Moses Kotane, I came across a passing mention of Ralph J. Bunche attending the Silver Anniversary meeting of the African National Congress in Bloemfontein in December 1937.[1] I was immediately curious why Bunche, who won the Nobel Peace Prize in 1950 for his role as a United Nations mediator in the Middle East, had visited South Africa in the first place. Biographical studies I consulted lightly touch on his travels in 1937.[2] Only after further digging did I learn that Bunche, a professor of political science at Howard University in the 1930s, had stopped off in South Africa for three months during a two-year, round-the-world research odyssey funded by the Social Science Research Council. The purpose of his journey was not research per se but instead to hone his fieldwork skills by studying the methodology used by anthropologists to study culture contact between Western and non-Western societies.

I then turned to Bunche's private papers at the University of California, Los Angeles, to learn more about his South Africa trip. I found several file boxes jammed with 5″ x 8″ typed file cards containing Bunche's copious field notes on South Africa. He had planned to use the notes for a book on South Africa that he could not pursue past this initial

1

period of research. I have edited the note cards into the present collection of travel notes.

Bunche's notes are invaluable for several reasons. They provide one of the few "outsider" accounts of South Africa by a black person; they are also a rich repository of information on black life in South Africa in that period. Bunche did not arrive bearing an intimate knowledge of South Africa. Yet he drew on his experiences and instincts as a radical political activist and a seasoned researcher and capitalized on, as he put it, "his Negro ancestry," to gain access to people and places few others could or would seek out. Because his grant did not require him to formulate a precise research agenda, he was free to report on whatever caught his eye. So he journeyed throughout South Africa randomly recording his observations, impressions, and reflections on an assortment of issues: race relations; black living conditions in the reserves, mines, and townships; African political and labor leaders and organizations; education; health and mental care; journalism; sports and culture; social life; business; religion; and the legal system.

He cast a selective gaze on his subjects. He was interested in the impact of segregation on black life, so he concentrated most of his attention on the Indian, Coloured (people of mixed-race ancestry), and African communities; whites played an interesting, but secondary, role. Furthermore, his perceptions of South Africa were selectively filtered through the views of a small group of interlocutors—white liberals and radicals and his racial counterparts, educated professionals in the small black middle class. But even with these limitations, his snapshots, when pieced together, create a vivid montage of life in segregated South Africa.

Bunche is probably the best-known African American to have visited and recorded his or her experiences in South Africa, but he was certainly not the first. Since the late eighteenth century, hundreds of African Americans had made their way to South Africa under different guises. The earliest visitors were sailors who crewed American ships docking in Cape Town. Some of these sailors (along with West Indians) later settled permanently in port cities such as Durban, Port Elizabeth, and Cape Town. Still others moved into the interior, setting up small businesses or seeking work and adventure on the diamond and gold fields. A notable case was Yankee Wood, a ship steward, who turned up in Port Elizabeth during the American Civil War. After building his nest egg in the diamond fields, he opened up hotels in Kokstad and Johannesburg, where he also staked out a few gold claims.[3]

African Americans also made notable contributions to South African music. Between 1890 and 1898, Orpheus McAdoo's Jubilee Singers spent five years touring South Africa. Their singing, music, and entertainment—spirituals, folk songs, and minstrel presentations—left an indelible impression on African choirs, performance clubs, and music styles. American jazz, dance and recording styles later made their way to South Africa and laid the basis for a distinctive urban music tradition among Africans.[4]

The most influential group of African Americans to arrive were missionaries. The National Baptist Convention first founded a mission station in 1894 in Cape Town. Following them came the African Methodist Episcopal (AME) Church and the Church of God and Saints of Christ.[5] Motivated by a desire to uplift and redeem Africa, they attracted many adherents into their folds. They influenced black education through their schools and religious philosophies. Booker T. Washington's self-help and industrial education ideas also had a major influence on black (and white) educational circles and were implemented in schools such as John Dube's Ohlange Institute at Inanda and the AME Wilberforce Institute in Evaton.[6]

It was in the terrain of ideas and images that African Americans had an effect on black South Africans that far outweighed their numbers. African Americans were a potent political symbol for black South Africans, who applied the African-American experiences of struggle to their own predicament.[7] Leaders such as Booker T. Washington and W. E. B. DuBois had followings in educated circles. But the figure who most captured the imagination of a popular audience was Marcus Garvey with his message of race pride, unity, and self-determination for Africa. His Universal Negro Improvement Association set up branches in South Africa after the First World War. On occasion the Garvey message took on a life of its own as local politicians transmuted it to serve local needs. In one Garvey offshoot in the Transkei in the 1920s, Wellington Butelezi tapped into a wellspring of millennial fervor and recast the African American into a liberator who was coming to free South Africa from white oppression. The image of an African American savior lingered on after Butelezi eclipse, and Bunche picked up its reverberations as he moved through South Africa.

Black visitors usually communicated their observations and viewpoints of South Africa through private correspondence, journal and magazine articles, and letters to black newspapers in the United States. Only a handful left accounts in book form. Perhaps the most colorful tale, *The Pedro Gorino* (1929), is by a sea captain, Harry Dean, whose dream to found an "Ethiopian Empire" inspired his exploits during the

South African War. Not surprisingly most accounts are by AME missionaries and teachers. These include Levi Coppin's *Letters From South Africa* (n.d.), *Observations of Persons and Things in South Africa 1900–1904* (n.d.), and *Unwritten History* (n.d.); Fanny Jackson Coppin's *Hints on Teaching: Reminiscences of School Life* (1913); Charlotte Crogman Wright's *Beneath the Southern Cross: The Story of an American Bishop's Wife in South Africa;* and A. J. and Luella White's *Southern Africa: Dawn in Bantuland* (1953). Because they were aimed at educating and winning over supporters for mission activities, missionary accounts have an evangelical flavor. But they also contain useful anecdotes about South Africa and offer valuable insights into missionary attitudes and perceptions.

The reminiscence most similar to Bunche's notes is Eslanda Robeson's *African Journey* (1945), which chronicled her impressions of a three-week South African stopover in mid-1936.[8] Her itinerary covered much of the same ground as Bunche's. At the time of her trip she was an anthropology student at the London School of Economics on her way to carry out fieldwork in Uganda. By the time she finally published her account almost a decade later, she was a leading participant in the Council on African Affairs, a left-of-center black activist group. From this perspective, she wove an explicit political message into her travel narrative.

Bunche's research notes are also of interest because they provide us with a glimpse into the inner mind of one of the twentieth century's leading black personalities. There is, of course, a wealth of documentation on his highly publicized official life. Yet deciphering his inner thoughts is not an easy task, partly due to the nature of the paper trail he left behind. Nathan Huggins, at work on a study of Bunche until his death in December 1989, concluded after thoroughly examining the massive collection of Bunche's private papers, that from the time Bunche entered government service during the Second World War, he wore an official mask that is difficult to penetrate. "There is little in [his] papers one could consider private or personal in character. Seldom does Bunche commit to paper true confidences or judgments which might reveal something beneath the public self. Bunche seems consistently aware of a public self and an office which demands discretion."[9]

At one level, Bunche's research notes, written before he went into public service, are an exception to this rule. Because he did not write them with an audience in mind, his comments are unguarded and candid. He allows various aspects of his personality—his wry sense of humor, his intolerance of pomposity and pretense, and his irreverent views on authority and leadership—to shine through. At another level, however, one should not read too much into his notes. Although he injected his personal reactions to people and events, he did not keep his notes for introspective, cathartic, or moralizing purposes. While his inner feelings about South Africa do spill into his notes on occasion, generally his comments on race, discrimination, and segregation are restrained and dispassionate. Quite simply, this may be an honest reflection of Bunche's personality. By all accounts he was a person who prided himself on his ability to maintain a calm demeanor in difficult circumstances. But it is also a measure of how he defined his role in South Africa: a disciplined social scientist recording what he was observing as accurately as possible. His intent was not so much "writing race" as writing about it.

II

The details of Bunche's celebrated life are well known. However, a brief account of his academic and political career will provide a useful context to help understand the background of his visit to South Africa. Born in Detroit in 1904, Bunche spent his teenage years in the home of his maternal grandmother in Los Angeles. An exceptional student, he won an academic scholarship to the University of California at Los Angeles, where he graduated summa cum laude in 1927. He continued his education at Harvard University, where in 1928 he earned an M.A. in political science and government. He interrupted his graduate studies to accept an offer from Howard University's first black president, Mordecai Johnson, to establish the university's Political Science Department. However, his ambition was to begin his Ph.D. studies at Harvard, so in 1932 he accepted a Rosenwald Fellowship.

Bunche's move into African studies was in fact prompted more by his sponsor's prejudice than by personal interest. He planned to focus his doctoral dissertation on mixed-race people in Brazil and contrast their experience with that of American blacks. Bunche believed that the head of the Rosenwald Fund, Edwin Embree, had deliberately blocked his proposal because he "thought that U.S. Negroes might get 'dangerous' ideas in Brazil."[10] Instead, Embree steered Bunche into studying Africa, where he concentrated his research on a comparison of the impact of French colonial administration on Africans in Togoland, a French-administered territory under the League of Nations mandate, with its impact in Dahomey, a French colony.[11] He spent seven months in archival research in England, France, and Switzerland and three months in

West Africa and submitted his dissertation on "French Administration in Togoland and Dahomey" in 1934. He was the first African American to earn a doctorate in political science.

By then, he had returned to Howard University. He undertook an assignment as an assistant to President Mordecai Johnson in 1933–34 and then resumed his chairmanship of the Political Science Department. Howard University at that time boasted several thousand students— about a sixth of the black students in American colleges—and more than 150 professors. Educators rightfully celebrated it as the "capstone of Negro education" and the academic apogee of black university life in America. Yet it was also an intellectual cul-de-sac, since at white institutions most African Americans were excluded from competing for jobs. Johnson took advantage of that fact to recruit an extraordinary group of black scholars, who created a vibrant intellectual community in which Bunche himself played a leading role.[12]

Howard's heavy teaching and administrative loads and Johnson's autocratic leadership style frustrated Bunche. But these were minor problems compared to those of dealing with the racially claustrophobic atmosphere of Washington, D.C. Although Bunche was no stranger to Jim Crow, the stifling segregation that pervaded every aspect of life in the nation's capital was new to him. An 1872 equal rights law had for a time guaranteed blacks equal access to public facilities. By the time Bunche arrived, however, Southern Democratic congressmen had rewritten city statutes as part of their broad assault on the rights of African Americans. With few exceptions, therefore, blacks were unable to eat at restaurants or lunch counters (unless they ate at a stand-up counter). They could not attend white nightclubs and could not even sit in the balconies at motion picture theaters. They could ride on public transportation, but not in white taxi cabs. City parks, water fountains, playgrounds, and schools were divided along distinct racial lines. Even though Bunche eventually moved into a white neighborhood, his daughters had to take buses to black schools elsewhere in the city. When he accepted a United Nations appointment in New York City, he did not look back fondly. The indignities he and his family had suffered were one reason he turned down President Truman's offer to return to Washington as an Assistant Secretary of State for Near Eastern and African Affairs in 1949. "Living in the nation's capital," he bitingly remarked, "is like serving out a sentence. It's extremely difficult for a Negro to maintain even a semblance of human dignity in Washington."[13]

Bunche's political views veered sharply to the left during his years of teaching at Howard. The crisis of the Great Depression drew many black intellectuals to leftist causes during the 1930s, and Bunche and his Howard colleagues were no exception. The Howard cadre of left-leaning academics—Abram Harris, E. Franklin Frazier, Doxey Wilkerson, W. Alphaeus Hunton, Alain Locke, Emmett Dorsey, Eugene Holmes, and Sterling Brown—reinforced and refined the Marxist analysis that had made its way into his writings by the late 1920s. Despite their attraction to Marxism, however, narrow Communist Party dogma put most of them off and the majority, including Bunche, did not become Party members. The group would meet on a weekly basis—often at Bunche's home on the Howard campus—to debate and dissect topical national and international issues and articles appearing in magazines such as *The New Republic, The Nation,* and *New Masses.* Within this circle, the economist Abram Harris probably had the most influence in the shaping of Bunche's thinking.[14]

The Howard group commonly shared the view that problems facing the black community were not uniquely racial but were an outgrowth of class exploitation. As Bunche phrased it, "Racialism is a myth, albeit a dangerous one, for it is a perfect stalking-horse for selfish group politics and camouflage for brutal economic exploitation."[15] His critique of Franklin Roosevelt's New Deal programs illustrates this line of argument. New Deal programs, he maintained, aimed at striking a balance between serving big business and the working class. But they ended up favoring Northern industrialists and the Southern landed aristocracy, who sought to preserve, not overhaul, the capitalist system. As a result, the New Deal's trickle-down philosophy undermined the independence of the working class and gave more power to capitalists. Under the New Deal, Bunche believed, the ruling class had not shifted its traditional antiblack attitudes to keep blacks in a servile condition and squeeze profits out of the working class. Racism was the tool by which the ruling class pitted black and white workers against each other.[16]

The concept of class, according to Bunche, had more potency than race for addressing black problems. He had little faith, however, that black leaders were prepared to change strategies he viewed as outdated, since their leadership roles depended heavily on appeals to race and because they were unable to comprehend how the black condition fit into the broader economic and social forces at work. As he put it, they were "unable to see the social forests for the racial saplings."[17]

Bunche leveled his sharpest criticism at reformist black organizations such as the National Association for the Advancement of Colored People (NAACP) and the National Urban League whose focus on civil and political rights won meager gains at too much cost and appealed more to the small black middle class than to the much larger black working class. "The fights for civil rights—for the right of Negroes to serve on juries, for equal salaries for Negro teachers, for the admittance of Negroes to white colleges, and even for an anti-lynch bill—do not carry an appeal to the Negro in the mass which is designed to arouse him."[18] He also disparaged former NAACP official W. E. B. DuBois's ideas on black self-determination as hopelessly misguided. Blacks, he argued, achieved nothing by bottling themselves "in a black political and economic outhouse."[19]

In addition, he belittled as an escapist fantasy the strategy of blacks advancing themselves through black-owned businesses. Because under-capitalized black businesses were incapable of competing with "larger-capitalized, more efficient white businesses," Bunche contended that black consumers took their business elsewhere. Preaching racial solidarity—blacks buying from blacks—appealed primarily to middle-class blacks, but offered little to black workers, who were not able to find jobs in their own community. Black workers were penalized by any plan that pitted them against white workers threatened with the loss of jobs. Moreover, he saw no evidence that the black businessman was "any less reluctant to exploit his fellow blacks as employees than any other employer."[20] The real issue, according to Bunche, was an economic system that did not provide jobs for all workers, whether black or white.

Another issue that disturbed him was the extent to which black organizations such as the NAACP were financially dependent on white liberal patrons. This reliance circumscribed the independence of black organizations because they could not make decisions without first conferring with their sponsors—and their sponsors consistently steered them in the direction of caution, moderation, and compromise. On occasion, white liberals acting on behalf of black organizations had won limited gains, but Bunche rejected this "half-a-loaf" approach: "this is no storming of the bastions of racial prejudice nor does it even aim toward them. In its very nature it is a defeatist attitude, since it accepts the existing racial patterns while asking favors and exceptions within them."[21] To move forward, black organizations had to set agendas based on their own needs rather than catering to white liberal sensitivities.

Since he believed "economic interests" would prevail over "racial prejudices," Bunche maintained that building a coalition of black and white workers was an attainable goal. Yet the starting point for Bunche had to be in the black community. His recommendation for an alternative to existing black organizations was a new organization devoted to black working-class and trade union interests. He became one of the principal founders of the National Negro Congress (NNC), which aimed at providing an umbrella structure for unifying black groups and politicizing the black community at the grass roots level. The NNC grew out of a May 1935 Howard University conference on the "Status of the Negro Under the New Deal" convened by Bunche and John P. Davis of the Joint Committee on National Recovery.[22] An informal meeting at Bunche's home laid the base for the NNC's first meeting in Chicago the following February.

Although the NAACP notably did not endorse it, the NNC's inaugural conference still attracted 817 delegates representing 585 organizations with 1,200,000 members. The NNC's goal was to come up with a minimum program on which black groups could concur so all black groups could focus on "economic and social betterment as well as upon justice and citizen's rights." In reviewing the conference, Bunche thought the NNC had paid too much attention to black business and had unwisely endorsed interracial organizations. At the same time, he believed the NNC had begun addressing black working-class issues and could serve as a viable alternative to the NAACP's moderation.[23]

The NNC got off to a promising start by setting up local branches in cities around the country. For a while, it threatened the dominance of the NAACP. However, because of its emphasis on working-class issues, the NNC lost the support of black clergymen, businessmen, and professionals. Bunche pinpointed the problem when he remarked that the NNC mistakenly expected race would be "enough to weld together such divergent segments of the Negro society as preachers and labor organizers, lodge officials and black workers, Negro businessmen, Negro radicals, professional politicians, professional men, domestic servants, black butchers, bakers and candlestick makers." He counseled the NNC to remain focused on its working-class constituency.[24]

The NNC held its second convention in October 1937 while Bunche was overseas. At its next meeting in April 1940 in Washington, D.C.—attended by 900 black and 400 white delegates—Bunche was present as Communist Party members, who had remained in the background in earlier proceedings, played a decisive role in forcing NNC president A. Phillip Randolph to step aside for Max Yergan. Communist Party members also pressed the NNC to adopt strongly worded anti-imperialist and anti-war resolutions that dovetailed with Soviet foreign policy concerns. In Bunche's view, the Communists had hijacked the NNC and "reduced [it] to a communist cell."[25] His bitterness over the experience was a factor in softening his critique of the New Deal.

III

    Despite his deep involvement in the NNC throughout 1935, Bunche did not lose interest in African issues. He organized a Howard conference on "The Crisis of Modern Imperialism in Africa and the Far East" in May 1936, and he published several articles based on his West African research.[26] His major effort was a monograph, *A World View of Race,* which drew on his dissertation and applied his class analysis of the United States on a global scale.[27] He focused his attention on colonialism in Africa, where he saw colonizers manipulating race as an instrument of domination and exploitation and the imperialist state protecting and promoting capitalist interests overseas.[28] Drawing heavily on writers such as Parker Moon, J. H. Hobson, and Leonard Woolf, Bunche argued that the driving force behind Europe's grab for African territory in the late nineteenth century was industrial capitalism's hunger for exporting goods and surplus capital as well as its insatiable need for new sources of raw materials. The colonies also served as dumping grounds for white—especially working-class—settlers, which led to even more discrimination, land expropriation, and conflict with African societies. Colonialism's aims were served by driving a racial wedge between colonizer and colonized, whom Bunche defined as "certain peoples as helplessly and incapable of keeping step with the modern industrial world." Although the base motive for colonial rule was exploitation and profit, colonizers still found it necessary to give their rule an altruistic facade by introducing ideas like trusteeship, "white man's burden," and *mission civilisatrice.* The real loser, Bunche concluded, was "the African, [who] must pay dearly for his introduction to Western 'civilization'."[29]

    Bunche's analysis presaged the Africanist "radical pessimists" of a later generation by maintaining that the solution to Africa's plight lay in the destruction of the capitalist state. He predicted that a global conflict between the working and owning classes would supplant race conflict. "Race war," he contended, "then will be merely a side-show to the gigantic class war which will be waged in the big tent we call the world."[30]

    Africa also figured in Bunche's search for a new research project that would afford him a respite from his burdensome teaching and administrative duties at Howard. As he confided to Melville Herskovits, "the more I can stay away from here the longer I'll hold my job, I think."[31] He considered writing a book on European imperialism in Africa. He also sounded out Donald Young, a race relations specialist at the Social Science Research Council (SSRC) in New York, about funding prospects for a new project that would go beyond his dissertation research to assess the impact of colonial rule and Western culture on Africans, through the eyes of Africans. Young was sympathetic, but advised him that since the SSRC was more interested in "equipping research personnel" by giving them new methodological skills, he would be more likely to receive SSRC backing if he agreed to undergo training in the field methods cultural anthropologists were using to study culture contact.[32] Bunche had attacked old-style colonial anthropologists for treating Africa like a private museum;[33] yet, he believed the new acculturation studies were suited to examining colonialism from the bottom up, and he agreed to recast his proposal to include a study of anthropological field methods. "The problem," as he eventually framed it, was "of the *effect* of imperial rule on retarded [*sic*] peoples. This approach to the subject regards colonial policy and administration as devices which support and give momentum to a much more profound social process, resulting from culture contacts."[34]

Bunche would have gladly settled for a year's funding. But Young pleasantly surprised him when he proceeded to sketch out a two-year program for him. It included having him study with three leading anthropologists: Herskovits at Northwestern University, Bronislaw Malinowski at the London School of Economics (LSE), and Isaac Schapera at the University of Cape Town. Young also encouraged him to visit Holland to study Dutch colonial policy, devote six months to field research in East Africa, and cap his journey in the Dutch colony of Indonesia. In the end, his two-year sojourn conformed closely to the program Young mapped out.

Young's selection of Herskovits was not unusual since Herskovits was one of the academic "gatekeepers" for private foundations funding research on Africa. The foundations shared the attitude that white experts on race relations had to sponsor and vouch for the integrity of African-American scholars because they were not likely to be "objective" on African issues. Through his previous experience with the Rosenwald Foundation, Bunche was alert to the maze through which African Americans had to pass to meet the standards of the white foundation establishment. Even though he railed against white foundations in his writings, Bunche was pragmatic enough to recognize that it was essential for him to make the pilgrimage to Evanston to serve an apprenticeship with Herskovits.[35] As a result, Bunche became the only African American funded by a private foundation to go out to Africa for research until the 1950s, when the Ford Foundation began funding African fieldwork.[36]

Whatever the SSRC's expectations, Bunche did not view his association with Herskovits as one of patron and client. Indeed, Bunche looked forward to working with Herskovits because he had already carved out a reputation for his work on the African contribution to African-American culture and had carried out field research in Dahomey in 1931. Moreover, Howard faculty members knew Herskovits well, since he had taught there in 1925. A mutual Howard friend, Abram Harris, had introduced the two in 1932 before Bunche went out to Dahomey and Togoland for his dissertation research. Herskovits saw himself as a mentor to younger black scholars. He had high regard for Howard scholars like Harris, Bunche, and Brown because they downplayed the importance of race and analyzed situations in cooler, less passionate terms. They were "the only group known to me among the Negroes able to approach the tragedy of the racial situation in this country with the objectivity that comes from seeing it as the result of the play of historic forces rather than as an expression of personal spite and a desire to hold down a minority people."[37] In Bunche, Herskovits saw an individual who could emotionally distance himself from a racially charged environment in carrying out fieldwork. Apprising Schapera of Bunche's ability to deal with South African segregation, he wrote: "one thing you can count on, and that is that he will meet these situations as they arise with a very clear head and a detachment that is as admirable as it is unusual."[38]

The correspondence that flowed between Bunche and Herskovits in the 1930s confirms that Bunche regarded Herskovits as a confidant with whom he could candidly share his feelings. The two respected and admired each other's work, though this did not prevent Bunche from criticizing Herskovits's work. For instance, in reviewing Herskovits's *Dahomey,* Bunche took him to task for not acknowledging how much French colonialism had distorted the kingdom of Dahomey. He argued that Herskovits was so fixed on reconstructing pre-colonial Dahomey through its remnants that he "did not see the imperialistic trees for the ethnological woods."[39]

How to relate to Malinowski was another matter, since Bunche was not a disciple of functionalism, but he relished the opportunity of going head to head with him in his celebrated LSE seminar.

IV

In February 1937, Bunche, his wife, Ruth, and their two young daughters, Joan and Jane, set sail for London. After the family had settled in, Malinowski quickly baptized Bunche into his seminar. Although Bunche attended seminars run by Lucy Mair, Audrey Richards, and Raymond Firth, his primary interest was Malinowski's Comparative Study of Culture seminar on Thursday afternoons because it was the center of the British anthropological universe—or at least that of the functionalists. As Bunche put it, "Malinowski is not only the founder [o]f functionalism—he is it." Malinowski had taken up a position at the London School of Economics (LSE) in 1920 and had carved out a reputation as a pioneer in the methodology of anthropological fieldwork. His seminar regularly attracted about fifty participants from diverse backgrounds, including colonial officials, African students, white settlers, and anthropologists.[40]

"Vain and dogmatic" was Bunche's impression of Malinowski after they first met in Malinowski's apartment, but Bunche had no reservations about acknowledging Malinowski's formidable intellect. Indeed, his seminar generated such creative energy that Bunche admitted he had never enjoyed himself more in an academic setting. He was less charitable, though, when he sarcastically described the band of acolytes who clustered around Malinowski. They were the "Malinowski-wow-wow-ites" who played "stooge" to "Bwana Mkubwa [Swahili for "big boss"] Malinowski." And he was certain that he did not want to worship at the functionalist altar. "There's never been a primitive religion so demanding as 'Malinowskism' is here. But I ain't converted. The Baptists dipped me in a tank and couldn't convert me and I know damn well I can't get no kind of religion in a classroom."[41]

One area where Bunche sharply differed with Malinowski was over his belief that scholars could not reconstruct the history of pre-literate societies. Writing to Herskovits, Bunche recounted one seminar exchange where he deliberately drew Malinowski into discussing whether history had a useful function in uncovering African survivals among African Americans, an area that Herskovits had pioneered. This had led to a circuitous Malinowski discourse on functionalism:

> the answer to my question seemed to be that there was ordinary, garden variety anthropology, and functionalism, and this latter type is practical and applied. Kroeber came in for some hard raps but one Melville Herskovits was specifically excepted. This exception was explained in

some such terms as the following: Herskovits employs history to some extent and chooses to adopt a semi-historical label for his work, but his method is essentially functionalist. He makes functionalist analyses of West African cultures and then draws parallels with Negro societies in the New World. So you're a historical functionalist, I conclude! The suggestion was that though you may seem a bit unorthodox, your work is essentially sound and commendable. But when I finally pinned him down he came forth with this gem: except for such formalized cultural attributes as language . . . , studies of cultural survivals are dubious, because it is virtually impossible to separate cultural origins in such a culture-contact situation.[42]

Outside Malinowski's seminar, Bunche devoted time to meeting people familiar with the South African scene, such as Don M'timkulu, who was in Malinowski's seminar; Julius Lewin and Jack Simons, who were studying at LSE;[43] Max Yergan, who had recently left South Africa after serving fifteen years as a YMCA missionary and who had veered sharply to the left:[44] Frieda Neugebauer, a Fort Hare lecturer and a companion of Yergan's; Essie Robeson; Leonard Barnes, a Labour Party adviser and anticolonial critic; and William Macmillan, a prominent South African historian who had left Witwatersrand University for London in 1933.[45]

They gave him extensive, but often conflicting advice on who to see and how to move about South Africa. For instance, Macmillan recommended that Bunche "gain status" by staying for a few days at the Mount Nelson, a prestigious Cape Town hotel, and to "pass" for white wherever he could. Bunche pointedly ignored his suggestions. Others wondered how he would react to the raw racism in South Africa. When an acquaintance asked him if he would have to walk in the gutter in South Africa, he replied, "I told him that I never walked in the gutter, at any time or anywhere, & that goes for So. Afr."[46]

In addition to his South African contacts, he mingled with members of London's compact black community, such as Paul and Essie Robeson, Arthur Davis and Eric Williams and key members of the Pan Africanist movement, including Ras Makonnen, C. L. R. James; Jomo Kenyatta, I. T. A. Wallace-Johnson, and George Padmore.[47] Bunche had actually taught Padmore at Howard in the late 1920s, when Padmore was an organizer for the Communist Party. By 1937, he had become an ardent Pan Africanist who, according to Bunche, was also "a fine rabble rouser." Although Bunche mixed a lot with the Pan Africanists, he was not sympathetic to their ideas. Pan Africanism clashed with his class analysis and he considered it another variant of the racial chauvinism he abhorred. As he expressed it in his book review of Padmore's *How Britain Rules Africa,* "the surest road toward liberation of the African masses is not through Pan Africanism, but rather the road which leads inevitably to a fundamental reconstruction of the political and economic systems of the imperialistic nations at home."[48] He was also wary of the Pan Africanists' penchant for romanticizing the pre-colonial past and ignoring the authoritarian aspects of the "old despotisms," those African kingdoms in which blacks exploited other blacks. Echoing his criticism of black businessmen, he charged, "it is scarcely more pleasant to be exploited and oppressed by privileged members of one's own race than by members of some other race."[49]

Of all this group, Bunche spent the most time with Kenyatta, who agreed to tutor him in Swahili at 12s6d a lesson.[50] Kenyatta, whom he considered "to be an intense racial chauvinist rather than a Marxist," was a student in Malinowski's seminar and often made ends meet by giving language instruction to missionaries. Malinowski called on Bunche to help mediate a dispute Kenyatta and an English student had been waging over the rights to certain research materials they had worked on together. In early June, Bunche went with Kenyatta to Malinowski's office, where the English student was waiting outside.

> Latter in hall [o]f Malinowski's office and walked up to Kenyatta, called him a *shit* & threatened him if he should say anything to Malinowski. Tried to keep Kenyatta out [o]f the office when he went in. I came on in; Malinowski scared. G. [the English student] called Kenyatta a swindler & unable to substantiate it had to withdraw the statement. They finally agreed that the material should be turned over to Malinowski & nothing should be written on subject without due acknowledgement. G. stuck close to Mal. when Kenyatta & I left.[51]

In his diary, Bunche speculated that the real cause of the trouble between the two was likely over a girl friend.

Bunche also attended many rallies and concerts centered around the Spanish Civil War and the Italian invasion of Ethiopia. Ethiopia's plight had aroused passionate outrage and concern in the African-American community. He contemplated taking a side trip to Ethiopia. Though Herskovits warned him, "though you might get in, getting out again would be something else,"[52] Bunche decided against the trip—not because of the risks, but because it would reduce the amount of time he could spend elsewhere.

Bunche unexpectedly had to devote a lot of energy in London to arranging permission to enter South Africa. He thought he had already settled the issue when he arranged for a South African visa in Washington. However, in London, he learned that a visa counted for little unless he had a more critical document, a landing permit, that allowed him to disembark from his ship and enter the country. On 5 April he took the first step towards securing a permit by filling out a South African immigration form. The form required applicants to declare whether they were "European, Hebraic, Oriental or African," but Bunche inserted "American" to express his objection to the racial categories.[53]

Several weeks later he took his permit problem to the Dominions Office, where Malcolm McDonald arranged an appointment for him at the South African embassy. On 26 April he met with the political secretary, Scallon, who had earlier served five years in the South African embassy in Washington. Scallon distrusted the motives of any African American who wanted to visit South Africa unless they were missionaries—and even they were suspect.[54] After carefully scrutinizing Bunche's application and inquiring about his proposed research work, he bluntly spelled out the kind of researcher his government objected to:

> [He] emphasized that missionary work was unpopular. When I assured him that I was engaged in scientific study rather than missionary work, he explained that Govt. was encouraging scientific work. Made it clear that if this were not the case I would be refused entry. Said govt. would be very annoyed if I were to make any speeches. Said missionaries would like to have a fellow like me working on their behalf and would try to get me to speak.[55]

Bunche came to the meeting armed with letters of introduction from the U.S. Department of State and the Department of Interior. In addition, he had a cautiously worded letter of endorsement from Charles Loram, a leading South African educator teaching at Yale University, which read: "I realize that is not wise to encourage all and sundry of the American Negroes to visit South Africa, but I have every reason to believe that Dr. Bunche will . . . refrain from saying or doing anything which might make the position of the South African Government in any way more difficult than it is."[56] In the late 1920s, when Loram had broken with the South African government over its policy toward African education, it had branded him a liberal. So after hearing Scallon's admonition, Bunche discreetly withheld Loram's letter.

Following his meeting with Scallon, Bunche tried another tack by requesting an American embassy official to write a letter on his behalf. The official brushed him aside on the grounds that he had to deal with South Africa through the British Foreign Office. In addition, American officials could not ask for favors on immigration matters with other countries since American laws were so strict and they were not able to reciprocate. Scallon later informed Bunche that the American official's explanation about using the British Foreign Office as an intermediary was incorrect.

In the meantime, Bunche had appealed to Schapera and Malinowski to intercede on his behalf. Malinowski had already expressed his doubts to Bunche about any African American carrying out fieldwork in Africa, contending that he was in a no-win situation—Europeans would discriminate against him and Africans would treat him as "white."[57] But Malinowski did not let his misgivings stand in the way of his helping Bunche. He and Schapera contacted a highly placed friend, South African Minister of Interior Jan Hofmeyr, about his plight. Their appeals bore fruit and Schapera wrote Bunche that Pretoria had cabled its London embassy with the permission for Bunche to enter South Africa. When Bunche went to the embassy on 25 June, Scallon informed him he had heard nothing. Bunche proceeded to show him Schapera's letter, and when Scallon called for Bunche's file, he found Hofmeyr's cable in it. He made a feeble excuse about his work overload and then lectured Bunche again on South African race relations. Scallon

> expressed his dislike of white Amer. missionaries who came to So. Afr. preaching brotherhood [o]f man and equality to "So. African niggers" tho they knew this is impossible because of the attitude of the So. Afr. whites. . . . Said all natives are savages & immoral. . . . Said there is no Jim Crow in So. Afr., but "reserved" sections on trains for natives & colored. Said I could ride 1st class, but would be given a whole section to myself if I was only colored on train.[58]

After delivering his homily, Scallon finally issued him a landing permit.

Bunche controlled himself in the meeting, but he fumed over Scallon's dillydallying and described him in his diary entry as "a real S.O.B." Writing to Herskovits a short time later about the permit affair, Bunche admitted that he had prevailed, but only at the cost of having ". . . to swallow my pride several times, stifle any number of impulses to cuss out the officials, and maintain a forced air of bewildered and sweet innocence."[59]

Bunche was not the only African American who had to maneuver his way through a bureaucratic thicket to enter South Africa. In the 1890s, European officials allowed African Americans to reside in South African colonies as "honorary whites." After the Anglo-Boer War, first the British and then the South African government strictly limited the number of African Americans admitted into South Africa.[60] Their scapegoat was African-American missionaries, whom they singled out as agitators whose pernicious gospel of racial solidarity and resistance to European rule was responsible for Africans breaking away from European missions and establishing independent churches.[61] European missionaries reinforced this image. The Dutch Reformed Church Secretary for Mission, Rev. A. C. Murray, expressed a common sentiment: "American Negroes have done a great deal of harm to mission work and also politically here in South Africa. The Union government is very reluctant to allow them to enter this country because of the way in which they have stirred up the uneducated natives and prejudiced them against Europeans."[62]

The South African government had the same mindset. It framed a policy that African Americans could enter South Africa only if they were carefully screened and monitored. It set down three conditions for accepting applicants: "1) that the permit would be temporary only. 2) that he or she would be attached to some organization preferably in the hands of white people. 3) that the post was one which could be filled by a native African."[63] For instance, government officials delayed granting a visa to Max Yergan until the Ghanaian educator, James Aggrey, interceded to assure them he was a safe risk. Based in Alice from 1921 to 1936 as representative of the Student Christian Association, Yergan was very aware how white officials resisted letting him in; and he consciously refrained from taking controversial public stances, even as his South African experience was radicalizing him.[64]

Although Bunche's permit issue had been resolved, the problem of transportation to South Africa was not. The Holland-Africa Line, the shipping company he had booked for his trip to South Africa, had already complicated his plans by requiring him to put down a deposit for a return fare in case he did not get a landing permit and immigration officials turned him back in Cape Town. Now he began to worry that he would have to surmount other racial barriers after Lewin advised him the Holland-Africa Line might place him in a cabin with a white man and this might give the shipping line the pretext to bump him off at the last moment when it discovered he was black. Lewin's call to the Holland-Africa Line confirmed that although company policy was to segregate the races on board their ships, they could accommodate Bunche since they had had dealings with West Indian and "Negro" passengers. They rewrote his ticket and placed him in a different cabin, though his roommate was a Dutch employee of the shipping line, Rees, who was taking up a post in Durban. By that point, he was so sensitive to racial code words that he wondered if the designation USC on his boat ticket meant "US Colored" rather than "US Citizen."[65]

V

Bunche's wife and daughters returned to Washington, D.C. in late August, and, on 12 September, he embarked from Dover on his African journey on the Boschfontein. He referred jokingly to his seventeen-day journey to Cape Town as "86 Boers and Me," but the fact was that most of the passengers in first class were English-speaking South Africans, whose race attitudes differed little from those of Afrikaners.

Although he thought it likely that he would have had "a tougher time on a boat headed from Florida or Texas," he did not expect a great deal of camaraderie on the trip. During the first few days on board, other passengers steered clear of him, which led him to lament, " 'a nigger is a nigger even in the middle of the ocean'—sociologically speaking, of course." He prepared himself for an isolated existence by staying in his cabin and reading—notably the poems of his Howard colleague Sterling Brown.[66]

Table tennis broke the ice. He was an excellent table tennis player, and after several games with Rees led to games with other passengers, he found it easier to strike up conversations. White South Africans made a distinction between him and black Africans. South Africans he had met in England had already impressed on him "the great difference—the vast gulf separating the American Negro from the 'Kaffir.' " Europeans had educated, Westernized, and civilized African Americans over centuries of contact, while their African ancestors remained mired in savagery and backwardness. White South Africans assumed that Bunche automatically understood—and perhaps even shared—their perception. As the trip wore on, passengers began to approach him more freely and unburden themselves about their feelings toward black people in the U.S. and South Africa. His diary recorded the following conversations:

16 September. Mrs. Goldberg of So. Africa . . . told me how fond she is [o]f her native maid, Sarah, how no account one of Sarah's sons is, how vicious "detribalized" natives are, how women don't dare walk on streets [o]f Joburg alone at nite, etc. Mentioned bands [o]f evil marauding natives . . . of Joburg who run about sticking knives (I wonder) in defenseless women. My Jewish ping pong friend (whom I licked) claims

to be a negrophile. . . . Has been to Cotton Club in Harlem and met Metcalf and Owens in a Negro nite club in London—was charmed by their modesty.[67] He thinks N. [Negro] has "something"—a very elusive and undefinable something, that white man hasn't got. Says prob. isn't an indiv. one—a man like himself may love Negroes, but must respect attitudes of his white friends.

18 September. In evening Mr. Harries of Rand Gold Mines got to talking to me about his diggings in caves for bones & stone-axes, etc. Talked about "the niggers" in the compounds, how backward, ignorant & child like they are, etc. they are clearly so many animals to him.

19 September. Talked with a Mr. Helen, who calls himself an anatomist & "scientist"—we are "fellow scientists"; he whispered that I will have no trouble with the English in So. Africa, but that the Dutch are hopelessly narrow. His view is that native is hopelessly mentally inferior—he can be educated but still has no intelligence. I just keep mum and listen.

22 September. Mr. Harris came by & engaged me in conversation until midnite —more tales about So. Afr. & its (to him) "humorous niggers"—all of whom are liars, thieves, cheats & drunkards, in his opinion.

24 September. Mr. Domisse, head [o]f Dutch bank in So. Afr., sat down beside me & we chatted for 1/2 hour or so. . . . Discussed race situation in So. Afr. Mr. Domisse spoke [o]f die-hard Boer farmers, who feel that their only chance as a minority white pop. in So. Afr. is to keep native under heel. Says they pursue a deliberate policy [o]f oppression. . . . Says So. Afr. gold prod., tho on highest mechanical efficiency basis, is based on dirt cheap labor. . . . Says he believes that natives must be educated & trained & must be paid higher wages—but he doesn't see how this can be done now without ruining half [o]f So. Afr. gold companies.

27 September. Then struck up conversation with Mr. Bowen, the Amer., who also came to bow. He has strong opinions re So. Afr. Says So. Afr. farmers are lazy & inefficient. Try to be 'gentleman' farmers. Depend on govt for financial aid & get it. Says Boers particularly bad. Says wrong people in control in So. Afr. Should permit a better class of immigrants—several millions. Says natives grossly under-rated. The farmers often leave their farms completely in control of native managers—some go on vacations for 6 mos. or more. Says Boer farmers are very lazy. Says many native workers show rare ingenuity. Says missionaries ruin natives. Thinks So. Africans don't get maximum out of native labor. Thinks white farmers should be replaced by black, and former

settle in cities. Thinks natives are not dangerous. Says poor whites are lowest elements in society. Favored some sort [o]f pass system for natives, but not great abuses in present one—ex. marching natives rounded up sans passes thru streets each morning. Doesn't like mixed up situation in Cape Town. Thinks solution is in separation of races, with each getting a break. But blacks must be kept out [o]f skilled labor in competition with whites. Blacks as farmers & more intensive mining to give them work.

However much some white passengers opened up to Bunche on a one-to-one basis, they reminded him in subtle and not so subtle ways there were social conventions he should not breach. For instance, Mrs. Morris Alexander[68] was chatting with him at a dance, but maneuvered around the issue of dancing with him by disclosing it made her dizzy to dance on a ship. He "gallantly countered by suggesting that it was much too hot for dancing anyhow." He also tactfully declined to participate in a treasure hunt the purser was organizing but not before another passenger pointed out to the purser that she was deliberately ignoring him. On another occasion, Mrs. Alexander told him that a Dutch woman sitting next to her had taken her to task for even talking with him and firmly lectured her on how to treat folks like Bunche.[69]

Given the racial and class obsessions of the first-class passengers, it is understandable that Bunche found relief socializing with the passengers in steerage. When the boat docked in Dakar, Senegal, they went to a Chinese cabaret and had a rollicking time. Likewise, the steerage passengers complained that they were dealt with as if they were second-class citizens; one remarked that "the So. Afr. Dutch" went so far as to "treat all the crew as tho they are natives."[70]
Whatever minor slights Bunche suffered on the trip, all in all, the other passengers treated him with civility. He quipped at its end that it had been so "damn dull that I was sorry that no one took a crack at me or at least called me a 'nigger' so that I might have had something to write about in my sociological notes."

VI

When he landed in South Africa on 29 September, Bunche had not mapped out a carefully planned schedule. One immediate goal was to participate in Isaac Schapera's seminar on African Social Organization at the University of Cape Town, which was looking at Schapera's new study on Tswana societies in Bechuanaland. Despite hosting Eslanda Robeson when she visited Cape Town in 1935, Schapera still went to the trouble of sounding out the University Council about whether there would be any problem having a black person attend his seminar. The council accepted the idea.[71] Bunche sat in on Schapera's seminar, and he benefited from his help in framing a field project studying the "powers and the sanctions behind the authority of native chiefs." However, after a while, he admitted to "getting slightly bored with my schoolboy role" in Schapera's seminar and anxiously looked forward to moving out of the classroom into the community.[72]

In making his plans for traveling around the country, Bunche determined that he was going to break out of the pattern of white liberals' hosting and programming visitors in South Africa. He told Don M'timkulu that he was only going to stay in black homes, a goal that he achieved with some success.[73] In Cape Town, he stayed with Dr. A. H. and Cissie Gool; in Basutoland, with Oswin Bull; in Alice, with Dr. Alexander Kerr; in Thaba 'Nchu, with Dr. James Moroka; in Mafeking, with Dr. S. M. Molema; in Johannesburg, with Joe and Ellen Hellman and at the Bantu Men's Social Centre; in Bloemfontein, with Mac Lepolesa; and in Durban, with A. I. Kajee. His black and white hosts, all educated professionals, represented an interesting cross-section of moderate, liberal, and radical opinion, and it was they who eased his entry into black communities.

Bunche's travels eventually covered a wide swath of South Africa, touching on Cape Town, Lesotho, Alice, Thaba 'Nchu, Bloemfontein, Mafeking, Johannesburg, Benoni, Pretoria, and Durban. When he moved from town to town, he took trains. Although segregated train compartments were the norm, he had an advantage since he could afford first class accommodation. Conductors usually seated him in a well-appointed "reserved compartment." Both black and white railway employees treated him solicitously, though some were not sure whether he was white or Coloured. He had this problem elsewhere. A clerk at Thomas Cook travel agency in Cape Town mistook him for a Filipino, while in Johannesburg, some people thought he was Portuguese.

Within cities, he relied heavily on black and white friends to escort him around.[74] It is striking that he had no problems traveling around with liberal whites, who were helpful in running interference with government officials. In turn, officials regarded white liberals as acceptable escorts for "outsiders" entering the black community. In contrast, he would later face a far more difficult time upon his return to the United States when he traveled through the South with two white colleagues, the Swedish economist Gunnar Myrdal and a Southerner, Arthur Raper. They had to extricate themselves hurriedly from several explosive situations in Alabama and Georgia after whites took offense at their pointed questions about race issues. White violence was a very real possibility, and the thought of a lynch mob crossed Bunche's mind on more than one occasion.[75]

Bunche commenced his South Africa trip as a detached chronicler, but he soon discovered that as an African American, he was a subject of curiosity and interest to many black South Africans.[76] Over the decades, they had transformed the African-American experience into a metaphor for achieving racial progress and success in a white-dominated society. In their eyes, America was a "mecca and oasis" and the African American was seen as a "paragon of virtue." They lionized such celebrated personalities as boxers Joe Louis and Henry Armstrong, track star Jesse Owens, musicians Fats Waller and Duke Ellington, and singer-actor Paul Robeson. Indeed, there had been several attempts to bring Robeson to South Africa, where he had long been idolized for his triumphs on the stage, film, and records. Bunche confirmed Robeson's reputation when he wrote him: "Paul you surely are an idol of the Bantu. . . . when one mentions American Negroes they all chorus 'Paul Robeson and Joe Louis'—the more sophisticated may also add Jesse Owens and Duke [Ellington]. The rumor still persists that you are coming down to the Union soon; if you do the black folk will mob you with enthusiasm."[77]

Confronting these expectations challenged Bunche's self-defined role as a neutral observer, and he came to accept the fact that "any American Negro visiting South Africa is [emphasis in original] a missionary whether or not he wills it." (p. 137) Despite his earlier assurances to South African officials that he would avoid public speaking in South Africa, he decided to deliver a series of extemporaneous "pep" talks aimed at countering the negative self-image he believed black South Africans suffered from. His talks underscored the importance of race pride by highlighting the notable accomplishments of African Americans who had become civil servants, judges, lawyers, scientists, and university presidents in the face of discriminatory barriers. "This all goes to show," he advised a Coloured audience in Cape Town, "that despite all the colour prejudice, the black man, if he sticks to his task, can with ability, reach the top."[78] Likewise, when he addressed a group of African school teachers in Pretoria, he brought several of them to tears by relating instances of "white teachers serving under black presidents and principals and black judges trying white cases in America." (p. 238)

However much Bunche hoped the African-American example would inspire his audiences, not all of his talks worked out in the manner he wished. At Fort Hare College, his theme that black people could rouse their "self-confidence and pride" by stressing their heroes and cultural and artistic accomplishments did not evoke a response. He therefore concluded that his listeners looked negatively on their past in much the same way as many African Americans viewed their slave experience. For them, education was to be an escape route, not a reminder of an inglorious past. Indeed, at this Fort Hare meeting, Prof. D. D. T. Jabavu held that Africans should emulate African Americans precisely because they had discarded their African cultural traditions and thus were more open to new ideas, trends, and leaders. (p. 135)

Nevertheless, other African-American visitors found that extrolling African-American achievements struck a responsive chord with black audiences; and they repeatedly touched on the theme in their talks. When David Henry Sims, bishop of the AME church in South Africa from 1932 to 1936, addressed an assembly at Amanzimtoti Institute in August 1934, he titled his lecture, "The Contribution of the Negro Race to Civilisation."

> The modern contributions of the Negro date from the time of the enslavement of the Negro. The American cotton industry owes its origin and maintenance to Negro muscles. No soldier in U.S.A. is as loyal as the Negro. In times of National crises, the Negro soldiers alone are commissioned to guard the Capital. The Negro is the greatest source of popular music the worldover; in science, the Negro is represented by men like Dr. Moton; in commerce, Law, Education, Religion, etc., the Negro is holding his own among other races.[79]

Another visitor was Eslanda Robeson. After attending the second national meeting of the All African Convention in Bloemfontein, she experienced first hand the intimidation of blacks in Kroonstad, a small Orange Free State town. When she spoke a short while later to a meeting of the African Order to Elks at the Bantu Men's Social Centre in Johannesburg, she emphasized the significance of race pride and unity for all peoples of African descent.

> The unity of Negroes in the United States of America was slowly but surely giving them more power. . . . Negroes in all parts of the world had the same problems, faults and virtues, and although the race was di-

vided because of the colour bar and geographical position, all its members were Negroes and should not be ashamed to admit it. They had reason to be proud of their race, because it had a great culture and background. Africans she had met in London had led her to believe that the culture and background of the race in Africa was of a high order. . . . Negroes, however, had an inferiority complex for which there was no foundation. . . . "If an example is needed," she said, "I am an African."[80]

Although Bunche was not expected to define a research project, he embraced Schapera's suggestion that he undertake an informal study on the repercussions of South African government policies for black communities. This became a theme on which he repeatedly commented in his field notes. As he phrased it in a letter to the Robesons: "I've been knocking around in South Africa trying to find out what sort of magic is employed to enable that handful of very ordinary pale-faces to keep the millions of black and colored so ruthlessly under the thumb."[81] Indeed, discussing the "sort of magic" roughly two million "pale-faces" conjured up to maintain control over 6,597,241 Africans, 767,984 Coloureds, and 219,928 Indians is important for understanding the system of racial domination Bunche encountered in 1937 as well as how it contrasted with the system in his own country.[82]

VII

The starting point for any such discussion is the last half of the nineteenth century, when two formative processes took shape in South Africa. The first was European conquest, as Afrikaners and especially the British accelerated their conquest and dispossession of African societies from their ancestral lands. The second was the discovery of diamonds in Kimberley in 1867 and gold on the Witwatersrand in 1886. Tens of thousands of African migrant workers recruited from throughout the region fuelled the mines. And the white-owned mining houses went to great lengths to control black workers by housing them in prison-like compounds, restricting their movements with pass laws, and setting poverty-level ceilings on their wages.

Even with these developments, white power was not firmly entrenched, so after 1910, when the British transferred political power to white settlers, the new Union of South Africa government began to consolidate and refine their instruments of control. Though whites were sharply divided by ethnicity and class, they normally found common ground on one point—that blacks were to play a subordinate role in the political economy of South Africa. As the historian C. W. de Kiewiet put it, "South Africa quarreled about everything but its native policy."[83] But even at that, white interest groups constantly battled each other to frame government laws and policies that protected their particular interests.

For instance, commercial farming interests were served by the Natives Land Act of 1913, which enshrined the European monopoly over land.[84] The act froze the black-white land division by prohibiting whites and blacks from purchasing each other's land. The government claimed the law protected blacks from losing even more land to white buyers, but its real intent was to block Africans, who were beginning to form land syndicates, from buying up additional land. The act also mounted an offensive against the thousands of African sharecroppers who managed to retain a semi-independent existence on white-owned land. This was intolerable to certain white farming interests who wanted to ensure a reliable pool of cheap black farm labor. Although the act did not destroy the black sharecropper overnight, it went far in turning sharecroppers into wage laborers or pushing them off the land.

Another facet of rural policy was the "native" reserves, where most Africans lived. Scattered about the countryside, the reserves were the bits of land (about 7% of all land) left over for African occupation after conquest. Over the decades overgrazing, erosion, and overcrowding sapped the reserves' agriculture productivity and transformed them into rural slums incapable of feeding their own people. The result was a steady stream of migrant laborers for the European economy.

Urban areas also fell into a segregationist pattern, but the government did not formalize policy until after the First World War, when the expansion of the manufacturing sector forced the government to reexamine its thinking.[85] One line of approach was to create a stable urban African population to satisfy the labor needs of manufacturers. The government-appointed Stallard Commission of 1923 expressed another point of view—that urban areas were the white man's preserve and any black person who moved there served Europeans until they were no longer essential. The Stallard vision eventually won out and set the tone for urban policy for the next sixty years.

The cornerstone of urban legislation was the Native (Urban Areas) Act of 1923, which aimed at removing Africans from mixed residential areas and placing them in separate living areas known as locations. It prevented Africans from owning property in new locations (in contrast to some of the older locations such as Sophiatown and Alexandra) and obtaining trading licenses. It created a system of administration for the locations under the control of municipal native affairs departments assisted by Advisory Boards on which Africans served. Locally generated revenues such as rents, fines, fees, and the sale of "Kaffir beer" to location residents were to finance the costs of administration as much as possible. Even if the 1923 act laid down a set of uniform guidelines and was periodically amended, the government did not systematically apply it. Therefore, the urban centers that Bunche reported on—Cape Town, Bloemfontein, Durban, and Johannesburg—represented a patchwork of approaches, even if the locations he described had a depressingly uniform appearance.

Whatever their intentions, the new regulations failed to stem the flow of Africans to the cities. The urban African population increased from an estimated 587,200 in 1921 to 1,146,600 in 1936; and, as the manufacturing sector expanded during the Second World War, an additional 650,000 Africans moved to the cities between 1936 and 1946.[86] Prime Minister Jan Smuts acknowledged the reality of African urbanization in 1942: "Segregation has tried to stop it. It has, however, not stopped it in the least. The process has been accelerated. You might as well try to sweep the ocean back with a broom."[87] This did not deter the Nationalist Party from passing the Group Areas Act in 1950 and ruthlessly carrying out its aim of purging blacks from the urban areas.

The control over black land and labor gave South African segregation a decidedly different look and feel than American segregation, but there was one area, separate public facilities for racial groups, where the two systems mirrored each other.[88] In this respect, South Africa was not "a very strange society" to Bunche since he had already experienced the same kind of (and no less restrictive) barriers in Washington, D.C. As he wrote Herskovits tongue-in-cheek: "The Jim Crow set-up is quite familiar to me, of course. I get nostalgia every time I see a sign 'For Europeans Only.' "[89] His notes are full of anecdotal material recounting the pervasive measures that separated blacks and whites from cradle to grave —in hospitals, public meetings, churches, movie theaters, elevators, building entrances, buses, taxis (and hand-pulled rickshas in Durban), prisons, and cemeteries. Written laws rarely codified this kind of separation, so there was considerable variety in the way municipalities enforced and practiced it. In certain situations, Africans had to negotiate the rules on an ad hoc basis. For instance, Bunche noted the confusion of Johannesburg Africans over whether they could ride upstairs in double-decker buses, since conductors often made up their own regulations. This led some to board buses and beg conductors to let them stay on. (p. 179)

Outsider accounts of South African segregation rarely reveal its human side, but Bunche's material adds considerable insight into how black people went about constructing their daily lives in the face of considerable barriers. However sympathetic he was to their plight, he did not hesitate to criticize developments in the black community that he believed sustained white domination. Two in particular stood out in his mind—the lack of racial solidarity among Coloureds, Indians, and Africans and inert political leadership by the educated elite.

Bunche catalogued examples of cooperation between Coloureds, Indians, and Africans, but he was disturbed by the degree to which black groups separated themselves from each other in ways that went beyond what law and custom mandated. He saw this manifested in many ways: Africans, Coloureds and Indians competing with each other for student offices at Ft. Hare (p. 126); the principal at a Benoni Indian school refusing to admit Coloured students to his school on racial and national grounds, even though many of his teachers were coloured (p. 202); and Jack Phillips's night club in Johannesburg having distinctive names for different clienteles—the Ritz Palais for Coloureds and the Inchcape for Africans. (p. 180)

Bunche was especially troubled by certain middle-class Coloureds distancing themselves physically and psychologically from Africans— some of them even objected to his referring to himself as a Negro since it implied he identified himself with Africans—because he could readily identify with the physical appearance and lifestyles of Coloured people.[90] This should not be so surprising because of all the communities in South Africa, Coloureds shared the most common ground with African-Americans. Many in both communities were racially mixed, Western-oriented and Christian (though many Coloureds were Muslim), and many of their forebears had experienced slavery.[91] One of Bunche's first observations on landing in Cape Town was: "The Negroes are so mixed up here the place looks like Harlem."[92] And at a reception for him, Bunche remarked: "In Cape Town, he could not see anything different in the Coloured community's lives to that of the United States' Negro."[93]

Bunche was at a loss to understand why some Coloureds were so antagonistic towards Africans until he gained insight into the cultural and linguistic differences between many Coloureds and Africans and how South Africa's racial hierarchy was structured. Coloureds (and Indians) constituted an intermediate caste between Europeans and Africans. By the late nineteenth century a Coloured identity began to crystallize as white authorities offered Coloureds slightly better educational and employment opportunities and exemptions from pass laws so they would not ally themselves with Africans.[94] From time to time some Coloureds and Africans found common cause politically, but middle-class Coloureds were divided over whether they should accommodate themselves to whites.

At the same time as South African segregation was driving a wedge between Coloureds and Africans, American segregation was moving in a different direction—bringing light-skinned and dark-skinned blacks closer together. This was due to the "one-drop rule," which gained currency around 1915. The rule categorized as black any person with a "fatal drop" or a small percentage of black blood. Fine distinctions were not made between African Americans on the basis of skin color and culture; and anyone defined as black was discriminated against with the same intensity.[95]

Bunche also came to appreciate that even within South Africa's mixed-race community, there were differences in opportunities based on the lightness of one's skin. Doors to higher status and educational and economic opportunities opened for those who could pass as white, so lighter-skinned Coloureds devised "passing" strategies for themselves and their children. One favored scheme was for parents to give their lighter-skinned children European identities by sending them to "border line" or "fading" schools, which prohibited darker-skinned children and hired only white teachers. Other parents encouraged their daughters to marry white males, though Bunche thought the girls were more likely to end up with illegitimate children than husbands. He wondered about the psychological damage "passing" could have on individuals, especially children, who denied their own identity.

He also uncovered some interesting twists to "passing" strategies. Friends told him about one Coloured woman who was accepted as European, but chose to pose as a Coloured so she could live in cheaper accommodations. And he learned of Cape Town Africans who passed for Coloured or married Coloured women so they qualified to stay in urban areas.

Another issue that came under Bunche's scrutiny was the anemic challenge black political organizations were mounting against white rule.[96] During his stay, he talked with a range of white and black opponents of the government, and he attended three major political meetings: the first sitting of the Native Representative Council, the third meeting of the All African Convention, and the silver jubilee of the African National

Congress. On the whole, the caliber of black political leadership did not impress him, and his portraits of them were unflattering.

His visit came at a critical juncture for black political movements. They had been thrown into crisis by segregation bills that Prime Minister J. B. M. Hertzog had navigated through Parliament in 1936 after a decade of effort. The Native Land and Trust Act allowed for more land to be added to the 'native reserve' areas, but set a ceiling on the amount of land that Africans could eventually occupy—some 13 percent of the country. The Representation of Natives Act took the vote away from the only enfranchised group of Africans in the country, Cape Africans, who could vote if they met education, property or salary qualifications. Cape Africans made up only 1.2 percent of all voters, but they constituted a significant bloc of voters in a handful of eastern Cape constituencies. In a closely contested national election, they could make a difference, since most of their votes went to Hertzog's rival, the South Africa Party (SAP).

Hertzog could not easily do away with the African vote because a constitutional clause prevented him from altering it unless he won over at least a two-thirds majority of both Houses of Parliament. His franchise bill had foundered in the late 1920s because he could not marshal enough votes. But he diluted the African vote first by enfranchising white women and then by removing the property and literacy qualifications for white male voters. After a merger with the SAP in 1934 created the United Party, he finally realized his goal. Part of the compromise of merger was that he could now rely on former SAP members of Parliament to support his franchise bill; and, in 1936, he finally mustered the necessary votes for its passage.

As a trade-off for eliminating the African vote, the Representation of Natives Act created a group of white "native" representatives to act on behalf of Africans in Parliament. Cape African voters directly elected three representatives to the House of Assembly and Africans nationwide indirectly elected four to the Senate. The Act also established a Native Representative Council (NRC) composed of twelve indirectly elected Africans, four government-nominated members, and key white "native affairs" officials. The NRC's limitations became immediately clear. Sitting in Pretoria, a thousand miles away from the all-white Parliament in Cape Town, the NRC was purely advisory and was never intended to be more than a sounding board for African opinion.

At the time the most prominent African opposition movement was the African National Congress (ANC). Founded in 1912, the ANC sought to create a broad alliance of Africans to protest the exclusion of

Africans from political rights, to air African grievances, and to uplift and advance Africans on a range of fronts. Its ultimate goal was not so much African majority rule as equal opportunity for all South Africans. Dominated by mission-educated professionals (teachers, clergy, lawyers, journalists), the ANC largely eschewed militant protest in favor of gradual change through constitutional and nonviolent means. Its leaders preferred petitions, delegations, and appeals over strikes and boycotts. The ANC had gone through occasional spasms of radical activity, but by the mid-1930s, the ANC was languishing under the feeble, conservative leadership of Pixley ka Seme, elected president in 1930.

When Seme's ANC did not provide the leadership to combat the Hertzog bills, 400 black delegates from all over South Africa converged on Bloemfontein in December 1935 to launch the All African Convention (AAC). The AAC elected D. D. T. Jabavu, a Fort Hare professor as its president, and A. B. Xuma, an American-educated medical doctor as its vice president. Black politicians hailed the AAC meeting as the most representative meeting ever of black leaders from throughout South Africa. And they invested much hope in several AAC delegations sent to Cape Town in 1936 in an unsuccessful last-ditch effort to stave off the Hertzog legislation.

However, once the legislation was passed, black leaders lacked a coherent political strategy on how to respond to the dilemma posed by the NRC's creation—whether they should boycott it or use it as a platform for challenging and wringing modest concessions from the government. Most leaders eventually took the latter tack, so when Bunche attended the NRC's inaugural meeting, he found himself in the company of such eminent African leaders as John Dube, R. V Selope-Thema, Richard Godlo, T. M. Mapikela, A. M. Jabavu, and C. K. Sakwe, all of whom were on the AAC executive.

Bunche's rare behind-the-scenes account of NRC proceedings sheds light on the NRC's impotence. The high-handed tactics of its European chairman, D. L. Smit, Secretary for Native Affairs, quickly dispelled any hope the NRC might prove to be a credible forum. Smit presided autocratically over a council that was supposed to be reviewing the policies of his own department. He set and controlled the meeting's agenda and "steamrollered" items through the council. He brooked no challenges from councillors and left little time for debate. He treated the councillors like errant "schoolboys," scolding three of them and threatening to dock them a day's pay when they turned up late for the second day's session. And he manipulated provincial rivalries by trying to drive wedges between councillors on education, budgetary, and land issues. Although

Smit's divisive tactics were transparent, Bunche still had little sympathy for the councillors whom he found unprepared, timid, and frivolous.

After the NRC meeting, Bunche went on to the AAC and ANC meetings in Bloemfontein, but his estimation of black political leadership did not markedly change. The leaders seemed to him more concerned with style and status than with addressing programs and tactics to combat the government. He cited the telling example of the AAC president, D. D. T. Jabavu, who left the AAC meeting before it had adopted a statement of policy—and the AAC was not due to meet for another three years. Of the two groups, Bunche was more critical of the ANC, which was more intent on celebrating its silver jubilee than in addressing serious issues. ANC officials had given little thought beforehand to organizing their conference and hastily patched together a program on the spot. They scurried about, begging outsiders like Bunche and Jack Simons to deliver speeches. The two resisted speaking until Selope Thema told a story about God paying a visit to Africa and finding Africans in such a state of poverty and backwardness that they had invited in white men to make use of the continent's vast mineral resources. Thema's speech so offended Bunche that he felt compelled to offer his own advice that blacks could not take their country back unless they first harnessed their own labor power and their own organizations.

His apprehension about the ANC's unhealthy reliance on outsiders was especially directed at the white "native" representatives, who he thought played a parasitic role around black groups.[97] Their presence struck a raw nerve since he had leveled a similar indictment at African-American organizations for depending on white liberals. By and large, the South African white liberals were drawn from the ranks of missionaries, educators, social workers, and academics, and they clustered around organizations such as the Institute of Race Relations and the Joint Councils. Although the "native" representatives had an official capacity at the Native Representative Council, Bunche was not convinced their presence was warranted at the AAC and ANC meetings. He believed their true role was to defuse any hint of militancy by African movements by promoting the idea that the white Parliament was a legitimate institution for dealing with African grievances. He concluded:

> The role of the European reps. [representatives] is a dangerous one—they are now counselling extreme moderation among the natives so as not to inject the native issue into the coming election, and also so as not to offend the Afrikaners and thus make their task more difficult in Parliament. They can't see anything they do of significance for the native is bound

to offend the reactionaries and that it is impossible to please both sides. They lack the courage to take a strong stand. (p. 274)

The 1937 meetings were a low ebb for black political organizations, but they also marked a turning point for the ANC, as disenchanted members began resuscitating it several years later. In 1940, the ANC elected Dr. Xuma President, and he put the organization on a firmer footing and broadened its base of support. He cultivated a younger generation of activists who, in 1944, launched the ANC Youth League. The Youth Leaguers, who included such future ANC leaders as Nelson Mandela, Oliver Tambo, and Walter Sisulu, in some ways echoed Bunche's reservations by criticizing the ANC's moderation, passivity, and reliance on whites. They especially singled out the NRC, labeling it the "toy telephone" and calling on African leaders to boycott it. When the government finally abolished the NRC in 1951, all but a few die-hard African leaders had already abandoned it. Eventually the Youth Leaguers were a key force in pushing the ANC to adopt a more challenging posture—as expressed in its 1949 Programme of Action.

NOTES

1. Brian Bunting, *Moses Kotane: South African Revolutionary* (London: Inkululeko Publications, 1975), 88.

2. Studies on Bunche include Jean Cornell, *Ralph Bunche, Champion of Peace* (Champaign, Ill.: Garrard Publishing Co., 1976); Roberta Feuerlicht, *In Search of Peace* (New York: J. Messner, 1970); Souad Halila, "The Intellectual Development and Diplomatic Career of Ralph J. Bunche" (Ph.D. diss., University of Southern California, 1988); James Haskins, *Ralph Bunche: A Most Reluctant Hero* (New York: Hawthorn Books, 1974); Ann Johnson, *The Value of Responsibility* (La Jolla, Cal.: Value Communications, 1978); J. Alvin Kugelmass, *Ralph J. Bunche: Fighter for Peace* (New York: J. Messner, 1962); Peggy Mann, *Ralph Bunche: UN Peacemaker* (New York: Coward, McCann & Geoghegan, 1975); Patricia McKissack, *Ralph J. Bunche* (Hillside, N. J.: Enslow Publishers, 1991); and Benjamin Rivlin, ed., *Ralph Bunche: The Man and His Times* (New York: Holmes & Meier, 1990). Rivlin's book contains chapters on Bunche's African interests by Nathaniel Huggins, Martin Kilson, and W. Ofuatey-Kodjoe.

3. *Kokstad Advertiser*, 22 July 1982. For accounts of other African-American visitors, see E. De Waal, "American Black Residents and Visitors in the South African Republic before 1899," *South African Historical Journal* 6 (1974): 52–55; Clement Keto, "Black Americans and South Africa, 1890–1910," *Current Bibliography of African Affairs* 5 (1972): 483–506; Thomas J. Noer, *Briton, Boer, and Yankee: The United States and South Africa 1870–1914* (Kent State University Press,

1978), esp. chap. 6; Willard Gatewood, "Black Americans and the Boer War, 1899–1902," *South Atlantic Quarterly* 75 (1976): 226–44; John Hope Franklin, *George Washington Williams: A Biography* (Chicago: University of Chicago Press, 1985), 197.

4. Veit Erlmann, " 'A Feeling of Prejudice,' Orpheus M. McAdoo and the Virginia Jubilee Singers in South Africa, 1890–98," *Journal of Southern African Studies* 14 (1988): 331–50; David Coplan, *In Township Tonight!: South Africa's Black City Music and Theatre* (Johannesburg: Ravan Press, 1985).

5. James Campbell, "Our Fathers, Our Children: The African Methodist Episcopal Church in the United States and South Africa" (Ph.D. diss., Stanford University, 1990); J. Chirenje, *Ethiopianism and Afro-Americans in Southern Africa 1883–1916* (Baton Rouge, La.: Louisiana State University Press, 1987); Carol Page, "Black America in White South Africa: Church and State Reaction to the A.M.E. Church in Cape Colony and Transvaal, 1896–1910" (Ph.D. diss., Edinburgh University, 1978); Beulah Fluornoy, "The Relationship of the A.M.E. Church to its South African Mentors," *Journal of African Studies* 2 (1975–76): 529–45.

6. Perhaps as many as several hundred black South Africans made their way to the U.S. for higher education. A number came under the sponsorship of black mission societies and attended American black colleges. See R. Hunt Davis, "The Black American Educational Component in African Responses to Colonialism in South Africa," *Journal of Southern African Affairs* 3 (1) (1978): 69–84 and R. Hunt Davis, "John Dube: A South African Exponent of Booker T. Washington," *Journal of African Studies* 2 (1975–76): 497–528.

7. Robert Edgar, "Garveyism in Africa: Dr. Wellington and the American Movement in the Transkei," *Ufahamu* 6 (1976): 31–57; Robert Hill and Greg Pirio, " 'Africa for the Africans': the Garvey movement in South Africa, 1920–1940," in *The Politics of Race, Class and Nationalism in Twentieth-Century South Africa* (London: Longman, 1987), Shula Marks and Stanley Trapido, eds., 209–53; A. P. Walshe, "Black American Thought and African Political Attitudes in South Africa," *Review of Politics* 32 (1970): 51–77; T. J. Couzens, " 'Moralizing Leisure Time': The Transatlantic Connection and Black Johannesburg (1918–1936)," in *The New African: A Study of the Life and Work of H. I. E. Dhlomo* (Johannesburg: Ravan Press, 1985); Alan Cobley, *Class and Consciousness: The Black Petty Bourgeoisie in South Africa, 1924 to 1950* (New York: Greenwood Press, 1990), chap. 3; and Helen Bradford, *A Taste of Freedom: The ICU in Rural South Africa 1924–1930* (New Haven: Yale University Press, 1987), 213–45.

8. Comparing Robeson's published account with her original diary would be an interesting exercise, but her son has not opened to scholars her original diary, deposited in the Robeson Papers in the Moorland-Spingarn collection at Howard University.

9. Nathan Huggins, "Black Biography: Reflections of a Historian," *CAAS Newsletter* 9 (1985): 1, 6–7. Huggins addresses related issues in "Uses of the Self: Afro-American Autobiography," in *Historical Judgments Reconsidered* (Washington, D.C.: Howard University Press, 1988), 171–80.

10. Halila, "The Intellectual Development," 49.

11. A synopsis of his thesis is contained in Robert Harris, "Ralph Bunche and Afro-American Participation in Decolonization," in *Pan-African Biography* (Los Angeles: Crossroads Press, 1987), 120–23. For discussions of Bunche as

Africanist, see Nathan Huggins, "Ralph Bunche the Africanist," and Martin Kilson, "Ralph Bunche's Analytical Perspective on African Development" in *Ralph Bunche: The Man and His Times* (New York: Holmes and Meier, 1990).

12. An excellent insight into the world of one academic at Howard is Kenneth R. Manning's *Black Apollo of Science: The Life of Ernest Everett Just* (New York: Oxford University Press, 1983); see also Michael Winston's "Through the Back Door: Academic Racism and the Negro Scholar in Historical Perspective," *Daedalus* 100 (1971): 679–719.

13. Mann, *Ralph Bunche,* 87.

14. I have profited from discussions with Harold Lewis, St. Clair Drake, and John Hope Franklin. A conversation Bunche recorded in Paris with the historian Carter Woodson confirms the attraction of Communism to black intellectuals. Bunche records that Woodson, who ordinarily took a nationalist line, "claims he's a communist really as every Amer. N[egro]. must be." (Ralph J. Bunche Diary, 16 July 1937. This is a daily diary Bunche maintained throughout 1937 and 1938; he kept it separate from his research notes. I refer to this diary hereafter as RJB Diary.)

Reading the writings of this Howard group confirms that their views were very close to one another on many issues. On Harris, see William Darity, Jr., ed., *Race, Radicalism, and Reform: Selected Papers Abram L. Harris* (New Brunswick: Transaction Publishers, 1989); on Frazier, see "E. Franklin Frazier," in James Blackwell and Morris Janowitz, *Black Sociologists: Historical and Contemporary Perspectives* (Chicago: University of Chicago Press, 1974); on Locke, see Russell J. Linnemann, ed., *Alain Locke: Reflections on a Modern Renaissance Man* (Baton Rouge: Louisiana State University Press, 1982).

15. Bunche, quoted in James O. Young, *Black Writers of the Thirties* (Baton Rouge: Louisiana State University Press, 1973), 54.

16. Ralph Bunche, "A Critique of New Deal Social Planning," *Journal of Negro Education* 5 (1936): 59–65. Because mainstream journals shut out black scholars, most of Bunche's academic writings appeared in the *Journal of Negro Education.* In addition, see John B. Kirby, "Ralph J. Bunche and Black Radical Thought in the 1930s," *Phylon* 35 (1974): 129–42 and John Kirby, *Black Americans in the Roosevelt Era: Liberalism and Race* (Knoxville: University of Tennessee Press, 1980), 202–17.

17. Ralph Bunche, "The Programs of Organizations Devoted to the Improvement of the Status of the American Negro," *Journal of Negro Education* 8 (1939): 549.

18. Raymond Wolters, *Negroes and the Great Depression: The Problem of Economic Recovery* (Westport, Conn.: Greenwood Press, 1970), 220. The clearest presentation of Bunche's views on black organizations is his "Programs of Organizations," 539–50.

19. Kirby, *Black Americans,* 205.

20. Note how closely Bunche's views paralleled those of the economist Abram Harris, who shared his suspicion of black businessmen: "The real forces behind their disabilities and discomfort are masked by race which prevents them from seeing that what the Negro business man wants most of all is freedom to monopolize and exploit the market they provide. They cannot see that they have no greater exploiter than the black capitalist who lives upon low-waged if not sweated labor, although he and his family may, and often do, live

in conspicuous luxury." Abram Lincoln Harris, *The Negro as Capitalist: A Study of Banking and Business among American Negroes* (College Park, Md: McGrath Publishing Co., 1936), 184.

21. Quoted in Kirby, *Black Americans,* 234. See also Bunche's comment on white liberals in Wolters, *Negroes and the Great Depression,* 319.

22. The conference created headaches for Howard's president, Mordecai Johnson, who had to fend off Congressional accusations that he was harboring radical teachers on his staff. Despite Bunche's eventual break with the NNC, the U.S. Civil Service Commission's International Organizations Employees Loyalty Board investigated him in 1954 for his earlier radical leanings but cleared him of any wrongdoing. See Robert Harris, "Ralph Bunche and Afro-American Participation in Decolonization," 119–20 and Charles P. Henry, "Civil Rights and National Security: The Case of Ralph Bunche," in *Ralph Bunche: The Man and His Times,* 50–68.

23. Ralph Bunche, "Triumph? or Fiasco?" *Race* I (Summer 1936): 93–96.

24. Ralph Bunche, "Programs of Organizations," 547.

25. Writing to Lewis Hanke in 1941, Bunche observed: "The Negro has been misled and duped by many groups, the Communist especially. . . ." Bunche to Hanke, 3 July 1941, Box 2, Ralph J. Bunche Papers (hereafter RJB Papers), Special Collections, University of California, Los Angeles. Lawrence Wittner argues that the basis for the NNC breakup was not a result of Communist Party interference, but because NNC members wanted the organization to take partisan stands on political and labor issues and its alliance with the labor federation CIO ran counter to its nationalist emphasis. ("The National Negro Congress: a Reassessment," *American Quarterly* 22 (Winter 1970): 883–901. On the NNC's break-up, see also Wolters, *Negroes and the Great Depression,* 370–76.

26. Ralph Bunche, "French Educational Policy in Togo and Dahomey," *Journal of Negro Education* 3 (1934): 69–97; "French and British Imperialism in West Africa," *Journal of Negro History* 2 (1936): 31–46.

27. For a broader view of African-American critiques of colonialism, see Mark Solomon, "Black Critics of Colonialism and the Cold War," in *Cold War Critics: Alternatives to American Foreign Policy in the Truman Years* (Chicago: Quadrangle Books, 1971), 205–39.

28. Ralph Bunche, *A World View of Race* (Washington, D.C.: Associates in Negro Folk Education, 1936), 64.

29. Ralph Bunche, review of *An African Speaks for His People* by Parmenas Mockerie, in *Journal of Negro Education* 4 (1935): 113–15.

30. Ralph Bunche, *A World View,* 96.

31. Bunche to Melville J. Herskovits, 4 October 1935, Melville Herskovits Papers (hereafter MJH Papers), Northwestern University Archives, Evanston, Illinois.

32. Bunche to Herskovits, 4 October 1935, MJH Papers. Bunche was one of thirteen postdoctoral research training fellows in the social sciences. Thomas Wallbank was also given a grant to study ". . . the culture of native peoples in relation to current problems of colonial administration."

33. For instance, Bunche observes: "The colonial anthropologist revels in the discovery of an isolated, untouched primitive culture, which may be analyzed in its condition of pristine purity, and it is not many years since Africa

afforded him an excellent playground." Ralph Bunche, review of *Reaction to Conquest* by Monica Hunter, in *Journal of Negro Education* 6 (4) (1937): 639–42.

34. Emphasis in original. File "SSRC Fellowship 1937–38," RJB Papers, Box 126. Bunche's use of the term *retarded* is not accidental since he used it again in his article "French and British Imperialism," 45. He was taking his cue from general attitudes of academics writing on Africa. His Harvard adviser, Rupert Emerson, backed Bunche's proposal with the following comment: "Without the ability and knowledge to do some trained and intelligent thinking on the question of the *effect* [emphasis in original] of imperialism on backward peoples there is no question in my mind that one is merely somewhat futilely playing around on the surface of politics." ("SSRC Fellowship.") To Bunche, the words *retarded* and *backward* did not imply that Africans were inferior or were incapable of advancing themselves, but that they had been isolated from developments in the outside world and had fallen behind in technological and material achievement. Environment, not race, was the factor hampering Africa's development.

35. Consider Bunche's comment in writing about higher education for blacks: "Negro scholars even more completely than white, are subject to the munificence of the controlling wealthy groups in the population. Negro institutions of higher learning, particularly, are the inevitable puppets of white philanthropy." Ralph Bunche, "Education in Black and White," *Journal of Negro Education* 5 (3) (1936): 356. For a general discussion on how private foundations influenced black colleges, see James Anderson, "Philanthropic Control over Private Black Higher Education," in *Philanthropy and Cultural Imperialism: The Foundations at Home and Abroad* (Boston: G. K. Hall, 1980), 147–78.

36. St. Clair Drake noted that Herskovits began to change his attitude toward African-American researchers after 1950. (St. Clair Drake, telephone interview by author, August 1989).

37. Letter from Walter Jackson to author, 12 June 1989; Herskovits to Henry Allen Moe, Guggenheim Foundation, 6 January 1937, quoted in Walter Jackson, "Melville Herskovits and the Search for Afro-American Culture," in *Malinowski, Rivers, Benedict and Others Essays on Culture and Personality* (Madison: University of Wisconsin Press, 1986), 117.

38. Herskovits to Isaac Schapera, 9 August 1937, MJH Papers. For additional comment on Herskovits's approach to African research, see Robert Harris, "Segregation and Scholarship: the American Council of Learned Societies' Committee on Negro Studies, 1941–1950," *Journal of Black Studies* 12 (March 1982): 315–31.

39. Ralph Bunche, review of *Dahomey* by Melville Herskovits, in *Journal of Negro Education* 8 (1939): 212.

40. RJB Diary, 23 June 1937; Bunche to Herskovits, 27 May 1938, MJH Papers. Few who judged Malinowski did so with equanimity. For additional comments on him and his seminar, see Adam Kuper, *Anthropologists and Anthropology: The British School 1922–1972* (New York: Pica Press, 1973), 13–50; and Hilda Kuper, "Function, History, Biography: Reflections on Fifty Years in the British Anthropology Tradition," in *Functionalism Historicized: Essays on British Social Anthropology* (Madison: University of Wisconsin Press, 1984), 197–200.

41. Bunche to Herskovits, 20 May 1937 and 27 May 1938, MJH Papers.

42. Bunche to Herskovits, 30 June 1937, MJH Papers.

43. Simons and M'timkulu returned to South Africa while Bunche was there and personally helped him around various places.

44. David Anthony has assessed Yergan's South African experiences in his "Max Yergan in South Africa: From Evangelical Pan Africanist to Revolutionary Socialist," *African Studies Review* 34 (2) (1991): 27–56.

45. Leonard Barnes had served as a civil servant in the colonial service and worked as a farmer and journalist in South Africa until 1933. His books included *Caliban in Africa* (1930), *The New Boer War* (1935), *The Duty of Empire* (1935) and *Zulu Paraclete: A Sentimental Record* (1938). Macmillan was at work on *Africa Emergent* published in 1938.

46. RJB Diary, 11 September 1937.

47. For more details on the Pan African crowd in London, see J. A. Langley, *Pan-Africanism and Nationalism in West Africa 1900–1945: A Study in Ideology and Social Classes* (Oxford, Clarendon Press, 1973), 337–47 and Imanuel Geiss, *The Pan-African Movement: A History of Pan-Africanism in America, Europe, and Africa* (New York: Africana Publishing Co., 1974), 340–62. Bunche's contacts with this group brought him to the attention of British intelligence, which was monitoring their activities. A communication went out to British officials in Dar es Salaam, Tanganyika, where Bunche planned to visit: "I think it well to tell you that while he [Bunche] has been in England he has apparently been pushed into touch with some of our black undesirables. We do not know what his relations with them are, or whether he is in any degree sympathetic with them. It is quite on the cards that he has simply been led astray by names and did not realise the sort of people that he was going to meet, but I pass this on to you. . . . I ought to add that there can be no doubt about Bunche's credentials, so it is to be hoped that his connexion with the scaly lot is purely accidental." (J. E. W. Flood to Merrick, 29 June 1937, Colonial Office (CO) 323/1517/7046/3 (Public Record Office, London).) I thank Marika Sherwood for sharing this document with me.

48. Ralph Bunche, review of *How Britain Rules Africa* by George Padmore, in *Journal of Negro Education* 6 (1) (1936): 75–76.

49. Ralph Bunche, *A World View*, 95.

50. Bunche's diary and other notes record useful biographical information on Kenyatta. For instance, Bunche took down an extensive conversation with Kenyatta about his early life (RJB Diary, 25 May 1937). See also Bunche's notes in Box 69, miscellaneous note cards, RJB papers. Kenyatta's London years are chronicled in Jeremy Murray-Brown, *Kenyatta* (London: Fontana/Collins, 1972).

51. Emphasis in original. RJB Diary, 8 June 1937. I have refrained from mentioning the full name of the English student.

52. An indication of Bunche's interest in the Italo-Ethiopian war is his book reviews in the *Journal of Negro Education* 5 (1) (1936): 133–36. For a discussion of how African-Americans reacted to the conflict, see William A. Shack, "Ethiopia and Afro-Americans: Some Historical Notes, 1920–1970," *Phylon* 35: 142–55; Joseph Harris, "Race and Misperception in the Origins of United States-Ethiopian Relations," *TransAfrica Forum* 3 (Winter 1986): 9–23; and William R. Scott, *The Sons of Sheba's Race: African-Americans and the Italo-Ethiopian War, 1935–1941* (Bloomington: Indiana University Press, 1991).

53. RJB Diary, 5 April 1937. When Eslanda Robeson had applied for a visa a year earlier, embassy officials gave her such a runaround that she decided to

start her ocean voyage without knowing whether she would be allowed to disembark at Cape Town.

54. RJB Diary, 26 April 1937.

55. Folder, "Correspondence re: Africa 1937–38," RJB Papers, Box 62.

56. Loram's lukewarm letter was a step forward for him. In late 1928, Alain Locke, one of Bunche's Howard colleagues, had been proposed as a visitor to South Africa on a Carnegie grant, but Loram had written the Carnegie Corporation that "anti-Native feeling is strong at present and it would be difficult to persuade people that Locke was not a propagandist." (Quoted in Richard Heyman, "C. T. Loram: A South African Liberal in Race Relations," *International Journal of Race Relations* 5 (1) (1972): 44); see also R. Hunt Davis, "Charles T. Loram and the American Model for African Education in South Africa," *African Studies Review* 19 (2) (1976): 87–100.) In 1935 W. E. B. DuBois requested a Carnegie travel grant to visit South Africa to study race relations, but the Corporation turned him down. He applied again in 1939, but the Corporation rejected his request after J. D. Rheinallt Jones opposed him. This incident is mentioned in Walter A. Jackson, *Gunnar Myrdal and America's Conscience: Social Engineering and Racial Liberalism, 1938–1987* (University of North Carolina Press, 1990). I thank him for sharing this with me.

57. RJB Diary, 29 June 1937.

58. RJB Diary, 25 June 1937.

59. Bunche to Herskovits, 30 June 1937, MJH Papers.

60. Although the 1913 Immigration Act did not specifically exclude black people from entering South Africa, they were covered under a clause that allowed the government to block "any person or class of persons deemed by the Minister on economic grounds or *on account of standard or habits of life* [my emphasis] to be unsuited to the requirements of the Union. . . ."

61. See Chirenje, *Ethiopianism and Afro-Americans* for additional discussion of South African government perceptions of African-Americans.

62. Rev. A. C. Murray to Rev. A. L. Warnshuis, 9 May 1923, Box 1127, file 1913/1923, International Missionary Council Archives (IMCA), School of Oriental and African Studies, University of London

63. Box 1226, file C, "American Negro Missionaries," IMCA.

64. Yergan's transformation is dealt with in David Anthony, "Max Yergan in South Africa." I thank David Anthony for clarifying the point about Yergan.

65. RJB Diary, 13 July 1937; 7 September 1937; 9 September 1937; 12 September 1937.

66. RJB Diary, 12 September 1937; 16 September 1937.

67. Jesse Owens and Ralph Metcalf were American track stars who had won gold medals at the 1936 Berlin Summer Olympics.

68. Bunche met Mrs. Alexander's husband in Johannesburg. See p. 185.

69. RJB Diary, 19 September 1937; 23 September 1937; 28 September 1937.

70. RJB Diary, 18 September 1937.

71. Letter from Prof. I. Schapera, 21 November 1935, University of Cape Town Council Minutes (1935). I thank Howard Phillips for this reference.

72. Bunche to Herskovits, 7 October 1937, MJH Papers.

73. Don M'timkulu, telephone interview by author, 13 December 1989. M'timkulu remembered that Bunche did not think through his travels in South

Africa before he arrived in a place. When he came to Durban, he believed that he could locate the M'timkulu family through the telephone book, but when he could not, he called A. I. Kajee to ask for help and Kajee invited him to stay at his home.

74. Eslanda Robeson describes her South African travel experience: "This traveling about Africa reminds me of traveling through the Deep South in America. You are passed from friend to friend, from car to car, from home to home, often covering thousands of miles without enduring the inconveniences and humiliations of the incredibly bad Jim Crow train accommodations and lack of hotel facilities for Negroes." *African Journey,* 65.

75. Mann, *Ralph Bunche,* 79–83.

76. In Johannesburg, when Bunche included a question about how Africans perceived African Americans in a limited survey he carried out, he received a variety of reactions. He heard one response that others had already directed at him—that African Americans were too proud to come to the rescue of black South Africans. However, most of the feedback he received was positive.

"They are very progressive more than our Negroes here."
"Because the source of our origin is the same."
"Because we are looking at them as Leaders of Education."
"I have a brotherly attitude towards Negroes partly because of their kinship and partly also because they are interested in the welfare of the African."
"One of brotherliness and one [views] him as . . . an advanced Black African. I'm afraid I've not too much of that belief that he can do much towards the betterment of the life of the S.A. [South African] black."
"favourable in that in them is seen what a people can do when actually freed from slavery."

77. Bunche to Essie and Paul Robeson, 11 January 1938, Correspondence files, Paul and Eslanda Robeson Papers (hereafter Robeson Papers), Manuscripts Collection, Moorland-Spingarn Library, Howard University. See also the editorials on Robeson in *Umteteli wa Bantu,* 3 June 1933, 25 July 1936, and 1 February 1941. Robeson was the role model for a fictional character, de la Harpe, an African American who visits South Africa in Ethelreda Lewis's *Wild Deer.* T. J. Couzens has written an illuminating introduction that probes Lewis's fascination with Robeson in *Wild Deer*'s 1984 edition published by David Philip.

78. *Cape Standard,* 25 October 1937.

79. *Iso Lomuzi* 4 (1) (October 1934): 2; see also Bishop Sims' "Future of the Non-European in South Africa," *Imvo Zabantsundu,* 30 October 1934. Other references are Dr. F. H. Gow's speech reported in the *Cape Standard,* 4 July 1939; Bishop R. R. Wright's speech in *Cape Standard,* 19 September 1939; and Prof. Amos White's lecture in *Cape Standard,* 26 July 1933.

80. *Umteteli wa Bantu,* 11 July 1936. See also her comments in Cape Town: "Too often we have that inferiority complex. . . . Perhaps this is because the great culture of the Europeans—which, after all, only grew out of the culture of the Coloured races of the East and North Africa—made the White man loud-voiced and caused the black races to be quiet. . . . Because of our attitude towards ourselves, we, as non-Europeans, made ourselves vulnerable." (*Cape Standard,* 22 June 1936.)

81. Bunche to Essie and Paul Robeson, 11 January 1938, Robeson Papers.

82. These figures are taken from the 1936 census.

83. C. W. de Kiewiet, *A History of South Africa: Social and Economic* (New York: Oxford University Press, 1941), 141.

84. The impact of government policy on the lives of rural Africans is detailed by Timothy J. Keegan, *Rural Transformations in Industrializing South Africa: The Southern Highveld to 1914* (London: Macmillan, 1987); William Beinart, et al., eds., *Putting a Plough to the Ground: Accumulation and Dispossession in Rural South Africa, 1850–1930* (Johannesburg: Ravan Press, 1986); and Colin Bundy, *The Rise and Fall of the South African Peasantry* (Berkeley: University of California Press, 1979).

85. On urban policy, see Paul Maylam, "The Rise and Decline of Urban Apartheid in South Africa," *African Affairs* 89, 354 (1990): 57–84; T. R. Davenport, "African Townsmen? South African Natives (Urban Areas) Legislation through the Years," *African Affairs* 68, 271 (1969): 95–109.

86. Paul Maylam, *A History of the African People of South Africa: From the Early Iron Age to the 1970s* (Cape Town: David Philip, 1986), 148–49, 177.

87. Jan Smuts, *The Basis of Trusteeship* (1942), 10, quoted in Leonard Thompson and Monica Wilson, eds. *Oxford History of South Africa* (New York: Oxford University Press, 1971), vol. 2, 189.

88. The best studies comparing the United States and South Africa are George M. Fredrickson's *White Supremacy: A Comparative Study in American and South African History* (New York: Oxford University Press, 1981) and John W. Cell's *The Highest Stage of White Supremacy: The Origins of Segregation in South Africa and the American South* (New York: Cambridge University Press, 1982).

89. Bunche to Herskovits, 7 October 1937. MJH Papers.

90. For another commentary on Coloured-African relations by an African American, see R. R. Wright, "South Africa Has Its Own Color Lines," *Opportunity* (May 1937): 138–41.

91. Fredrickson, *White Supremacy,* 255–57.

92. RJB Diary, 29 September 1939.

93. *Cape Standard,* 1 November 1937.

94. The Coloured community is treated in Gavin Lewis, *Between the Wire and the Wall: A History of South African "Coloured" Politics* (New York: St. Martin's Press, 1987); Ian Goldin, *Making Race: The Politics and Economics of Coloured Identity in South Africa* (Cape Town, Maskew Miller Longman, 1987); Richard van der Ross, *The Rise and Decline of Apartheid: A Study of Political Movements among the Coloured People of South Africa* (Cape Town: Tafelberg, 1986); and Mary Simons, "Organised Coloured Political Movements," in *Occupational and Social Change among Coloured People in South Africa* (Cape Town: Juta and Co., 1976), 202–37.

95. Joel Williamson, *New People: Miscegenation and Mulattoes in the United States* (New York: Free Press, 1980). In London, when Lord Noel Buxton engaged Ruth Bunche in a conversation, he expressed amazement that she defined herself as an "American Negro" since she was light-skinned. She explained that in the United States, all it took was a "fatal drop" to be considered black. (RJB Diary, 21 June 1937.)

96. African political and trade union movements are chronicled in Peter Walshe, *The Rise of African Nationalism in South Africa: The African National Con-*

gress, 1912–1952 (Berkeley: University of California Press, 1971); Thomas Karis and Gwendolyn M. Carter, *From Protest to Challenge: A Documentary History of African Politics in South Africa, 1882–1964* (Stanford, Cal.: Hoover Institution Press, 1973), vols. 1 and 2; Jack and Ray Simons, *Class and Colour in South Africa, 1850–1950* (Harmondsworth: Penguin, 1969); Tom Lodge, *Black Politics in South Africa since 1945* (London: Longman, 1983); Gail Gerhart, *Black Power in South Africa: The Evolution of an Ideology* (Berkeley, Ca.: University of California Press, 1978); Francis Meli, *South Africa Belongs to Us: A History of the ANC* (Bloomington: Indiana University Press, 1989); and Baruch Hirson, *Yours for the Union: Class and Community Struggles in South Africa, 1930–1947* (London: Zed Books, 1990).

97. On white liberals, see: Paul B. Rich, *White Power and the Liberal Conscience: Racial Segregation and South African Liberalism 1921–1960* (Johannesburg: Ravan Press, 1984); Saul Dubow, *Racial Segregation and the Origins of Apartheid in South Africa, 1919–36* (New York: St. Martin's Press, 1989); and J. Butler et al., eds., *Democratic Liberalism in South Africa: Its History and Prospect* (Middletown, Ct.: Wesleyan University Press, 1987).

Bunche receiving an honorary degree from Howard University, 1949. Pictured in photo—Bunche, President Mordecai Johnson, Vijaya Pandit, Oscar Chapman

Bunche (on right) in Senegal

Comments on Editing

Ralph Bunche kept
two records on his visit to South Africa, a handwritten daily diary and
typed research notes. He used his diary, which runs from late 1936 to
the beginning of 1938 (a second diary covers the rest of 1938), to log
personal observations as well as day-to-day appointments. The diary is
very detailed on his experiences before he arrived in South Africa, and I
have relied on it for information on his London stay. Once he arrived in
South Africa, his personal diary was primarily kept to note appointments, but it has performed an important function in my research—
helping to reconstruct Bunche's precise movements in South Africa. I
found Bunche's research notes in jumbled order and often undated.
Thus, when I could not determine when he did certain things or made
particular observations, I turned to his diary for leads.

His daily diary also contains detailed entries on his boat and train
travels that are not covered in his research notes. I have therefore
spliced in passages from his personal diary to add transitional passages
to his journey. I have inserted these passages in the following places: his
landing in Cape Town on 29 September 1937 (pp. 53–4); his trip from
Cape Town to Basutoland from 3 November to 5 November (pp. 97–8);
his layover and departure from Bloemfontein, 8 and 9 November (pp.
120–1); his arrival at Thaba 'Nchu on 14 November (p. 143); and his
departures from Bloemfontein on 17 November (pp. 156–7) and 18
December (p. 282) and Durban on 1 January 1938 (p. 310).

Bunche regularly made entries in his research notes. He did not contemplate writing about South Africa before he left the country, but presumably he kept the notes as part of his training in field work methodology. He also does not indicate whether his notes were handwritten first and then typed on 5″ x 8″ file cards after he returned to the United States. If he handwrote his notes first and typed them up later, then the uneven quality of his typed notes suggests it is likely that he faithfully transcribed his original notes.

When he was in towns in South Africa, Bunche's normal schedule was to sleep late and write up his observations before he set out on his appointments and socializing, which often kept him busy until the early hours of the morning. He would also take advantage of his lengthy train rides to make notes.

When Bunche had a chance to reflect on his experiences, his notes read smoothly and required little editing. But some of his notes were obviously written in haste. Bunche often did not write sentences with a personal pronoun subject or verb or both. I have added words in brackets wherever I felt they were necessary. All ellipsis points in the text indicate where I have editorially excised words from Bunche's notes.

I have supplied the complete forms of Bunche's abbreviations wherever I felt they were necessary for clarity. A listing of Bunche's more common abbreviations follows this section.

Bunche was inconsistent with verb tenses. He might use several different tenses in one paragraph. However, I have retained Bunche's original verb tenses.

Where Bunche has misspelled a person's name, I have inserted the correct name in square brackets: Kadale [Kadalie]. Where he has spelled a name inconsistently, but provided the correct spelling, I have given the correct spelling throughout to avoid confusion.

Words or phrases that Bunche underlined appear in italics.

Bunche usually began paragraphs—and often sentences—with two dashes. I have omitted those dashes. He also would string together a series of complete sentences with double dashes between each sentence. Where he was connecting two sentences or thoughts that could be joined by a semi-colon, I have used a dash. But where he was connecting a series of three or more sentences, I have omitted the double dashes and made them into separate sentences.

Except in cases of obvious typographical errors, I have not changed any of Bunche's original wording. For instance, Bunche used the words *native, Bantu* and *African* interchangeably. Even after he was alerted to the fact that *African* was the preferred word among politically conscious Africans, he still repeatedly used the word *native* in his notes.

I have also kept Bunche's American spellings. Thus, when Bunche refers to mixed-race South Africans, I have retained his American spelling, of *colored* rather than the South African *coloured*. Depending on the context, his use of the word *colored* could imply one person or many persons.

Where Bunche has used American colloquialisms or unusual spellings, I have provided definitions or placed the word in brackets. Thus, *cullud* [colored] and *massa* [master].

Finally, I have not included all of Bunche's notes. Some of his notes were one-line factual statements and he sometimes quoted extensively from government publications. For instance, he had extensive notes on Indians in South Africa taken from government publications.

The original note cards can be found in Boxes 64 and 65 of the Ralph Bunche Papers, Special Collections, University Research Library, University of California at Los Angeles. I have also deposited photocopies of the cards in the Moorland-Spingarn Library, Howard University, Washington, D.C., the Institute of Commonwealth Studies library, London, and the Church of the Province of South Africa Archive, Witwatersrand University, Johannesburg.

ABBREVIATIONS USED BY BUNCHE

A.A.C.	All African Convention
A.M.E.	African Methodist Episcopal (Church)
col.	colored (Coloured)
cong.	congress
C.P.	Communist Party
C.P.S.A.	Communist Party of South Africa
ct.	court
C.T.	Cape Town
d.	pence
D.C.	Washington, D.C.
Exec. Com.	Executive Committee
I.C.U.	Industrial and Commercial Workers' Union
Ind.	Indian
indiv.	individual
J.C.	Jim Crow
Joburg	Johannesburg
K.B.	Kaffir beer
lang.	language
Min.	Minister
M.O.H.	Medical Officer of Health
munic.	municipally, municipality
nat.	native
nat'l	national
N.R.C.	Native Representative Council
Nat. Rep.	Native Representative
O.F.S.	Orange Free State
organ.	organization
Prov.	Provincial
ry. (r.r.)	railway
S.A. (So. Afr.)	South Africa
secy.	secretary
Stan. (stand.)	Standard
t.b.	tuberculosis
union	Union of South Africa
Xmas	Christmas
Wes.	Western

An
African
American
in
South
Africa

CAPE TOWN

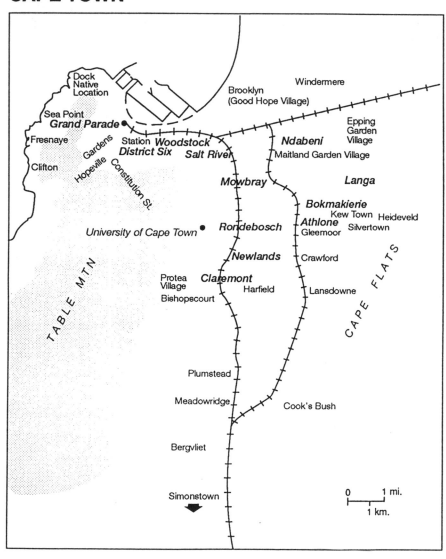

Cape Town

September 28

Last day on board ship—thank the Lord! Everyone showing signs of irritation. We are tired of 17 days together in close (too close) quarters. Rather unpleasant weather—some rain and very little sun. Wrote letters, packed, paid off bills and tips, etc. Visited briefly down in 2d [class]. They were bemoaning the strict class system on board etc. Many people annoyed by arrogant vanity of the purser. Of all the self-puffed up pigs, he's the worst I've ever seen.

Mrs. Alexander told me last night that the Dutch lady who sits in deck-chair next to her took her to task severely for talking with me. Read her the riot act, it seems, and told her how to treat folks like me. Talked some with Mr. Reuben. He gently reminded me that one lady noticed that I had been talking to another with a cigarette in my mouth. It's not done, etc. Ho hum!

Wondering how my reception with immigration will be tomorrow a.m. Hope Schapera or Snitcher will be on hand to meet me.

Room steward woke me up at 5:50 a.m. Dressed, finished packing, and went on deck to see Cape Town nestling beautifully at the foot of Table Mountain. A striking picture. Got through immigration officer okay after a wait of half an hour and a payment of a £ 5 deposit for "good behavior." I'm allowed to stay until December 31st. Then went back on deck and saw Abe Desmore[1] on the dock with two white men whom I later met as Snitcher[2] and Swanstein. Couldn't get the customs declaration straight on deck, so I got my bags together and went down to meet Desmore et al. Turned customs business over to a [Thomas] Cook's agent and finally got through without paying any duty (though customs officer tried to soak me £ 2.10 for my bedding, etc.) by arranging for Cook's to store the tropical equipment for me and to hold it until I am ready to leave South Africa. Cook's representative said I can have the stuff whenever I want it.

Went out to Snitcher's beach cottage for a ham and egg breakfast. It was then only 8:30. Then Swanstein drove me by Cook's and I got plenty of mail, including a fat letter from Ruth and one each from Joan and Jane. Then out to Mrs. Gool's . . . where I am staying.[3] Fine new stucco bungalow and very modern. Her 15 year old daughter is beautiful. They are Malays. Mrs. Gool is attractive, left-wing and talks a mile a minute. Reminds me of Katherine Beard. House up high right near the mountain.

Went down to Cook's and Post Office to mail letters in p.m. Strolled about a bit and watched [a] negro and his woman sing, clown and dance on his hands at the Parade.[4] Drunken white men loafing and enjoying show. One snapped a picture with his hand over the lens.

I have a nice large room and all of my things were put away when I came back this p.m. Dr. Schapera called—will see him at 10 a.m. tomorrow.[5] I met Snitcher's brother and Sam Kahn.[6]

Negroes so mixed up here the place looks like Harlem.

Up too late and had to take cab to university [of Cape Town] for my appointment with Schapera.

University lying at foot of majestic mountain rising in background. Looking away from Jameson Hall, I see a great range of mountains in the near distance, blue-hazed, some snow–capped still.

Schapera is small, trim, reserved and cold-eyed, but he was quite friendly. I had a long talk with him. He had received a letter from the High Commissioner extending me the privilege of visiting Basutoland. He advised me to do so. He introduced me to his seminar students, and I remained for it. It consisted of his reading from one of the chapters in a new book he's writing and asking for criticisms. He told me there are about fifty colored students at the university. Told me I might be able to visit him at his hotel but would not be allowed to eat with him there.

No Jim Crow on buses, but colored and natives* can only ride 2nd and 3rd [class] on trains—even on the train to Mowbray for the University.[7]

Went to the University by train to Mowbray. Rode 1st class on train—no segregation. Saw colored and blacks mostly in 3rd class coaches (wooden seats), but a good sprinkling of colored in 2nd class. [I was] only colored in my coach in 1st on return.

Lavoratories marked "For European Gentlemen" in Cape Town ry. [railway] station. No such designation in station at Mowbray.

Heard a fattish, bald, dark-brown Negro soap-boxing at the Parade.[8] He apparently represents the African National Congress.[9] Inveighing vs. the "pick-me-up" raids on the location and the government's brewing of Kaffir beer.†

Used American Negro as example constantly. Said they have brains and wealth and don't stand for foolishness. Says American Negro says Africa belongs to Africans, and are ready to come back home, but are Africans ready to receive them? Advocates joining the U.N.I.A. and spoke highly of Garvey.[10]

Says brown men (colored) are afraid of guns and "run 25 miles an hour" whenever they see one. But says guns only make the native "wild" and the more he sees the wilder he gets. Says Indians are chasing the white man out of India and African must regain his own country too. Says if white man "doesn't play the game" he will be chased out. Says Japanese are chasing white[s] out of China, especially Russians, and apparently that this is a good thing.[11]

Said American Negroes can strike, but South African natives can't

---

*Native refers to an African. At the time of Bunche's visit, native had generally been discarded by Africans, who resented its paternalistic overtones. Bunche also used the word colored; I have kept Bunche's spelling throughout the text. In the American context, the term referred to anyone of Negro descent. In the South African context, it was spelled Coloured and generally meant anyone of mixed descent. However, the term is loosely defined and, in South Africa law, it can mean anyone who is regarded as neither African nor European.

†Kaffir beer is any home-brewed beer made from malted grain, usually sorghum.

and warned that being dressed up didn't make a person a human being. American Negro demanded to be treated as human beings and are equal of any people in world. Praised Joe Louis as a great man—a black man and world champion.[12] No white man in all of Africa can challenge him.

Attacked Smuts. Said natives must join organizations and use their power.

Crowd snickered as he began, but he soon had many nodding their heads in approbation. He spoke vigorously and often cursed. A few white[s] stood by listening; others walked boldly back and forth between him and the crowd. He had a girl selling copies of the *Bantu World*.[13] Police not far away, but they didn't molest him.

A short distance away another native was speaking to a crowd in Bantu. Called Dutchmen "dumb." Pointed to a picture of Negroes marching in *Courier*[14] and said: "See here how 10,000 American black men march to show the world that they are equal to any people on earth." Said black men in Africa asleep.

Denounced poor whites in South Africa—said they would take all black men's jobs.[15] Attacked the rich. Said rich are sitting on their riches, on the gold and diamonds that rightfully belong to the natives, and that time had come for poor men to demand their share. Said white men had robbed natives of their own gold and diamonds in their own country. But said native is changing. He is oppressed by white man's laws—liquor laws, poll-taxes, pass laws, etc.,[16] and white man must change them and give him good laws or native is ready to die. Being starved to death anyway.

Said native is shoved off on location because white man doesn't want him near him, and then white man invades the black man's location with "pick-me-up."* Natives say white man must stay away from his place.

Attacked religion. Says bishops give natives only religion. Natives shouldn't fall for it—God doesn't help lazy men—helps only those who think and act for themselves. Says "a blinking bishop" prayed (in [news]-papers last night) for the war in China to end and this drew a big laugh.

One native speaking to another in "fancy" English. One sporting a new watch.

---

*Pick-me-ups or pickup vans are police vans. Eslanda Robeson described the pick-me-up as: "a cross between a dog-catcher's wagon and a police patrol wagon. Africans call it, simply, 'Pick-Up.' If they cannot show a pass or permit to be out on the streets, they are seized, loaded into these vans, and taken to jail." (*African Journey* (1945), 72.)

"Ken you tell me the time, I *do not* suppose?"

"Ah yes, eet is quarter to the clock."

"Oh god-damn, let again!"

Talks with Kahn, Eddie Roux,[17] and Harry Snitcher. Criticism of C.P. [Communist Party] policy in deciding to support South African Labor Party.[18] Latter has been consistently bad in [its] attitude re natives. Some mixed unions in Cape and a few elsewhere, but colored and natives generally excluded. Labor Party a white man's party. Kahn and Harry believe that [Communist] Party's tactics should be in accordance with strength and ability of the particular candidate.

Roux points to difficulties of organizing whites and blacks:

1. Backwardness of natives and their lack of effective native leadership.
2. The lack of organizational experience.
3. The lack of direct competition for jobs between blacks and whites because blacks are unskilled and whites skilled workers.
4. Government subsidy to white farmers and employers helping them to keep up higher levels of wages for whites. In fact any attempt to raise the wages of natives would be at expense of whites either by increased taxation, higher price for commodities, or lower wages for whites.
5. Government laws also protect white workers from attack by native workers through the Color Bar Law restricting natives to unskilled labor.*

Thus, white worker runs risk of harming himself thru helping native to higher wages. Therefore, solidarity between white and black workers extremely difficult in South Africa.

Never any stimulus for white workers to get thoroughly warmed to the "religion" of C.P. in order to join up with native workers. The best policy would be, that C.P. and other left wing groups devote most of their attention to the problem of (a) educating (social consciousness) of the native; (b) [giving] thorough attention to organization of black

---

*The Color Bar Law or Mines and Work Amendment Act of 1926 restricted skilled jobs such as blasting and engine driving in the mines to "Europeans, Cape Coloureds, Mauritius Creoles and St. Helena persons."

workers. Under present conditions, they are more significant and afford greater possibilities than the white.

Black man has been used as a strike-breaker in some cases. However, [he] is always a potential threat to the white worker (the color bar laws tend to protect the white skilled worker). Blacks used as scabs in a strike of white workers on the [Witwaters]Rand and during strike mine [owners] made more profits than before due to meager wages paid blacks in contrast with whites. On other hand, whites have been used as strike-breakers when [black] dock-workers struck. Feeling is that even white middle-class is so anti-native that it would never tolerate wide use of black as scabs. But condition of white worker is not good—much severe exploitation of him.

Vereeniging riots have whites stirred up and afraid.[19] No real lynchings yet in South Africa, tho there was almost one when a native was badly beaten up by a mob after the riots. Feeling here is that lynchings will come as natives become more threatening to the system. [They] say there are many individual killings of native workers on farms by [white] farmers.*

They all say here that many of the fair colored pass over into white race as in U.S.[20] Say that in some workshops, where white and black (or colored) are segregated, members of families are segregated—fair one with whites, dark one with coloreds.

One sees very brown mothers with very fair babies and vice versa on the streets.

Cape natives have never before been required to carry passes, but they will have to now under a new law.[21] They go about streets with long walking sticks in tatters, often barefoot and usually smoking pipes.

See many native and colored nursing maids—some in neat uniforms.

The block in which Mrs. Gool's house is located is full of white families, but the property is not covenanted and colored cannot be kept

---

*The South African state officially sanctioned violence against Africans through the punitive use of its police force; in the United States, white mobs resorted to lynching because their control over black people was so tenuous.

out. Beginning at the corner, however, the property is covenanted vs. colored. These [covenants] have been upheld in the courts.*

Dr. and Mrs. Abdurahman[22] and Mrs. Gool were vigorously resented when they first obtained the beach cottage. But no law to prevent them and so they have it today. Recent adoption of segregating blacks and colored from whites on main beaches.

The house of Mrs. Abdurahman, where I took dinner last night, is very old. The first South African Y.M.C.A. meeting was held in it over 100 years ago. It's still in good condition, however. It was very solidly built. It is on edge of colored district—close by Hanover Street and opposite the Parade. Castle is just a block away.

Americans cars are very popular here. Dr. Gool has a Nash.

Hanover Street is main colored street.[23] Bus runs up it. Crowded with colored of every description, with flower vendors lining the curbs.

Familiar Jewish shops all along Hanover Street—just like "U" Street.[24] The colored theatres are owned by whites (Jews?) and also the two colored Cape Town newspapers, the *Standard* and the *Sun*.[25] These are edited by colored but have white owners. Therefore, they are not independent nor are they representative of the attitudes of the non-European population.

The Star Cinema a rather largish, plain, barn-like structure. Every type of mulatto represented in the audience, which was very responsive to comical situations and wise-cracks.[26] They paid no attention when "God Save the King" was played at end—just moved on out, unlike England.

Saw two incidents of cops arresting colored drunks. One cop was handling the drunk alone in the P.M. and had to keep pulling him up from a prostrate position in the gutter. Tonight two were scuffling with one inebriate, while a third cop stood by. Were having a lively tussle.

Dirty urchins of all shades playing all up and down Hanover Street. Maybe I've become insensitive to smell, but the odors in the colored section were neither strong nor offensive to me.

Saw some skollys,† but they didn't look so tough or dangerous.

---

*Covenants restricting the sale of white-owned property to blacks were a common practice in Washington, D.C. By coincidence, in October 1937 the U.S. Supreme Court upheld covenants in that city by refusing to rule on a case where a white owner had tried to break a covenant and sell to a black man.

†*Skolly* refers to a Coloured street tough. The term is probably derived from the Afrikaans word *schoelje*, meaning "rogue" or "rascal."

They were too small—most of them are. Yet everyone seems to have much indignation toward and plenty of respect for them and their knives. Claim is that they knife you if you refuse their demands for coins. Shaheen [Gool] was knocked out by a couple of them at the movies not so long ago.*

The local water is vinegar-colored—a very dark brown. Even the drinking water has a pronounced brown tinge.

■■■■■■ **October 5**

The National Liberation League of South Africa represents all non-European groups—colored, Bantu, Indians, and Malays.[27] The "Non-European oppressed people irrespective of race and religion," as they put it. It has no color bars and Europeans are members, but its leadership is predominantly non-European.

Has been recently flirting with the idea of colored (non-European) business enterprise, etc. Too high brow and above the masses.

At Liberation League meeting yesterday, Le [La]Guma asked me in front of several others if I am "in the movement."[28] I abruptly parried and changed the question. Today, in my conference with Abe Desmore, after carefully leading up to it, he, too, asked me point- blank if I am a "member of the C.P." I emphatically replied, "No!" and went on to explain why. Then he said he had joined "the Party" in New York, which I think is a lie. He spoke deprecatingly of the party members here.

Many colored here say, and this is corroborated by white social scientists at the University [of Cape Town], that many Cape colored find escape in Joburg [Johannesburg], where problem is more strictly defined as white vs. native rather than white vs. colored, as here.

The "sociology" of South African tea drinking. Tea in Schapera's seminar at 10:30 every a.m. No apparent reluctance on part of white students to sit and drink with me. Would this be true in So. [southern] United States?

---

*Mrs. Gool's son, Shaheen, committed suicide in 1946.

Cissie talked some more about her father, Dr. Abdurahman. He is part Indian and part Malay. Has been a leader in local politics here for years, and long held the significant colored vote in palm of his hand. He ruled the colored roost politically. Until formation of the New Reform Party locally, he was one of the "Big 5" which had everything sewed up.* Elective member of the Municipal Council. He fought chiefly for more municipal jobs for colored, more clinics, etc. Often supported white rather than colored candidates, however. A follower of Smuts.[29] New Reform Party has frozen him out, he has lost chairmanship of Street and Drainage Committee.

A clever and ruthless politician now nearing end of his rope. Ruthless, a bitter fighter, now dealing in recriminations.

So many of even the young girls here have all their teeth pulled and wear false teeth. Marcina claims it's "fashionable."†

■■■ **October 7**

Got haircut in a dinky little colored barber shop on Hanover Street. My barber was a half Indian and half Malay.[30] He talked very broken English. Is crazy to go to America. Was terribly shocked when I told him I have no religion. Then I must be *anti*-religious, was only conclusion he could draw. But what a haircut he gave me!—regular prison cut, leaving the back of my head looking like a battlefield. And he worked the scissors like a madman—almost played a tune with them. The little two chair dump was equipped with electric clippers, though.

Sidwell, the native Xhosa boy from near East London, who works for Cissie [Gool], told me he likes to cook but doesn't like to do the washing because his friends kid him about it. He was awfully amused today when I told him I wanted a glass of plain cold milk. At first he was unable to believe me—he tried to induce me to take cocoa. Then he insisted that at least the milk should be hot, and when I remained adamant, he suggested that maybe the milk wasn't good (tho admitting it was fresh this a.m.) and brought the bottle for inspection. When he watched

---

*Founded in 1937 with the aim of promoting more efficient municipal government in Cape Town, the Reform Party died out in 1939.
†Marcina is the fifteen-year-old daughter of Cissie Gool.

me take my first drink of it, he stood chuckling and shaking his head in amusement.

October 8

Dr. Lestrade told me how much of a "mongrel" he is—some 15 European races in his ancestry, including Jewish—but hastened to assure me that there are no African strains.[31] [He] claims this is excellent insulation [against] racial prejudices [since] he can't foster prejudice to a particular race without insulting one of his ancestors.

Lestrade referred to me as a "European" inadvertently and then went on to explain that the natives would look upon me as a European or else as colored, and that I would have no advantage over whites in field-work among natives. Said that he, knowing the language, would be better than I. In fact, being regarded as colored, [I] might well be at a disadvantage in eyes of natives. Said he has no prejudice but never feels "free" when in contact with natives in this country. Says some natives bitterly hate all white men, without discrimination. Referred to ridiculous chauvinistic "ignorant people." Says only one native ever got free enough to speak to him without giving him a title, and that this was done by a native agitator and it seemed forced. Says Jabavu, who knows him well enough to do so, never addresses him informally.[32]

Professor Lestrade says even educated natives get only superficial aspects of European culture. [He takes an] adaptationist attitude that it takes a very long time for native to absorb European culture.

Cites two examples to prove it. Says Dr. Jabavu was working with him on grading papers and protested that papers written on a three hour examination should be graded on a basis of 300% rather than 100% (i.e., 100% for each hour). Thus, he concludes that even Jabavu does not understand European culture despite his training in England.

Xuma, from Joburg, he cites as another example.[33] He is a fine and fully able young doctor, educated in U.S. But when Xuma was called on to move vote of thanks at a meeting in Joburg at which Lestrade spoke on adaptationist attitude, Xuma, instead of moving the vote as a formality, took the occasion to make an 1/2 hour speech before the motion, in which he severely criticized Lestrade's speech. This Lestrade says has been repeated elsewhere on him, and this he interprets as an evidence of the inability of natives to absorb European culture.

Lestrade cited how native children being taught about their local rivers, Bushmen, etc., in English did not understand who or what these were until they were explained (by him, of course) in their native tongue. Also cites cases of native children stumbling over addition in English and having no difficulty with same sums in their native tongue. When asked why of this, one of the native pupils explained that "sums in English is arithmetic, while those in native tongue are figures" and easy to do.

Also cites cases of natives having difficulty with words and meaning for working for oneself and working for Europeans.

Lestrade, in speaking of his favorite native boy in a group picture of Venda youngsters, called him a "nigger."

Bishop Wright told me of difficulty he has had in getting permission to enter South Africa for American Negroes.[34] Says he has gotten four in so far . . . [including] Professor and Mrs. Amos White[35] at Wilberforce Institute (near Joburg).[36]

Bishop Wright has to get his permit renewed every six months.

Bishop Wright says some of natives are very well off and live well, tho not having same opportunity for expression as American Negroes.

Schapera tells me that Chief Immigration Officer informed him when he was interceding for me, that there is an unwritten law that no alien Negro shall be admitted to South Africa—because of my work with Schapera, an exception was made in my case.

Reverend Gow (who was born here, but whose father is American)[37] says time is coming when the Cape Colored will be pulling at shirt-tails of the native population. In the professions, education, etc., except for Indian group, [Africans] are outstripping the colored population.

More swarthy, frizzly-haired, "suspicious looking" "white" people here than any place I've ever been.

Many people allege that Prime Minister Hertzog has colored blood and many other prominent officials and families.[38]

■■■■ **October 9**

Signs in court house: "Male witnesses colored"; "Female witnesses colored"; "Male—European"; "Female—European." The rooms are at opposite ends of corridor.

In Civil Court D, Snitcher arguing civil damage suit for a colored plaintiff who was abused, and allegedly unlawfully arrested and prosecuted by a guard on a suburban train. Harry demanding £250 damages. Harry's arguments very potent. The magistrate is quiet, dignified and honest enough looking. The magistrate takes his own notes on the case, noting citations carefully. Harry avoids the color issue.

Harry described the plaintiff as a "respectable, dignified colored man, who wouldn't use the abusive language defendants charge him with."

Snitcher demanded that opposing attorney (a government attorney defending a government worker) cease referring to his adult colored plaintiff (a middle-aged dignified man with a flowing moustache) as a "boy."

Colored fellow behind me says colored [and] natives are treated terribly on the trains and that most of guards are recruited from the country. Says this is first case of its kind and [it] will have a good influence.

Harry said bilingualism is general in courts, tho not universal. Said there are no laws requiring Jim Crow in Cape Town, but that public discriminations have never been tested in courts here. Thinks common law capable of interpretation to the effect that, e.g., a proprietor of a bioscope, holding a license from the state, could be compelled to admit the general public without discrimination. [His] only fear is that a favorable decision and attendant publicity would lead to a positive segregation law. But this would probably be counterbalanced by educational value of such a fight to non-European community. At least it would clarify and define the existing anomalous situation, which is much like D.C. in re absence of laws. Tacit agreement between groups re separate groups.

Used a lavatory boldly marked "For Europeans Only" in Snitcher's building.

Frequently see cops pulling hand cuffed colored and natives along street en route to jail.

Dropped into a tobacco shop near the courthouse and saw many colored men and women buying snuff. They handed small metal cups or containers to the salesman, who filled them and handed them back.

Secretary of Railway Union (European) told me that no one dares scratch beneath surface of South African racial situation and that everyone realizes this. His sister married a colored man and their daughter has been teaching as white for years.

Said more and more white workers (except highly skilled artisans) were realizing their common interests with black workers. Said there are some mixed unions. There are many casual white laborers on docks and at mines—working at same rates and under same conditions as natives.

Referred to many injustices against workers. Said bilingual system imposes an injustice on railway workers, lorry drivers, etc. Bilingualism and Standard VI education are qualifications for attaining maximum pay class by lorry drivers. Drivers having both qualifications receive 10s per day, while drivers on same job who know only one language, get only 8s for same work. Said general pay for dock workers is 4/6 per day for very uncertain and irregular work.

▬▬▬ October 10

Discussion with Gomez [Gomas],[39] Kotane,[40] Van Gelderen and Sam Kahn. Native mine workers living in compounds do proletarian work, but retain peasant psychology. They are thinking of what's going on at their kraals—of their families, cattle, etc.

Sidwell, tho living and working in C.T., worries chiefly about the 12 cattle due him and not yet paid as lobola for his sister's marriage.*

Kotane thinks development of political consciousness and organization among the natives is most important need now, along with trade unions—due to transient nature of mine workers.

Difficulty re lack of common language medium. Most natives have probably not yet heard of Vereeniging. It will be kept carefully from the mine workers.

Feeling that a National Organization is necessary. Doubt that I.C.U.[41] or African National Congress can fill the bill—many natives were disillusioned by them.

The National Liberation League is not yet clear in its thinking—much of membership still thinking in terms of special status for colored. Many now hope for development of non-European business as a way out, are emphasizing the stronger economic position of the American Negro.

---

*Lobola, or bride price, is an African custom in which cattle are given by the groom to the parents of his prospective wife.

Coloreds and natives—tho more native than colored—worked together in the I.C.U. Taking natives in the mass, they have been taught to belittle the colored people and to regard them as nobodies. They have been told that colored have no chiefs, etc., and therefore are insignificant. Absence of a common language medium has emphasized these differences.

Colored group which, because of its position in industry and politics, and its more advanced intellectual status, should be providing much leadership for the native masses, is doing nothing.

▰▰▰ October 11

In Schapera's office, the young Dutch Reformed Church missionary told how when he took up his native mission work, one of his superiors—an elder in the European church—lectured him on how to conduct himself with the natives—e.g., he must never shake the hands of natives in the street, though, if he should feel so inclined, he *might* take their hands *inside* the church.

We all emphasized that if the church expects to get young or old natives to give up what, in the eyes of the church, are unchristian customs, substitute activities must be provided. Schapera told how one pastor took over the circumcision rites in his church and gave medical circumcisions—so that even heathens were coming to ask for his ceremony.

Reverend Gow, Desmore and Golding[42] all asked me if I "had yet met any of Cape Town's more solid and substantial citizens." Typical of Negro intellectuals everywhere—tho these here have difficulty enumerating their "solid and substantial citizens," since they lack businessmen, professional men, public office-holders, etc.

▰▰▰ October 12

Dr. Friedlander thinks that one possible explanation of scrawniness of cape colored (in addition to gross malnutrition, of course) is in fact that they are mixed with Malay and Indian coolie strains—these being slight people.[43] He says incidence of T.B. is very high among colored here (and among whites too) and that with such rotten living conditions for the colored masses, T.B. is essentially "an economic disease."[44]

Dr. Friedlander drove me out to the municipal housing project for colored at Bokmakierie (named after a bird that makes this sound).[45] A good-sized village of trim little white plaster and stucco duplexes with fruit and vegetable gardens in every front yard, well paved streets, a large, airy school, and modern improvements, including electricity. Project subsidized by city of Cape Town and units rented at sub-economic rates. But it is rather far from the city—some 6 to 8 miles (out past Mowbray—near Athlone)—and this is a hardship, since the colored workers are almost all engaged in town.

There are some very poor sections in the vicinity of this project, however. One sees scores of corrugated iron and tin shelters, which must be terribly cold in the winter and unbearably hot in the summer— little square tin shanties housing large families. Back in the wattle bushes, and reached by uncertain paths, are scores more of pitiful lean-to's, which, according to Dr. Friedlander, afford virtually no protection when it rains. As a doctor employed by the city, he has attended patients in these shanties, [which] are surrounded by pools of water from the rains. The roads in these sections are unpaved and become impassable quagmires after rains. Dirty, ragged, rickets-stricken children are seen everywhere. There is a C. T. birth control clinic, but these can't afford the purchase of expensive contraceptives. They can't afford children either.

We also visited a privately owned group of comfortable-enough looking bungalows at Jamestown and the older municipal housing project at Garden Village. This is not so attractive as Bokmakierie since the streets are unpaved, but it is a vast improvement over the crowded living conditions in the colored sections in town. There is plenty of fresh air out there, tho the dust is picked up plenty when the southeasters sweep over.

In terms of convenience for the town workers, the municipal housing project of flats along Constitution Avenue (near Trafalgar School) are better. They are quite modern looking.

It would appear that the vast majority of the colored population live in dire poverty and squalor. En masse, economically they are worse off than the natives, who living at their kraals, on the locations and reserves, are at least more certain of getting sufficient food. The colored group is completely at the mercy of the white, because it must work for the white in order to get food. The natives, on the other hand, must work for whites, only to be able to pay poll taxes. The colored group has no economic foundations at all—it is suspended between black and white. It has sacrificed much initiative, enterprise and aggressiveness by pursuing a double illusion (for all but the very few) of escape into the white race and faith in the continuance by the white man of the special status and privilege originally extended the bastard group. They have shied from black skins but yet expect to exploit their own dark skins by requesting special consideration from the whites. Very little progress among them—few business or professional men, no wealth, meagre property holdings, etc.

Some day they will be whining at the tails of the Bantu, whom they have traditionally looked upon just as the white man looks on them—i.e., as inferiors. E.g. Abe Desmore justifying difference in educative policy for colored and black on grounds of "different culture" of the two groups.

October 13

Conversation with Kotane. At outset I.C.U. was a trade union organization—organized in 1919. It began in Cape Town among dockworkers, under direction of Kdale [Kadalie].[46] Then it began to spread, including ry. [railway] workers. Then went to farms and began to get muddled in its objectives, including women, preachers, etc.

It then became a national organization. In 1925–26 it reached peak in membership, boasting about 100,000 members. The organization too big and cumbersome. As a national organization it began to take up all issues—all national demands, re pass, liquor laws, etc. But its progress became less specific and paid less attention to the demands of workers.

It began to betray strikes. In about 1929 workers in a government laboratory at Pretoria went on strike, and Kdale went in person as general secretary of I.C.U. And without any investigation at all, [he] immediately called strike off and sent workers back to work. His subsequent negotiations were totally unsuccessful.

In 1928–29 at Joburg, the workers in Joburg railway goods shed went on strike, invited Kdale and same thing happened as above. In 1930 at E. London, the dock workers went on strike under Kdale's leadership; strike was on for several days and had paralyzed industry there. Finally, some of leaders, including Kdale, were arrested, and as soon as he was arrested, he ordered workers back. Such incidents caused I.C.U. to lose its influence.

Graft in I.C.U. was terrible. Money squandered like water. Officials drank heavily, including Kdale, who was a big boozer.

The government, as result of I.C.U. agitation, passed the Native

Administration Act (1927).[47] Contained a clause forbidding more than 10 natives to congregate except for church affairs or tribal matters. Law administered so strictly that strangers had to have a special police permit to enter locations. Riots and Assemblies Act[48] [and] Pass Laws all made organization work difficult.

From 1917–24 in South Africa there was a great deal of fighting caused by the I.C.U. E.g., in 1920 in Port Elizabeth a meeting was called to discuss an increase of 1s for all location workers. Date for a strike set, [but] police came before day set for strike and arrested the [I.C.U.] secretary, Masabalala,[49] and held [him] in custody without any charges preferred. A big demonstration of natives marched to the charge office and sent a deputation in to demand release of Masabalala. But before deputation got in, an officer from top of building fired into crowd and some score or more natives were eventually killed; also three Europeans who were in the crowd.

Another incident in Bloemfontein in 1925. Unemployment among workers led to many arrests, beer raids, etc. Natives held meeting to protest arrest of some natives, including an I.C.U. leader, Msimang.[50] But police, instead of releasing prisoners, called in surrounding white farmers and also white railway police. Ordered native protest meeting to disperse and to end their strike. Shots fired and natives scattered and were hunted down [and] clubbed, and there were some deaths and many wounded.

Kdale used to get jitters when fighting occurred.

The African National Congress—organized in 1912. At beginning, a collection of tribal organizations, burial societies, etc. Founder was Dr. Pixley Seme who, tho a natural South African (Swazi), had studied in U.S. (England?).[51] [Its] first meeting at Bloemfontein—representatives from all over the country. Came into being on eve of Land Act of 1912–13[52]—sent delegation to England to protest vs. Act. Unsuccessful. War broke out and they had to return. Two delegations were sent. Most of leaders were liberals and strung along with government during war. Engaged in nothing to embarrass government during war. But agitation by some of young members began in 1917, leading to strikes in mines and on farms (1918). In 1919 there occurred a big strike in Joburg, accompanying the first pass-burning demonstration.[53] Mine workers shot. The Congress responsible for all these early demonstrations.

Government stool pigeons led to break up of the A.N.C. and whole thing collapsed. But it reached thousands of people in its active years; many chiefs supported it.

The organization received a great deal of money from the people. It also suffered from graft.

After 1919, African National Congress subsided, and began to lose its indus. [industrial] interest and more and more to enter and confine itself to political matters.

African National Congress divided into several factions today. Seme head of what is called the "official" Congress.

[Kotane stressed the] difficulty of organization work among natives—strict regulations make it almost impossible for organizers to get to natives in mine compounds. Place to reach natives is at their kraals, even before they come to the mines.

On his two trips to Russia Kotane has had to travel with false passports.[54] Government wouldn't have let him out otherwise, unless he was sponsored by missionaries or someone like Rheinold [Rheinallt-] Jones.[55]

Kotane, who is editor of the *African Defender*,[56] told me that Reverend Gow travelled on the same boat with him when returning from England (Kotane had been on a trip to the U.S.S.R. a few years ago). Reverend "Dr." Gow was with his family, in a cabin next to the one in which Kotane and a native, who was servant to a white man, was placed (on Union Castle Boat). Gow never spoke a word to Kotane and the other fellow during the entire trip, tho several of the Europeans came to talk with them. In the dining room Kotane and his room-mate were stuck off in a corner by themselves, but "Dr." Gow and his family, because of his rank and status, were given a table among the Europeans. (Gow emphasizing in his newspaper interview today that he represents the "*respectable*" colored community.)

Kotane says many of the native constables are very brutal to the natives. They are recruited chiefly from uneducated Zulus. He says the educated boys are not wanted because they are too gentle with the natives. Says Zulus have too much tendency to kow-tow, bow and scrape to whites.

October 14

Visited Bethel School. Rev. Gow's church, Bethel A.M.E. church, rents its buildings to the School Board.* Is a primary school. Over 500 students. George Golding is Principal.

---

*Bethel Memorial AME Church in Blythe Street was established shortly after Bishop Henry McNeil's visit to Cape Town in May 1898.

Talked with Rev. Gow and he said that invitations extended to Chief Magistrate and Mayor to attend colored meeting vs. the skolly evil, had been refused. Mayor expressed regrets but gave no reasons. Gow incensed but wouldn't give story to white papers, wishing to protect the mayor. Police against meeting and won't let the Boy Cadets' Band Corps wear their uniforms when they play at it.

Then accepted Golding's invitation to play tennis. [I] met Eddie Simms and Baku—both colored school teachers. Golding lives well. [He] drives a new studebaker, has a big house, a H.M.V. radio-victrola, makes home recordings, boasts and displays many handsome tennis trophies, dresses and eats very well, has two or three colored servants about the house, and has two little girls. He's very bourgeois. [He has a] big picture of his wedding about three years ago, which he freely admits was "one of the biggest weddings ever held in the colored community." Has a couple of big pictures of it on the walls—one, a metal affair, was specially made in London. [In it] Golding all dolled up in morning trousers and tails, his attractive but very buxom wife in a beautiful wedding gown. The attendants, most of whom are relatives, are all extremely fair—look like whites. His father-in-law, who lives across the street in a huge house, well furnished with billiard table, etc., is a rich Indian real estate dealer, who once was a dock-worker.

Golding told me that he canvassed, spoke and loaned his car for Adams,[57] the Reform Party candidate, in the current municipal elections, because Cunningham, whom Cissie is working for, is nothing but a parking lot attendant and a poor white, while Adams is a respectable gentleman.

Golding thinks Cissie is very intelligent, but too "communistic"—a pattern reaction.

Golding would himself like to stand for the [City] Council if he wouldn't have to give up his school job to do so.

Eddie Simms and Mrs. Golding queried me re American Negro. Simms raised question as to why I refer to my group as "Negroes." Says South African colored always refer to us as "colored." Said they reserve term "Negro" for black Kaffirs.* He cautioned me not to call my group "Negro" before South African colored. I told him I would have to do so as we are proud of our dark skins and to be known as "Negroes." He replied that people like me and Bishop Simms [Sims] could

---

*Originally derived from an Arabic word meaning "infidel" or "the ungrateful," *Kaffir* was first applied by European colonists to refer to the Xhosa. Later the word was generally applied to all Africans. The word came to connote inferiority and was used in the same fashion as "nigger."

not be regarded as Negroes by South African colored.[58] He admitted that American Negro must have more initiative and aggressiveness than South African colored. Said he thought it would be a big help if South African colored had some big business men like the American Negroes.

Mrs. Golding said the Desmores hadn't told them about the attitude of the American Negro on color; they indicated that we take same attitude toward it as Cape colored. [She] said the Desmores reported that all American Negro women straighten their hair and pile on cosmetics, in an effort to look white.

Golding said many parents of fair colored girls encourage them to go with white fellows in hope that they will marry white. But they get more illegitimate babies by far than white husbands.

They all seem to think entirely in terms of color.

They play a very patchy sort of tennis; no good stroke-making.

They have a colored national tennis organization. They are very proud because some of the local "European" tennis stars come up to Trafalgar Park (where the courts are) "to have a knock."

Conversation with Eddie Roux. Spoke of changes in the C.P. position re blacks. First held to a totally white ideology. Then Bunting,[59] Roux et al. emphasized necessity for organization of blacks. C.P. worked closely with such black organizations as the I.C.U. and African National Congress. This led to exodus of many whites from the Party. But great progress was made among the blacks. Until outbreak of internal factionalism, the African National Congress was closely linked to the C.P. of S.A. [Communist Party of South Africa]

Then came purge of "rightists" [who] criticized the Moscow-dictated policy of the independent "African Republic" as unrealistic.[60] Eddie thinks there was too much dictation from Moscow. Eddie and others in the Party had to give up the "African Civil Liberties League" on orders from Comintern.[61] The Party became narrowed down to a small group of extreme revolutionaries who opposed the membership of any but the strictest Marxists. Party had at one time 5000–6000 members.

The present policy is one of concentrating on war and fascism, and purging "Left" elements, ignoring natives and playing with Labor Party and other soc.-dem. [social democratic] organizations.

Kdale [Kadalie] is washed up. Physically a wreck with advanced syphilis, tho still retaining some of his former glamor in eyes of natives. Still talks in Joburg of reviving the I.C.U.

At one time C.P. had 500 native members on the Vereeniging location.

Saw a colored "pansy" in C.T. station—dressed in flaming red silk shirt, flowers in his hat and "switching" his rump to beat the band. He attracted plenty of attention.

October 15

Wesley Training College, Salt River. Mr. E. A. Ball principal.[62] Mr. Ball is a Welshman. Training college for colored teachers. Work begins at Stand. VI through Stand. VIII, and then two years training courses for teacher's certificate.

17 teachers on staff—only one colored. [Ball's] explanation is that no colored students [are] adequately trained. Desmore says this is accurate view.

Mr. Ball said most of teaching is in English, though majority of students speak only Africaans [Afrikaans] in their homes. This he explained on a two-fold basis: a) that of race feeling, i.e., that even though most coloreds are Africaans speaking, they dislike the Dutch, and prefer to learn English; b) the economic advantage of knowing English in the towns, where it is the principal language.

Ball said if he did the logical thing, his school should be committed to Afrikaans medium, with English only as a secondary language. But if he did so the students and their parents would strenuously object.

Said English affords wider cultural possibilities in teaching; Afrikaans still being refined and this is a process only begun in recent years. Until very recently all text-books were in English.

Mr. Ball said regulations were against admitting natives, though he had some who were listed as "colored." This is because education funds are ear-marked—14 gs. per child for whites (per year), 5 gs. per colored child and 2 gs. per native child.* Therefore, if natives are admitted to a colored school, they are poaching on colored funds. Says at another school where he had 20 native students in a colored school, they were ostracized by the colored students, their early training was of inferior standard, and they suffered greatly.

Ball favors complete educational segregation. Thinks if, say, a 100 coloreds flock out to the University of C.T., the University will close its doors to colored. Says that now they are academic students only and are not permitted to participate in University activities. He thinks this

---

*Gs: guinea. A one-guinea coin equalled £1.1s.

is bad for colored students there, tending to develop an inferiority complex. Says his one young colored teacher (she's very fair and new this year) is the best teacher he has on his staff.

Says Education Department stubbornly insists on a double standard for white and colored teachers. Whites must finish Standard X before entering training college course. Colored need finish VIII only, and until a few years ago, only Standard VI. Whites command more money, of course.

Says Education Department is limiting the number of students to be accepted in training college classes for colored. This is because there are too many with certificates for available posts—though girls are still needed. But if there were compulsory education for colored, "they'd have to use the lame, halt and the blind."

[Ball] dislikes the Dutch and says Education Department is afraid of them. Says regulations of Education Department require that when a white teacher in a colored school drops out, place must be filled by a colored teacher, if one qualified is available. This now being applied to secondary and even training college students.

I raised the question as to whether attempts to teach both languages doesn't retard the development of the child's learning. No tests have been made yet. Desmore's opinion is that it does definitely retard the child.

There seems to be no real policy in operation re the languages. Each school [I] visited has a different policy. So-called Africaans medium schools teaching plenty of English; "Bilingual" schools teaching almost entirely in English, etc. In answer to my repeated questions as to what was basis for determining which subjects are to be taught in English and which in Africaans, only explanation was that arbitrary determination is made. As far as I can gather, the whole thing is left to discretion of principals and teachers.

Trafalgar High School. Mr. Henek [Heneke], colored, assistant principal.[63] Henek holds an M.A. from the University of C.T. Very dignified, cultured gentleman, who has subscribed to *Crisis* for 20 years.*

[The high school has a] modern building equipped for metal work, wood-work, domestic science, cooking, etc.; science laboratory, etc.

Staff of 17 and only 3 are colored teachers.

---

*Edited by W. E. B. DuBois, *The Crisis* was the journal of the National Association for the Advancement of Colored People (NAACP).

The principal is white and is retiring in March, but Mr. Henek, who has taught for 21 years, and is logical successor, doesn't think he will be given the job. Says nationalists are dead set against letting any colored man hold a job in which he will be over whites. But school has had colored principal in the past—in fact, first principal was colored—the first colored man to get a degree from University of C.T., Mr. Cressey.[64]

[The school has] 415 colored students. Only a few natives—special cases who are required by the Education Department to come from a "fading school."

[Heneke] says coloreds find it difficult to get proper training to qualify for many of the teaching jobs.

The Cape Town traffic cops, with khaki uniforms, white gloves and white over-sleeves, have the "fanciest" gestures I've ever seen.

Many Indian-looking girls and women with silk cloths over their heads, bandana-like. Blue seems to be favorite color.

Gow took me down to C.T. broadcasting studio, to witness rehearsal of the Coleridge-Taylor Quartet with a white group in a radio minstrel show for tomorrow nite.[65] Gow's discomfiture was great re song his quartet has to sing. It is called "Sleep," an old "Coon" song, referring to "Niggerland" (in very first line), pickaninnies, etc.! Gow told me it is the first time he's ever been called a "minstrel." Composer of book habitually refers to Gow and group as "boys" or "lads," etc. In minstrel their song is announced as that "beautiful darky lullaby, Sleep." The whole bunch also sang another "Coon" song—"The Coon Drum Major." Gow does a little not too subtle "kow-towing."

About 9·30 [p.m.], we drove to the Pavillion, Woodstock, where I discovered a big reception by the A.P.O. in my honor.[66] About 40 people present. Reagon of the Board of Education presiding, with me on his right and Gow on his left.[67]

Reagon and Gow gave me a big send-off with a lot of inaccurate statements, and then I spoke for one-half hour on the American scene. Refreshments and then discussion. Speakers like messrs. Maurice[68] and Kay[69] gave the Cape colored group hell for its apathy, stupidity, lack of initiative, etc. Each emphasized the curse of *division* among the colored group. All agreed in blaming the Church, both black and white, for its divisive influence in colored group. All seemed to regard the American Negro as a paragon of virtue. One speaker told how objective of most colored here was to be able to "pass over" into white group.

Reagon also claimed (with considerable exaggeration, I think) that the A.P.O. (African People's [Political] Organization), founded by Abdurahman at beginning of century, though a colored organization, had consistently fought the battle of the natives.[70] He intimated that colored must recognize an identity of interest with the native.

Deplored report in day's press that Agent General for South African Indian community, had made a speech in which he cautioned Indians against linking their interests with the causes of the colored and native populations, though professing great cordiality for both.[71]

A very mild group. No aggressiveness indicated; merely polite speeches. A rather pitiful sight, if these are, as I was assured, representative of leading public-minded colored citizens.

Dr. Gow told me that Ball out at Wesley Training College is having trouble with his staff, who claim he is dictatorial, and who threaten to walk out if he proceeds with his policy of bringing in colored teachers.

October 16

Effendi, the Turkish reporter for the *Standard,* claims Turkey is the only country in the world entirely free of race prejudice.[72] He says English are responsible for the introduction of race prejudice here, as black and white (Dutch) were getting on very well before the English came.

Visit to opening of primary school at Bokmakierie. School a nice, low lying plaster building. Big crowd in open air. Union Jack flying, but no South African flag. School had been opened only nine weeks ago, but already it is over-crowded, with 293 students, though it was built to accommodate only 270.

Deputy-Mayor [of Cape Town] arose and almost deliberately insulted Negro group by calling attention to the three main drawbacks of the colored people in Cape Town: (1) the skolly menace, (2) drunkenness, and (3) cruelty to dumb animals.

Mr. Nyman[73], councillor, soon spoke and he arose and answered the Deputy-Mayor very pointedly, by indicating in crisp sentences that these evils among the colored are entirely due to the *"horrible environment"* and slums in which they have to live. He said the evils will be automatically eliminated when these bad conditions are removed, and not before. He said they don't exist in Bokmakierie.

Reagon fully seconded Nyman's stand a bit later on. The President of the School Board emphasized the great manifestations of enthusiasm for education among colored. As fast as a new school is opened, it is immediately over-crowded. He reproached white people for their dilatoriness in providing obvious remedies for slum and crime conditions; and for economic and health opportunities too.

One city councillor, Ross from Salt River, was so dark and "colored" looking, that everyone was commenting on him.

▬▬▬ October 17

Saw a native group of about 25 in baptism ceremonies in sea at Woodstock beach. Church of Christ group.[74] Cold, raw, windy day. Singing hymns (strange) and Bible printed in Xhosa. Weird harmony. Only three women; one with a baby on her back. One English speaking native in the group—a little cringing, bearded fellow, dressed like a dandy, told me they are from Langa and have about one hundred members in their flock.[75] Pastor was a tall, brownskinned, serious-eyed, bearded native. In short testimonial sermons after the baptisms (in English), one native, while quoting the scripture like Ford quotes the party line,[76] stated that the scriptures and religion made no provision for the color-bar.

▬▬▬ October 18

Dr. Gow took me to Reagon's office (A.P.O.) and we all sat in on the meeting of the 12th Quintennial 10-day conference of the Dutch Reformed Mission Church Synod, held in the Gesticht Church, Long Street.[77] Hard-looking Afrikanders [Afrikaners] in black hats and frock coats ran the meeting, though more than half of the members were colored looking.* Assistant pastors (colored)—most of them seemed pretty old. They sat for several hours without making a peep. Not an

---

*Afrikander and Afrikaner were used interchangeably, but English South Africans could use Afrikander in a pejorative sense. With the evolution of the Afrikaans language, Afrikander has been little used since the 1940s.

ounce of social protest in a carload of them. Saw one or two with a gold ear-ring in left ears.

Reagon thought he had it arranged through one fair-skinned "assistant parson," to let Reverend Gow address the group briefly. But when Gow presented himself, the chairman turned him down point blank. Didn't even introduce him to the group. We then left. Whole proceedings was in Afrikaans.

There was virtual Jim Crow at the Dutch Church meeting, for the colored all occupied entire rows and the whites similarly. There was no race mixture on any particular row, though the rows were mixed—sort of alternating. There was a tall, tense looking [man] in frock coat, who seemed to be a sort of door-keeper, page boy, messenger. No fraternization between black and white delegates.

Saw "Sister Nannie," the mountainous, black sister who got the King's medal recently (Dr. Gow also received one several years ago) for her work in running a hostel for "unfortunate girls"—i.e., a place where they can drop their fatherless babes.[78] She's connected with the Dutch Reformed Church, and was all dressed up in a nurse's uniform, serving tea to the delegates.

Reagon a pompous, conceited ass in an Emmett Scott sort of way.[79] Thinks himself a great leader and financier. Talks of the people as though they are children or subjects who would flounder and perish without his astute hands.

He makes all sorts of extravagant claims for the A.P.O. Says it is the only South African non-European organization that has ever done anything. Poppy cock! He didn't even mention the I.C.U. or the African [National] Congress.

He runs a couple of "semifraternal" business enterprises—building associations, industrial insurance and the A.P.O. burial association, out of all of which he undoubtedly gets his ample cut. He's a smooth and fluent talker.

Thinks Abe Desmore always puts himself ahead of any cause.

October 20

Sierfogel [Zierfogel],[80] librarian of the Hyman Liberman Institute,[81] is a "self made" colored man. Says he has never been inside a school and used to be what they now call a "skolly." Loves books and has a very good private collection. Says he has been written up in the *Cape Times,* *Christian Science Monitor,* etc. Says his board (European) won't let him keep his private library on the public shelves of the Institute because he has too many "dangerous" books. Says he has "left" inclinations, but he states that he "hates white people and can't help it."

October 22

These American consuls and legation secretaries are pretty lousey [*sic*] when they are confronted with an American Negro. Went down largely on Gow's advice to see the American Consul-General today—a Mr. Denby[82]—just to ask a single question about my permit—and largely on Reverend Gow's advice. He was a fairly young, blue-eyed guy who said he hails from D. C. and has been here ten months. He was just as taciturn, curt and unsympathetic as the guy at the Legation in London was. The only place they treated me decently was in Paris.

Passed by a hotel with a big printed sign in black letters, painted along wall in entrance: "Europeans Only."

Colored medical students can't go beyond the third year at the University of C.T. because they can't get clinical work there, so they must complete their work abroad. They aren't allowed to work on colored patients even for these are needed by the white students!

Very little colored business, but Indians have a number of shops, though small, up Hanover Street. Some colored printers, some small builders, etc. But there is no real bourgeoisie. The teachers tend to affect the psychology of the bourgeois class, but have no economic foundation for it.

When I was introduced to Dr. Abdurahman at his sick-bed last week, he merely confronted me with a nod and a dull, glassy stare. This morning, October 22, he is gravely ill and Cissie has had to rush over at 7 o'clock.

The colored workmen putting down the pavement on Exner Avenue all speak to me genially and never fail to ask how Dr. Abdurahman is getting along. (Cissie says that one of her father's main achievements was to get about seventy-five per cent of the street improvements' labor for coloreds.)*

Tendency of Cape colored to lay back and wait for equality of status with whites to be handed to them—they "fall" for such pronouncements as Hertzog's promise of ultimate equality made in 1924.[83]

Cissie and Sam tell me there are (approximate figures) for following professional colored in Cape Town:
 Doctor—ten (mostly Abdurahmans and Gools)
 Dentist—one Pharmacist—one (Dollie, the municipal councillor)
 Architect—one (and not well qualified—several draughtsmen)
 Lawyer, one (and he's in jail)
 Law student—one
 Minister—(many—see Gow)
 Teacher—(see Golding)
There are among these two women doctors, one woman medical student, and three qualified nurses.

Children forced out of school at very early ages by economic circumstances. E.g., saw large number of 7 and 8 year old kids in Desmore's Trafalgar Junior evening school classes. Desmore said they had to leave day school and go to work.

Lestrade, Du Plessis[84] and Schapera agreed that education for submerged groups is important, because it makes possible contact between groups on an equal social and cultural level. Lestrade emphasized that his home is open to one of any race who is on his intellectual and cultural level, but that it wouldn't be to an illiterate native, or for that matter, to an illiterate poor white.

Du Plessis agreed that there is a wider cultural and developmental gap between white and native masses in South Africa than between white and black masses in the Southern United States. Tried to apply same argument to the difference between white and colored, but gave in when Lestrade and Schapera demanded.

Lestrade and Du Plessis had never before heard it said that Cape colored find it easier to escape and to get along in Joburg than in C.T.—because the issue there is strictly white vs. native. They agreed that it sounds logical.

---

*Abdurahman had this influence because he was chairman of the Cape Town City Council's streets and drainage committee (1923–37).

Schapera was the butt of many a reference to his "Jewishness."

Lestrade liked my story about how I was introduced as an "Egyptian," etc. in West Africa.

Malay girls are most attractive. Some are mistresses of leading whites in town. One big white politician recently had to pay £ 600 for return of some letters he had written to his Malay mistress.

October 23

Everywhere I go people are discussing Dr. Abdurahman's prospects of recovery.* The city has roped off the streets all around his estate, guards are stationed nearby to caution "hooters," etc. Gow says he has undoubtedly done a great deal for the colored people, even though it may be said that he has been a selfish political leader.

Gow claims to have definite information that it is the intention of the powers that be to remove practically all of the C.T. colored population out of town entirely or to its outskirts. Said idea is to expand colored townships and housing projects like Bokmakierie—says they already plan to add 2,000 cottages to Bokmakierie. . . . Daily transportation is a great expense from out there. Says most of the colored out there have had to begin to ride 3rd class on the train, to which they are unaccustomed and which causes them to "lose caste and status."

He says there are many onerous restrictions imposed upon the renters. E.g. there is no electricity during the day and for only a few hours at nite—all lights are out at 10:30. Thus mothers cannot take advantage of infant care etc. programs that are broadcast during the day.

Another rule requires tenants to get special permission from the supt. of project in order to permit friends or relatives to stay with them for a short time. He says tenants object to the long list of restrictions and prohibitions imposed on them.

Last nite Schapera told me that many colored families here lavish their favor on their light-colored children—giving them clothes, education, etc. at expense of darker children, in order to aid the fair ones to escape into white community.

---

*Dr. Abdurahman was not to die until 20 February 1940.

81 Cape Town

What must be the psychological effect on the dark children of this sort of parental favoritism is not only re question of color, but also re their parents.

The point is, of course, as Sam [Kahn] suggests, that the lighter child will have greater economic opportunities.

The economic opportunities for colored are very limited—about highest paying position obtainable is that of teacher and their salaries are pitifully small, for C.T. is not a cheap place in which to live.

Schapera had a party of eleven to dinner at the International Hotel before going to the Khalifa.*

When I arrived, dinner was over, but he had the waiter fetch me a chair and I sat at the head of the table between him and a large Dutch lady, who yelled to me to come up there. (The help at the hotel, incidentally, is white.) I was served with beer and coffee along with the rest. Schapera, who is very timid, I think, told me that he had spoken to the hotel manager about the possibility of including me in the dinner party. The manager indicated a quick mind by asking Schapera how many people were to be served already. Schapera replied, "Twelve." The manager then conveyed his negative answer to Schapera by saying that if I were included there would be *thirteen,* and he was sure his guests would not like that! So Schapera let it drop there.

I was driven to the Khalifa in the American, left-hand drive car of the California Talbots.

The Khalifa—8:30 p.m. Held in small *Slamse Saal* (Malay Hall). The hall was about 30′ x 50′. At the back, there were stairs leading up to a loft. There was a large opening in the loft, like a trap-door, and some Malay people were peering down through there. It was very hot and stuffy inside but we felt better when the few windows were opened.

---

*Ratiep, a Malay variant of the Arabic retieb, is the actual name for the ceremony. Khalifa is the title of the person who presides over it. The ceremony was part of a festival celebrated annually on the eleventh day of the Islamic month, Rabi' al Awwal, and marked the birthday of Serda Alribchar, Muhammad's successor. The sword ceremony is supposed to represent the power of the flesh and spiritual purity over the steel sword. The ceremony became very popular in the mid-nineteenth century among Cape Muslims, but after citizen complaints about the noise and clerical displeasure over its abuse, it was curtailed to a once a year observance. By the time of Bunche's visit, the sword ceremony was largely being performed for commercial purposes for white audiences.

When windows on the front side were opened, crowds of Malay children pressed against them to watch the performance.

This was a private demonstration, arranged by Professor Du Plessis for the benefit of some 30–40 of his friends. He works with the Malays, organizing their choir, etc. Some one [*sic*] has said: "Were it not for the Malays what would Professor Du Plessis do?"

We sat on long wooden benches. I was on the front bench, next to Dr. and Mrs. Sachs [Sacks].[85]

When we entered, the fourteen male performers were squatting in two rows before the Khalifa or leaders who were behind the gaily flower-bedecked, altar-like framework or "ratip [ratiep] bank." They were praying and chanting in low voices.

The Khalifa is supposed to be held on the 12th day of the 4th month of the Mohammedan year. The institution has degenerated somewhat now and has a commercial as well as religious significance. Du Plessis claims this ceremony is truly Mohammedan and not at all Europeanized. There are several troupes, some of whom have appeared before large audiences at the City Hall.

"Khalifa" is really not the "show" at all, but the designation for the leader. He is not a priest. All the participants are laymen.

The idea [behind the Khalifa is] the power of the flesh, fortified by the Mohammedan religion, to resist steel.

The red and black flags hanging from standards at either side of the ratip bank, were covered with Arabic inscriptions which one of the performers told me are holy words. The names of the gods and prophets were in gilt Arabic letters at the top and center of the ratip bank.* The flowers were artificial and in pastel shades. The intoning of prayers was quite solemn.

The Khalifa sits behind the ratip bank and leads prayers and chants. A young boy of about fourteen sits beside the Khalifa.

Du Plessis explained that different drums are used for this ceremony than for the choir. The men beat thirteen large tambourine drums (raban[n]as) and one barrel drum (ghomma). The rabanas were the circumference of a dish-pan; the ghomma was about three feet high and with the same circumference. The drums were beaten by hand and very skillfully through intricate rhythms. When the drummers got down to

---

*Bunche is clearly mistaken about the names of "gods" being inscribed on the ratiep bank, but it is difficult to determine what he is referring to.

it, they created a great din. Two of the men were elderly, the rest were middle-aged and younger.

The rabanas beat the slow rhythm while the barrel drum (ghomma)—beaten by hand—carries the fast beat. Very loud. The chanting is vigorous.

Swords are suspended on the ratip bank in front of the Khalifa. The Khalifa drops incense in the small bowl on the ratip bank. There was a spell of chanting without the drums.

Men now come around displaying the steel skewers to the spectators. They are very sharp and about 1/2″ in diameter. One pair [of men] has one fork and the other pair has three forks. They were like heavy ice-picks.

Two men now dance with the skewers and bring them down forcibly on their chests and abdomens. They keep their shirts and sashes on, however.

The old man uses the two skewers with the three forked points. The timing, rhythm (aided by the drums) and muscular control of the younger men are especially good. They raise them above their heads and then with a powerful, downward thrust, seemingly drive them against their chests and abdomens. But I could only see slight pin pricks in their bright blue satin sashes afterwards. It was realistic looking, though.

They now bring large swords around—the same two men. The swords are sharp all right, as we discover when we run our fingers along them. Mrs. Sachs cut her finger testing one of them. The men bare their arms and slash viciously at them with the swords, raising them high in the air and bringing them down blade-first on their extended left forearms. The old man was not at all convincing. He draws his arm away too quickly and it is clear that there isn't much impact. But the younger fellow is much more convincing. They are clever at mimicking pain (like [professional] wrestlers).

Some of the men are barefooted and some in socks. Their shoes are all over in a corner. They keep their red fezzes (two of them are black) on, however.

The old man stops, wearily. The younger man slashes at his cheek and draws slight blood. When he displays his left arm, it is very red and with many slight abrasions running across it.

The older and darker man's arms shows little as results of this performance, but his arm bears several ugly scars running across it—indications of previous performances more seriously done. It is said that he once nearly severed his arm.

Now a young, stocky built lad with a poker face, sits in front of the ratip bank and takes off his shirt. The Khalifa then beats [heats] long, extremely sharp-pointed skewers with metal crescents at their heads, in coals in the incense pot. They are about 18″ long.

The Khalifa then comes out and with great deliberation pokes them one by one through first the ears, the cheeks, the shoulder tops and the flesh over the ribs of the standing, motionless lad, who doesn't change expression.

To get them through the cheeks, the Khalifa opens the boy's mouth and pushes them through the fleshy cheek. We could see the point gradually work through. They then hung out of his mouth, pushing his lower lip down with grotesque effect. Those on the shoulders were pushed through the loose flesh.

It took several minutes to get all eight of them through and then the boy slowly walks around among the spectators, gripping the two rib skewers with his hands. There was no blood in evidence at this time.

Another Malay walked behind him with an inverted drum for the collection.

When the old man carefully draws the skewers out of the boy, however, there was a considerable amount of blood drawn, particularly from the cheeks. The skewers were about the circumference of an ice-pick, but a good deal longer.

Next a man with body bared to the waist, lays flat on the floor. The Khalifa stands above him with a sword.

The Khalifa first saws on his (the prostrate man's) arm with a heavy sword. Plays on it like a fiddle. [The prostrate man] mimics anguish. The Khalifa then saws his cheeks, forehead and neck with the sword.

Then the Khalifa pounds the stomach of the prostrate man with the cutting edge of the sword. The victim just raises up casually and adjusts his fez. From no more than 6 ft. distance, it certainly seemed to us that the man was being hit with great force. His stomach muscles were powerfully contracted, it was noted.

The Khalifa then proceeded to saw heavily on the man's body—chest, back and side—as he rolled back and forth. Only slight cuts and abrasions, specked with blood, were in evidence. Then the Khalifa sawed the man's neck with a wobbling motion.

Then the Khalifa takes a heavy wooden mallet and pounds hell out of the sword, resting blade down on the victim's abdomen. The sword was seemingly embedded in the abdomen. He diffidently reached for his fez again. This was very impressive.

The victim displayed only superficial cuts, chiefly on his sides, back and abdomen. His cuts are wiped off. There were no marks at all on his neck.

They next bring around a sort of double sword contraption. Two swords fastened together at the ends. Two men hold it tightly between them and a third man in the middle brings his arms down on it with great force, the bodies of the sword bearers shaking with the impact. He then displays the slight cuts and redness on his arms.

Then he drives his neck into the swords, now held horizontally—though by gripping it with his own hands, he is probably able to break the blow.

He now rests his neck on the sword edges held vertically without touching them with his hands, and a boy of about fourteen climbs up from another man's back and jumps up and down on the back of his neck. It seemed that his head must surely be severed from his body.

Next he vigorously drives his abdomen into the sword. Then he climbs up on the swords and in his bare feet stomps up and down on the swords suspended about four feet from the floor.

There seemed little chance of denying that he struck the sword heavily. The bodies of the men holding it quivered at each impact and their arm muscles were straining to hold it. He displayed many superficial cuts on his arms and body.

Throughout these episodes there was continuous drumming and chanting, and this in itself was very impressive. It often bordered on the furious.

Some had said that perhaps the boy with the skewers through him was drugged, but as soon as they were removed, he assumed his place and began beating the drums with great enthusiasm. I could see no holes in his face or body afterwards.

All of the performers were good at dramatics. Good showmanship.

An intermission was called and we went upstairs for tea and cakes. Some of the women in our party "couldn't take it" and covered their eyes at some of the episodes—particularly the skewer business. I didn't enjoy that too much either. I've had too many inoculation needles stuck in me.

One of the Malays told me that the men had to be "pure" or "clear" when they came for the ceremony—i.e., they must abstain from contact with any women other than their own wives. If they cut themselves badly and bleed, that is evidence that they were not "clear."

Dr. Gool says they go through a rigorous school of training, reciting names of gods, etc.[86] They often start training at the very early age of 8.

The performance was to be continued after the tea, but my party had had enough, and so we left.

October 24

Trip to Mamre—Moravian Church colored mission village, about 33 miles from C.T. and 10 miles from Malmesbury.[87] Resting unobtrusively on a dirt road down in a valley. [The mission station] covers about 2700 morgen (original grant of land to the church).*

Conversation with Rev. W. Winckler, the tall, bearded, bespectacled mission pastor, with a cold eye, but who speaks fluent English. We first saw him looking after the counting of the collection in the back of the church, following the Sunday morning service and communion. The collection was mainly pennies, tickeys† and sixpences, but there was plenty of it.

Rev. Winckler said the Hottentots‡ were still living on the outskirts of the farm when the Moravians started the station in 1808. The people are descended from the Hottentots, but today the people resent any reference to it. There are about 1300–1500 actual residents of the village though the church rolls carry 2000.

Rev. Winckler freely admitted the great amount of miscegenation that is responsible for the present very mixed population there. He cites many cases of present inhabitants of the village whose fathers are known Europeans. Some very Dutch and German-looking mulatto types there.

There is a great deal of illicit intercourse between young and a great spread of venereal disease. Also much adultery. Winckler mentioned one case where a married man had been having a clandestine affair with another woman over a period of years. He had children by both women, though the children knew nothing about their kinship as they grew up. One son by the legal wife fell in love and had an intimate affair with his half-sister—daughter of the mistress. Is this incest?

---

*A morgen is a Dutch land measure equivalent to just over two acres.

†A tickey is a threepence coin. The name is derived from a Malay word *tiga*, meaning "three."

‡*Hottentot* refers to one of the indigenous groups of the Cape who made their living through pastoralism. However, because the word is linked to negative stereotypes of blacks, the word has been discarded in favor of *Khoikhoi*. See Richard Elphick, *Kraal and Castle: Khoikhoi and the Founding of White South Africa* (1977).

About 1/4 [of] births are illegitimate. Community and parents very tolerant toward unwed mothers. Only the church condemns them. He [Winckler] told me of one girl who twice bore children to her unwed lover—one in the village and another when she later met him in town.

He said the young folks find it hard to make a living in the village and therefore migrate to town. When they get to town, they don't want to come back. He says there is not much tendency among these people to "pass."

High infant mortality rate—about 6 to 8 out of the approximately 50 annual births. They have lately acquired a resident nurse, though this is strenuously opposed by the old mid-wives, who only attend the actual birth and give no pre or post natal care.

He said murders are rare, but assaults are fairly common. This due to easy accessibility of liquor supplies in nearby towns. It is also easy to smuggle wine off farms. Petty theft and theft from gardens are common.

Many of villagers work on surrounding white owned farms. They get from 6 to 12 "tots" of dreg wine per day.* Even the children who work on farms are charged for tots which are given to their parents.

The farm workers get house and rations—latter for workers *only* and not his family. They get from £ 1 to £ 2.6 per month. They often leave their families in village and return from farms only on Sundays. The farm workers are usually kept in debt to the farm owners. The villagers also get considerable employment on the road gangs.

There are between 280 and 300 school children in the 3 room schoolhouse. There are 9 teachers in the school. The school goes through Stan. VI. But many of the children leave before then because their families need their economic subsistence from work on farms.

The principal, a slender, light-brown-skinned mulatto with European features and a timid air, told us that workers on the farms are virtual "slaves."

The people build their own mud huts or houses. Mud huts painted white, with straw-thatched, sloping roofs. Many of the houses have only mud floors. Winckler says they often cost as much as £ 100. They do not hold full title to them—only right of occupancy. They have right to the resale of the houses.

The Mission doesn't manage the village anymore. Mission control of the village ceased in 1912. The village is run now by a village Board of Management.

The village Board of Management is composed as follows: the vil-

---

*A tot is a mug of wine.

lage elects six members; the government appoints three, one of whom is recommended by the mission. There is universal suffrage for those who have paid their annual taxes.

People, excepting the old folks, are tending to dress in modern style now!

They attend church faithfully.

Rev. Gow's meeting on "skollyism," at Bethel Church, Sunday, p.m. Church nearly full. Cadet Corps band playing; two choirs to sing. Two whites on platform—few, if any, in audience.

First speaker: Mr. Van der Ross, secretary of Non-European Teachers League.[88] Referred to fearless white friends and those who were falling away in hour of need. Alleged that there is a determination in some quarters "to put colored in their place." Said "fight is a fight for our existence—almost." Claimed that compulsory education seems to be the *one* remedy the European population could apply to prevent vice among colored. Charged christian churches with letting the government use them as a catspaw in education.

Second speaker: Mr. Ball, principal of Wesley Training College. Pledged support to Dr. Gow. Described skollyism as a festering sore. Congratulated railway authorities on decision to appoint 17 colored railway guards.

Third speaker: Dr. Gow. Pled for breaking down of the color caste within the colored group. . . . Said "Dr. Abdurahman is now hovering between life and death because he chose to serve before he chose to guard his health." Referred with scorn to "the custodians of civilization— our guardians." Suggested that maybe "colorphobia" is the *real* cause of skollyism. Demanded employment for colored and a living wage. Said Europeans have the remedy for vice in their hands.

Meeting closed on this note—no discussion, no selection of a continuation committee—like a bubble burst.

Ball and Gow both emphasized very significantly that this meeting signifies a "turning point" in attitude of colored people toward their problems. Audience not very enthusiastic about anything—mere polite applause.

Visit to Parade on Sunday p.m. Too many representatives of the Liberation League holding forth from a soap-box with a small audience. Preaching working class ideology.

Not far away was a young Garveyite (formerly an African National Congress member) preaching race chauvinism to another small group.

All of the Garveyite speeches I've heard there, including this one, were praising Japan's rape of China on color chauvinism grounds.

At fruit stall end of Parade was a Dutch Reformed Church troupe of men and girls with guitars, led by a mulatto preacher who looked a lot like Elder Michaux and who was talking the same hokum.[89]

I've never seen any white speakers on the Parade.

October 26

Golding's reception. Desmore said he was surprised that I expressed bewilderment at the inability of colored and natives to get together here. He said the American situation is different from that here in that there is a vast cultural difference, both contemporarily and by heritage, between coloreds and natives. Said Colored are descended from Hottentots, who were not Bantu.* But he admitted that sociologically and economically the colored were being pushed down to the level of the natives, despite their different cultural heritage.

Bishop Wright spoke and expressed amazement that Dr. Gow's moderate, well-controlled meeting could provoke such attention from the Europeans. He said significantly, that the A.M.E. church came over here because it was convinced that the welfare of the American Negro depended upon the establishment of an independent black nation in Africa—because the American Negro is a minority group. He said he was in agreement with me that union between colored and natives in South Africa had a significance which could not even be described, but that "it would not come before I die."

October 27

Experience at [Thomas] Cook's. In booking my railroad ticket to Maseru, Joburg, and Durban, the agent asked my "nationality." I told him "American." He hesitated and asked timidly, "You're not an American Negro, are you?" I replied, "Of course, I am—what do you

---

Bantu means "people" in Nguni languages. The term was applied to all African peoples, but fell into disrepute when the South African government began using it in association with apartheid policy in the 1960s.

take me for?" He then sheepishly said, "I thought you were a Filipino or something."

Visit to Zonnebloem School, an Anglican church school.[90] Grants teachers certificates for primary schools (like Wesley College) and also has secondary and primary schools. Low, flat bungalow-type, white plaster buildings. Not very large. One colored teacher, and she is very light—"border line," as Sierfogel [Zierfogel] says. 400 students in advanced classes. 1200 in whole school, including primary practice schools. Used to be a native college. Many chiefs used to attend, including Chief Yeta, who stopped to visit en route to Coronation.[91] Principal, Miss Waters, is white, though she could pass for colored.

A few native children in primary school, but principal says that the law does not permit natives to attend the training college. Watched several lessons taught. They believe in group recitation. Neither teachers nor teaching was very impressive. School gets many pupils from Rhodesia—through an arrangement with the Rhodesian government.

In discussion with Schapera, [Jack] Simons,[92] and young Dutch Reformed Church missionary, it was brought out that the Catholic Church has suffered less from native separatist sects than any other church in South Africa.* The missionary claims there are some 300 of these sects, though the government report (National Affairs Committee Report, 1936) states there are only 180. He says Dutch Reformed Church has had few because it has only recently begun to work among natives in South Africa. Until about 20 years ago, Dutch Reformed Church confined its work to Nyasaland, the Rhodesias, etc. Wesleyan church has suffered most from dissentient sects.

He accounts for lack of separate Catholic sects by the greater liberalism of Catholic Church toward native—[and] fact that Catholic priests often actually live with natives, that Catholic Church ordains native priests; and the appeal of Catholic ritual to the native.

He and Schapera feel that while appeal of nationalism had some ef-

---

*In the last quarter of the nineteenth century, groups of Africans dissatisfied with European missionary racism and control over mission leadership and finances and their attacks on African customs began breaking away to form their own "independent" or "separatist" churches.

fect on natives in early days of separatist sects, the chief explanation is to be found in the personal disgruntlement of individuals who break off from the mother church and take small groups with them. He includes A.M.E. church among separatist sects, though he admits this is inaccurate and says he does so only because government does so—[and] because A.M.E. is Negro, of course.

Says Dutch Reformed Church is bitter toward the Catholic Church and sets aside one Sunday each year on which sermons are to be preached vs. the Catholics—"Reformation Sunday."

Sam and Cissie say that there is preferential marriage among Cape colored—amongst the educated group, at least—men preferring light wives.

They also say that Malay women do more than 50% of the washing. Many Malay men are tailors and artisans.

My wisecrack that a man has no business wearing a full-dress [tuxedo] unless he can afford a valet to lay it out for him. When Golding met me at his door in tails the other nite, he was usurping the function of a butler who should have been there but wasn't.

Dr. Gool says Indians are right in not tying up their cause with that of the other colored, because the Indian must turn to India for his salvation. The Indian can maintain cordial relations with the colored, but must not identify his interests with those of the colored.

Schapera says that whites distinguish Indians from rest of colored population and give them preferential treatment.

The basic factor in division of colored group is that of religion. Physically they seem greatly mixed up.

███████ **October 30**

The other day in Schapera's seminar, Robertson,[93] the C.T.U. [Cape Town University] economist ("equilibrium economist," Dr. Sachs [Sacks] calls him) interrupted me to state that not only does the employer exploit the racial conflict situation, but the situation also exploits the employer. This stumped me until Sachs and I figured out last night that he meant this was true in South Africa only, where government protection of white worker makes employer pay higher wages than he would have to in a free market. But I answered this is really insurance against ultimate labor unity trouble for the employer, and therefore a good investment.

Betty and George Sachs told me that a few years ago the Carnegie Foundation offered £70,000 for a medical school to train native doctors and the South African government refused it. When forced to make an explanation later, Hertzog offered the lame excuse that the government did not wish any outside interference with its policy re natives.

Betty Sachs says she can't see why Cape colored are so bitter vs. the Labor Party. George explains it on basis of Labor Party's past of segregation and discrimination vs. colored worker. I said that colored tend to identify Labor Party with the poor whites. Betty claimed that Labor Party is not the party of the poor whites—that they support the Nationalist Party.

One of Eddie Roux's poems re the tot system. This was written when it was proposed to extend this system to the natives beyond the Cape. Eddie says it has not been extended and is still confined to the Cape. It was published in one of the native papers, I think:

> In the future it seems we shall have one right,
> When all other freedom is taken away,
> The right to get drunk on a Saturday night
> And lie in the gutter till break of day.
>
> The Congress is broken and I.C.U. dead
> And Bunting deported across the foam
> And everyone who's the least bit red
> Is spending his time in a "government home";
>
> Tho you've taken our vote in the Cape, and tho
> With tear gas bombs you're collecting your fines
> It will thrill dear old liberty doubtless to know
> We still may get drunk on South African wines!

Dr. Bodmer[94] said that the University of Cape Town Council had met to consider the question of colored students.* It has been partially

---

*In the end, the controversy came to nothing since university officials decided not to establish a separate institution for "Coloureds." At the time, there were about 50 Coloured students registered at the university.

decided, he claims, that in the near future a policy will be instituted whereby colored students will be barred from the University and "parallel" courses taught for them by university professors at the colored Technical High School in Cape Town.

Many folks in C.T. were trying to credit me with being the guiding hand and influence behind Gow's "skolly" meeting. They think it more than a coincidence that my arrival and this unusual (for C.T. colored) meeting came at the same time. Nothing to it. I only gave Gow advice when he asked for it.

██████ November 1

Clerk at Cook's pulled one on me. I went in and told him that on advice of friends I wanted him to see that a "coupe" would be reserved for me on the train Wednesday nite (a "coupe" is a single compartment—one berth). He smiled genially and replied: "With your color you'll be sure to be assigned to a single compartment." That floored me.

Dr. Norwich has been collecting data on a sampling of some fifty colored families resident at Bokmakierie—all christian colored. Families of eight, averaging two to three pounds per week, and pay rents varying from 8 to 11 shillings per week. The figures he has on expenditures for food indicate that they spend from 14s to £1 per week and eat very sparingly—with little or no milk, butter, eggs, or meat.

Some women told him that they did not use contraceptives because they are Catholics. On the other hand he has evidence that many women are refused permission to use contraceptives by their husbands, who allege that these will induce their wives to be unfaithful. One clinic (private) distributes contraceptive devices gratis.

An angle of dual use of the color[ed]-European situation is indicated by one very fair colored woman among his group, who is registered as European, but who goes as colored in order to take advantage of the cheaper rents and better living conditions at Bokmakierie.*

---

*The woman was registered to vote as a European. The definition of a European was based not only on one's physical appearance, but on one's lifestyle, customs and acceptance in the European community. This vague definition was carried over to the Population Registration Act of 1950.

It gets powerfully painful ducking all these signs—for "non-Europeans"* and for "Europeans Only" etc.

Observing the colored folks on the streets here one sees familiar sights—colored delivery boys on bicycles and driving trucks and wagons; colored men and boys dressed up in "monkey" suits; poor colored women gazing longingly into shop windows, etc. The white folks on the street—especially the women—are too ugly for description.

Saw two natives—one tall and lean and the other short—the latter with the familiar walking stick and in rubber boots—the former with a yellow lumber-jack's cap—strolling languidly down Plein Street, and stopping at every shop window to point and exclaim excitedly. They seemed to ignore the whites all about them.

Discussion with Mr. and Mrs. Desmore. Told about how Reagon, colored member of the Board of Education of C.T., fought against and had abolished the two "border line" schools (one in C.T. and one in Wynberg). These schools were "winked at" by the Board of Education—[and were] being maintained short of sub-rosa to appease the parents of "border-line" children, who didn't want their kids mixing with the more "colored" appearing kids. No dark children admitted to these schools. The fair children were not admitted to white schools, but associated with exclusively "fair" children in these special schools. Only white teachers taught at these schools. Reagon had them abolished about two years ago and now they are ordinary "cullud" [colored] schools.

The Desmores were obviously in favor of them—"necessary to face realities," says Desmore. He refers to the "economic advantages" in passing and clearly condones it. Says Reagon thought he could get colored teachers in these schools, but only one very fair one has been placed so far—claim is that white teachers would object to the use of same lavatory as colored.

Desmore says "borderline schools" are essential in places like Salt River and Wynberg where population is so mixed up that races are indistinguishable.

He continually harps on fact that the vast majority of whites are tainted with colored blood here, and this is basis of his argument for equal treatment and assimilation: since most of whites are "colored"

---

*Non-European refers to any person of color, whether of African, Coloured, or Asian descent.

and so many of colored are "white," therefore they are all in the same boat and should row together. He doesn't seem too much concerned about the non-passable colored—apparently they can fend for themselves. He and his family are in the borderline category. But he's dying to get to America for good.

Desmore says he tried to get all the colored groups together in Durban—but found difficulty because the Christians charged that while Indian fellows associated with their Christian girls, the Indian girls were kept under lock and key—no reciprocity!

Mr. and Mrs. Desmore say that Christian boys may go around with, but seldom marry the Malay girls, who, tho pretty, are "coarse" and mature very early. They say there is an even stronger prejudice against Malay boys marrying Christian girls.

They think Indian and Malay men treat women cruelly and indecently. They also said so many of the pretty light colored girls married white.

The Desmores were speculating as to how the press would treat the delicate "widows" problem if Dr. Abdurahman should die. Which wife would be recognized as the "widow"—the white, under Wes. law, or the colored, under Moslem law.[95]

[Mr.] Desmore referred to one colored family, living as white, in which the light children are sent to white schools and the dark ones are kept at home—since they are too dark to be accepted at white schools.

They claim there are many South African colored married white in England.

Mrs. Desmore told story of how the one (very fair) colored teacher at Zonnebloem (Miss Hendricks—from a known and recognized colored family—her sister is fairer still but doesn't try to pass) though known to staff as colored, has nothing to do with colored people. Says one day she cautioned her class, "you colored people shouldn't color your nails." One boy chirped up: "Shouldn't you say 'we colored people,' Miss Hendricks?" The lady is still seeking an answer!

Desmore says he fell out with Dr. Abdurahman back in the early 20's, when as an A.P.O. man, he was standing for election to the Prov. [Provincial] Council. Said he and his supporters came to Abdurahman for his backing and he told them bluntly: "If there are any plums to be handed out I'm handing them to my lieutenants."

Desmore claims that Bishop Sims told him that the reason the A.M.E. bishops don't tell the American Negro about what the real situation is in South Africa, is because they (the Bishops) don't really want the American Negro to know that there is any civilization here for the black and colored population—if that were known, money would not be forthcoming so readily for "missionary" work.

November 3

Monty and I were hunting my compartment—a double affair all to myself—when the guard told me "this section is for non-Europeans" and tried to shoo us on.[96] I found my compartment in that section. Talked to my friends till the train pulled out. I was fooled by the sign "Col. [Colored] Male" typed on card outside the car—I mistook it for a reservation for some colonel. Sam [Kahn] had a big laugh. At least they had "Mr. Ralph Bunche" typed on my reservation cards. In these state-owned railways, a colored man has no trouble getting first-class accommodation—he really exploits his color because, as there are few colored travelling first class, the colored man is almost always given a whole compartment (the spare berth is mine). I heard the conductor warn the guard to keep the door of the coach behind us locked as there were prisoners there.

The train is slow and has already (11:15) made 3 stops. A European steward came in shortly after we left and asked me what would like for breakfast. The colored porter is very attentive.

━━━━━ **November 4**

Slept very well. Was awakened by the steward at 7:30 to inquire if I wished coffee. Had breakfast in bed—orange juice, buttered toast and soft-boiled egg. Bleak, sparsely settled brush country. We're riding through the Great Karoo this a.m.* The mountains to the right are beautiful with a bluish haze about them. The bedding boy informed me that this is an especially good coach and compartment I have—it has a heavy spring mattress. He says they get one of these on this line very rarely—"once in 6 yrs." (was this "special for me?")—or was it for the Indian who had a crowd of fezzes to see him off last night?

There's a wash bowl in my compartment and the bedding boy brings me a pitcher of hot water in the morning. Good service. Chief

---

*The Karoo is the dry interior region of the Cape Province.

steward dropped in and asked me if I was being properly served. A large table [was] let down and set with white table cloth. Good meals and cheap.

C.T. Indian on our train en route to India, referred to our slow train as a "Kaffir train" because it stops at every village to pick up natives.

The same Indian alleged that the Jews in South Africa are trying to drive out the Indians from the country because of business competition. Had obvious dislike for the Jews.

The Indian was very proud of me and wished me all luck. He thinks Indians in South Africa will never get their rights until they stop dividing their time and interest between South Africa and India.

██████ **November 5**

Up at 6:30 in order to be ready to change trains at Bloemfontein at 7:20. Fine weather at Bloemfontein. Talked with 2 of the colored bedding boys on our train. They get only £ 4.70 per mo. (a few of the older employees get as much as £ 6. The tips are meager and they work from 5:30 a.m. till 1 a.m. (or later often). At times they had had two boys to look after 7 cars. They are agreed that this is a rotten country for colored. The lighter one told me that he had had to have his sister take his 2 children to a Europ. school for as soon as they are registered as colored here there is no future for them. They are all very proud of Amer. Negro fighters like Armstrong and the Louises.*

---

*Henry Armstrong, John Henry Lewis, and Joe Louis. For Armstrong and Lewis, see note 26 in Johannesburg I; for Louis, see note 12 in Cape Town.

Sam Kahn

Sam Snitcher

99 Cape Town

George and Betty Sacks

Jack Simons

Abe Desmore   Christian Zierfogel

George Golding   Stephen Reagon

101   Cape Town

Trafalgar High School

Mamre

Coleridge–Taylor Quartet

Sister Nannie Tempo

Arthur McKinley

Basutoland

Caledon River is boundary bet. [between] Basutoland* and Orange Free State—a twisting, deep gorge, not much water.[1] On the Free State side is the "Conquered Strip"—taken from the Basutos and inhabited by them still—the most beautiful part of the Free State.[2]

The country, though still a bit brown in spots, is beautiful. In another month it will be much greener. Rolling plains, mountains and deep valleys, cut up by hideous dongas.† Peaceful, cattle grazing, clean blue sky, scattered clumps of trees; sculptured, low lying mountains; native village huts (brown) nestling against hill sides.

I defined my project here as follows (on culture-contact basis): (1)

Basuto is the British corruption of the word *Basotho*. *Basutoland* is the British colonial name for the country of *Lesotho*.

† A donga is a gully created by wind or water erosion.

European customs which are helpful to the natives, e.g. soil erosion control, etc. (2) Native customs which are worth preserving, e.g. laws.

Conversation with Mr. Thornton, head of Agricultural Work.[3] Econ. [economic] pressure today did not exist in early days when natives could roam freely—but now native is restricted to districts. White man stopped natives from blotting each other out. White man (1) confined the people. (2) stopped diseases from wiping out both people and herds; stopped overstocking and overbreeding. (3) Livestock and people have increased enormously. (4) But land has decreased—i.e. depleted.

Capt. Blyth visualized small land holdings for natives—a peasant population like France, etc. . . .[4] Rhodes took Blyth's idea but adopted idea of giving an extremely small holding which would keep the indiv. just on the starvation line.[5] His object was to secure labor for the diamond mines and this system would make natives come out and work. It was employed in Glenn [Glen] Grey district in the Cape and was known as the Glenn Grey Act.[6] Was applied to 8 districts in the Transkei. Has not been extended elsewhere, for there are no advantages shown by this indiv. title to land over other native methods of tenure. Only restriction in title was that they could not sell to Europeans—or they would have lost it long ago. Thornton used to be strong advocate of indiv. tenure—but no longer.

The 3 field system [is in practice] in Basutoland.[7] The chief allocates 3 fields to each individual . . . —man would work two fields and 3rd would lie fallow. Land belongs to tribe, but is handed down from father to son. Chief could expropriate land only with consent of council and there is now the court of appeal.

Natives gradually breaking away from old system and accepting new crops at advice of Agriculture Dept. As old feudal land passed away in Europe, so he (the chief) will pass away here. Native society passing through feudal stage. Chief has great power which is to advantage of the admin.

Soil erosion and such questions are taken up with chief. Chief told work is necessary if Basutoland is to be saved. Meant cutting off corners of fields, etc. Chief asked that work be done first on his fields. But in Transkei, no soil erosion work has yet been able to cut thru a cultivated field—whereas thousands of such, on order of chiefs, have been cut thru in Basutoland.

In all progressive agricul. schemes govt. has had full support of Paramount Chief and his council.

Natives, even the uneducated ones, appreciate fully the signif. of the erosion work and ask that their fields be cut up more as "wash can still take place." They don't merely follow blindly the advice of their chief.

Basuto a good business man. Basutoland natives relatively well off; no poverty-stricken population. Last year, Basutos raised a surplus of foodstuffs. 200,000 to 250,000 bags of wheat for export.

Thornton says much more grain is now being stored by natives. They had a surplus last year, they didn't sell it. They are learning to protect selves vs. the future.

Biggest export is wool. In 1930, 3,000,000 sheep and 1,000,000 goats of inferior quality. . . . Enormous drought of '33–'34 reduced numbers thru natives eating and selling [their stock] and this was followed by interval parasites. Now these losses are checked and herds are on increase as result of universal dosings at native's cost. End of '36, 75,000 horses, 4,000,000 cattle . . . 1,264,000 sheep and 410,000 angora goats.

No institutionalized markets. All indiv. barter. Admin. has started one market at Mafeteng and it is doing well. Thornton wishes to estab. livestock markets here.

No cooperatives yet. [Thornton] says it is necessary to go slow with them and that they haven't thrived in the union [Union of South Africa].

Lobola practiced. Out of about 120,000 family heads (based on population of 600,000 and family unit of 5) there are only 26,000 cattle owners. There are many things creeping into dowry system which didn't exist yrs. ago—incl. [including] all types of livestock, farm implements and *cash money.*

Conversation with Mr. Richards, Resident Commissioner of Basutoland.[8] Richards [was] impressed when I mentioned Margery Perham's name re Indirect Rule.[9] [He] said she didn't start Indirect Rule, "but we did," and she's just writing "what we have already said and done." (He served under Sir Donald Cameron in Tanga. [Tanganyika]—hence, his enthusiasm for Indirect Rule.)[10]

Said Indirect Rule could not be instituted all over Tanganyika because the Germans had broken down tribal institutions in many places and there was nothing to build Indirect Rule on.

Said there had been a few good and efficient chiefs in Tanga. One was particularly great, but he absconded with a considerable sum of money "and had to be deposed" by the govt.

Richards pointed out that native treasuries as in Tanganyika increased temptations confronting native chiefs, but said that they are an important part of the native's experience in running things. Otherwise able chiefs have sometimes had to be deposed for misuse of funds.

Richards says there are no native treasuries here—no need for any, he says, as there are no white settlers here and there is no need for separate or parallel treasuries. There is only one central treasury here (is this because native revenue is insufficient to support native treasuries?)

He says Basutoland has the best system of Indirect Rule. Only one Paramount Chief [Griffith Lerotholi][11]—he's old— descendant of Moshesh[12]—and who suffers from diabetic trouble.

He is said by Richards and others to be very intelligent and clever. Has a marvelous memory. Doesn't speak English. Has a clerk to type his letters for him.

Richards says that the modern chiefs have many duties. They are often not too busy, as they delegate many of their jobs to relatives and friends. Their clerks also handle many of their jobs, such as writing letters, etc. Richards said I might go out to see a chief and find him doing nothing but drinking beer.

He said Pim . . . advocated individual land tenure for natives.[13] Richards is opposed to this, as it would break down tribal organ. [organization] and thus make impossible the operation of Indirect Rule. He agreed that it would lead to development of a few wealthy, large land holding people (mainly chiefs and relatives) at expense of rest of population. But neither Richards nor Thornton could explain how to get around fact that communal tenure of land does make it very difficult for the native farmer to progress—especially where fencing is prohibited.

Richards defended keeping of illiterate and seemingly backward chiefs in their positions. He said they had abandoned separate school for sons of chiefs— latter now go to regular schools and mix with others, and this is better for them.

He says there is no point in having the chief too far educated beyond his people. Young educated natives could be put in chief's position and do a much better job from the standpoint of the administrator— theoretically; but the young chief would not have his people with him and could hope to do but little. Desideratum is to educate masses of people to a higher standard of life and chiefs along with them.

Richards says the Basuto are very fastidious and astute in their purchases from traders. They want nothing but the best quality of goods and expect to pay more for it; e.g. they want *all wool blankets.*

Richards said they are to build a new high school as it is more desirable to educate the natives at home instead of sending them out into the union.

Richards said it is a good thing so many Basutos go to work in mines and on South African farms, quite aside from the money they earn, for the country is overpopulated anyway.

In the evening I saw 26 boys rehearsing their outdoor singing. They assumed different formations—sometimes in two lines facing each other about 30 feet apart; sometimes with 4 men facing a semi-circle of the others, etc. They changed places with military precision and their leader gave signs very inconspicuously. They sing lustily, and like to harmonize.

Heard the technical school boys sing their Sesuto "Threshing and Braging" (softening leather) songs on Fri. nite. A group of the singers act these out in front of the singers. Very impressive. For my benefit apparently, they also sang "Glory to the Men of Old"—not nearly so impressive as the other two.

Bull[14] and Thornton said Moshesh, the great old chief, was opposed to witchcraft.[15] They claim that he used to hide things and tell the witch-doctors to find what he had "lost"; then laugh at their consternation when he would produce what they had failed to find.

When a delegation of Basuto natives were sent into union [of South Africa] to investigate mine compounds sometime ago, they were told secretly by their chiefs to inquire of union natives re their condition, in view of proposed incorporation of the protectorate in the union.[16] The delegation came back with the report that the union natives invariably told them: "if you want to go to hell, join the union."

There are 2 or 3 small schools for Europeans—up to Standard III only—for the approximate 70 European school-age children in the territory. After Standard III, their parents must either have them taught at home or sent outside for their education.

There are no soldiers, either black or white, in Basutoland, only police under European officers. There are about 300 native police in the country.

Bull told me that if he had been at C.T., he would have "fixed me up" for my train journey by seeing the station-master for me and having him write me a letter telling the r.r. [railroad] missions to "look after me" properly—"Mr. Charlie" looking after the "good nigger."*

---

*Mr. Charlie is a term African-Americans used to refer to a white man. Miss Anne referred to a white woman. The origins of these terms are not precisely known.

They all here employ that same cliche about how "happy" the natives are. They don't look so "happy" to me.

November 6

Conversation with Mr. Lovett, Basutoland recruiting agent for the mines.[17] Said on deferred pay scheme natives of Basuto[land] sent back much of their money from the mines thru the recruiting office (these figures do not include postal order remissions).

1929	£ 15,800
1930	£ 37,800
1933	£ 96,800
1934	£ 104,400—famine period.
1935	£ 90,900
1936	£ 131,800

He says that in early days [of] recruiting, the spirit of adventure was the main incentive behind workers going to the mines. He claims this is giving way to the idea of mine work as a permanent livelihood.

Lovett says that the educated natives who get the better jobs in the mine compounds, are the only ones who in any numbers tend to stay at the mines. Their children become completely detribalized.

He said there was a good crop last year—particularly in Kaffir corn*—and this has meant a revival of many tribal customs—such as circumcision schools, beer drinks, visits from kraal to kraal, etc.† The six weeks spent by the boys in the circumcision schools (after which they enter manhood), greatly restricts mine-recruiting during that period.

Lovett says there is an average of about 40,000 Basutos annually in mines—mostly on 9 mos. [months] contracts.‡ He says % of desertions is almost negligible, even among those who go out on free or open contracts. On such contracts (specifying no partic. [particular] mine and no period of work) the company allows the natives three months grace before charging desertion.

The 9 mos. contracts are based on 270 shifts, usually taking about 14

---

*Kaffir corn is a species of sorghum ground up for making porridge or beer.

†*Kraal* is a Dutch word denoting an enclosure for farm animals made of wood and/or stone.

‡In 1936, 38,200 out of 163,838 workers from Basutoland in South Africa were working on the mines.

109   Basutoland

mos. to complete. Those on A.V.S. (assisted voluntary system) contracts, work an average of about 11 mos.

Lovett says the average period of service in the mines is far greater than the average period of work at recruitment—and the term of service is growing longer. Many just stay on.

Lovett says that as a result of idle rumor and gossip, some mines are very unpopular and natives are very reluctant to sign up for them.

He says that the Basutos are very good workers. They are "almost invaluable" to the mines as they do most of the shaft-sinking work—the hardest but best paid work at the mines. Some of them earn up to £15–£16 per month.

Lovett said the mines have a "carding system" for native agitators and once they are "carded" it is difficult for them to get employment on mines, at least until they "all been good" for a yr. or so.

He says the union system of deporting Basutos for mine offences works a great hardship on them, for it debars many of the means of livelihood. For often they are without land when they get back home and they are forced to become criminals. They are sometimes deported for such things as failure to carry a pass, etc.

Lovett alleges that most of the women who bootleg* beer and act as prostitutes on locations near mine compounds, are Basuto women and he says they were chiefly respon. [responsible] for the Vereeniging uprising. Bull argues that they may be Basutos but not necessarily come from Basutoland, tho he admits that a great many Basuto women go into union to work as domestics, harvest crops, etc., tho many others smuggle across the boundary when the Caledon River (the boundary line bet. Basutoland and the Orange Free State) is low.[18]

[Lovett says] the Basuto are much more proud and independent than most of the union natives.

Lovett and Bull say that the Basutos are very humorous, love fair play, are amenable and "easy to handle."

Lovett says that the Basutos are now saving their money, too. They are tending to eliminate the trader as a medium for exchanging and business. He says they are anxious to buy stock, but do so from each other or in the expensive union market, but not thru the trader. He says formerly if co. paid out £300 in checks about £200 would come right back from the trader. But not now. Recently £300 was paid out and only £25 came back thru trader.

---

*Bootlegging is the illegal brewing or selling of liquor.

Visit to trading stores. Europ. clothes become more popular each year in sales. Frasers selling quite a few 2d hand overcoats—at 15s and 2d each.[19] They come from the U.S.—tho he doesn't know how they get here nor how they can be sold so cheaply.

In Colliers native women are beginning to buy cloth hats—tho they wouldn't wear them 3 or 4 years ago.[20] They wear hdkfs. [handkerchiefs] and caps. Colliers sell a good deal of men's underwear (long drawers)—mostly made in U.S. and retailing at 5s. They buy sardines and tinned beef too (latter became popular among nat. [native] soldiers during one of the wars). They are also buying such modern articles as thermos bottles, tea sets, cups and saucers (one large lot of latter sold out in a jiffy—retailing at a tickey for a cup and saucer).

They only want the best quality in blankets, good quality in shoes. The blankets are wool and are made in Ger. [Germany], Eng. [England] and So. Africa. They have very striking designs which are specially made for this trade. Many have much color, others mild. Formerly green was abhorred by women but now it's in demand, because they've learned that green dyes are now fast.

Colliers creates interest in new articles by giving one or two away and letting women wear them. Wool blankets sell at from 8/6 to 22/6—more expensive ones most popular. Some of them are in very mild colors. Wool shawls are popular with the women and retail at from 15s to £3.

Saw native prisoners, male and female, being marched out to work in Maseru. They have very fancy and "loud" uniforms. The women prisoners are mostly guilty of bootlegging Kaffir beer.

Visited Ladybrand, a little town in the Orange Free State, nestling in a valley. Here, as in most Afrikander rural towns, the Dutch Reformed Church is the central feature and towers above all else in the town as one approaches it.

Bull suggested that I talk to his schoolboys "about the boys in French W. Africa." I didn't—I talked about American Negro boys.

I spoke to boys at Lerotholi Technical School tonite. Emphasized necessity for pride, adventure and achievement.

They sang two negro spirituals in my honor—"Steal Away" and "Walk into Jerusalem" (not too well). They also sang the Sesuto National Song and the Xhosa National Song.[21] They sang a Sesuto war song which tho simple was very vigorous. Some of them did war dance up front as they sang.

At Bull's home, Sat. night, discussion with Tomae [Thamae][22] (govt. secy. in educ. dep't and former secy. of Yergan[23]); Rev. Janke [Jankie] (an old man);[24] the ed. [editor] of nat. [native] newspaper; an interpreter in the leper colony (the most talkative and least liked by Bull); and 3 other young educ. [educated] Basutos, one an intermediate school teacher. 3 are from Fort Hare.[25]

[They say] in old days the chief's court was given more discretion in deciding cases. But today the chiefs are arbitrary. Many abuses by chiefs deciding cases today.

The chief keeps the fines and abuses his power. In the old days the chief heard cases themselves. But today most of the chiefs let their "chairman" of court hear the cases. Existing chiefs are corrupt and "multiply like locusts" due to polygamy. (Bull says one of Richards' forthcoming proclamations is to limit the no. of chiefs.)[26]

In the old days only the sons of chief's first wife were recognized as his heirs. But now the chiefs have often insisted that the sons of other chiefs divide their domains amongst all these sons.

In the old days there was mutual love between the chief and his people. This is changed today—because the chiefs are out for self and gain.

The situation is changed today because of the British government. Before the British, people could desert the bad chiefs (the Basuto rarely killed them). This is impossible today. The chiefs have indirectly gotten privilege and security under indirect rule.

The alternatives of the Basuto today are to either stay under bad chiefs or go into the union—"out of frying pan into the fire." They admit that the masses of people still cling to the chiefs—but the signs are that they are slowly breaking away from the chiefs. They will still plough for the chiefs, even tho they don't like it.

Chief Setsomi in the Leribe District was thrashed by his people for maladministration and had to be hospitalized. They cited another instance of a native subject firing (tho missing) a gun point-blank at a chief because the chief had expropriated his horses.

Another common abuse by chiefs is in unjust reallocation of lands. "The chiefs take advantage of commoners."

They admit the fund. [fundamental] conflict between the educated African and the chief, tho they say that the chiefs are under the misapprehension that the educated natives hate them.

The masses of natives still regard the hereditary chief as having a special status and would prefer a bad hereditary chief to an efficient, educated commoner (educ. [educated] chief might be *too* efficient).

A system of elected chiefs wouldn't work now—people are not

ready for it and the hereditary chiefs are too strong. They would control elections anyway. Similarly any kind of "recall" system would be too advanced.

There is a power of appeal from the decisions of chiefs; but there are not many appeals tho some are upheld. Those who appeal from decisions of chief are left in his bad graces.

[The chiefs] find native masses bitterly opposed to incorporation, due to rough experiences in working for Boers and at hands of union police. [The Basotho] fear pass system also. Many Basutos in jail in the union merely for being without passes. They are also opposed to union taxes—e.g. dog, bicycle, beer taxes. All of the chiefs are against incorporation and the masses of natives follow their chiefs.

Many Europeans—traders and officials—in Basutoland also opposed to incorpor. [incorporation].

Basutos prefer to go to mines rather than to farms in union. But many young men who go to mines come back—broken in health with mine diseases—yet the young men are eager to go. Many younger men who go to mines desert their families at home and never return.

Without incorpor., how will Basutoland support its population?

Prospecting for minerals not allowed in Basutoland—the chiefs are opposed to it. "They won't hear of mining here." Afraid of losing their land to whites. For same reason, the chiefs are opposed to the introduction of railroads in Basutoland.

There is much cattle raiding still in Basutoland. Armed raiders (local) steal livestock and sell them in the union [of South Africa].

The chiefs are much more wealthy than the rest of the people. The educated native does accumulate more wealth than the others.

Complaint that "a matric" (one who has passed the matriculation exam.) returning from Fort Hare and entering the Civil Service in Basutoland gets only £3 per month. A native policeman without any education gets as much.

There are 4 govt. intermediate schools and they pay from £3 to £10 per mo.

They were all impressed by what I told them of the color unity among Amer. Negroes.

Bull disparaged the most voluble one of their [group] (an interpreter at the leper colony). He is obviously the boldest and the best thinker.

Bull told me of McKinney's [McKinley's] visit to Basutoland recently and the subsequent suit for defamation of character brought by a native school teacher (at McKinney's urging) who had been dismissed for inefficiency and insubordination. Suit brought against European supervisor who made the rec. [recommendation] for dismissal and lost. McKinney is the W. Ind. [West Indian] Garveyite who soap-boxes on the Parade in C.T. Bull called him "an American Negro."

Disadvantages of men going to the mines : (1) immorality; (2) broken health; (3) broken families.

Aspects of native culture worth preserving:
1. Native herbalists or medicine men as distinguished from witch doctors.
2. Native law is good—*but* it is badly administered by the present chiefs. They administer it capriciously.
3. Circumcision schools. These are dying out. Christians and school boys and girls will not submit to them (tho Richards says that several of the Sesuto boys at Fort Hare had been circumcised). Their rites are very secret. Richards says they should be abolished because during the initiation period the boys are very spunky and rude. Some chiefs still encourage circumcision rites, but leading chiefs discourage it.
In former times the Basutos were more kind-hearted, hospitable and generous than today. There was more respect for parents and elders—this was due to the circumcision schools.
4. Folklore—(a good deal)
5. Music—(some).
6. Dancing. Basutos are good dancers, but traditional dance steps are dying out. Bull said he was asked to judge a native "singing" contest, and when he got there he had to judge a fox-trot contest instead.

Educated Africans feel that people have great respect for a Fort Hare man—though there is always the matter of conflict with the chief when they try to influence the people.

■ **November 7**

Sunday morning and afternoon trips with Mr. Thornton . . . , Sir Alan Pim, Mr. Milligan, Mr. Wecher and Mr. Moudell, to see soil erosion control work, farm experiments, etc.
Thornton says natives take eagerly to new vegetables. They are

particularly fond of cabbage (they don't leave a leaf), peas and to lesser extent, carrots. They are also growing potatoes, lettuce and beans in their gardens now. Peaches are plentiful and thrive in this country.

The natives are eating more European vegetables because the mine boys get them at the mines and want them when they come home.

We visited a native's garden. The man has a herd of 200 sheep over in the Free State. His wife does the gardening—very difficult terracing.

The local cattle are not good dairy cattle and Thornton is planning to import Swiss goats for milk. He says the natives like goat milk.

The country, tho beautiful, is terribly eroded and cut up by gaping "dongas" (arroyos) which Thornton is trying to control by furrowing, banking, dams and control at the top, and planting trees (mostly poplars). They are also experimenting with various kinds of sturdy grazing grasses.

Thornton estimates the cost at an average of about £1 per acre for erosion work, though some flat lands can be worked as cheaply as 5s per acre.

Sir Alan Pim asked Thornton Sunday how they would get money to maintain the erosion banks, furrows, etc. Thornton replied, "Through the chiefs, sir." One chief has already made it compulsory by law.

Thornton has requested no ploughing on slopes over 20 degrees. Has to depend on chiefs to carry this out and says they are cooperating extremely well in all the agricultural work—even giving him their best fields for experimental farming (one chief offered him his race track). He says the chiefs are competing with each other in this.

Some valleys have been reclaimed already. One 750 acre valley we visited has been reclaimed and is now good grazing land.

The white sub-officials are as deferential to their superiors as the natives are to them. They were "Sir-ing" Sir Alan and Milligan all over the place all day.

The European officials in our party showed great respect for the native village women whose gardens we visited—tipping hats, [giving] pretty speeches of thanks to [them] through the interpreter, etc.

England seemingly gets nothing from a possession like Basutoland. For long it has been self-sufficient, but recently England extended a loan of £160,000 (without any interest charged) for erosion control work.

Elsewhere the struggle is to protect the natives' land from Europeans; in Basuto[land] it is to protect native land from the elements and the natives themselves.

European influences in huts of natives—beds, clocks, chairs, tables, pots and pans, pictures, oil lamps, clothing, etc. Saw a clock with a music box in one.

We all took tea at the Maseru European cafe—no question raised about me.

Frank, the senior secy. in the Educ. Dept. and headman of his village of 60, said that natives of his village go to work in the mines only because they have to. He said that the young men seem lost in the village when they first return from the mines. They buy cattle with the money they bring back.

Bull said that the Financial Secy. (now on leave) had been penalizing Frank because he was an active member of a native govt. clerical workers organization or "union"—tho all members were very loyal to govt.

The native women (and some men) buy a lot of hair pomade and use it. But they haven't acquired the straightening iron yet.

A question is continually in my mind: How can this handful of whites keep these millions of blacks down?

The blacks can't be but so dumb—they show too much adeptness at handling the white man's contraptions—bicycles, cars, carpentry, forges, football, cricket, languages, etc.

November 8

Left Maseru at 8 [a.m.]. "Alexander," the much mouthed Sesuto, driving, Ma and Pa Bull in back seat.

All along the road the natives were industriously ploughing the fields. They appear to be a real peasant people—farmers and herders, though the men are scarce and one sees mainly women and children in the fields. The men are at the mines. They use oxen before the plough and sometimes as many as a full span.*

Umbrellas seem very popular with the native women. I saw many of them along the route—walking down road with babies on back, strolling across fields and even on horseback—with umbrellas unfurled.

We saw scores of neat, unobtrusive villages on hills and mountain

---

*Depending on the weight of a plough and the strength of the oxen, a full span can vary from two to eight oxen.

sides all along the way. Many are a ruddy brown color—built with red clay. Many use the local sand stone for part of their huts. The huts blend into the background thatched tops. Some square and some round. Mrs. Bull says that the square huts are thot [thought] to be "more advanced" than the round [ones].

We attend a court in Masupha's village in Leribe.[27] The court is held every day but Sunday. The court is presided over by the chairman of the court and not Chief Masupha, who has gone into town and taken some members of the court with him.

The court is held outside with members of the court seated on chairs underneath trees. Moshesh established custom of holding courts under a Monkhoane tree,* and most village courts continue it. Spectators perched in a circle about the court on rocks. The members of the court are nominees of the chief—headmen and elders. They serve at pleasure of the chief.

The first case we observed is over a cow. The plaintiff is a ragged old man who claimed that a cow he has bought has been sold by the husband of the defendant, an old widow, and that a substitute cow was being pawned off on him.

The widow sat under a Mexican aloe (cactus) plant, her grown daughter squatting beside her. She claimed that she knew nothing about the change. The litigants and the court yelled back and forth at each other with questions and answers.

The cow, it develops, had been sold by the son to another party. Due apologies were made to the plaintiff at that time and he was offered the return of the £2 he had paid for the animal—but this plaintiff refused because he maintained that the cow belonged to him in the first place.

The old lady defendant got very "hot" and proceeded to bawl out the court, telling the chief questioner on the court to "shut up," and claiming that the plaintiff had misrepresented the facts and that the court's questions favored the plaintiff.

The case was complicated by the fact that the cow had had 4 calves—during period of dispute, and issue involves their ownership.

The court finished its questioning and reserved its decision until after it had held later deliberation on the case.

Another case was called. 2nd case: defendant had married and had

---

*The monkhoane tree or parsley tree (*Heteromorpha arborescens*), has a special association with Moshoeshoe's birthplace, Menkhoaneng, "the place of monkhoane trees."

to pay "bohali" (lobola). He paid 13 of the 16 cattle demanded for his wife, and chief ordered him to [pay] the other 3. A chief's messenger was sent out to collect the other 3 cattle.

Messenger set out to collect them and he demanded a fee of 2/6. But defendant didn't have it at the moment, and then messenger seized 1/2 [a] bag of peas.

Defendant says he now has the 2/6 and wishes his peas back. Messenger hasn't shown up yet and so case was postponed for the time being.

3rd case: land dispute between 2 headmen. The defendant was a tall young fellow and a headman, who talks very rapidly and eloquently. He refuses to give a statement to the court because he alleges that the plaintiff has introduced some extraneous issues into the case that he is unprepared to discuss.

The plaintiff is a fat man with khaki suit. He claims that case is not heard by plaintiff's chief because that is plaintiff's father and therefore the defendant demanded a change in venue to this court.

The defendant claims that plaintiff took 2 fields because the plaintiff claimed they belonged to a man who had moved away from the defendant's village and plaintiff claimed the fields because he is higher in rank (as son of a chief) than defendant.

Court orders defendant to go and *write* down all his objections.

Had a short conference with the District Officer, Mr. Cannon. He discussed the difficulties with the "educated" natives, who are "too far advanced" for their people, and who criticize the chiefs. He dismissed them by saying "if they don't like it here, they can go elsewhere."

Cannon told us that the head chief in the district is Masupha Molapo, who is "acting" for his brother, Motsoene Molapo, "who has been virtually deposed" because he has outbursts of temper.[28] Cannon says all chiefs must be deposed through the paramount chief, on the recommendation of the administration, however. Cannon complained that old Motsoene doesn't accept the situation too well and keeps sticking his nose into district affairs.

Bull says he thinks Yergan exaggerated the physical inconveniences he suffered here. He thinks that Yergan was treated very well in that respect, tho he added piously: "it is not for a white man to say what *spiritual suffering* a colored man undergoes in such a situation."

Bull emphasized that Yergan underwent a change after his trip to

Russia.* He wanted everything to be "more radical" in the union after that.

Said Yergan lacked organizational ability, tho he was a good contact man. Said Mrs. Yergan's work would be more lasting than Max's and both Mr. and Mrs. Bull had more praise for Mrs. than for Mr. Yergan.[29]

Said Yergan cooked his Y.M.C.A. goose in South Africa when he wrote a stinging, discourteous letter to the International Secy., charging that as a white southerner he was prejudiced and blacking Max's work (re Denmark conference).†

Bull mentioned how unusual it is that Harris, a South African Jew, should be appointed as a school inspector for Basutoland, in London— tho hastening to assure me that it made no difference to him that Harris is a jew.

Bull, in introducing me, continually refers to fact that "the Dominion Minister, Mr. MacDonald and the High Commissioner for the Protectorates," sent me here and wished me to be shown around.

Bull praised the way natives are treated in the mine compounds. But when I raised the question of the deprival of families he could only say that many native mine workers are unmarried.

Bull says that while there is a good hospital here, and natives can get the best medical attention, the chief criticism of the med. work is that it has not been *aggressive*—i.e., there is no real maternity welfare or infant care work. Med. authorities have waited for natives to come to them. Good med. attention plus hospitalization for a nominal fee of 1 shilling.

Bull says there are no age requirements among the Basuto; they still have clan names but no clan organizations; they are both endogamous and exogamous.‡ The villages seem to vary greatly in size.

Bull claims that no Indians are allowed in the Orange Free State.§

---

*Max Yergan's shift to the left came before his trip to the Soviet Union in the winter of 1936.

†In 1932 Yergan had resigned from the executive committee of the World's Students Christian Federation when he wrote its director, F. P. Miller, a Virginian, accusing him of "gross conduct" and of meddling in Yergan's work in South Africa.

‡Endogamy is the custom of marrying within one's own clan; exogamy is the practice of marrying outside one's clan.

§An 1890 law passed by the Orange Free State Volksraad prohibited Indians from permanently settling or remaining in the Orange Free State for more than two months. In addition, Indians could not buy property or own a business. This law remained in effect until the late 1980s.

There are only 2 or 3 Indian traders in Basutoland, he says, but they do very well. One has given £350 for a library for the new high school. He has several trading counters in the north [of Basutoland].

November 8

Ficksburg-Bloemfontein. Drunken, talkative Basuto chief in my compartment. Got in while I was out. Was insistent that he had right to stay though he had only a 2nd class ticket. Ticket examiner put him out with a sharp command. He came by later and apologized. I then invited him [in] and he told me he is a cousin of Chief Masupha, whose village I had just left. Says he got his education at Fort Hare. I told him I am American Negro and he waxed effervescent about how American Negroes like [have pride in] their color and understand and sympathize with the African. Said Sesutos are a great people, but they need education and great leaders. Said Richards, the Resident Commissioner of Basuto[land], is a fine man and shows love for black man externally, but deep in his heart, he is like all white men. Wants to break the African. Says Basutos are excellent politicians.

He told me I ought to see the Council of Chiefs at Maseru next week—then I would hear some fine speeches.[30]

I was put into a smelly compartment at Ficksburg, even though it was a double compartment all to myself.

Ludicrousness of putting me in a jim crow compartment (the jim crow on these South African trains are the coaches marked reserved). The bedding boys always occupy one compartment in them; the native 3rd class coaches are usually on either side, even if it is 1st class, and having a white waiter in a blue monkey suit to serve me my meals here, and to bow to me and inquire "will that be all, Sir?" and "Is that satisfactory, Sir?"

I'm a curiosity because I travel first class—even the chief travels only second. The ticket examiner very pleasantly inquires what I'm travelling for, and the waiter, seeing all the equipment in my photo apparatus bay while [I am] down changing film in my Rollieflex, asked me if I'm "selling them."

I told ticket examiner in answer to his inquiry that I was doing research in cultural anthropology for the S.S.R.C.* He just gave me a queer look and walked out.

---

*The Social Science Research Council, Bunche's funding organization.

I'm transcribing these notes on the train—over a bumpy roadbed and in relative comfort at that—thanks to Mr. Bull, who told me that writing in a train is relatively easy, if one puts a pillow in one's lap.

Leo Marquard met me at the station at Bloemfontein.[31] Marquard drove me to his home for dinner. He and his wife and I chatted until 10:30 ⌊p.m.⌋ and then went to station to catch 11:45 train for Fort Hare. But we found that Bull was in error re connections and I had to lay over here until tomorrow a.m. at 7:15.

Returned to the Marquards for the nite. Marquard told me that his father was a Boer. He and his wife claim to be Socialists. They are friendly.

Mrs. Marquard . . . emphasized the drink evil among the Cape colored. She said the stuff sold by the liquor dispensaries and freely obtained by the colored is of terrible quality and greatly contributes to the moral and physical degeneration of the Cape colored population. She sees this as a greater evil than the tot system there.

She said many of the colored are skilled artisans but that they are terribly dishonest and untrustworthy.

She shares the popular impression that the Cape colored are physically very weak and under-developed. A renegade, bastard population.

November 9

Up at 6. A girl brought me a glass of orange juice. A taxi came at 6:40 and I went to the station. The train left for Fort Hare at 7:15.

They can't seem to figure me out on this train (from Bloemfontein to Naauwpoort). I had to get my compartment reserved this A.M. and alone with no "good white man" to intercede for me (Ken also told me that a colored man has no difficulty if a white man intercedes for him). Two ticket examiners went into a huddle and put me in a coupe in a white coach. They first started to put me in a double compartment with a white man. I still don't know whether I'm "passing" or not on this train, brown and kinky headed as I am.

Waiter insisted that I come to dining car. He said chief steward told me to come as I wanted a full lunch. I went and was "Sirred" plenty. Nobody got up and walked out, though the colored kitchen boy was peeping out at me. So I guess I was passing.

I may have "passed" from Bloemfontein to Naauwpoort, but they had my number at Naauwpoort. On the ticket examiner's orders sheet from Bloemfontein (I had a whole sheet to myself) was scrawled the tell-tale word "colored"—clear across the page. I am colored a whole page full.

Naauwpoort Junction—a terrible, dull joint; it is, according to the sign at the station, "4884 feet above sea level, 270 miles to Port Elizabeth."

Had 3½ hours to wait for connecting train. It is just a railroad junction. What a dump. The seats at the station, the lavatories, buffets, etc. are marked "for Europeans Only" and "for non-Europeans." The Post Office has 2 entrances—one for Europeans and one for non-Europeans. Plenty of mulattoes in evidence. Colored and native folk look frightfully poor.

The natives use "bloody" plenty—at the stations one can hear the men and boys using "bloody" while speaking the native language.

So they put me in a 1st class "Reserved" compartment—which means that though I have a double compartment all to myself, I'll have to change trains at Cookhouse at 12:30 A.M., whereas I should have been in the E. London coach and then I could go to bed and the coach will be switched off and picked up by the E. London (and Alice) train. I was in a Port Elizabeth coach. The colored porter who handled my bags at Naauwpoort on my arrival and called me "massa" [master] was terribly disappointed and puzzled by it all and I wanted to protest but didn't.

I raised hell with the ticket examiner. He meekly said he had just gotten on this train and hadn't been through the train yet—but that he would see what he could do for me.

The waiter came in soon afterwards and was very solicitous about what I would like to eat—even asked me if I'd have a beer. I did and it was cold. So maybe ticket examiner spoke to him. It pays to raise hell even though colored.

Lesotho scene with British officials

Man standing in front of plant

School scene

Two men at court

Eastern Cape

November 10

Met at station at Alice by Mr. Kerr,[1] (principal) and Matthews[2] at 8 a.m. Mr. Kerr wouldn't let me give the boys who carried my bags at the Alice station a shilling tip—insisted that a tickey was enough.

Have a room at Kerr's home—had breakfast there.

130 students at Ft. Hare; 10 girls among them; a few colored [and] Indians. Not many sons of chiefs here.

The costs [are] £ 32 per yr. for everything, but due to [government] subsidies, Kerr says they can make it on about £ 20.

Kerr says there is no difficulty in placing their graduates; the demand exceeds the supply.

2 Negro teachers, Matthews and Jabavu, on a staff of twenty.

The issue of admittance of a few white students arose here once and the vote was negative by the Board of Control.

Conversation with Mr. Kerr.

Referred to divisions among students at Fort Hare. Colored, Indian, and native students, though housed together, etc. tend to form separate social groups, e.g. natives, who are in the majority, never permit election of an Indian or colored student to the student elective body—despite Mr. Kerr's talks about the rights of minority groups, etc.

Then there are tribal divisions and jealousies among the natives. The 3 main tribal groups are the Fingoes (Xhosa speaking),[3] Xhosa and Basutos. The Fingoes, who are more adaptive and quick, tend to be numerically dominant at present.

Kerr says there is no difference between capabilities of the students of the various groupings. The good native student is the equal of any Indian or colored student.

The natives are taught their native language or that of some other tribe. They have a course in Social Anthropology, giving them knowledge of and respect for their own customs, and there is a course taught in native law (both by Matthews).

Kerr doesn't believe that much of native custom can be retained. Too many influences working for changes. . . .

But the development toward European culture is very uneven—e.g. he has seen native initiation rites for girls not five miles from Fort Hare, in which old native men danced around completely nude and with decorations on their penii.

Kerr says many of the boys still spend their money for circumcisions—for they feel this is necessary in order to attain manhood.

He says most of the boys here are individualists and are looking forward to government jobs (in some of which they will start for as much as £180 per year), but that a few have group and social consciousness. Thus there are 2 wide gaps opened between the educated African and the masses—one of ideas, education and thinking and culture, and the other in economic status.

He says that to all intents and purposes the Protectorates* are already in the tension because of their great reliance upon union mines and farms for economic employment. What would happen to them in case of a depression in union? [Will "natives"] all [be] thrown back unemployed into the Protectorates?

Kerr doesn't think development of secondary industry will help the native much because the government, controlled by the conservative

---

*The Protectorates are the British High Commission territories of Bechuanaland, Basutoland, and Swaziland.

farm population, will interfere and keep native from improving his position too much.

Kerr said while South African judges are on the whole very capable and fair, the jury system leaves too much to be desired where color question is involved. Says a new law has been passed giving people before the court the right to choose either jury trial or trial by judge and 2 assessors. Kerr says whites prefer jury trials and blacks invariably the judge.

Kerr says there are only a handful of educated and socially sophisticated natives, and that American Negro can still be a great help to South African native if only through showing a good example. Kerr named: Jabavu, Matthews, Drs. Bokwe[4], Xuma, Moroka[5] and M'timkulu[6]—and says that is about all.

But why doesn't Fort Hare insist on a training that will better and more realistically prepare them for life?

Kerr said Jew is friend of black man in South Africa. Feeling against him [the Jew] has only recently developed.

Matthews told me that the Presbyterian church is the dominant church group in Ft. Hare's Board of Control (Council). There are some 24-5 members of the Council and some are natives. The mission groups insist on religious training—hence the daily chapel, the Sunday services, etc. The Presbyterians gave the land and the religious groups have been responsible for building the new hostels for students.

But the Council refused to permit the Catholics to contribute a hostel, since the Catholics made a condition that Catholic students would not have to worship at the Sunday common service.*

I visited the library—good selection of basic texts. Not much on the American Negro.

Livingstone Hall made possible by Chamber of Mines Deferred Pay Board [which gave money] in 1935. . . . Building opened this year. Chamber of Mines gave £75,000 for whole scheme (building cost about £20,000).

The course is called "The Medical Aid Course." Part of rural medical service for natives. Fellows have trained to be assistants to district surgeons. Students in this course get free education, and are guaranteed employment upon completion of 4 year course. Candidates must have

---

*This dispute with the Catholics over the construction of a Catholic hostel eventually led them to found their own university, Pius XII College, in Roma, Basutoland (Lesotho) in 1945.

matriculation of University of South Africa for entrance—this would entitle them to full medical training. People are against scheme and despite monetary advantages, they are having difficulty in getting students—only about 10 students now. They have been forced to let students in without full qualifications.

They get a special certificate from Fort Hare on completion of the course, but this does not entitle them to practice medicine. If they wish to take up medicine later, they must take a complete medical course and get no credit for work done in this course. The South African Medical Council insisted on this.

The first director of the Medical Aid Course (while well qualified) stayed a year and quit in protest. [He] said students were being duped. If they are training sanitary inspectors they should be called that and not led to think they are studying medicine.

"Official" version is that national health has greatly deteriorated and something must be done to improve health conditions in rural areas. But nothing said or done about the main cause of ill health—malnutrition through cheap wages.

The native mine workers union of Joburg gave £1,000 to this project. They have a plaque too in Xhosa: "This stone is given by the Native Mine Workers Union as a memorial to Mr. H. M. Taberer their protector and friend." Taberer director of the native recruiting organization and was liked by the native mine workers for his efforts on their behalf. . . .[7]

Visited one of student hostels and main dining room. They were getting a small loaf of bread, a tin of green jam and tea for supper. Nothing else.

Met Dr. and Mrs. Bokwe, who had supper with us. He's the sole native doctor for some 40,000 people on the reserve. He has many white patients, too, including Dutch policemen. He has recently been appointed District surgeon by the government—the first Bantu to be so appointed in the union. It's all been done quietly and Kerr is afraid the newspapers will make a stink about it, since it can be misrepresented so as to imply that white patients seeking government medical service, *must* come to him. In fact, says Bokwe, he's always done all the European medical work at Middledrift and now many of his former white patients come to him for free government medical service.

Bokwe said that except for the few thousand natives (about 11,000 now, says Kerr—some years ago there were 15,000 exercising the suffrage), there is no suffrage for natives in South Africa.[8]

It's good to live in Africa—the attention one does get from the black servants—and everyone has so many of them. Tea in bed in the mornings, shoes always shined (the maid came in for mine this morning). I got my washing done on the same day, etc.

Took trip out toward Middledrift and stopped at trading store to buy native beadwork. The land in the nearby native reserve is wretched-looking—barren, arid and crowded with native huts.

The trader said business is not so bad despite the drought because the men are working on the local soil erosion control, in the gold mines, and the diamond mines are open again. The trader is a Brooklyn Jew who came out here 20 years ago. He wants me to look up his cousin in N.Y. [New York] and gave me an extra native money belt for nothing—all for sentiment.

Practice in union and protectorates for traders to buy mealies* from natives at about 5s per full bag of 200 lb. and then sell it back to them later on when they need food at 15–20s per bag. The educated natives say that the sale must be made in order that money can be gotten to pay the tax.

Kerr told of purchasing a lock and key from a trader, who told him "tickey to you, shilling to a native."

Many of the Xhosa women and girls are nice looking. They are colorful in their ankle-length, ochre-colored (orange or burnt orange ?) robes. Many of the women and some men too use ochre or white chalk over their faces and look rather grotesque. The green turbans (tocques) worn by the girls also look nice. The married women can always be recognized by the apron about their waists in addition to their ochre robes.

Talked (Matthews as interpreter) with a fine looking Xhosa boy, who at 20 said he had already done 2 years at the mines—underground work too—and is going back after Xmas. He earned £3.10 per month—and said he saved his money by the deferred payment plan.

Matthews says after a couple of shifts like that they're done for.

Matthews also said that the mines pay no interest on the millions of £'s of men's wages they hold under the deferred payment plan. This in-

---

*Derived from Afrikaans mielie, mealies is the South African word for maize or corn.

terest is the money they use for "native philanthropy"—e.g. they recently gave a building to Fort Hare.

Matthews is very critical of the missions. Says they oppose State control of education. He sees . . . the conflict between state and mission in any societies . . . [as an] added division among whites which will redound to benefit of natives.[9]

Matthews says Jabavu is becoming a mistrusted leader—feeling is growing that he will sell out to the whites or compromise too greatly. They say he was tickled pink when some white M.P. protested against the extension of the native curfew laws "to educate[d] natives like Jabavu"—and flattered that his name was mentioned in Parliament; gloated that he had been thus able to save the educated native from this humiliation.

He [Jabavu] is said to have been hard hit by the new native franchise acts. While his franchise (as a Cape native) was not entirely taken from him, it was virtually, for he and the 11,000 or so other native voters in the Cape who can vote (and no others in the union can), can elect only 3 European representatives to look after their interests.

Matthews thinks it would have been better for all the natives to have [been] disfranchised together—this would aid unity.

The white Methodist be-robed person who conducted the "silent service" today (Armistice day) in the Assembly Hall (gotten by money obtained by Yergan) read his eloquent statement which I also read later, word for word, in the morning edition of the *East London Daily Dispatch*.* And what stinking religious crap he dished out!

There was very obvious Jim Crow at the meeting to hear the German professor from Rhodes College[10] lecture on the "Jewish Renascence" at the Lovedale library.[11] The whites sit down in front and the natives, students and teachers, in back. Matthews and others say it is an unwritten law and is respected; and that most of whites present are Lovedale teachers, whose staff is about 50-50 black and white.

Talked to Fort Hare students on necessity for development of group self-confidence and pride. Pointed out that their cultural background, their folklore, music, art, great chiefs and political institutions could become valuable cultural devices in the hands of educated Africans, in moving toward progress.

---

*Built with funds raised by Max Yergan, the Assembly Hall was opened in 1930.

They are very dubious about my suggestions re retention of their culture. They dislike looking back (as American Negroes dislike to look back to slavery). Many young Africans seem to be already ashamed of their culture and look upon education as an escape. Want to adopt all of the white man's standards of value.

In evening I talked to a group of native Lovedale teachers and found them too a little suspicious about the retention of what is African. I preached group chauvinism to them plenty—that it [is] justified at just this stage.

November 12

Dr. Dingemans, a Moravian German from Rhodes University and a typical "Christian," handed me a long line about South African conditions. Things are not perfect, he admits, but improvement is certain though slow, etc. Referred to "conservative, but kindly patriarchal" Afrikander farmers, who are so "human" in their regard for the native. Says it's true that natives don't get much money but they do get kindly treatment, etc., etc., ad nauseam. He's highly critical of the mines and the unnatural situation created by their taking so many native workers from the farms.

Mrs. Ballinger speaking to some of her native constituents at Gipira district of Middledrift. . . .[12] About thirty present.

[She] referred to her conference with Hofmeyr, Minister of Labor, re necessity for establishment of a minimum wage for natives.[13] Discussed also difference in price of mealies when natives buy and sell them.* European farmer is getting a better price for indiv. mealies, but natives are not. But all, black and white, pay more for them.

Mr. Ballinger spoke re wages.[14] Made reference to me and American Negro.

Sen. Malcomess, big business man in district, who formerly represented Europeans in this district and was elected native senator at the last election, also on hand and spoke.[15] He referred to fact that white farmers can get mealies cheaper for livestock than natives. . . .

Sen. Malcomess raised question as to what attitude of natives is re right of natives to buy land as individuals. Malcomess said that it is apparently the intention of government to give land to natives only under communal tenure. Do natives also want Malcomess to agitate in government for private purchase of land by natives?

A native, in answer to Malcomess's query, arose and vigorously replied that not an Amagqunukwebe[16] man would stand up and ask for right of individual native to buy land in Khama's [Kama] country.[17] Pointed to traditions of people.

Another educ. native arose and pointed out that government was taking individual pieces of land and asked group if they wanted to continue to live in that old way. This created a slight furore.

An old native farmer spoke next. Said he has no confidence in government to do anything. From a paper he read figures re livestock, ploughs, etc. owned and tax paid by natives in 1875. He then pointed out that in the 62 years since the native group here has increased in numbers, and had paid more and more in contributions to the government, but have less land—[and] that many of the "released" lands in this area were lands formerly held by Khama. Said natives weren't asking for more lands but just to keep the land originally granted to Khama. He pointed out that natives here have been buying back lands which were originally theirs.

In answer to Malcomess' question, the old native affirmed that there are Europeans now holding farms in the original Khama land grant. Some of these lands have been reobtained by native purchase through tribal levies.

Malcomess arose and said he would like to see natives holding new land like small German settlements with each native holding 20-30 acres of land around his hut, but emphasized that he didn't want to interfere with any tribal custom.

Malcomess very deferential to wishes of natives—says he can come at any time to discuss native wishes.

A. M. Jabavu,[18] editor of *Imvo*[19] and member of Native Representative Council, spoke re poll tax.

Dr. Bokwe (he was campaign manager for Mrs. Ballinger) next spoke. Discussed mealie quota in re malnutrition and ill-health of natives—t.b., chest diseases, lack of milk. Referred to Dr. McVicar's[20] statement at Lovedale yesterday to effect that if native wages could be doubled, native t.b. would be cut in half. Demanded that question be raised in Parliament as to why [European] farmers can get mealies for livestock at a cheaper price than natives have to pay for foodstuff. European farmers get mealies for livestock for 5/9 (in drought stricken areas—by government subsidy), while natives in same areas pay 17/6.

Another native arose and advised that the native should hold a meeting of their own to discuss these questions.

The old native farmers weren't afraid to stand up and talk to their ofay representatives,* Ballinger and Malcomess, nor to express their doubts re what they could do.

Mrs. Ballinger seems sincere. Sen. Malcomess is a typical professional politician—full of bluff and hypocritical glad-handing.

Sen. Malcomess is a wealthy trader in ploughs which he sells to the natives. He has to make a lot of noise, at least in favor of the natives. When he was in the Provincial Council, he got his seat through the former native franchise.

Only three native representatives in an [House of] Assembly of 153.[21]

Mrs. Ballinger—(English, South African) backed by English organization called Friends of Africa.[22] Her main campaign plank was demand for improvement in industrial wages, etc. She has keen interest in the urban native [but] knows little about the rural native.

Moltino [Molteno][23]—advocate—an Englishman (South African)—interested mainly in constitutional and political questions. Seems to have leanings toward Dominion Party.[24]

Advocate Hemming—head of a legal firm in Umtata—mainly native business.[25] More interested in rural and land problems. Also has Dominion Party leanings.

4 native senators in a Senate of 44 (elected by people) plus 4 more senators nominated by the cabinet on basis of their supposed knowledge of native affairs. These 8 are in the Senate which has no influence in the political affairs of the country.†

The four nominated senators: (1) Thompson—known as "Matchele" Thompson—grandson of man who was prominent in the conquest of the Matabele. (2) Smith—son of a missionary. (3) Spies—high Afrikander—no one knows how he got in. (4) Van Niekerk—another Afrikander—apparently a purely poli. appt. [political appointment].

Senators for Natives: C. H. Malcomess (South African of German

---

*Ofay is a term African-Americans used to refer to whites. Its origin remains unclear, although it is commonly thought to be pig Latin for foe.

†The Senate had no special powers. It could not initiate bills dealing with finance and taxes. Although it could amend or reject bills sent up to it from the House of Assembly, it rarely did so and it was often a rubber stamp for bills sent forward from the House at the end of a parliamentary session. The South African government abolished the Senate in 1980.

extraction), W. T. Welsh,[26] Rheinold [Rheinallt] Jones and Dr. Edgar Brookes.[27]

Welsh—former Chief Magistrate for Transkeian territories—now retired and on government pension. His record was not good and people didn't like him. He got in by 2 votes over a Mrs. Stuart.

Dr. Brookes—ex-professor of Public Administration at Pretoria and now principal of Adams College, now a Buchmanite.[28] Encountered much opposition in his campaign because of his book, *The History of Native Policy in South Africa,* which was published by help of subsidy from Gen. Hertzog,[29] and people felt that it made Brookes the father of present native policy. Brookes admitted that when he wrote this book, he had these ideas, but a subsequent visit to U.S. caused him to change his views (this was his explanation during the campaign). He was later cut off by Hertzog. The real reason for his success in the campaign was because he was the lesser of 2 evils. His opponent was a second rate lawyer who was making plenty of money out of a big native practice— he wasn't in Brookes' class intellectually. Brookes received a comfortable majority.*

The Bursar of Fort Hare, a young South African, trying to convince me that Basutoland would have been much better off under the union, because whatever may be said of the white man's treatment re the native, the white man conserves the soil and Basutoland would not be the barren, bleak country that it is now, etc. But what about the erosion on the Free State side of the Caledon River—in the "conquered strip"?

Dr. Bokwe (and Jabavu too) told me how the South African [blacks] became all excited about Garveyism and the slogan was "the American Negroes are coming to save us."[30] They, too, grasp frantically at any sort of hope for escape. Matthews says this feeling was so intense that Pirow had to send airplanes to the Transkei to break up demonstrations.[31] They were saying that "the Americans were coming in big ships to save us."

Two old fellows out at the meeting today told me how happy they are that an American Negro is with them and they knew that we, too, are Africans.

Matthews says there is little camaraderie between whites and blacks

---

*Brookes claims that he ran on the urging of Chief Mshiyeni, the Zulu regent, who could not bear the thought of a Shepstone (in this case, Denis Gem Shepstone, a Durban attorney) representing Zulu interests in Parliament. Brookes won 180,000 votes to Shepstone's 160,000.

on either the Fort Hare or Lovedale staffs. He said that the Jim Crow seating arrangement (Negroes all in rear and to one side) at the Dingemans lecture at the Lovedale school library the other night, was accepted as an unwritten law. He said that some of them broke down an attempted segregation seating arrangement for members of Lovedale and Fort Hare staffs at a Lovedale native athletic meeting last year.

Matthews told me they had tried to carry out a policy of Jim Crow entrances at the Alice post office, but that the boys had refused to recognize it, had protested vs. and violated it, and finally a ruling came that it could be ignored and abolished there, since these were "educated, respectable natives."

Midnight meeting of the Fort Beaufort and Victoria East Teachers Association, affiliated with the Cape African Teacher's Asso.[32] 35 teachers present [at] all night meeting. The group present is about 50-50 male and female, mainly young.

Difficulty of having day meetings because of unavailability of conveyance and also because so many teachers have lands to look after. Many of these have to walk great distances to get to the meetings.

This one is held in a small one-room combination church and school. Room lighted by one candle and kerosene lamp; several wooden benches and a few wooden desks. Dirt floor well pitted.

They were discussing change in constitution and change from nite to day meetings when we came in.

I spoke at 12:30 a.m. with Jabavu acting as interpreter in Xhosa for some who cannot understand English.

I was thanked profusely for my "eloquent address." I found it difficult talking through an interpreter. The pauses disconnected me some.

Jabavu is a really comical old fellow. He had my sides splitting with the travelogue, graphically illustrated by grotesque gestures, of his recent trip to America to attend the Quaker meeting in Philly [Philadelphia].[33] Everything impressed him—the big boats, the elaborate furnishings, the luxurious "Y," the lifts, the expense, the traffic, the roads, the colored customs officials, the speakers, etc.

Jabavu again took occasion to disparage, for my benefit, the policy of the African holding on to his old culture—this he considers as a drawback. He said it would be better for the African to be, like the American Negro, with no cultural roots, and therefore willing and eager to clutch at every new idea, leader or movement. He praised the gullibility of the American Negro and his eager attendance at meetings, etc. He also laid emphasis on the tremendous amount of organizations among the American Negroes, which he regards with envy.

The chairman of the meeting, a young Fort Hare grad. [graduate], stressed the fact that I had mentioned that our Howard Teacher's Association is a *labor* union, affiliated with a working man's organ[ization].* He pointed to this as a lesson for the African teachers.

The teacher's temporarily adjourned the meeting after Jabavu's speech in order to eat supper—at 2 a.m! And then the meeting will go on until about 7 a.m., I'm told.

These people are coming along. But all of the educated ones seem cognizant of the fact that through differential treatment, flattery, back-slapping, special privileges, social acceptance, government posts, etc., subtle influences are at work to create a wide gap between the educated African and the native masses. There are evidences among the younger men, while not violent yet, that they resent these influences and scorn older Africans who are duped by them. There is a kindly, somewhat tolerant criticism of Jabavu on this score.

Some of them are beginning to assail vigorously and intelligently any suggestion by whites that the African is not capable of holding responsible posts directing institutions and generally doing anything that the whites can do when given a chance for training.

They all seem impressed by American Negroes (tho unable to discriminate between "Christian" Negroes like George Haynes[34] and Yergan and me) and feel that we are sincerely interested in Africa's welfare.

Among themselves these young educated natives are very scornful of the whites, ridicule and caricature them, and relate how the whites have been duped and tricked on this or that occasion.

The educated Africans here have very few African art objects on display in their homes.

Educated Africans feel that people have great respect for a Fort Hare man—though there is always the matter of conflict with the chief when they try to influence the people.

It would pep these people up if they could develop, say, even, one or two outstanding native athletes. They take such pride in the American Negro athletes—especially Jesse Owens[35] and Joe Louis.

Among both black and white there is widespread respect for America but little knowledge of or understanding of it.

---

*Howard University had had a chapter of the American Federation of Teachers since 1918.

I insisted to Scallon at South Africa House in London, that I am not a missionary. But any American Negro visiting South Africa *is* a missionary whether or not he wills it. But he doesn't have to be a *religious* missionary.

November 13

Met Senator Welsh, who had been attending the Fort Hare Governing Council meeting, at the station and chatted with him and Matthews until train came—late—enroute to Bloemfontein.

I don't know whether Welsh, who was ushered on to the train by the ticket examiner, spoke a word on my behalf or not, but at any rate the old boy was unusually congenial toward me. Put me in a coupe, lifted my bags in the train and talked to me about his planned trip to America next year, etc.

I am in a 1st class coach—not a "reserved" coach—whites on either side of me and no bedding boys.

It takes this "Kaffir train" 3 hours to cover the 50 miles between Alice and Blaney, the junction where I change trains.

I just had a 20 minute wait at Blaney—which is railroad junction and nothing else. Senator Welsh leaned out of the window, chatted affably, wished me a pleasant trip in South Africa, wished to be remembered to Dr. Moroka.

A European boy portered my bags. I sat on a European bench and was given a coupe in the 1st class coach. The dining room steward came through and said since I was the only one eating lunch he'd set me up a single table. Plenty of "sirring." They surely are deferential to first-class here.

The bedding boys (who are always light-colored) tell me that these coupes are mainly used by married couples. I'm just 1/2 of a married couple, but I'm sure using them on these trains.

Small native boy at a village stop just beyond Blaney begged for pennies: "Please, Baas [Boss], give one some penny. One so hungry Baas." And when I didn't respond immediately, he cried, "Shame, Baas." So I tossed him a penny and received a profuse "thank you, Baas."

Beautiful driving car on this train, excellent food and service. I was only one in it. Heavy plush arm chair seats, finely appointed in every way. And the ofay stewards are too polite for words. And this darkey was drinking Castle beer, not Kaffir beer! For 2/6 I got soup (paysan), stock fish ringed with mashed potatoes, choice of curried turkey and rice, roast lamb or cold meats, vegetables, lettuce and tomato salad, pineapple fritter and custard, cheese and crackers, and fresh fruit, tea or coffee, bread and butter. Beer is 1s extra. The train must be the cheapest place to eat in South Africa and quick, polite service.

Roseberry T. Bokwe

Z. K. Matthews

D. D. T. Jabavu

William Ballinger addressing Ciskei meeting

Mrs. Ballinger sitting at Ciskei meeting

141 Eastern Cape

Four Xhosa women

Thaba 'Nchu
and Mafeking

Slept restlessly and awoke at 5:30 a.m. At 6 the ticket examiner came in to tell me we would reach Bloemfontein in 1/2 hour. The steward arrived a minute later to ask me if I wished coffee. Dr. Moroka had his chauffeur Alexander to meet me at the station in one of his two Hudson Terraplanes (the Coupe). He drove me to Thaba 'Nchu in about 1 hr.[1] A bath was drawn for me and I had breakfast with Dr. and Mrs. and 4 yr. old son Kenosi ("I am alone"). Dr. Moroka is a quiet, dignified man, well-dressed and poised. Definitely mixed and also Mrs. Moroka. Both very friendly. Dr. Moroka had work to do in his surgery and Alex. took Mosaka and me on a tour of the reserve.[2]

Thaba 'Nchu native reserve in the Orange Free State. Thaba 'Nchu means "black mountain." It's 41 miles from Bloemfontein. Main source of wealth for natives is farming and work in the mines. Mealies, wheat, kaffir corn, beans, sheep, cattle main agricultural activities. The land in the reserve is terribly inadequate.

21,000 natives in Thaba 'Nchu district and approximately 500 colored. About 10,000 natives on reserve itself.

Not so many of the Thaba 'Nchu men go to the mines—most work on farms, roads and in Bloemfontein. Average pay for native farm workers here is 15s per month.

The native houses on Thaba 'Nchu reserve are of much better and more modern construction than the mud huts on the Middledrift and Fort Hare reserve.

The white population is mainly composed of traders. The small town of Thaba 'Nchu is in middle of reserve, but natives are not allowed to live in it.

The coloreds live right among the natives in the location. Some have timidly pressed for separate residential quarters. Not much mixing socially. They have their own social functions. Practically all the colored speak Tswana.

Land in the reserve is held communally by native tribes. But colored graze their animals on reserve land, are given plots and land to cultivate by chiefs, and in general, are treated as children of chiefs in the same sense as the natives.

In Thaba 'Nchu some natives still own expensive farm lands outside the reserves.

Several churches for natives—Wesleyan, Anglican, A.M.E., Dutch Reformed. All except A.M.E. have schools. Visited two churches—both Wesleyan—one for colored and one for natives—just opposite to each other.

The government regulations account for the necessity of separate schools for colored and native—but that doesn't account for separate churches.

Nhlapo[3] [told me] the colored can't support their own church. There is a general treasury for the two churches, and so the colored church is largely supported by native contributions. They tried a complete separation at one time, but couldn't carry on financially. (This is all Wesleyan church [affairs].)

A European missionary came here 4 years ago and encouraged this separation for the three separate churches—white, colored and black—entitled him to *three separate allowances*.

All the folks in the churches visited wore European clothes. Some quite well dressed in hats, silks, etc.

The natives at the Dutch Reformed Church . . . are more poorly dressed and seem definitely less well off than at the Wesleyan Church. This church and school bldg. [building] was built in 1932—at some distance from the others. It has 58 school children now and goes up to Stand. III, but has no recognition (and therefore no subsidy) from the government. They don't seem to know what to do with children above Stan. III.

The local churches have devoted their attention to the salvation of souls; only recently have they even begun to talk about social, economic and political questions affecting native interests—in their conferences, not in their local meetings. They have made great contributions to education, of course, but are now fighting government control of education bitterly; despite the fact that native education would best be served by this control today.

The African Advancement Association, an organization of men only at Thaba 'Nchu. Now three years old. Meets once per month. Organized to consider land etc. questions and to bring speakers. The Assoc. has had several speakers to come to discuss modern methods in agriculture. Chief Fenyang is the chairman;[4] Dr. Moroka is the moving spirit.

In Thaba 'Nchu the people are more advanced than in other native communities. They have their own lands and some do quite well. But there was no organization except the church [until the association was founded] to consider comprehensively the problems involved in the advancement of the people. Organization to date has been supported chiefly by the educated members of the reserve—about 36 of them— mostly chiefs, teachers, pastors and Dr. Moroka, the only African doctor on the reserve.

As soon as organization was started the Native Bills arose and the organization has had to devote most of its attention to those matters ever since.* Its attention has been chiefly devoted to the question of land under the released lands provision.†

The govt. land commission (Nat. [Native] Affairs Commission) came here in Dec. 1936 and the Advancement Assoc. acquired an advocate.[5] [It held] several public meetings of natives and Dr. Moroka pre-

---

*Hertzog had fought for the "Native bills" or "Hertzog bills" from 1926 to 1936, when Parliament enacted the Representation of Natives and the Native Land and Trust acts.

†The 1936 Native Trust and Land Act provided for the government to transfer additional or "released" land to the reserve areas so long as it was adjoining or adjacent land.

sented opinions and desires of reserve popul. [population] before the govt. commission.[6]

Assoc. argued before Commission that land is inadequate and that if govt. cannot give more land than it has promised, then natives cannot accept less. The govt. is now prepared to give all that was originally promised.

About 80,000 morgen are to be released by the govt. for native occupation. Dr. Moroka was offered £ 30,000 for his farms (by govt.) and refused it. About 50,000 morgen of the above 80,000 morgen are already privately owned by natives.

Organ. [has] an humble treasury; money used for organizing meetings, notices of meetings, constitution, etc. The land question absorbed some £ 60 of the organization's funds.

Last week it was decided to encourage farmers to organize a Farmer's Assoc. as in the Cape. The Farmer's Assoc. would deal with both cooperatives and educ. for modern agricultural methods.

African Students Associations are arising throughout the country. There is 1 in the Transkei, 1 in the Cape (at Port Eliz. [Elizabeth]), 1 at Queenstown, 1 in the Transvaal (at Joburg called the Rand Students Get Together—started by Paul Mosaka), 1 at Kimberley (Cape), and 1 in the Free State (provincial). No Natl. organ. yet.

The Fr. St. [Free State] organization has been in existence for 3 years and has been struggling over the const. [constitution] most of the time. Mainly get acquainted groups and training grounds for the teachers organizations. They play a lot—tennis, football, etc. They have debates, lectures by prominent men, competition in music, dancing. Little discussion of student's problems. Getting to these meetings puts a drain on parent's purses.

The Status of Chiefs. District's only head and chief in Thaba 'Nchu is John Pahetogane [Phetogane] Moroka.[7] Moroka is a hereditary chief descended from Chief Moroka,[8] Dr. Moroka's great grandfather, now 68, educated at Lovedale. [He lives at] Sediba Reserve—about 12 miles from Thaba 'Nchu. . . .

Chief [John] Moroka is recognized by govt. and gets an allowance of £ 2.10 per month from govt. In addition he gets all the fines on civil cases and has power to invoke police to help collect the fines. These amount to a goodly sum (approx. £ 10 or more per mo.).

Chief Fenyang, nephew of Chief Moroka, is the big chief's headman for the principal location (Chief Moroka's location). Fenyang has about 5,000 people under him. There are 3 other headmen beside him—one for each of the 4 locations.

Hereditary chieftainship is retained; but headmen are elected by people in location for life, and must be confirmed by government. Chiefs are really government chiefs now and must be recognized by government.

The chiefs' powers now are nothing like their past powers. Now they try only civil cases between natives, impose fines, keep order on the reserve through headmen.

Not much of tribal organ. left. Only recently the power of chiefs to try native civil cases was revived by govt. [in] 1932. In 1884 at time of annexation of this district due to fight between two chiefs, this power of chiefs was taken away.

The chief's court meets every Wednesday. The composition of the court are the *matona* (councillors) and the chief. There are 3 councillors and a secretary. But any man is allowed to speak at the court. He also tries cases among colored people.

Native law is applied in these cases. There is power of appeal to the Native Commissioner from these cases. Very few appeals. They can also appeal to the Native Appeal Court, from Native Commissioners. Two such appeals have been made—one was rejected and one upheld. No record need be submitted to the Magistrate except on appeal. No complaint here against exercise of this power by the chief.

[The chiefs have] no power over taxation—the Reserve Board controls that. The Reserve Board is chosen by people except for 1 man appointed by government. The people elect 5 members of the Board and the government appts. [appoints] the other (who now is Dr. Moroka).

Only those who own residential certificates thru payment of 10s hut tax can vote. This 10s goes to treasury of the Reserve Board—used for road repairs, construction of latrines, putting up windmills, etc.

Members of Reserve Board are elected for 3 years. Members of Researve Board are paid 10s per mo.

The government collects the poll tax directly.

All lands now held communally. But rts. [rights] to cultivate pass onto children. Headmen allocate lands to new people. Many plots have not been cultivated for 10 years or more. Tribal law says headmen cannot expropriate land.

In old days a man could claim as much land as he could fence. One old man has 150 morgen obtained in this way (under tribal law before annexation fencing was not allowed). This was why the 50 x 50 yds. law [limiting residential sites] was made by the Reserve Bd. [Board].

There are 4 locations in the Reserve and after a residential certificate is obtained from the Reserve Bd., the headman in the desired location allocates the site. No one can hold more than 2 residential sites.

Only residential sites can be fenced. Unlimited grazing rights. Stock are removed from cultivated areas. One man employed by Reserve Board impounds stock poaching on cultivated lands and pockets fines himself.

The whole reserve is Christian. No circumcision rites on reserve. No age nor class organizations left. No clan names left. Tribal dress lost. No training in tribal customs for the young, though they are conscious still of their tribal affiliation.

Lobola is still paid by all natives, even the Christians . . .—and is recognized by government. Money is often substituted for cattle (4 sheep equal one cow).

Dr. Moroka and the others say there is still too much consciousness of tribal lines.

Police don't bother natives out here. No pick-up van ever comes here.

Govt. interest in Joe Louis here, too. Moroka had made reservations to fly to fight via Imperial Airways, and one week before time to go he was turned down. Color bar.

■■■■■ **November 15**

Visit to Moroka Mission Institution. Teachers training school. Gives the J.C. 54—total enrollment. 29 students enrolled in teachers training work. 6 teachers, only one native. Under Methodist (Wesleyan) control. School in its first year. Large new classroom bldg. under construction. English medium.

The Methodist native primary school headed by Mr. Mosaka has 500 pupils (up thru Stan. VI) and 16 native teachers. The small colored school is separate, but on the same grounds. The colored children play separately at recess.

The primary school choir sings to beat the band; good harmony and they follow their director so intently. They even get good bass.

Songs sung by choir: "Gauteng" by the late Monaisa;* "Thaba 'Nchu" by Mokgothie, a local teacher; "The Special Pass" by Sidgiys. They protested audibly when an Afrikaans piece was announced by the director.

They all sang Nkosi Sikelel'i Afrika (Xhosa Natl. Anthem) very lustily.[9] It's now the Natl. Anthem of all South Africans. . . .

I spoke (thru an interpreter) for about 15 minutes to about 300 children of the Methodist primary school after they had sung for me. They gave me a flattering response.

Spoke to about 20 teachers at 2 p.m. Was tough though somewhat chauvinistic. Was well received.

Dr. Moroka is 46. He is said by some to be the wealthiest black man in South Africa.

Visited 2 of his farms. One covers about 1000 morgen; another about 600. Well cultivated. [He is] bldg. a huge dam on one. Dr. Moroka has a white man for a farm-manager.

Dr. Moroka keeps about 30 children (non-relatives) at his place. Some of them have simply been left by their parents. He feeds them and sends them to school. He estimates that he spends £200 per year on students at Fort Hare, etc.

Plenty of cars in front of Dr. Moroka's surgery. Crowd of natives waiting in two rooms, and a pretty young white woman waiting for him in the front waiting room. Dr. Moroka has a large number of white patients.

The color line seems to break down re native doctors and European patients. Dr. Moroka says that his [European patients] used to come to him only at night, but now they come openly. He told me that he used to notice that his name would be scratched out on the printed labels for the medicine bottles he gave to his European patients. So he put blank labels on the bottles.

He said that before he went to Vienna for his post-grad. [graduate] work (about 1930) the govt. promised to build a hospital at Thaba 'Nchu. But when he got back they told him it must be used for the natives only, and since this meant all of his time would be taken up with natives and he would have to give up his lucrative European practice, he declined to accept the offer of heading the hospital and it wasn't built.

---

*Gauteng is the Sotho name for Johannesburg.

149 Thaba 'Nchu and Mafeking

Dr. Moroka says that many white patients come to him for treatment of V.D. [venereal disease] due to shame about going to white doctors. Many white women come asking for abortions, too.

Dr. Moroka says about 40% of the natives in his district have syphilis. They have the unfortunate belief that one must get it once to acquire immunity, and are very reluctant to take injections. He says V.D. was unknown among his people before the coming of Europeans.[10]

Dr. Moroka says morals among the Thaba 'Nchu natives are not very high. He says that to estimate 50% of the girls are unmarried mothers is conservative. If a girl goes to Bloemfontein to work and doesn't come back with a baby soon, it is almost certain that she is sterile. He thinks the morals of the white girls is equally low but that they know how to protect themselves better. He says this definitely makes it more difficult for the girl to marry well—such a girl must usually marry an old man whom none of the girls want. He was a bit incredulous when I mentioned that there were chaste women and girls in America and asked me to repeat the statement.

Dr. Moroka told me of [his cousin] Ginger's recent fine by the native chief's court at Thaba 'Nchu. Ginger, among so many other women so treated, knocked up a colored gal living on the reserve and a son was born of whom the girl alleged Ginger to be the father. The parents charged Ginger before the native court and the court fined Ginger £15 because the girl was colored and a colored girl wronged was a more serious offense than a native girl wronged—the fine for knocking up a native girl being only £10. The court reproached Ginger for picking out a colored girl and said he should have wronged a native girl. Ginger hasn't paid the fine yet and denies paternity.

Dr. Moroka's great grandfather, Chief Moroka (whose people are still often called "Moroka's people"), came down from the Bechwana* country and Moshesh, to avoid a fight, sold them the Thaba 'Nchu country for 17 goats.[11] This was in 1833 and is attested by a deed of sale witnessed by the missionaries assigned to the two chiefs. Moroka's people didn't trust Moshesh's word. The land purchased is worth millions of pounds today.

Dr. Moroka is very harsh in his criticism of present Basuto chiefs, who have many wives, are dissolute and selfish—quite unlike Moshesh and the other old Basuto chiefs.

He says no young girl is safe in Basutoland today. There is no such

*Bechwana (or Bechuana) is the British corruption of BaTswana, which refers to the Tswana people.

thing as rape. If a man wants a certain girl he gets his friends to help him kidnap her, seduces her on the spot, and the whole thing is satisfactory under tribal custom if he pays lobola to her parents. He alleges that many educated Basuto girls will not go back for this reason.

He says many Basuto chiefs don't know their own children.

He also says that old chief Moroka was a tough and cruel guy and would take any woman he wanted.

Old chief Moroka died in 1881 of dropsy. He thought he had been bewitched by a Zulu witch doctor who had planted something that he had stepped on, and, says Dr. Moroka, Moroka's people or the Thaba 'Nchu people, hate the Zulu to this day.

Dr. Moroka says the witch doctors are still very active at Thaba 'Nchu and that it is lucrative business.[12] The people all still believe in magic, charms and witchcraft, even though they are Christians. Young men and women still believe that the witch doctors can give them love potions through which they can seduce favored ones. Most of the witch doctor's divinations of evil involve relatives in the role of enemies and Dr. Moroka says this is why there is so much animosity and hostility among the members of Thaba 'Nchu. Everything that occurs, the witch doctors interpret as being connected with some evil omen. They also peddle herbs, many of which have proved medicinal value, but dosages are not standardized and consequently too little or too much is usually given.

Moroka feels that ordinary A.B.C. educ. is not enough to break the spell of witchcraft on these ignorant people.

When Dr. Moroka had a recent auto accident and a miraculous escape from death when his car, travelling at 70 miles per hour, left the road and jumped over a culvert or donga 12 feet wide and 5 ft. deep, for the fun of it, he called in a witch doctor to do his stuff.

The doctor, a middle aged fellow who inherited his "powers" from his father, was very ominous after "throwing his bones." He said that the trouble is that Dr. Moroka is trying to be too much of a European, that he thinks people on the reserve like him, but in fact they hate him, and among his relatives—his uncles, etc., on the reserve—he has many bitter enemies who are resolved to dispose of him. This time they failed with the car accident, but he is unprotected, and next time, he will be killed by lightning—sometime during this summer.*

Dr. Moroka says that neither colored nor natives are allowed to live in the towns in the Orange Free State. He says separate native and

---

*Dr. Moroka did not die until 1985.

colored sections are established in the locations as at Bloemfontein, but that at Bloemfontein, many of the colored choose to remain in the native location and have not moved across the road to the colored section.

He says the Transvaal also is moving toward getting the colored out of the towns through the establishment of colored townships, as at Joburg.

He says they didn't want to let Mrs. Moroka in to the Joburg location, claiming that she is not a native and didn't belong there—though she was scheduled to make a speech on her welfare work. By speaking the native tongue, she convinced them and was let in but not permitted to stay overnight.

Dr. Moroka says the Rhodesias are even worse than the Union and that the natives are fenced—almost locked—in the locations and are checked in and out like sheep.

He is president of the Orange Free State Native Sports Assoc. and says that on his native football and tennis teams he often has colored players. But he adds that this is never true of the Transvaal and Natal teams.

All of the educated Africans seem hep to the folly of native-colored divisions and see the white man as cunning in his many efforts to foster and encourage it. But Dr. Moroka pointed out that the colored have developed no great men and have not gotten much education; being content to train themselves to become skilled artisans. He likes Dr. Abdurahman and Goolam Gool because they have identified native and colored interests in their speeches.[13]

Says most of the natives don't appreciate the value of land when privately owned and are too entranced by motor cars. Some of them have large acreages in private land, but that most . . . mortgage it heavily for shiny new cars and then lose it. This is particularly unfortunate at Thaba 'Nchu, for land there brings a good price. (I think he said £6 per morgen).

He despises the Dutch and thinks they are lazy and poor farmers. They, too, go in for cars (mostly American made) in a big way and many go bankrupt because of the expense.

He is a good businessman. A Jew offered him 10s (a good price) per bag for his 2000 bags of mealies in storage. But knowing that there is a drought on and that in all likelihood there will be a very short mealie crop, he is hanging on to his mealies and expects to get a much higher price and probably will.

He says that the mealies (like our hominy) which the govt. aids European farmers in stricken areas to get for 5s per bag are the same quality mealies that are sold to natives at prices varying from 15s-25s per bag.

Dr. Moroka says that there are approximately 20 South African natives (including one girl) studying medicine abroad now (mainly at Edinburgh and Glasgow) and chiefly because their parents hoped them to be "successful" men like Moroka and Molema.[14]

When Mosaka spoke to Rev. Mears,[15] white director of the Wesleyan set up here about my being here, he asked Mosaka if I am "sober and stable."

Mrs. Moroka handles the big car like a man. They have 2 cars—a Hudson coupe (new) and a Terraplane sedan.

The educated natives at Thaba 'Nchu are very skeptical about the time ever coming when black and colored will pull together in South Africa. They all see the division as one fostered and encouraged by the whites in order to keep both groups weak. They feel that the feeling of superiority and aloofness is with the colored and are reluctant to make any advances for fear of being rebuffed. They feel that since the colored help to perpetuate the caste any advances should come from them.

Wise sayings: "In Africa, it's a wise traveller who carries his own toilet paper."

November 16

Trip to Mafeking—340 miles.[16] Dr. Moroka's cousin, Ginger, driving. Desolate, drought stricken country all the way. Not many mealies being planted because of drought. We passed through some miserable looking reserves and locations enroute. On none of them did the natives seem as well off as at Thaba 'Nchu.

Stopped at Dr. Molema's house in Mafeking—another native doctor who is doing well and inherited a lot of land from his father who was a chief. Dr. Molema is "nearing 50" he says, though he doesn't look it.

The 8 or 9 native doctors in South Africa seem to be the most wealthy group in the popul. [population]. All seem to be doing very well—many, like Molema and Moroka, with white patients—and were educated abroad, chiefly at Edinburgh or Glasgow, for their med. work.

Moroka and Molema have big houses, well equipped surgeries, nurses, tennis courts, cars, many servants, radios, rugs, papered walls, beautiful gardens, etc.

Visited Dr. Molema's nursing home in which he treats and operates on white patients. He has a staff of white nurses and one of them had to serve us (Mrs. Molema, Mrs. Moroka's sister and me) cold water on a tray. The nursing home is well appointed and has a large number of rooms. It has been open for 2½ years. He opened this for his own white patients after a law was put through whereby he couldn't operate in the white hospitals.

Dr. Molema went in for the private nursing home with a German doctor, because the nurses at the public hospital in Mafeking protested against "taking orders from a native doctor." Subsequently the Provincial Council passed an order permitting the hospital boards to determine who could enter and practice in the hospitals. The hospital board excluded him. So now he treats his patients in his own hospital ("nursing home") and employs his own white nurses.

Dr. Moroka says that while natives seldom have enough dough to enter a nursing home, Dr. Molema will accept them.

The irony of Dr. Molema having a nursing home, and a surgery in town, tho the law will not permit him to live there.

Mrs. Molema holding a Bible reading session after dinner—had 5 of the household youngsters (one only 5) reciting passages and all of them except me plopped down on their knees when Molema prayed. Reminded me of the Kerr's habit of calling in the help for the before breakfast rel. [religious] sessions at their table.

Dr. Molema's wife is a 7th Day Adventist—she defected from the Wesleyans.

Dr. Moroka and Dr. Molema are not well liked by the old-timers on their reserves—they are doing too well. In fact Dr. Molema has had a law suit and for long was not on speaking terms with his chief.

Educated Africans like Dr. Moroka, Mosaka, Nhlapo, Molema, Matthews, etc. are becoming quite critical of religion and the church and are only half-hearted Christians. They see religion as a drawback to the progress of their people.

Dr. Molema, like Dr. Moroka, has an elec. [electricity] generator and his is giving trouble tonight.

Dr. Molema recently was kidnapped by a white man who forced him into his car at the point of a pistol and told him he was going to drive him far enough from town to avoid detection, and then kill him, because he is doing too well for a native. He drove him out and then changed his mind, robbed him of £10, pushed him in a donga, and fled in Molema's car. He was apprehended later, but escaped from jail and was laying for Molema at Joburg again when the police nabbed him.

Tour of Mafeking in Dr. Molema's new Packard Six sedan, Mrs. Molema driving.* (Dr. Molema also has a Chevrolet coupe.)

We first visited Chief Lotlamoreng Montshioa.[17] He is the hereditary chief of the Ratshidi Barolong—the paramount chief of the Ratshidi clan of the Barolong.[18]

The chief is a nice-looking, brown-skinned fellow—and fairly young. He was quite sporty in a cream linen suit, a grey hat and a silver-headed walking stick. He has a charming smile, with what seemed to be a bit of sarcasm in it, and he uses it constantly. He would not talk directly to me, but talked in Barolong and to me through an interpreter—a young fellow—who is one of his secretaries. He was not very communicative and, according to Mrs. Molema, a bit suspicious. He told me when the interview was ended. I told him of the American Negro and he asked me what aspect of the life of the American Negro I thought might be helpful to the African. I replied: "the lesson of organization," but this elicited no response. On the whole I didn't like him. He did consent to pose for a picture. . . .

The natives here live in two places—the stad or reserve, characterized by its mud huts—many of them quite modern—and the mud walls or fences surrounding them—many of which are artistically decorated. Here the lands are tribally owned, and while the chief said there is insufficient land, Mrs. Molema says there is plenty.

The other natives live on the location run by the town and on which they rent sites for 24s per year. It is a typical location, not at all attractive. Mud huts, and other structures and quite dismal looking. On this one there is no public hall for meetings, but a private one owned by a Chinaman and which he rents out.

There is a colored colony in the location, which inhabits a separate section. Mrs. Molema says this is through choice of the colored and not by town regulation.

There are the usual churches in evidence in the Stad and location. One Wesleyan church and school in the Stad dates back to 1880's.

---

*Shortly after Bunche's visit, Mrs. Molema tragically died following an appendectomy.

There is no training school for teachers—often Standard VI local pupils must go to Lovedale and such places.

The people ["natives"] work in town and not any men at the mines.

The *peco* (assembly)* is held in the *kgotla* whenever need arises. The chief presides and anyone can voice views and protests. . . . No definite meeting time is set but Molema says one is held about every week.

The chief still exerts power over the people in the Union [and] Bechuanaland. Chiefs here have far more power still than elsewhere in the Union. The chiefs still try all civil cases here—also criminal cases except serious assault, murder and witchcraft.

Chiefs retain power to allocate lands. People still feel a "sense of duty" toward chief and weed, plough and reap his lands. He no longer has any power to compel this.

The whole fabric of tribal lines is broken down. Occasionally [there is] conflict between chiefs and educated Africans, though relations are generally good between them. Situation [is] markedly different in Bech. Prot. [Bechuanaland Protectorate]† where petitions have gotten out vs. the autocracy of chiefs.

Now the chief is the chief Govt. official in tribal life. This often brings on conflict between chief and people, who regard him as a policeman.

November 17

Woke up at 6 a.m. and got ready for return trip. Had tea and scones and started back at 6:40 a.m. (a 340 mi. drive ahead). Uneventful except for Dr. Molema stopping the car at 8 to take shots at two partridges walking about in a field, with his 22 rifle. His first shot nicked the door glass as he shot across my face. But on his third he crippled one bird and stunned the 2d a couple of shots later. But this one got away when we went to retrieve it. We ate as we drove and arrived at Thaba 'Nchu after a terribly hot and dusty drive at 2:20 p.m.

I had lunch, shaved, took a tub bath and was ready to come to

---

*The *peco* or *pitso* is the public gathering place for adult males to discuss issues of local or national importance. The *Kgotla* is the place where legal or judicial proceedings are held.

†The British colonial name for the territory that became the independent state of Botswana.

Bloemfontein to get the Joburg train. Alexander drove me in, I called the Marquards, drove around in the location, went out to the Marquards for supper and Leo drove me to the station.

The ticket examiner on the Joburg bound train didn't seem to know what to do with me. He finally took his agitation out on the white porter who carried my bags. Marquard talked to him although I don't know what was said (it was something confidential). After a few minutes wait, I was given a coupe in the 1st class coach. Marquard stayed at the station till train pulled out. When the ticket examiner came through he was pleasant enough and asked me if I was satisfied. I assured him I was, for this is the most modern coupe I've seen.

Mr. Marquard said that Dr. Moroka is especially noted among whites for his ability at diagnosis, which they attribute to some magical native power.

Dr. and Mrs. Moroka (standing to the right/ Paul Mosaka kneeling)

Dr. and Mrs. Molema

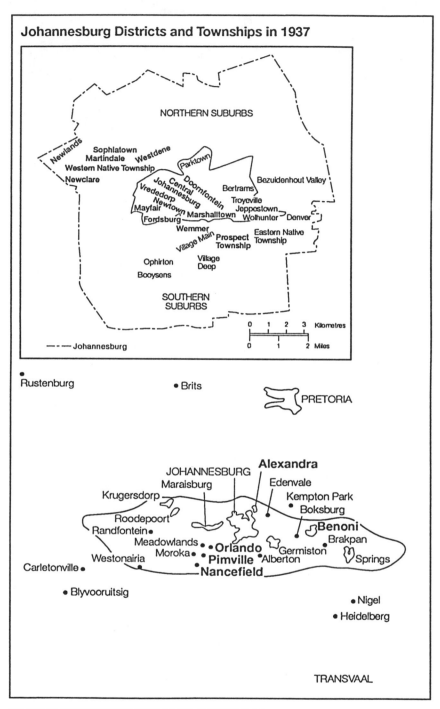

THE WITWATERSRAND REGION

Johannesburg I

November 18

Johannesburg is a big, bustling town of about 500,000, of whom half (when the townships and locations are included) are non-European.[1] The mine dumps, like huge sand-hills, ring the city. It has beautiful residential suburbs running to some distance. It currently seems to be the rule that the richer you are the further away from town you live.

My first direct encounter with prejudice here was in the Exploration Building, where William Ballinger has his office—with a "Friends of Africa" sign on the door. There are two elevators—one with an operator for Europeans, and a self-operating one for non-Europeans. When I first called on Ballinger, I rode upon the European elevator and the operator took me up with only slight hesitation. When I later came down with Ballinger, however, he brought me down in the non-European one, explaining that "Europeans often use it too."

Later I came back with Masole, a native, and walked into the European elevator.[2] The operator, *a German Jew refugee*—an old man with a Prussian moustache—glared, said nothing, but made motions toward the elevator on the other side. I said that's all right, when Masole hesitated about stepping in, and the old guy took us up. Later on I came back alone, and after another hesitation, he took me up, but was obviously flabbergasted.

Ballinger very talkative and . . . believes in sounding horn for Mr. and Mrs. Ballinger.

Ballinger is a European with a "martyr complex"—always referring to fact that he is considered "dangerous," that Europeans want to shoot him, deport him, etc.

While walking down the street with Ballinger discussing the severity of South African problems, he protests violently against the violation of the Int. Lab. Reg. [International Labor Regulation] re the maximum load to be carried on bicycles.

Ballinger says there is no law fixing the Jim Crow in public places here—it is an "implicit Jim Crow." Non-Europeans have the right to ride on public conveyances (in Jim Crow section; e.g. upstairs on the buses) where no alternative non-European service is offered.

Ballinger, like Lewin et al.,[3] voices a complete despair re the white man's future in South Africa. He sees violent conflict and bloodshed as inevitable. He thinks this is sure to come when the gold boom fades out. He sees [the] Vereeniging [riots] as a vital warning.

Ballinger refers to the "white aristocracy" of South Africa and the "white oligarchy" in control of govt. The standard of living for whites here is much too high for the poor white group to live under.

Ballinger says this repressive system has made the natives very sharp and cunning. He refers to the dumbness of the Afrikaner police, most of whom come from the farms—and many of whom can't read English. When a native shows a pass on demand, the cop must often ask the native to read it for him. Many of the sharp natives will read it to the cop in Afrikaans and will then be sure to be let go.

The colored district here closely resembles district 6 in Cape Town, though the Malay element is not in evidence.[4] The slums are plenty bad.

Many natives here "pass as colored" so as to be able to live in town. Others are married to colored women and thus have right to live in town.

Colored and Indians are permitted on the buses and trams, but natives only when with white employer or on repair missions.

The color line breaks down in many places—e.g. Europeans go to native doctors (Molema has a big practice in Joburg, too). Permits to live in town are issued to native workers who can give good reasons for the desire.

November 19

Rheinold [Rheinallt-] Jones says he is a democrat and is forced into disagreement on fundamentals with the govt. officials, many of whom are anti-democratic and totalitarian.

Rheinold Jones is skeptical about Jabavu—he thinks the old man is untrustworthy and far behind the caliber of Matthews. Jones can't see any chance for a compulsory education regulation for natives for a long time, because of the expense involved.

He says the Afrikanders are tough nuts on these questions and that the Afrikaans press is the only press that hops on the work of the Institute of Race Relations.

Rheinold Jones has doubts and worries about Desmore. He says Desmore is very sensitive and unhappy. Jones mentioned that Desmore has his children in a white school.

Jones stated that though in the past there had been some possibility that the colored would be given white status or at least equivalent privileges, the trend now was definitely against any possibility of that being achieved. He thinks the natives are making more intellectual progress than the coloreds.

The young English agronomist[5] who has been making a survey in the Transkei on nutrition and labor supply for the Chamber of Mines[6] thinks it would be best for more natives to stay on the land—they would be better off physically and morally. There will be a natural drift to the towns anyway. Thinks they should have more agricultural education. Says there should be more preventive medical work among them. Thinks the native should be encouraged as a peasant population. He says the silicosis the boys contract in the mines often develops into t.b. and glandular trouble and then becomes infectious.[7]

He thinks it tragic that whites are leading natives through same painful process that whites went through for last 200 years—i.e., whites are aiding to build up a small, economically well-off group of natives who become allies of whites in the exploitation of the native masses.

He says the system of Indirect Rule in the Transkei is far behind the present stage of development of the people. The chiefs are for it because it means favored position, more land and wealth for them and their relatives.

The young English agronomist told me that he knows of a recent strike among white workers in a gold mine—a local affair—in which natives, working under supervision of a handful of whites (compound supervisors, etc.) ran the mines without any trouble and trebled the profits of the mine during that period due to low wages paid to natives. He says mines would surely increase the number of native workers at expense of the whites, [if] the govt. did not constantly exert pressure on the mines to employ an increasing number of poor whites.

The barracks are for native workers like watchmen. Permits to live in town are issued to native workers who can give good reasons for their desire to be there.

Many of the native houseboys are recognizable by distinctive "uniforms" they wear—white shirts and pantaloons with red borders. They are usually barefoot.

Mrs. Hellman says reasons why native children don't attend school are (1) the very bad and inadequate system for them; (2) the natural indifference of the Bantu to such things as punctuality, attendance, etc.[8]

The civilized labor policy is much in evidence*—e.g. poor whites working in the service stations just like the natives, but the whites are dressed up in white jackets.

The standard of living for whites is much too high for the poor white group to live under.

In Bloemfontein the only conveyance non-Europeans can ride on are the location buses.

---

*A policy introduced by Hertzog's government after 1924, "civilized labor" aimed to protect white workers and prevent them from allying with black workers. It gave white workers unskilled and semi-skilled jobs in preference over black workers in state-owned enterprises such as the railways and harbors and the post office.

Mrs. Hellman and I met Dr. Sachs[9] and together we drove out to Orlando Township, a native location owned by the municipality.[10] It now holds 40,000 people and will be built to hold double this number.

Mushroom growth of Orlando like mushrooming of Joburg itself. The most impressive sight first greeting the visitor today are the scores of newly constructed brick out-houses which seem to be the most important item on the constructive side in these native housing schemes.

After the foundations are laid . . . private contractors build two room houses in twenty-one hours and three room houses in twenty-three hours, including latrines. They employ 6,000 workers—2,000 Europeans and 4,000 Africans . . . drawn from the location population.

Venables told Jack [Simons] that contractors make £5 per house but location officials said the profit is only £2.5 per house.[11] The contractor has his own concrete mixing plant and concentrates on location building. The municipality engineer also submits tenders, but is never successful. African workers get about 3/8 per day (Jack thinks)—i.e. at local building workers rate.

The Orlando and Pimville[12] locations are ringed about with barbed wire fences and native guards step out from sentry boxes to stop all who try to enter and to open the gates for those who have passes. Passes are required and these are obtainable from the Native Affairs Dep't. Mrs. Hellman and I got in both Orlando and Pimville through Dr. Sachs showing his M.D. prescription blanks.

The native guards also require natives entering the locations to leave their sticks and knobkerries in order to prevent brawls in the location—of which there are said to be many.

Some feeble efforts are being made toward landscaping at Orlando—a few trees planted. The houses are brick of 2 and 3 room units. The 2 room houses, with dirt floors and tin roofs, rent for £1.0.6 per mo. (the 6d is for medical service). The 3 room units rent for £1.5.6 per month.

One water pipe serves 16 houses and so they must carry water some distance. Water is free but lately restrictions have been imposed on its use, due to allegation that too much is being used for watering gardens, etc.

Orlando is 10 or 12 miles out from town and the transportation cost is 6d. return, with a higher charge of 1s on Sunday—to discourage visits of location natives to town on Sunday and other natives to the location! Mrs. Hellman says monthly tickets (not good on Sunday) can be obtained for 8/6.

The shop bldgs., also built by the municipality, rent for £10 per month. (Esther and her husband rent a shop and pay £1 more per month for a partition that was put in but which they can never own.) Many natives make improvements in their houses by finishing ceilings, walls and floors, but there is little incentive to do so because they can never own the houses. They make nice ornamental gardens at Orlando, with both flowers and clay statues.

Pimville (formerly Nanceville) is an old location and is in very bad shape—the houses are oblong tunnel-like affairs of tin, or ordinary mud huts.

We witnessed a wedding at the Pimville location—bride and groom were Zulus. They were fairly young and had been married first (last Wednesday) at the court. Today . . . they were married at the native Zion church.[13] £20 lobola has been paid by the groom.

The Sat. afternoon ceremony took place at the home of the bride. A white flag fluttered on a long pole above her clay hut, signifying the marriage. In front of the hut two groups of men, women and children were dancing—one group representing the bride's party and the other that of the groom's. Each had a leader (see pictures). They danced vigorously with the leg brought up slowly and the delayed stamp. They chanted as they danced in a simple, monotonous, but compelling rhythm. This continued for hours. There were about 50 dancers in all. There was evidence that Kaffir beer had been had recourse to.

True to tradition the bride, dressed in a blue silk dress of European style and a chic hat, was kept inside the hut and when she came out to be photographed, she hung her head as if in shame. She smiled very demurely as I snapped her. The groom was not at all self-conscious nor was he much in evidence.

The bride appeared and was, as confirmed by her sister, considerably pregnant—demure and innocent as she looked. Her husband cannot touch her until she comes to his home the following day.

When we came back on Sunday the ceremony was proceeding at the groom's hut (above which the white flag also flew). There was no dancing outside the hut as we entered, but bride and groom were seated behind a long table spread for a feast, together with their attendants and 5 old men dressed in flowing light blue robes who, we took it, were priests or elders in the Zion church. They were conducting a religious ceremony in a weird chant and then all knelt and a long prayer was pronounced by one. The spectators stood on the opposite side of the table.

Bride and groom were well dressed now—the bride in a flowing white lace gown and lace cap, with a bouquet of flowers, the groom in a white flannel sports jacket, dress collar and tie. They looked very serious and she still hung her head in shame. The door to the bridal chamber was open and the high wooden bed was spread with white linen all ready to receive the newlyweds.

Soon the groom's father stood opposite his son and in loud earnest imprecations admonished him to be good and do well. The bridegroom's father was attired in a black shirt (no collar), tuxedo jacket and trousers, and no socks or shoes. He had taken on too much Kaffir beer and soon had to be ejected for the sake of proceeding with the wedding.

In the bedroom was the food for the reception - the tarts, pies, etc.—and under the table were the bride's presents.

The bride and groom came out for a picture.

Soon the dancing began again, with both bride's and groom's party dancing opposite each other. The bride's party was definitely superior in this case, both in numbers and vigor. With regularity one or two of the fat ladies standing by under their umbrellas would start forth with a staccato yell (like an Indian war cry) and prance back and forth across the lines of the dancers.

Mrs. Hellman saw the bride getting in to her wedding dress Sunday morning and noted the vigorous efforts to fit her corset so as to hide her pregnancy.

We visited another similar Zulu wedding on the same afternoon—the only difference being that in this one both bride and groom danced, but neither very vigorously. The bride, dressed in a blue gown and hat, held her head very low and would raise it for a snap only very reluctantly. The groom wanted me to wait until the bride changed into her white dress to take a picture. He was well dressed in a double-breasted blue suit.

The baby of Esther, a shopkeeper, looks very weak and emaciated. Esther says that babies all over the Orlando location are sick and are dying like flies, and that all the mothers are complaining about [it]. Esther has a piano in her house, nice furniture and serves us tea. She wants to stop nursing her 8 month old baby so she can go to Natal (her home) for a wedding in December.

Esther says she is a Christian and doesn't believe in witch doctors, but admits that she has been to them and seems to know how to read the bones even. On Sunday she told us she wanted to join the Catholic Church because she can go and pray there whenever she wanted to and can always see the priest.

She says the main activity on the location is the choirs' sing-fest, and that these are very prolonged, since not only do the choirs sing their program numbers, but anyone in the audience can request a number from a particular member of the choir by paying 6d., a shilling or more, and that this person must comply or pay the amount offered.[14] The people running the thing make a racket out of it by letting the singer use the door money to back himself up in first refusing to solo, in order to push up the bidding.

Episode of "John," the medicine or witch doctor—the "Black Hamlet" of Dr. Wulf Sach's book.* He lives with his wife and children at Orlando and is 2 months behind in his rent. A beady-eyed, sly and cunning-looking fellow, with pouting lips and a head pointed on top. Medium stature. Shows a very good memory. Probably not at his best in English, because of limited vocabulary. Very temperamental and addicted to Kaffir beer. His wife, Maggie, is a big fat, roly-poly gal who giggles all the time and sort of bosses John about.

In my first "sitting" John was not too free as he couldn't figure out just who I am and was puzzled by my "doctor" title, since I told him I was not a medical doctor. He was sly enough to deduce that I was interested in some kind of work among natives, since he saw me in the company of Dr. Sachs and Mrs. Hellman.

I had to blow in the fur sack containing the bones and got my eyes full of dust on the rebound. The bones were not in good mood so he could see only bad luck for me. He read that I was a clever man, etc. and very good in my work, but couldn't figure out just what it is. He said I would definitely have bad luck in East Africa, though no enemies were trying to poison me; said I was worried about my health in East Africa, too. He mumbles something in the native tongue as he reads the bones and looks up cunningly through the corners of his eyes from his squatting position on the floor, in order to appraise the reception of his "readings."

He said I have a good wife but that she is pregnant, and that our next child will surely be a *boy*. I told him I had been away from my wife for 3 months and that she hadn't been pregnant during the first 2 months of my absence, but that made no difference. Later on, Dr. Sachs asked him if my wife is faithful to me, and John read "yes." So her pregnancy must be due to immaculate conception, we concluded, and John agreed.

He said if he were in my place he would definitely not go to East

---

*Wulf Sachs published *Black Hamlet* in 1937. A second edition updating John Chavafambira's life, *Black Anger*, appeared in 1947.

Africa, but said that he could give me some "medicine" to make things safer for me there. When he threw the bones again on request after I agreed to let him mix me some medicine, things looked brighter for me in East Africa, though Ruth was still pregnant and a boy is sure.

He also read the "male horn," a little black pestle in a small yellow cord. The clay pestle, cone-shaped, is balanced on the bottom of the gourd and he holds it out and the pestle "talks" when it circles about the rim of the gourd. But it was very reticent and wouldn't talk for me. That cost me 2/6 (in advance).

The next day, Dr. Sachs, a young Irish nurse and I went out again. This time John was ready for us and ushered us into the bedroom where all of his equip. [equipment] was lined up on the floor. Maggie also participated in this one. John was in ugly mood and everything was bad for the Irish girl—said she had to take medicine for her stomach, her relatives (especially her mother) are sick with worry about her, she must not stay in South Africa and must return to England to marry, etc.

He read me again and my luck was better. He was temperamental and made us stop smoking and ordered me to sit on the floor. Wanted 5s from us for the reading this time, but we remonstrated and he went ahead for 2/6 each. He consulted with Maggie often.

Dr. Sachs says the Afrikaner officials are very willing to be bribed by native shopkeepers, etc. in the locations who can thus keep their stores open on Sundays and after-hours.

I see the "barefoot proletarians" all over the streets of Joburg.

Natives certainly walk on the sidewalks here—I've seen none ordered off yet, and the whites rub up against them but say nothing.

Saw a couple of large batches (about 100 total) of new mine recruits hustling down the street past the Bantu Men's Centre.[15] They were very "kraal" looking and were afraid to cross Eloff St. because of the traffic. They had to be yelled at by the "city" native leading them and would scamper across the street in a wild rush and with laughing fright. There were many narrow escapes because these blokes drive fast in their American cars in Joburg.

Is it assuming a pattern in South Africa that Colored (as at Bokmakierie) and Native (as at Pimville) locations and housing projects should be built alongside sewage disposal farms?

Joe and Ellen Hellman have four servants—a native woman cook, a houseboy, a gardener and a European nurse for their cute 22 month daughter. The houseboy who waited on me at the table always calls me "massa [master]," and that gripes me.

November 22

Visit to the [Witwatersrand] University to attend non-European student group meeting. Professor John Gray speaker.[16] Meeting called for 7:30 p.m., but Professor Gray didn't show until 8. Masole introduced Professor Gray and made a bogus joke about "N.T."—native time— mild Uncle Tomming.

Professor Gray [asked] what exact biological meaning can concept of race have? Idea of race can be used to make nations war vs. nations and groups vs. groups within a nation. Biological classification of human races on same basis as animal kingdom unjustified. Concept of race has certain scientific importance in terms of human differences, but even these can be easily exaggerated. Social and cultural characteristics are always subject to change and often to rapid and easy change—much more quickly than biological change. These differences in social and cultural levels not so fundamental as biological ones and can be much more easily overcome. Race differences mainly in degree of social life—of culture displayed by certain groups.

30 or 40 students (mostly native) present—several sleeping vigorously.

Non-Europeans not allowed to use main reading room at University of Witwatersrand.[17] A small room is provided for them. Masole says Hofmeyr told them he is in sympathy with them but not to press their case now because the principal of the university is not in sympathy with idea of their using main reading room. They can draw books from the general university library, however. They have been promised more room when new building is finished in a couple of years.

There are three classification groups of pictures here by the Board of Film Censors (Ray Phillips was once on it).[18] The films are divided into three groups, viz: (1) Those which Europeans only can see; (2) Those to be seen by Europeans and coloreds; (3) Those which can be seen by everyone, including natives.

Non-Europeans can go into the Palladium Cinema (Paul Robeson's *Jerico* is showing there now) providing they get an advance permit for them to attend from the manager. They, of course, are put in a Jim Crow section.

All the educated Africans wail about the difficulty of getting anything written by an African published here. They say all native papers, or almost all, are controlled by the mining interests or at least get support from them.[19]

Vil-Nkomo,[20] a young native who works with the Benoni Medical Officer, Dr. Anning,[21] says that the natives are very clever at fooling these Dutch officials and employees. He says if a native wants to ride a prohibited bus or train he gets on and when the conductor rudely orders him off, he begins to cringe and plead in Afrikaans and to clown also, and the conductor will usually let him ride. But coloreds and Indians can ride upstairs.

He also told me of Mr. Durant, colored, a local head of a native burial society which gives him a good living, and whose son is a M.D. practicing among natives, who at the time of the Urban Act to move natives out of the towns, reported that some natives who had no right to be were actually living near and lounging near his place. In resentment at his action, Dr. Xuma and others here, formed a burial society of their own to squelch and punish Mr. Durant. But Vil-Nkomo says that a location is being built for Colored and that they will be pushed out of town too.

The straight of the Durant story is that young Dr. Durant was to be given a place in the United Burial Association, but when his old man turned on natives living in town, they turned thumbs down on him and formed the South African Society which immediately copped 2000 of the United members and now has 14000 members.

Masole says that only 2 1/2% of their members drop out for nonpayment of dues.

The insurance companies clean up on the natives for they know most natives will not and cannot continue to pay premiums.

Vil-Nkomo says in old days Dutch Reformed Churches (and he thinks some in rural areas still do) bore signs "Dogs and Kaffirs not allowed." He said at one time in Joburg natives had to wear badges on their lapels where possible and could not wear shoes, nor could a young native "walk out" with his girl. This was called "aping" the white man.

Vil-Nkomo, at the Professor Gray meeting, voiced the belief that large skulls were indicative of superior mentality, and included Mussolini in the list of great men and scholars whom he mentioned as having large craniums.

The Jews are life-savers on a trip like this—even many of the non-left ones are helpful.

Signs along the Main Reef road reading: "Caution - Beware of Natives"—in big letters.

Natives dislike the use of the term "native"—they prefer term "African."[22]

Saw non-European tram on Sophiatown route—"darkey tram" the natives call it.

Toilet tissue is a traveler's problem here. At Moroka's, Molema's and at the Bantu Center here, newspaper is the current wiping medium. I will always carry Kleenex in my pockets hereafter. My thin air-mail paper came in handy this morning.

████████ **November 23**

Visit to Van Ryn Deep Mining Compound with Webb and Masole, his native assistant.* Webb rep. [representative] of Durban sugar interests trying to sell a mealie meal porridge requiring sugar to the mine compounds. Called *Langalaza,* it merely consists of mealie meal soaked for 15 hours until it sours and then cooked with sugar. Idea is to substitute it for the ordinary mealie meal porridge and thus greatly increase sugar consumption. Webb, a slick English South African of 56, told me that he is working in the interests of the natives since "the Durban sugar interests already rich." But he was anxious to get hold of a letter from one compound manager to another so he could send it in with his monthly report, as the letter indicated the native mine boys like the sugar porridge.

Webb calls himself a "negrophilist," though I doubt if the ignorant bastard understands the meaning of the word.

He told me he could make no progress with the compound managers, so he hatched the idea of getting the company to permit him to employ a "native propagandist" to sell the new porridge idea to the natives in the mine compounds. So he hired Masole.

---

*The Van Ryn mine was near Benoni.

Masole, a middle-aged, well-dressed black man, acts as stooge for Webb—as his "boy" in fact—driving his car, etc. Masole is doing his work well for the men on several of his compounds are now demanding the new stuff. He gets the natives to ask for it and gets a rake-off from the company. It has been introduced at Van Ryn Deep.

Webb is a real crack-pot. Has an ambition to run for Parliament and all sorts of hair-brained [harebrained] monetary schemes. Thinks himself an economist and a financier, though he alleges he is not interested in money.

Bored me with an explanation of his pet monetary scheme enroute to Van Ryn Deep. He says the idea just came to him out of the clear blue. Says he would change the "I promise to pay" of the Governor General of South Africa on the South African currency with "we promise to pay"—meaning "the people." But this currency would be issued on a 20 year basis and each month during that period a 1d. stamp would be affixed to each £ note. (He got peeved when I innocently asked by whom and how these stamps would be affixed.) In this way . . . all of our financial troubles would be solved. He says he doesn't mean anything socialistic, but that everyone would still have money "according to his worth."

Another crackpot idea is for teachers to give every school child 1d each day (so that the child can buy sweets, of course—long live sugar!)

Because of his interests he even condescended to sit at table with 35 natives one evening at the Bantu Center. He financed the meal so that these natives would go back to the compounds and pump his product. What a sacrifice!

He also encouraged natives with a brilliant idea, viz—that they start a *Rotary Club!* And now he chuckles that they've started one and don't know what to do with it.

He says natives must develop gradually—that it wouldn't do to pay native mine workers 10s per day now. They wouldn't know what to do with it, but as they learn to live better they should be paid more.

His only even decent statement was that ill-nourishment, lack of housing and clothing and all such evils bred by low wages encourage inferiority complex among a people.

[We met] Mr. Thomas, a stuttering European, who has managed mine compounds for 33 years. Interested mainly in costs. Says his boys are good. Knows how to keep them in check. He says he never goes down into a shaft, probably from fear of what might happen to him from boys he has "hided" if he does.

6,000 natives and 750 whites are now employed there—gangs are of

30 men each. Recent labor saving devices have reduced the number of miners by 1,200. All now use "pack-hammers" (compression drills). This, he says, is a big saving for the mine since 1,200 boys cost plenty. Costs are too high and must be cut. But mine needs 400 boys now. Those now there are "working bloody hard" he says. They work a 10 hour day and work in day and night shifts.

The men sleep in brick barracks with cement rooms and on cement double-deck bunks. 20 bunks to a room. They eat in their bunk rooms and this is very unsanitary. Flies galore!

They have to buy their equipment—a lantern and rubber shin and knee pads (these latter now costing 1/6). Shower baths and washtubs provided.

The kitchens are big dark rooms with huge pots into which mealies, beans and stew are cooked by natives. Big sides of beef lying on floor in butchery. Bones being extracted for soup. £2000 being expended to improve these disgusting conditions now. Natives line up for their food and take it to their bunk rooms in tin pans.

Their diet consists of mealie meal, beans, stew, meat (twice a week), porridge (a recent innovation, as previously the men ate only once a day). They get beer twice a week.

There is a terrible monotony in diet which even the Compound Manager had to mention. Said if his wife gave him mutton 7 days a week he would throw it at her. Said he can't understand why there hasn't been more variety in diet on mine compounds.

Advised us on how to handle natives. Said one came to him recently and said he couldn't go down in the mines because "the devil is in me." So Thomas told him to bend down and then "I gave him a few and asked him is the devil still in you! And he said yes, and I gave him a few more and asked him again. And he said yes, a little, and I gave him a few harder ones and then he got up and said the devil is gone, and went down in the mines."

Said that the other day he gave one a hiding and he said, "Massa [master], I've been here 17 years, and have never been in trouble before."

Admitted that there is considerable sodomy among natives and said that some take others as "wives," but was reluctant to talk about it.

There are an average of 8 deaths per week and many injuries. They have loud speakers installed which they use in cases of accident "to inform natives that if they hadn't been careless in this or that way, the accident would not have occurred." Said some boys have been electrocuted from water dropping from high extension [tension] wires.

This is one of the three mines on the Reef having a miniature surface mine in which actual mine conditions are in replica to train natives how to work, avoid dangers, etc. Saw some recruits line up for this instruction.

Some boys have won first-aid badges and for these they get 2d extra pay each day (the mine saves more than this in accident costs, of course).

Bioscopes once a week.*

Peter Dabula, who is acting as my secretary here, has had many experiences about the pass laws.[23] Says he has been stopped four times and once arrested. He is an educated, young African and well-dressed. But he has been stopped three times by plain-clothesmen (European—but there are native officers, too, doing this work). He demanded that [one] plain clothes officer show his warrant and this infuriated him, but his passes were in order twice. The third time he was called out of court while serving Dr. Xuma and for this reason only was let go though he had no pass.

He says a monthly pass (costing 2 bob)† is also required here, in addition to the poll tax receipt.

On a fourth occasion he was accosted on a bus by a policeman after the curfew hour (now 11 p.m.—formerly 10:30 p.m.). He showed his pass only under protest but it was in good order and, after examining it, the young officer handed it back to him and slapped his face. He brought suit and the officer was found guilty by the Magistrate; but sentence was suspended, because, as the Magistrate explained, the plaintiff only desired to show that the officer was in the wrong and not to punish him.

On another occasion he had written out his own pass but had put the wrong date on it and was arrested after curfew hour by an officer while cycling home. He was taken to station, and after several hours detention, was allowed to pay 3 bob bail and gain his release.

He says any African who can write can make out his own pass. All he has to do to get a book of passes is to write a note saying "Please give bearer a book of passes" and take it to any bazaar where the pass books can be purchased. Then he can write out his own special passes. Peter has no monthly pass now and is liable to arrest at any time on the streets.

Says a group of educated Africans was stopped by an officer once

*A bioscope is a movie theater.
†A bob is a shilling.

who examined their passes but apologized when he heard them talk and knew they were educated and complained that it was his duty, but that badges should be given to be worn by educated Africans, so they wouldn't be molested.

Peter says rightly that the "exemption from pass certificates" are passes too since "exempted" natives are also stopped and must show their "exempted" cards.

They all agree that the whites couldn't do much if all of the Africans would simply refuse to carry passes. There wouldn't be enough jails to put them into. But too many are afraid of losing their jobs.

Jack Phillips is the local "nite club king."[24] He's been active in this work for 17 years. His club is large. Spacious, and well-appointed. He claims to recognize no insidious color distinctions. He is a mulatto of uncertain origin—an English accent mixed with bad grammar, airy, deep laugh, affected and somewhat "pansyish," though a large, stout man.

I went over to Jack Phillips' Ritz Hall and found a colored kids' show in progress with a full house of the Ritz colored. I was with Vil-Nkomo and Peter [Dabula] and this was a problem for Jack but he invited us in and made a surprise announcement and called me up on the platform to make a speech. I walked up and took a cute little girl with me, said a few words and offered to spar with Jack.

These were the fancy colored folk, well-dressed, many very fair. One fellow I talked with was really trying to put on the dog. They obviously want no part of the native.

The natives greatly resent the colored attitude and are very critical of the colored group—almost scornful.

From there we went to the Bantu Sports Club and found an entirely different picture.[25] There colored and natives were dancing together to the piano played by a light colored fellow and were having one hell of a grand time. Real friendship and amazing abandon in the intricate dances they performed. The dances had such names as the following: "The Caledonian," "Quadrille," "Lancers," "2nd Set," "Dr. Alberts." They swung each other around at a dizzy pace, dodged in and out and showed rare ability. And they enjoyed it so. They are much more real than the other crowd.

So there is a caste even with the colored group. Those colored at the Bantu Sports Club would not be acceptable to the fancy colored and so seek cowardine with the natives. The colored here were both young men and women and some were fair enough. They were very friendly.

Saw the local native jazz and dance band practicing—all young fellows and they are trying hard under difficult conditions. Saxes, trumpets, a piano and a banjo are the instruments and American Negro musicians, the inspiration.

Saw young native boxers working out in gym and their inspiration, too, is the American Negro boxers. They know all about Joe Louis, John Lewis, Henry Armstrong.[26]

The fellows working out in the center gym are all very keen on Negro fighters, and bewail the fact that they have no chance here to fight against white boxers. They all are eager to come to America.

The same wish is expressed by the young natives in the dance band. They look on America as a mecca and oasis.

The Empire Exhibition held here from September 1936–February 1937 started out with a policy of special days only on which natives could attend (also other non-Europeans could go on every day).[27] But when the thing was proving financial failure, after about 2 months, the policy was changed and natives were admitted on every day, including holidays, though the separate turnstiles were retained. But natives were not admitted to some of the stalls inside.

Dan Twala,[28] director of the Bantu Sports Club, said that after a route had been suggested by the City Commandant for the procession of a native pageant that he planned to stage on Dingaan's Day,[29] the City Commandant has now revoked the permit for the procession on the grounds that trouble might arise due to the fact that the Voortrekkers are also processioning on that day.*

Some of these fellows are real whizzes at table tennis, though I can hold my own with most of them.

November 24

The editor of *Umteteli wa Bantu* told me that the native printing companies cannot do job printing.[30] They are only allowed to print the paper. Native organizations must get their work done at European

---

*Voortrekkers are Boers who migrated out of the Cape Colony in the 1830s to evade British rule.

companies or at the native printer of Maseru.[31] This rule fixed up by the Nat'l Industrial Council, established by law, which has power to say what can be done and fix wages.[32] In order to do job work, the native printers would have to pay union wages as fixed by the Council, and this they cannot afford to do. The Council has made an exemption in re printing of native papers. One man shops can do this work.

Special exemption forms put out by the "National Indus. Council of the Printing and Newspaper Industry [of] South Africa."

"While engaged by the employer named below, and only while performing work comprised in the occupation or trade specified herein, the following employee may accept a wage other than that specified in the agreement of the Printing and Newspaper Industry, but not less than the special wage stated herein, or any work under such conditions as herein stipulated, which are a departure from the conditions laid down in the agreement."

On one Certificate of Exemption, one employee of the native P.P. Co. (*Umteteli*) with 40 years of experience as a compositor should have received an agreement wage of £ 6.19.0 but receives a Special Wage authorized of £ 2.5.0 per week. [The] reason for exemption is: "Native Newspaper."

But in visiting the composing rooms I noticed that a good deal of the work is being done for the mines . . . and large agreement sheets for the Native Recruiting Corporation. The give-away is that the Chamber of Mines controls the company.

The *Bantu World* is controlled by about 6 white men, including Rheinold Jones.

Europeans in control of Bantu Press:
(1) Mr. O. Maggs—chairman—member of United Party; Postmaster-General for Union.
(2) Senator Rheinold Jones—shareholder.
(3) B. G. Paver—managing director of the Bantu Press.
(4) Montague Pin—accountant.
(5) J. L. Hardy—accountant. shareholder.
A large number of non-European shareholders.

Sophiatown all freehold stands.[33] A few Europeans and many colored. Different from locations in that they are all controlled by the municipality and there are no freehold stands.

No curfew in the locations, but there is in a place like Sophiatown.

Much of the property in Sophiatown is owned by Indians who rent it to natives and colored. By Government Statute (some 30 years ago) this area was opened up as one in which black men can buy. It is now in the Municipal area. At time of the Statute it was made an exclusive black man's purchase area. The law then provided that colored and natives to buy land here but not Indians. But Indians do own land here which they buy through colored wives or native agents—mostly through colored. Less than 50 colored property owners here. Rest rent from natives and Indians. Rents are high. Room rentals go as high as £2 per room per month.

Visit to Dutch Reformed Church primary school (through Stand. VI). Native principal, 6 native teachers, 330 pupils. . . . The principal says though teaching is supposed to be in Afrikaans medium, much of it is in English, because parents and children don't like Afrikaans. Spoke to a group of the students and enjoyed their singing.

St. Cyprians Mission School—an Anglican school. 24 teachers [and] 1200 pupils through Standard VII. English medium; teaching in vernacular through Form 1.

At the Anglican School at Sophiatown, I noticed many colored children and the principal told me that only in the government schools were the lines between native and colored recognized.

Visited nursery school where kiddies, ages 18 months to 7, were taking afternoon nap on blankets and mats. 6 attendants—costs 2d a day.

Princess Alice Nursing Home (also Anglican) 32 bed capacity for women and children. White matron. Complete segregation of staff down to lavatories and kitchens.

Sophiatown rates about 15/6 to 17/6 per year. Water rates extra. No pavements, electricity or gas except on main streets.

Some fine looking homes owned by natives. Dr. A. B. Xuma's fine home in Sophiatown—called *Emphiweni* ("at the place of health"— Xhosa). Dr. Xuma, a Xhosa, was married to an American or West Indian mulatto who died at birth of her 2d child.[34] He has a dispensary in Joburg, too, and a large European practice.

Visited a dress-making and hair-dressing shop run by a native (Sesuto) woman.* She does plenty of hair-straightening which is becoming very popular with native women. Uses Val Mor products of Chicago. I put her on to Poro.[35] She rents her shop in a stone and cement building owned by a native and built by him.

Native shop signs must be displayed by stores selling to natives (or any non-Europeans) between 6 and 7 in the evening, if the shops sell soft

*SeSuto is an archaic spelling of seSotho.

goods—clothing, etc. Fruit shops, etc. need not display the signs. "Native Shop" signs displayed all over the town.

The Shop Hours Ordinance of 1923 requires the sign "Native Shop" to be displayed on all shops selling to natives after 6 p.m.

Private buses (3d and 6d return) . . . take people back and forth to Sophiatown. Municipal trams charge 2d each way.

Western Native Township—an older location than Orlando.[36] Built in 1919. £1.0.6 and £1.5.6 rental fees as at Orlando. Streets unpaved and no sidewalks.

Western Native Township is a municipal location; therefore, [it] is enfenced and has the tell-tale native guard and pill-box at the entrance.

Whenever white clerks at the municipal offices step out of their offices at the location superintendent's headquarters, the native officers pop up to attention.

In Western Township the municipality maintains no schools of its own, but only subsidizes those run by missionary organizations.

Talitha Home for Delinquent Girls. . . . [I] talked with 4 of the girls—one fair colored and 3 native—3 were 17 and one is 16. 3 of them in for stealing. One in for possessing yeast which she had brought from a Chinaman for her mother to make Kaffir beer. 2 white matrons, rest native.

"The Africa Co-operative Trading Society"—native cooperative store in Western Township.[37] Has three dep'ts—general trading store, butcher shop (the butcher complains the meat is "too expensive"—no ice, of course) and a tea room, which does good business on week-ends. Some 150 shop members.

Ballinger said the Western Township Cooperative Store, on basis of £300 capital, has a turnover of £20,000 per year. But he's afraid the organization may fold.

Visited the Bantu Creche run by Children's Aid Society in Western Township. For 2d per day native working mothers leave their children (from 6 months up) to be looked after and fed by 3 native attendants. Two room bldg. and they have from 30–40 kids daily.

Alexandra Township—another freehold township like Sophiatown.[38] No pavements, some big houses.

Alexandra Township is outside the boundary of Joburg and thus beyond control of the City Council. It is owned by an incorporated company, whose stock is almost entirely in the hands of one family (all but 46 of 10,000 shares). Plots sold to natives and Euro-Africans who have migrated there as a result of Joburg slum clearance.

There are not so many colored living at Alexandra. Indians cannot live there at all.

Mr. Baloyi director of the Alexandra Township Bus Owners Association.[39] He is M.R.C.—member of the Native Rep. Council.

Mr. Baloyi owns 5 buses and has been in business 9 or 10 years. Has a big garage for his buses behind his large modern brick house. Baloyi's buses are marked "For Colored Only"—this includes natives.

We pass scores of native workers cycling the nine miles from Jo-burg to Alexandra in a driving rain. They have 18 miles to pedal each day. Poor devils.

During the day I met the only native S.P.C.A officer, a sanitary inspector (there are 2 at Alexandra), a native recreational director, 2 native principals of primary schools.

The Alexandra Health Association is struggling to do good preventive health work there. The clinic is directed by a very nice American woman, Mrs. Sales. They are doing much vaccination, enteric injection, infant welfare, etc. work.

The natives here are themselves terribly confused about the J.C. [Jim Crow] situations on trams and buses. They say there are no specific rules and no signs and that it is left to the arbitrary decision of individual conductors as to whether a native can ride upstairs or not. There are no signs up here but by accepted custom the natives always sit in the back. They are indefinite as to just what happens to coloreds.

Peter [Dabula] and I went into the main Post Office to get stamps and mail letters. We used the European stalls. I didn't even know there was a segregated section as I saw no signs. I got the stamps okay and was standing at a desk affixing the stamps when a guard came up and asked me if Peter is my "boy." I mulled at him and said: "My boy? Of course not! He's my friend and companion." The guard smiled quizzically and walked away.

Had a long talk with Sophonia Poenyane of Bechuanaland—one of Schapera's informants. Tested him on his views concerning the standardized orthography that Doke,[40] Lestrade, et al. have been hatching for the Tswana language.[41] He is all for it but the only reason he could give was that it was recommended highly by "the professors." But he could give no answer to my insistent question as to what the natives would gain by the change and whether this was actually being done for the benefit of the natives or in order to make the language easier for

Europeans to handle. He finally admitted that the language as is, spelling and pronunciation, serves the needs of the natives well enough and is fully understood by them and they handle its present spelling and pronunciation without difficulty, and that the [new] language really would serve the interests of whites best.

With [Jack] Phillips, I had dinner at Mrs. de Villiers. She runs a boarding house and has to rely mostly on natives as colored don't support her.

. . . A young colored radical who is apparently in the [Communist] Party and has been to Moscow, said South, East, and West Africans there were astounded and shocked at the way American Negro comrades idolized white women and ran after them.

Attended the Ritz Hall to see the Bantu Players program as a guest of Jack Phillips. I sat in his office and watched—native players performing for an exclusively European audience in a colored hall! The players were better in their own plays. The American Negro play, "The Recruiter," by Matthews was poorly done. They also tend to sing too many hymns.

There were about 700 colored people present at the kiddies show last night (and some fair talent was shown there too). But only a handful of Europeans present to see the Bantu Players tonight. Maybe because it rained too hard. Another exclusively European night will be held tomorrow.

Jack Phillips told me that he has to use 3 names for his hall because of the racial situation here. The native people will not use the *Ritz Palais de House* because colored people use it; the colored will not use *Inchcape Hall* because natives use it; and old people will not use either—they use the *Majestic*. And some prefer to use just No. 5 Polly Street on their announcements.

The different names all appear on lighted globes in front of the building and all are lighted at once.

Natives can't attend colored bioscopes because of picture censorship.

Letter in Jack Phillips' file:

City of Johannesburg
Dept. of Traffic & Licensing
March 18, 1936

Mr. Jack Phillips:
Dear Sir:

Inchcape Palais de Dance

With reference to your letter of the 4th instant, relative to the above, I have to inform you that the General Purpose Committee. . . . resolved as follows: "That permission be granted to Mr. Jack Phillips to hold a performance on the 25th March, reserving the hall for Europeans on the conditions that no white females be employed and that he comply with the building by-laws in regard to the use of scenery, etc."

Yours faithfully,
License Officer

There is a local by-law or ordinance here which prohibits European women from attending native places of amusement; the law does not apply to men. Ballinger thinks it is *ultra vires*. Because of it, Phillips . . . had to put on a "European night" for his "million dollar review." It handicaps the Bantu drama work because they must depend on European attendance for financial support.

November 25

Visit to the Van Ryn Deep Mine with Mr. Webb.

Webb told me it was difficult to get me a permit to include me because when he told the officials that I am an American Negro, they demurred. They claimed to have no prejudice on the matter, but said that the policy had been not to take any dark people (including Chinese and Japanese) down the mines for fear that Afrikaner miners employed below might resent it and that they might drop something "accidentally" and cause injury to some dark visitor.

Webb told the official that if I was refused a permit I might tell natives elsewhere in South Africa that I was refused because conditions are so bad in the Van Ryn mine and that this would hurt recruiting. When they asked him what I look like, he replied, "Just like the de Villiers" (a prominent South African family whose members are swarthy and whom everyone alleges to be colored). So the permit was issued.

We first went to the office of Mr. Jack, the mine manager—a tall handsome, blue-eyed, courteous fellow, who told us the mine has about 10 years to go. We were escorted by a European employee, Mr. Lloyd. We were given mine torches and raincoats and were taken down 2500 feet to level one in the "skip."* Lloyd told us the great drop would cause our ears to buzz and to keep our mouths open. I had to.

We got out at level one after a fast and noisy trip down (about a minute) and followed the car tracks. There is a very sudden drop in temperature when level one is reached . . . and the perspiring native workers must be in constant danger from this.

Lloyd pointed out the "leaders"—the ribbons of pay rock—characterized by the spotted black rock along the side of the openings. There was much dripping overhead and muck underfoot. We had to stoop low most of the time as we wended our way, passing an occasional native boy. On the entire underground trip of 3 hours we encountered only 3 European miners.

The leaders were mined out on either side on a steep slope. Often a layer of only about three or four feet has been taken out—shelf-like. Some leaders were left untouched as props to be reclaimed later.

The tunnels and dug-outs were shored up by round concrete, wheel-like slabs and round wooden props. In many places that had been mined out the sand has been poured back into stockades to avoid death traps. Electric lights were lit all along the car tracks.

Often we could hear the compression drills working on rock above or at the side of us.

Often we had to almost crawl on hands and knees to get through tight places and had to be contortionists to get up narrow, winding ladders and steps. Solid rock walls were on all sides of us, and when we left the car tracks everything was pitch dark except for our torches. Many fungus growths on the wooden props and "pig stys"—stockade-like square props into which sand and rock are poured.

Winches grind as the loosened rock is pulled down slopes by scow shovels, to be loaded on cars and pulled up to level one in large cable cars which roared back and forth and skip the tracks about twice a week. From level one, it is taken to the top in the open skips, through the shafts.

It was cold at level one, but increasingly hot as we worked our way through holes to level two. (There are 13 levels in all.) They told us that on some of the lower levels where ventilation is poor, the heat is insufferable. There was a terrifying labyrinth of passages and it would be easy to get lost as many natives often do.

We stopped at a first-aid station and talked with the native attendant. There was a long concrete water trough outside, with disinfectant

---

*A skip is an open elevator car for carrying men and ore.

in it, through which injured native workers walked before getting their wounds dressed. The native attendant said mine work okay, but that he would work on a farm, too, if he were sent there. The air would be good, he said.

Another worker with whom we talked—a Xhosa—was re-threading pipe and did other mechanical work. Said he had learned to do it by "seeing"—i.e. watching whites do it. He was getting £ 3 per month. Still another young fellow of about 17 (he didn't know his age)—a Xhosa too—said he had worked for 5 months in the mines, his first experience, and that when his contract is up, he is going back to his kraal to his wife. He has family land and his father paid 8 cattle as lobola for his wife and he doesn't have to repay his father. He saves his money by the deferred payment plan and only draws 10s monthly of the £ 3 wage he receives.

He was ordered to take off his hat and headcloth by Mr. Lloyd's native boy who accompanied us, as were several other natives whom we encountered. (Lloyd explained that usually it isn't insolence when a native fails to bare his head to a white man, but usually "ignorance" of the raw farm and kraal natives.)

We talked with a young European contract miner who has earned as high as £80 per month and complains that now he only gets about £60 or £65, though working in a rich lode. Says the mine can't get enough native boys to help. He's been mining since 1926. He has a team of about 10 natives and one white with him (this subordinate white fellow got £ 1.1 per day and says he is fed up with the mines in which he has worked for 21 years—no money in it for the workers, he says).

The [white] miner gets a guarantee of 15s per day from the mine (in case something goes wrong and his gang can't work) and is paid on a monthly basis by the fathom of rock mined—based on a monthly survey. He was working in a lode that yielded 5 pennyweight of gold to the ton of rock—slightly above the average yield.*

His native drillers also get paid on a contract basis. There are two to a drill—and he said that one of his had earned as much as £ 15 per month ("a fabulous salary for a native," exclaimed Lloyd).

The chief duty of the European seemed to be that of placing white chalk marks on the rock where the holes are to be drilled for blasting (this is done when the shifts are out). The drills are about 6 feet long and tubular—water runs through them as they drill. They are about 2 or 3 inches in diameter—about the size of a water pipe and they bore a clean

---

*A pennyweight is equal to 1/20 oz. troy weight.

hole. It's hard work manning the drill and the drillers work an entire shift without relief. The miner said he had no trouble getting the natives to work.

Mr. Lloyd cuffed one young native away from the water spigot when we wanted to drink.

[Above ground] natives are lined up before 5 moving belts in a big tin shed, picking out waste rock as the belts move by. They are trained to distinguish between "pay" and waste rock, and a native boss boy moved up and down each belt to keep an eye on them. They have rubber pads on their hands and pick out waste rock as the belt moves along.

The European who showed us through the refining plant pointed to a pipe above the shed from which mine dust continually poured. He said that despite the continuous use of water in the process of mining and crushing, this dust could not be eliminated and it was this that causes phthisis, the miner's scourge.* He said the drillers below were also endangered by it, but conditions are not as bad now as formerly.

All the whites at the mine emphasize how "obedient and docile" the native workers are and how much trouble there would be if that many whites were thrown together.

There are more whites employed on the surface in the refining process and administrative offices.

Many of the native workers look to be very young—probably 16 or 17.

The native miners were anything but a happy-looking lot. There was no laughing or jostling—all had deeply sober looks.

One European miner referred to them as "coons" in my presence.

███████ **November 26**

Two of Peter's girl friends who are probationers at the non-European hospital, discussed the conditions at the hospital with me. There are some 45 African probationers at the hospital. They get only one lecture per week and paid at rate of from £ 1 per month to £ 3 per month in their 4th year. They say the food is impossible, and that there are no colored girls in training there because they can't stand the conditions.

The hospital has segregated wards for natives, coloreds, Indians,

---

*Phthisis is pulmonary tuberculosis.

and Chinese, but all native nurses. Non-European doctors can attend to private patients there—at rate of £1.1 for the theatre and £1.1 per day for the room. All the other doctors are young European medical school men. The hospital is overcrowded and some patients have to sleep on the floor. One of the girls told of her experience in acting as a nurse when Rathebe's daughter was having a tonsillectomy.[42] The first attempt was unsuccessful and at the 2nd effort the young medical students used no anesthetic at all. But Rathebe made no complaint.

The old Jew who runs the store next door to the Center [Bantu Men's Social Centre] came in to call on me and stood around with his hat on in my room. He was reluctant to give his hat to Peter when I invited him to do so but finally removed it when I insisted.

He thinks Malan is anti-everything, and that his anti-semitism is not dangerous, nor his fight for the South African Republic, but just so much political humbug.[43] He doesn't think the Nationalists will ever get in, nor that there will ever be a South African Republic.*

Peter told me about the "darkey-cabs"—run by Africans. It seems that now some European cabs will haul non-Europeans, though not always.

Lithebe and Sophonia took me to the African cab rank and told me I could get taken out to the Hellman's for 1s. But when I got in a new Studebaker, the driver told me it would be 4s (the European cab rate) because he would have to carry me alone as he "couldn't pick up his usual fares with this big man." (They had told him who I am).

Went to lunch with Dr. Sachs at the Plaza. He called up the manager before-hand and asked if there would be any objection to me and was informed that I would be entirely welcome. [I] met advocate Morris Alexander at one of the tables.[44] (Ballinger said that Joburg must be changing when he heard about it).

Visited Issy Diamond, formerly a C.P. [Communist Party] member and leader, at his hair-dressing salon.[45] He was very friendly and took me over to meet Solly Sachs[46] and Gana Makabeni,[47] union organizers. But he recommended a colored shop when I suggested that I had to get a hair cut—though his shop is adorned with huge pictures of Marx,

---

*The Afrikaner nationalist fight for republic status was extended, but they finally won the battle in a closely contested referendum in 1960.

Lenin and Stalin, and he has spent 18 months in the coop for leading a mixed demonstration. In sentencing him, the magistrate told him his crime would not have been so grave if he had been merely leading his own people; but that he had been leading black people and white people together.

Had dinner at the Sachs and went through some of his case histories of native inmates in Pretoria Asylum. I noticed that a number of natives were recorded as raving against whites—who had taken the land, against pass officers . . . etc. There were also several references to America.

Dr. Sachs believes that the Bantu mother's practice of nursing the babies whenever they want the breast and until an advanced age has a profound psychological affect on the Bantu people in later life. (cf. Margaret Mead and Ruth Benedict.) He thinks this accounts for the fact that even the educated Bantu today has a tendency to look for favors, for care and protection to the government and the white man—not aggressive—i.e. he has a strong "mother instinct."

With Dr. Sachs I visited two social functions—one for natives at the Bantu Center and the other for colored at the Ritz. "The Pioneers" are a group of young colored who were giving the "flannel ball" at the Ritz. One of them told me the crowd was handpicked, but there were very few who could even be called brownskin there. Some of the women were exceptionally attractive and many of the men were handsome. The women wore evening dress for the most part and looked very well. Many were only "sociological coloreds."

The eight piece orchestra was colored and played well. They waltzed, 2-stepped and fox-trotted, but their favorite dances were the square dances, each of which, such as the Caledonian, the Quadrille, the Lancers, the 2nd set, the Albert, lasted a long time and was danced with great enthusiasm, vigor, abandon and amazing joy. And they danced these complicated dances exceptionally well—and they do require energy.

On inquiry I ascertained that most of them, men and women, are factory workers—working in box factories, dress and hat makers, etc. The men are said to be expert wood polishers and some get £6 or £7 per week. Many of them pass as Europeans on their jobs—some of the girls work as sales girls. Very few of them would be well educated, but they talk very grammatically. Not much drinking in evidence. None of the women smoked in public. Many have Dutch names.

One big fellow—a school teacher—talked with me [and] said that whites are responsible for separation of colored and natives. Said he has no prejudice against the native; said his grandmother was a native woman; but that many of the colored have a deep prejudice against natives. Said no colored man could lead both colored and native, but that native leaders can.

Tremendous interest manifested in American Negroes, and especially Joe Louis, et al. Only one asked me about schools. Had to sign autographs, make a speech, etc.

One girl told me that she had seen American Negroes, but never an American "Colored" before. All agree that this is a tough town for the black man and the colored man. They say economic conditions here are so bad for dark-skinneds that colored business has no chance. No cafes, tea-rooms, etc. owned by coloreds. Some Indian places but some of these are run for Europeans only.

The colored people at the dance were very bourgeois in manners, thinking and dressing.

The natives at the Center were having a good time too, watching a western film. Two teams of native entertainers (one, the Darktown Strutters, were very clever, danced and sang well and had good poise) and dancing.[48] They were not "dressed up" like the colored, but the entertainers wore tails and white gloves, a la Layton and Johnson.[49] There were some colored sprinkled among the 300 or so natives present. They laughed heartily and seemed to enjoy themselves immensely.

Here, too, the American Negro influence on the entertainers was in evidence.[50] One act was announced as an impersonation of Fats Waller[51] and another of the Mills Brothers.[52]

Prof. White, prin. [principal] of Wilberforce, came in. Said he had told natives that if Government gave them a chance they could develop like American Negroes. Said a location superintendent challenged this; told him he didn't know the native and that there is no such thing as an educated native. He said also that among young natives there is great prejudice vs. the colored. Said that when Bishop Wright went to Kimberley, both natives and colored wanted to entertain him. . . . The suggestion that natives and colored combine in entertaining him was vetoed by colored, who gave a reception in the Town Hall, into which the native [AME] pastor dared not stick his head.

<hr>

November 27

The Indian barber who cut my hair told me that the black man had no chance in this country. He said they [Europeans] ran natives out of

Joburg and would soon be running coloreds out too. He pointed out that though they discriminated against the coloreds, Indians and even Chinese (because Chinese government is not strong) here, they handled Japanese with kid gloves. This is because Japs are backed by a strong government. He said in 25 years the Indians here will be backed by a strong independent Indian government too, and the Indian will get justice then.

Trip to Mental Hospital for natives at Pretoria (visited male-female sections).

Male section has accommodation for 490 but there are now 539 inmates—terribly crowded. Only two Europeans in attendance. No chance for treatment—merely an isolation hospital.

All sorts and degrees of cases—catatonic, schizophrenic, dementia praecox, etc. There are several cases resulting from advanced pellagra, contracted and neglected at the mines, and resulting in insanity.

They wander about in the yard all day long. The violent ones are kept inside a wire fence or cage in the yard. Place reasonably clean.

The beds in the hospital ward are almost touching each other, and the well ones sleep on mats on the floor toe to toe.

Many of the men are vigorously anti-white. They inveigh against whites in general and show much animosity. They refer to pass laws, land deprivals, police brutality, etc. A group tried to convince us that one badly paralyzed case was due to police brutality.

These attitudes are significant, for [though] they cannot be ascribed as the direct causes of insanity, they indicate what was preying on these men's minds before their breakdown.

Some of them claim either to have come from America, or that they or their parents had been there (indicating extent to which thoughts of America and American Negroes influenced their pre-insanity thinking).

Some of them are strapping fellows and look healthy and normal; others are terribly emaciated. A grotesque crowd of social debris.

One fellow in the violent cage claims to be "God"—says all he wants as "God" is some clothes and a job. He has illusions of grandeur on other matters—talks of cattle in terms of millions. He seemed to delight in being insolent and impudent to Dr. Sachs as he questioned him.

One grated bitterly about Smuts and yelled at us "why do you come, you don't do anything for us?"

The European attendant says that most of them come from the Joburg and Pretoria areas. Many were from the mines—men who were quite normal when examined and accepted for mine work, but who subsequently break down. The European attendant attributes much of this latter to "town evils"—such as dagga-smoking,* liquor, women, and V.D.

The attendants say not many of them come from the kraals on the reserves.

There are several young boys kept among the men. One of about 8 or 9—an idiot—refuses to wear any clothes and scampers all about naked. The attendant says the men treat them as tenderly as babies.

There were no apparent sexual reactions among them at the presence of Dr. Sachs' European nurse friend.

One of them gave me the Zulu hand-shake (hand-shake and then a thumb shake) as I left. They willingly posed for pictures.

Dr. Sachs claims their psychological condition and reactions are identical with that of Europeans, though Europeans are often far more violent and dangerous.

Women's section—also overcrowded. 275 inmates [but] the total capacity is 175.

They also sleep on mats on the floors of dormitories—in very close quarters.

Unlike the men, many of them talk sex all the time. Several were bold enough to walk around and rub up against us.

There are several cases of women who spend their entire days on their knees and with pails of water, scrubbing the floors and walks. One has been doing it for 7 years. Dr. Sachs likened this form of expression to Lady Macbeth's washing her hands all the time. [Jack] Simons and I argued that this form of expression was due to the women's prior occupation, though not arguing that scrubbing was the direct cause of insanity.

Discussion with Dhladhla and Makabeni. Dhladhla a former native C.P. [Communist Party], was kicked out of Party. Says there are no real revolutionaries in South Africa. He is bitterly critical of African leadership—says men like Jabavu (a "white minion") and Seme ("a crook") are hopeless. Says left wing faction in [All] African Convention tried to get the Native Representation Act boycotted—refusing to support the Native Representative Council and the Native Representatives and Senators. But Jabavu et al. decided this was a big step toward solution of the native problem and supported the scheme.

Makabeni an organizer of native garment workers—both he and Dhladhla have been recently expelled from the C.P.

---

*Dagga is marijuana.

Makabeni emphasized the corruption of educated native leaders, mentioning Kdale, Seme, etc. They said the corrupt and conservative leaders "pack" the conventions of native organizations and make it impossible for progressives to do anything. Makabeni isn't even going to the African National Convention [AAC], nor the Bantu Congress [ANC], which he said is an attempt to revive a dead organization.

They admitted the I.C.U. proved that language and tribal difficulties were not strong enough to prevent mass African organization. They said these are no barrier at all among educated Africans.

The fundamental problem of the African is to discover honest and self-sacrificing leadership.

Makabeni thinks most important work now possible is organization of Africans in trade unions. He thinks some support can be gotten from white workers too, e.g. miners—in self-protection. Said a number of white trade unions are organizing parallel native unions—though tendency is for whites to try to get native leaders that will be puppets for these unions. Whites want natives organized so that their threat to employers will be stronger.

They said practically nothing is being done in mine compounds. Difficult to get in these and reach the men. (Makabeni said Roux had to disguise as a priest in order to get in them.)

Makabeni said natives should be first reached at the kraal, so that they will have some basis of understanding when they reach the mines.

Had dinner with Mrs. Barnes, a colored widow who has a good deal of property. She and her sister, Mrs. de Villiers, bemoaned the lack of spirit and organization among South African Colored. Significantly they both endorsed the self-sacrificing efforts of a young colored fellow here whom they said is branded as a "Bolshevik." They said efforts are being made to get all colored out of Joburg too.

Visited W.N.L.A. (Witwatersrand Native Labor Association) Hall— at mine workers recruiting depot—a barn-like affair, owned by the recruiting corporation.

As we (four African boys and me) drove up to the gate at night, an old native guard yelled out, "Banumzana" ("Sirs"). Then he came up and peered into the car, saw the black faces, and exclaimed in disgust, "Aw! Ngabantu," ("Aw! They are Africans")

Natives in great variety of European dress—all extremely poor looking. But admission was 1s. One young fellow was attired in full dress and with his gal on his arm—amidst mine workers in working clothes. One fellow had on morning pants and a light blue stovepipe hat. Some of the women had on fur coats though it was hot as hell in and out of the hall.

Two troupes, one of men and one of 2 girls and 2 boys, sang Zulu songs, weird and with shuffling steps as they sang. Money was being paid to "buy" dances and to "buy" singers not to sing.

In the hall there was a chairman (sitting before a table laden with oranges and large bottles of "Society Pop"—not Kaffir beer) to announce items and to receive cash either for the request of a choir to sing or stop singing. That is, if one wishes a choir to sing one should go up to the chairman and "buy" that choir to sing. Small sums of even a penny are accepted. If, however, one is tired or not interested in the singing of a group, one can go up and "buy" the choir "off" with a slightly higher sum than the person who has bought them. There are cases where bidding in this fashion has been very keen and, of course, the highest bidder wins. I "bought off an act" for 6d. Wilfred for 3d got the chairman to "send one troupe home to bed."

November 28

Watched soccer at the Bantu Sports ground in shadow of mining dump and on former mining ground—very appropriate.

White policeman throwing the discus out on police athletic ground with a red-shirted native prisoner to chase it for him. Does the system here make these whites soft!

South African European police on adjoining sports field even playing lazy cricket—sprawling all over the ground, barely running after ball, etc.

More than one young African has said to me: "South Africa is a good place for *white* men." Africans do everything but move their bowels for them.

It is evident, as Peter avers, that the city natives are developing great scorn for whites and often an intense hatred. In private conversation, they evidence a great skepticism even of the white "friends of the native." They also show a great dislike for Jews, whom they regard as exploiting the African, even to write books.

Many natives scorn the Zulus as "Uncle Toms"; many whites say the Zulus are the "best" natives. Some natives say that the humility of the Zulu house boys and clerks is entirely affected—a means of pulling the white man's leg in order to get along (like American Negro pullman porters re "Mistah [Mister] Chollie").

Many Indians are severe on question of mixed marriages. They feel that a black man's duty and responsibility to his group should deter him from ever marrying white. They point out the bad example set for the young by prominent men who marry white.

Native cutter of clothing, employed for five years—gets only £2.15 per week. Has no fear of them putting in whites because under union wages whites must receive £5 to start with.

Native orderly at Municipal Building. Says he is "well paid"—gets £5 per month and room.

Saw Zulu war dance within five minutes walk of Bantu Center . . . at Salisbury Jubilee Compound, where the herbalists have their stalls and sell herbs, love potions, etc. Men, in loin cloths, goat's fur, feathered head-gear and with sticks, danced wonderfully well. Stomach muscles prominently used in dance and terrific foot stomp. They are all well built.

Shoemaker has the best troupe. A hard-eyed, nice featured Zulu. Four tom toms held by drummers who stand erect behind the dancers. A leader leads them in yells sounding something like a college yell. Mostly young men participating in the dance. 6d admission charged, and after the routine dances of the four participating groups, dances are "bought" later and I bought a dance by Shoemaker and his troupe for a shilling.

Some European influences evident in the costumes—e.g. Shoemaker had on a Scottish kiltie; the leader of another troupe had a bunch of bottle tops attached to one ankle to jingle as he stamped; others had on festival paper hats.

Dirt was kicked in the faces of the spectators squatting at the "ring side." Heavy shower failed to break up the dance. About 75–100 dancers present—some almost naked. Very few female spectators. Many participants and spectators had the discs (some of them as large as watches) in their ears.

Had supper as guest of Naransamy, an Indian accountant, together with Rev. Sigamoney,[53] an Anglican churchman, Mr. Ernest, an Indian sportsman, and two other Indians.

They agreed that [there is a] great need . . . for an organization of all non-Europeans in order to defeat the whites' efforts to keep the non-European groups divided.

They told me of the liquor laws. Special conditions apply to non-Europeans here. Under the Liquor Act of 1926,* non-Europeans are under strict liquor prohibition except by special and individual permits issued by the courts. Natives carrying "pass exemption" cards, are also allowed such permits. These court permits allow a limited monthly quota (including hard liquors) and are issued only after investigation of the individual's home, wage or salary, etc.

They said that in Natal, the colored are better off than the Indians. There the colored have the franchise and the Indians (excepting a very few who come under an older act) have not.

They said that there the St. Helenans would not speak to me because I am not light enough, nor would the Cape Colored who "pass" there as St. Helenans.

Rev. Sigamoney said that natives now have much prejudice against both colored and Indians and that they are now not willing to be led by either. He admitted that now the natives are making more progress educationally than either colored or Indians—they have more college graduates, professional men, etc.

Mr. Ernest told of Jim Crow situations in Cape. Said Joburg is really the best place for colored. Said in Grahamstown one bioscope will let Indians sit in the peanut gallery,† but not colored. An Indian with a colored wife cannot take her to the movie.

They say the Agent-General is merely representative of the English government and not the South African Indian people. They say he does not express Indian opinion when he talks of dissociation of interests of Indians from those of other non-Europeans.

They say the Indians, like natives and colored, have an inferiority complex here.

When they served me beer at the Plaza the other day [26 November] when I lunched with Dr. Sachs, they violated the law, as I had no permit to drink beer. The colored doorman at Jack Phillips Hall says

---

*The Liquor Act was passed in 1928, not 1926.

†*Peanut gallery* can mean the upper gallery in a theatre or a boisterous crowd of spectators. Bunche is referring to the former.

he has had a liquor permit for 4 years, but they carry on such an exhaustive investigation into one's pedigree in order to grant it, that he has given his up in disgust.

████████ **November 29**

Discussion with [Solly] Sachs. Says early white workers were from England and had a strong labor tradition, but they have been replaced by raw, unsocially minded, backveld Afrikaners who are bitterly prejudiced against natives. Thus, in the Garment Workers Union, [there is] tension, e.g., it is necessary to have separate native unions. Also said that no organizational work of any significance was being done amongst natives.[54]

No purely anti-trade union legislation in South Africa—no prohib. [prohibition] under Roman-Dutch law—no conspiracy act as in Eng. But restrictions make it virtually impossible to organize natives.

(1) night special pass—making it difficult for natives to attend meetings

(2) Urban Areas Act—keeping them [Africans] far from town[55]

(3) Masters-Servants Act making a breach of contract a criminal offense (all natives—even domestics—have to be employed under *written* contract). Applies only to the Free State and Transvaal.[56]

[In] 1928 Garment Workers Union [had] strike by natives—about 200 arrested while Sachs addressing them and charged with breach of contract.

Boycotting is a criminal offense under common law of country and picketing (police decide what is "peaceful picketing" and this is permitted) is made illegal under the Riotous Assemblies Act.

Native mine workers are not really proletarianized. They retain kraal and peasant psychology. This is deliberate policy of Chamber of Mines—to keep them from organizing. Tendency is for natives not to trust European labor organizers. Cannot approach native workers, as agrarians, in same way as Europeans. No proper techniques for approaching them yet worked out. Proper technique: main approach must be by natives. Native workers have no friends—neither employers, European trade unions or colored. Whenever an advanced European trade union makes a gesture of helpfulness, it is gratefully received by natives.

Laundry [workers] best organized of native workers in South Africa.

They have received support from European union and are employed on skilled and semi-skilled work.

Garment Workers have parallel unions—6,000 Europeans and 300 natives organized in Transvaal. Native garment workers are skilled and semi-skilled cutters and pressers. Unskilled native workers in garment industry are unorganized.

Garment workers also organized in the Cape and Natal. About 17,000 workers, white, colored and black in whole industry.

Proportion of black, white and colored in garment industry: Black—1500; White—11,000 (approximate); Colored and Indian—4500 (approximate). About 6000 are non-Europeans.

No color bar at all in Cape Town. In Durban, no color bar in union const. [constitution] and no discrimination vs. colored workers. Most of members of union exec. [executive] are colored there. Natives can be members but not enthusiastically received.

Transvaal parallel garment unions have separate executives but they meet together and cooperate. European union in position of big father—extends financial [assistance]. One paid native organizer.

On a holiday three of the European girls on cleaning work failed to show up. Employer put native men at their work on that day. The next day the three girls refused to sit on seats that had been occupied by natives the day before. Most of the European workers went out on strike—for about an hour until Sachs came and pacified them. Similar incidents in other factories where colored have been employed. These incidents Sachs attributes directly to racial prejudice.

About 1930, strike of European furniture workers [over] management grievances. European workers alone would have been beaten for non-Europeans did a lot of skilled and unskilled work (about 200 to 400 European workers). Europeans were beaten because natives carried on work (natives not members of union—colored were and went with Europeans). About 10 days later natives presented ultimatum to bosses that bosses must meet demands of Europeans or natives would stop work. About a month after reinstatement of Europeans (after Europeans acknowledged that natives had made it possible for them to win the strike), natives demanded the legal wage under the Wage Act, a group of them were arrested under the Master-Servant Act and some of the European workers stood by and jeered them as they were led away. This was in a furniture factory in Joburg.

[Sachs] advocated trade unionism and use of legal means to get proper wages for non-European workers. This would develop morale among European workers and increase their confidence in unionism.

Peter and Vil-Nkomo were refused service at the European section of the Post Office here. The European clerk and a native guard directed them to the non-European window.

Natives (probably on duty for whites) line up at the windows of the Barclay's Bank, however. White women have to wait behind black men.

Notes on labor force in South Africa (Ballinger):
S.A. labor force in three clearly defined groups:
1. European or "white workers" with some "colored" in Natal and the Cape Province.
2. Natives in urban areas who are classed as detribalized, i.e., solely dependent on a wage earned from some industrial or commercial pursuit.
3. Natives engaged in mining, pastoral and agriculture. This group is classed as semi-tribal because it has some connection with the Native Reserves or tribal lands. It is not entirely dependent on a wage and is therefore paid an adult wage or wage based on the requirements of an individual.

Ballinger mentioned anti-Jewish sentiment in Trades and Labor Council because of trouble with Sachs of the Garment Workers Union. De Vrees [De Vries] told Ballinger that he doesn't trust any Jew. Sachs suspended because an employer in Garment Industry in King Williamstown asked for rebate on the Wage Board rate of 2-1/2% because he could not pay the fixed rate. De Vrees knew that Sachs was prepared to give this rebate and De Vrees proceeded to try to arrange an agreement. Sachs resented De Vrees' interference and charges vs. De Vrees were made in a letter from Garment Workers Union, charging De Vrees with being too intimate with Min. of Labor, etc. In meeting of Trades Council, Sachs said he had not written letter, but was in sympathy with its charges. Sachs was asked to leave the meeting. New delegate was sent from Garment Workers Union and he refused to have letter withdrawn and apology made. So Sachs remains suspended from Trades Council. Sachs is challenging this suspension in the courts. He's alone—communists and conservative labor elements against him.

Economic condition of some of boys who come into Center [BMSC]: Two, working at *Star* Office as messengers for the editors, get £ 5.10 per month. Rent costs them £ 2 per month. Transportation (from Sophiatown) 15s per month and the rest goes for food, which they get wherever they can. One, at the same wage and expense, develops blue prints for a firm of contractors.

They say it is general that clothes must be purchased "hot"—i.e. from natives working for clothes companies and other stores who steal articles and sell them for what they can get. Everything is gotten in this way—even furniture and pianos. One native, working in a warehouse, shipped a load of furniture out to natives in some small town and was only detected because the people delayed too long in claiming it and the station master, fearing it would be damaged by rain, notified the company that it had not been claimed.

Peter [Dabula] says there is much stealing by natives working in stores. They are very clever at it and do not consider it stealing. They say they are merely adding to their meager wages by the only means in their power through the resale of the "hot" goods. Some use fences for the selling. Peter says he even knows cases of men getting away with bed-steads.

A large number of the young fellows are essentially "kept" men— sleeping and eating with their mistresses where domestics are employed—"Joburg marriages."

The boys with sticks and knobkerries, prowling about the locations and townships at night probably look more dangerous than they are. They do fight with these weapons, however, for one young fellow packed into the native "taxi" in which we returned to Joburg from Sophiatown (there were 10 of us packed into a 5 passenger car) was badly cut about the face from stick blows.

On Sunday, in the lot behind the Bantu Sports Ground, Kaffir beer is sold openly and I saw native and colored women digging the large bottles and cans out of the ground where they kept them hidden from the police. "Lookouts" are constantly on the watch for police intrusion. It is a big business.

Jack Phillips said the local colored are much impressed with me, but they don't like it when I employ the term "Negro"—even to my own group.

Peter's [Dabula] notes on the "stockvel." The word "Stockvel" has no satisfactory interpretation. It might be associated with the word "wholesale."*

In Joburg many African women form themselves into societies and organize parties called "stockvels." At these parties, usually a brass band is engaged for music. The woman who is organizing the party receives as her guests the other members of her particular society. There is a party organized on each Sunday, thus making it possible for each woman to be hostess to the others of her society. At these parties food is always provided.

But of primary interest is the contribution that is made by each woman of the society—the contribution being given to the organizer of the "stockvel."

Thus, if a society has 5 members, ladies A,B,C,D, and E, and A was hostess today, the rest would each donate say 10s, and A would have £2. When B's turn comes, the contributions would be made to her in rotation.

A profit is often made when after the hostess has served the free meal and beer to the members of her society, she levies a charge for extra eating and drinking by the members and all eating and drinking by the public.

A *stockvel* is, therefore, a pay party, but the society members invest their small contributions.

These parties are frequent on Sunday afternoons and members wear the distinctive dress of the societies to which they belong.

Visit to the Magistrates Courts.

Just before we arrived, there had been plenty of excitement at the arraignment of a young European charged with assault and murder of a school girl.

Before "G" court, a sweating, irritable uniformed officer was calling the roll of native witnesses and brow-beating and cursing them because they did not respond quickly enough to suit him.

In "C" court, the magistrate was shaming a native youth in the box for beating up his wife.

When some poor whites came up later on reckless driving charges they were treated deferentially, given [addressed with] titles, etc. which were denied to the natives.

Stockvels were income generators for women in the urban areas. Groups of women would band together and pool their money so that one of them could organize a party, where members and guests would pay an admission fee and buy food and drink inside. The privilege of hosting the parties would rotate to all the women in the club.

In "D" court, two degenerate-looking poor whites were up for assaulting and robbing a native of his passes while [they were] drunk. The native gave straightforward testimony and couldn't be confused by the defendants' questions.

The magistrate was Lugg—who is said to be a terror to the natives. But this was such a flagrant case that he had to give judgment for the native.

The defendants and their lone, almost moronic, woman witness, were obviously perjuring themselves and Lugg sharply warned the woman once.

The native spectators, for whom no seats are provided in the court and who must stand behind a rail at the back of the seats, followed the case avidly. (I stood with them—as did a few whites). The court bailiff once arose and cuffed a young native woman next to me who was resting her head on the rail, yelling at her, "This is no place to sleep—go home if you want to sleep." She stayed with a smile.

The whites were given a sharp sentence. The young white prosecutor, while not very brilliant, was determined enough to convict the whites, and did not handle them too gently.

The native was referred to as "boy," of course.

A humorous incident came when the magistrate had to call on the prosecutor to help him get into the snake-skin wallet and then emptied out half a dozen different papers that the native was carrying. All passes . . . and poll tax receipts.

The whites had gotten drunk in a Kaffir beer joint on Eloff Street extension.

Ruth said Peter will have to pay between 30 and 40 pounds lobola in order to marry her. She is in favor of it, she says, because her parents have spent a lot on her and she owes a debt to them which her prospective husband must pay off. She says she would not stand for her parents to demand too much lobola from Peter but that £ 30 to £ 40 would be enough. She says it will cost Peter 5 quid to open his mouth,* i.e., to open marriage negotiations with her father. She says some girls nowadays do like the fellows so well they run off and marry them without any lobola transaction, but she would not do so, as she wouldn't want to earn the enmity of her parents. She says also that a girl is proud when a man is willing to pay a high lobola price for her.

---

*A quid is one pound sterling.

199 Johannesburg I

Ballinger's speech on "Civilized Labor Policy" at Witwatersrand Church Council (Interdenominational). Natives and non-Europeans seemed to sit where they pleased. There were seven natives, one Indian and no colored present.

Ballinger indicated parallel between indus. develop. of South Africa and that of England from 1880–1910. He said the election of 1924 (the National-Labor Pact) marked the disintegration of a liberal native policy in South Africa. He said the Civilized Labor Policy, ambiguous as it is, is part of the economic color bar legislation of the country. He criticized the South Africa policy of promoting public prosecutors to be magistrates. He claimed wage rates for natives in South Africa have stood still for nearly fifty years. He said the Industrial Conciliation Act cannot apply to pass-bearing natives because of the conflict with pass laws and the Master and Servants Act.

He said the prosperity of South Africa and Joburg is based on the moral degradation of hundreds of thousands of native workers—on prostitution and sodomy.

He said he supports a "realistic" policy of demanding a wage for natives based on the cost of living in urban communities—i.e., an urban minimum wage which he fixes at £ 6.10.0. Ray Phillips suggested the determination of a minimum wage according to local conditions.

Ballinger warned that the European worker in general will have to pay the price for its neglect of the native worker.

Non-Europeans took no part in the discussion.

Another big ball at Jack Phillips. All colored, though it was the hall's 2d anniversary celebration and natives contribute greatly to its support.

Some of these colored can dance tangos, rhumbas, fox trots, etc. with more grace and fancy steps than any American Negroes I've seen outside of the Savoy.[57] They make the ditty Washington crowd look like novices.

Most of them bewail the lack of economic opportunity and say passing is justified *for that* reason alone.

These people here surely go in for singing in a big way. The kids are rehearsing for their choir contests, Eistedfodd, etc.*

Several people have asked me what I thought of the designation "Eurafricans" which some South African colored apply to themselves

---

*Created by a committee of Europeans and Africans in 1931, the Eistedfodd was modelled after the Welsh music festival of the same name and featured music, literary, oratorical, and dancing competitions.

and seemed tickled when I replied that I saw no reason for a people to parade their bastardy.

It's common for people here to tell me I would be taken not as colored, but as Portuguese.

Benoni is a city east of Joburg.[58]

Coloreds can stay in town but natives cannot. But there is a large colored section in the Native location and a municipal sub econ. housing project for colored. Though living in the same location with only a road between the native and colored sections, the colored must have a permit to enter the native section. There's no fence or gate, but the police hop on them when they cross the line. The colored teachers in the colored school have to get permits to come to the native clinic to join my discussion group.

There has been a proposed rebuilding of the native location at a cost of £1,300,000. Only a few of the location houses have been built by the municipality but most are built by the residents themselves at a 10s stand rent per month.

There is a fine new colored school on the location—a government school. . . . The government school for colored is the only school for colored in the Benoni area. It has over 500 pupils and 15 teachers. The principal, a colored man, attended Fort Hare and says it is the best non-European school in South Africa.

By Govt. order, Afrikaans is the teaching medium in the colored school—English is secondary.

There is only one government school for natives in all the Transvaal—the primary school at Pimville.

Conference with Dr. Anning, Benoni Health Officer. [He told me about] t.b. among native mine workers. T.b. definitely an economical disease. Incidence of death from t.b. greater among colored than either natives or whites throughout South Africa [because of] slum conditions and poverty.

No birth control or V.D. preventative work among non-Europeans at Benoni yet. Natives respond eagerly to birth control clinics, in the few instances in which they have been instituted, as at [Pieter] Maritzburg.

Says the Benoni location is one of the worst. Huts are ugly, dilapidated, dirty. No trees [and there are] pits and mud in the road. Littered with paper and trash. Asiatic Bazaar, a part of and separated from native location only by a road. About 15,000 natives on location. . . .

A few of the Benoni location houses are built by municipality but most are built by people themselves—at 10s stand rent per month. Many shacks of corrugated tin, etc.

Tin shacks in back yards owned by Indians [are] rented to natives at £ 1.10 per month.

Slums built up in the location. [We visited one place, where] 9 people—3 adults and 6 children—in one room, rented at L 1 per month . . . from an Indian shop-keeper. Cooking over a square tin in same room. Father and mother work in town, father as a store boy and mother as domestic servant. Walls covered with newspapers. One small window. They have been only a month in this room. Before that they lived in one room on another street.

Another one room place of tin, with window boarded up. 5—all adults—in one room—pay 17/6 per month rent from an Indian. Only one bed—tub sitting on bed to catch rain-water leaking through. Very old man sleeps on floor. Burlap bags tacked up to try to stop leaking. Washing on line in same room.

The Indian family of 5 who are the "landlords"—i.e., who rent the "Stand"—live next door in 2 rooms in more filth and squalor than their "tenants."

Visit to exercises of Ferreira Indian government school. Mr. Desai, principal. Some 200 Indian students. Standard III. The principal is opposed to the admission of colored students on nationalist and "pure racialist" grounds. (I noted how Rev. Sigamoney played on Indian nationalism, Indian traditions and centuries of culture, etc. in his remarks on my talk to his students). But many of Desai's teachers are colored (many of them living socially as "white") because there are not enough trained Indian teachers prepared for the jobs.

Peter tells me that this same Desai recently came to him in search of a good medicine man (in whom he has faith) to cure his ailing wife.

The Indian children participants were all well dressed and costumed. But the two Indians on either side of me were pointing out the particular Indian castes and types to which the children belonged—Hindus and Mohammedans, Parsees, Madras (black) Indians. One belonged to Aga Khan's group, etc. Many were coal black, though their hair is straight.

One of the acts was a group of Indian pupils in a Plantation scene.

They were blackfaced (though the skin of some of them was blacker than the greasepaint used). They represented the typical white man's caricature of the American Negro. They opened by singing a la minstrel "My Old Kentucky Home." Real minstrel stuff. I wondered as I watched it whether Indians have forgotten the Indian coolies on the South African sugar plantations. Beside me, Sigamoney and Naransamy voiced disapproval of the act as indicating bad taste.

The colored teacher who moved the vote of thanks for my talk at Benoni, voiced a timid, halting hope that natives and colored people could get together. But he said he didn't think the third group in the location community, the Indians, could be brought into the united group, because the life and outlook of the Indians are so different from that of colored and natives. He said there had been unfortunate leadership in the past and poor organization. He received acclaim when he said that one way of improvement would be through business and cooperatives.

I have noticed that whenever, in my "pep" talks, I criticize and condemn the church, I get an enthusiastic response from a large part of my audience. Similarly whenever I make reference to the interest of the American Negro in the African and to black chauvinism.

In discussion, they all bewail their economic suppression, their poverty, their low wages and don't seem to have any idea as to what to do about it.

I told them how vital it would be if there were organizations active on every South African location, with ultimate possibility of a federation of location organizations.

I'm getting sick of the deference (sometimes I wonder if it isn't mockery) with which all the blacks say, "Yes Doctor."

Under existing conditions the young African becomes completely demoralized. In every location groups of young boys can be seen shooting craps in the open. They scurry away when they first see me, thinking that I'm a cop—but when they are reassured, they return and resume their game for pennies and tickeys. Their dice have a very large black spot where the "1" is on ours. I accepted a shilling bet from one young fellow on the verandah of the Western Native Township Communal Hall during a dance there—and lost. I asked to see the dice and he deftly changed them on me, though my eye caught the act. I withdrew, minus the shilling. These kids are real sharp.

Miriam Gamiet, who types for an Indian company, and says she is one of the few colored typists in South Africa, says there is practically no opportunity for such work unless a girl can pass (as she can). She was amazed when I told her how common it was for American Negro girls to be typists, and how much employment of the white collar kind was found in the American Government by Negroes. She was also shocked by the salaries paid to Negro school teachers in places like Washington [D.C.].

Conversation with Jack Simons: says European workers are becoming good for nothing under the present system—e.g. painters who stand about smoking and receive painters' pay while natives actually do the painting at low wages. Both employers and unions connive in this state of affairs. Same condition applies on mines.

Jack says [white] unions have not protested against recent mine action in reducing number of European workers because of union agreement with mines not to press for increased pay, etc. in return for mine recognition of union.

Jack very much interested in attitude of native toward whites. He thinks some whites can win their confidence, but he realizes that beneath their pleasant exterior, the native is distrustful of whites and is often pulling their leg.

He says everyone but the police knows that natives who are even semi-educated, write out their own special passes.

Jack denies that there is anything to Dr. Wulf Sach's theory that long breast-sucking made the Bantu dependent. He says the Bantu in the towns is plenty independent and sharp. He thinks the black can dupe the white more easily than vice versa.

He feels that government policy has been shortsighted in that there has not been enough land for natives and coupled with food shortages and the attraction of higher wages, this has forced them into the towns. Here they have been living in slums which must be cleared out. He feels the native housing problem is well on the road to solution, but colored and Asiatic slums in places like Vrededorp remain.

Location conditions will force greater unity, cohesion and organization among natives. A place like Orlando, with an ultimate population of 60,000 would be a fine soil for proletarianization of native thinking and development of organizations. "But it will also be a fine target for bombing by the government," says Jack.

Jack does not believe that the municipality suffers a loss from maintenance of municipal locations. He points out that land and construction costs are listed at excessive figures, that salaries of European inspectors, health officers, . . . location superintendents, and . . . town inspectors who never go to the locations [and] the municipal native affairs department maintenance charges, are included in the cost of maintenance figures.

Jack says that there is much bribing of officers on locations re stores open at illegal hours, liquor, lodger regulations, etc. But that greatest abuse is in respect to transfer of permits to inhabit houses on locations. He says Venables has submitted that such abuses are frequent and that a couple of clerks have had to be fired for accepting bribes. . . .

He says Venables told him that location superintendents do no police work, but that in talking with location superintendents he discovered that they do this indirectly—by having the location—and often the state—police do the jobs for them.

He agrees that South Africa will follow America in institutionalized lynching (they virtually have individual lynchings now) as the natives develop and the conflict between the races becomes more acute. Then the vigilante groups, the S.A. equivalent of the K.K.K., etc., will crop up.[59] The existing greyshirt organizations are pointing the way.[60]

Jack says that living in his section (Braamfontein), there are no native trains (except when big days are held at the zoo) and that when he desires to have natives . . . come to his room, he must go and fetch them and bring them to the meeting on the tram-cars. A native cannot ride on these cars unless he is accompanying his employer.

Jack says it is a common subject for conversation among European matrons that their servant girls get pregnant—but that this is entirely their fault in that they insist on building their servant's quarters away from the house and affording their domestics opportunity for amusement.

Jack says Rev. Ray Phillips is minion of the mines and that Ballinger told him that Phillips is responsible for getting him kept out of the compounds for five years.

Phillips was overheard by a native messenger telling a Chamber of Mines official that "less niggers and more white men ought to be employed in the clerical positions of the mines." Also cf. Phillips' boast in his book that he stopped a native mine compound uprising by showing Charlie Chaplin films.[61]

The effect of Vereeniging and the publicity given to police abuse of tax and liquor raids, etc. has resulted in softening of police methods. The pick-up vans have been less in evidence on the locations.

Conversation with Issy Diamond [about his prison experience]. When he arrived, he found 150 naked natives standing shivering in a corridor—in winter—Sept. Whites have cubicles in which to dress.

Blacks bullied and shouted at; Europeans treated more courteously. Most brutal assault in his presence was a European warder hitting a native prisoner in the mouth with handcuffs. One comrade, Walton, received a term of imprisonment for exposing cruelty to native prisoners which could not be absolutely confirmed.

Complete racial segregation in the prison. Very filthy work, even in European prison, is done by natives, e.g., digging streets. All pick and shovel work.

European [prisoners are] given some sort of opportunity to learn a trade—but not natives.

No European prisoners are hired out of prison, but native prisoners are. Why doesn't Left movement protest this unfair competition with labor?

A lot of native prisoners are hired out to white farmers—the employer gives them board and lodging in camps, with European warder in charge.* They don't come back to prison at night. [White] farmers asking cessation of tax collection so that more natives can be imprisoned and hired out.

[Diamond detailed the] difference in diet between Europeans and blacks. During whole period of imprisonment, natives receive no bread—only porridge, mealies and *machau*†—a sour mealie—no matter how long they are in for—except meat once a week. The Europeans on other hand receive 8 oz. of mealie meal, 8 oz. of bread and a pannikin of tea in a.m.; 8 oz. of meat, 8 oz. of bread and soup (if chosen) at lunch (except Monday); 8 oz. of bread and tea in evening. At two intervals during day—also tea.

European prisoners have a library, but not natives.

Owing to herding of these natives together for such a long time, sodomy is very common and is well-known, but no interest is taken in it by officials. But it is punished on European side.

Native is just thrown on streets when released. A native ex-criminal has no chance of employment, for Nat. [Native] Affairs Department can check up because all native employees must be registered with a pass. This means discharge of natives.

---

*A warder is a prison guard.

†*Machau* (or *mahewu* or *maheu*) is a "drink made of thinned, slightly-fermented mealie-meal porridge." (Jean Branford, *A Dictionary of South African English*, 3d ed. (1987), p. 207.)

His mother employed a native and three days later a letter came from Nat. Affairs Department. "Dear Madam: the native in your employ has been sentenced to years and lashes for rape. Kindly keep this information secret."

He was not discharged and worked for her for 18 months and at end of period, the native told her, "Mrs., you have saved my life—I have been tramping and starving for 12 months. I have saved enough money now and I am going home."

Diamond thinks the Afrikander does not really hate the native—that the native is in his blood and that he has been brought up with him. But that before other whites the Boer feels it is necessary to affect a pose of hatred. He says this bitterness has been deliberately fostered by the Dutch church and the press.

At the Center entertainment the other night [1 December], the young natives booed when the African Entertainment Committee put on an Afrikaans skit and sang "Sarais [Sarie] Marais."*

The men danced with hats on as usual, but after all, there are no cloakrooms in these native halls.

The native school teachers at the Ritz last night were very timid about dancing and couldn't dance nearly as well as the colored. The explanation is that this was largely a church group.

They talk about "Native Time," but though natives come late to these functions, it is because they have to work so late for their European masters.

Real culture contact—the African Entertainment Company doing several black face numbers, including "Sing, Sister, Sing" and "Swanee River."

Children from local Methodist Primary School carrying on their concert from 8:30 p.m. to 4:30! Their excuse is that this is necessary in order to avoid conflict with the curfew hour and having children and parents stopped at night. They surely love to sing!

It is pitiful to see the scores of natives, including the entertainers and the bandsmen, crowd around the Secretary's counter after the functions asking for "special passes" so they can get home safely. Lithebe writes the passes out for "Willie," "Lucy," "May," "George," etc.

---

*"Sarie Marais" is an Afrikaans folk song probably written about the time of the Anglo-Boer War. The first two couplets were adapted from an American song, "Ellie Rhee." By the 1930s, the song had achieved widespread popularity among Afrikaners.

[Discussion with] Wolfson—Tailoring Workers Industrial Union.[62] Says there is a growing recognition that natives must be organized and must receive higher wages.

No natives in European unions in the Transvaal. In Durban, in Textile Union, natives and colored are in European union. In Joburg, natives have parallel union in textile industry. In Transvaal in tailoring trade, Europeans and Indians have separate unions; but executives meet together and exchange delegates. Natives in tailoring industry are unskilled and as yet unorganized.

Tailoring union just made an agreement for a week's holiday with pay for all workers in industry, including natives. Have also gotten a minimum of 30/ per week for natives.

Leather Workers have colored members—[and] a few natives who are skilled. During a strike in Leather Workers Union, though natives are not members, they too were pulled out and paid same rate of strike pay.

Large numbers of skilled native workers were kicked out of [furniture] industry a few years ago because white workers refused to work with them. Natives then started independent manu. [manufacturing] and European employers protested and European employees wanted to hold demonstrations on these native workers. But Kulk [Kalk][63] protested vs. this and a parallel union called "No. 2 branch of the Furniture Workers" was organized. An organizer employed at £ 1.10 per week.

Wolfson and Kulk say it is well-known that in mines natives actually do most of the skilled work. Mine management putting natives into jobs formerly held by whites.

In State Street Works at Pretoria, Europeans are being displaced by natives despite civilized labor policy. Work too hard for whites.

[Wolfson] says workers can be prosecuted for accepting less than the legal wage. Some tailor shops (small) employing "pickanins" do not pay union wage. Frequent cases of natives being employed and paid at unskilled worker's rate, but actually doing skilled work.

European unions are not yet ready to actively support development of native union organizations. Wolfson says he was almost lynched for issuing a union card to a native in his union. More willingness of Europeans to organize where they work side by side with natives.

Greater hostility often shown by South African Eng. than Boers even. They say Sachs is wrong in his interpretation and [that Boers are] often more progressive than traditionally conservative Eng. craft unionists. A lot of unions with Afrikaners are more militant than others.

De Vrees [De Vries],[64] Secy. of Trades and Labor Council,* says Afrikaners more opposed to native worker than English craftsmen.

National Trades and Labor Council has about 60,000 organized members, mainly Europeans.

Council feels that natives should organize themselves and council will give advice, etc. Labor Department will not recognize a union unless it is properly representative—union should have about 40% of workers for registration. No certainty as to whether pass-bearing natives can be in registered unions.

Organizations not urged to affiliate with Trades Council but they are welcome. Affiliation charge is 2d per member per month for Europeans and natives. Movement on foot to organize an African Trades Council.

Attitude of Trades and Labor Council is to let natives, on their own initiative, organize their separate unions. This has started and they are using the same constitution as the European Trades and Labor Council. Trades Council gives no financial assistance to organization of native workers.

Many of the S. A. [South African] trade unions have express provisions in their charters limiting membership to Europeans. About 50% of unions in Trades Council have color bar.

Unions with no color bar: Typographical Union—native, colored and Indians. Absence of color bar is most effective means of keeping natives out, as they must get same wages as Europeans and employers, under such conditions, would employ Europeans.

In Transvaal no natives working in typo. [typographical] industry but there are coloreds and Indians. In Cape all races are represented. In Durban, industry comprises Europeans and Indians. But in Cape, under Apprentices Act, colored who formerly controlled 75% of work in industry, have been pushed out, and now industry is 90% Europeans.†

De Vrees says it is his opinion that state here actually gives great protection to European workers. State has now taken over functions formerly performed by trade unions—through Unemployment Benefit Act, Apprenticeship Act, Wage Act,[65] Industrial Conciliation Act[66] and

---

*Although the South African Trades and Labour Council admitted all races to its ranks, there were only two black trade unions out of thirty-eight affiliated to the council in 1937. And these two unions were not included in wage agreements.

†By establishing minimum educational (a Standard VI education) and maximum age qualifications for individuals entering trades, the Apprenticeship Act (1922) boosted white workers by dramatically decreasing the number of Coloured workers who qualified as artisans.

Mines and Works Act.[67] Government now performs this function of protection gratis and thus weakens the position of trade unions which must charge for such services.

Natives have generally and willingly supported European workers in their strikes and demands. In several instances natives on strike have been given strike pay by European unions.

Miss Johanna Cornelius (Garment Workers Union).[68]

Under Industrial Council agreement European pressers in clothing industry are due to get £ 6.10 and natives £ 3. As result, many Europeans have lost their jobs and the jobs of others have been saved only by exempting them from the European wage. Only one European presser in the whole industry gets the agreement wage. A clear-cut example of native low wage pulling down white wage. The union is now pressing for a flat rate of £ 4 per week for European and non-European workers as protection to European wage rates.

Whites and blacks work on same basis in clothing industry. White men and white girls are willing to work in same factory with black men—but the white girls stubbornly refuse to work beside any non-European girls. The white workers in the industry are mainly Afrikaners.

Several shops in the industry are manned wholly by non-Europeans— colored and Malay girls and native men—except for bosses. Native men work in all the clothing factories. In some factories even the main cutters are natives. Natives do pressing—a very skilled job—in most of the factories. Colored and Malay girls do the machining.

Colored, Malay, and Indian workers are admitted into the European clothing workers union. They are jim crowed at meetings—but natives are not admitted at all.

Conversation with [Edwin] Mafutsanyana [Mofutsanyana], secretary of the local C.P.[69] There are now some 200 members in Joburg— mostly Bantu. In 1927 when he joined the Party, there were only a handful of natives in it; but subsequently real progress was made among natives in some places, as at Vereeniging.

C.P. pamphlet on Vereeniging is in preparation, but very little publication on native problem has been undertaken by the Party. Re C.P.'s attitudes toward the [South African] Labor Party—he says it is a policy subject to local variation. The strategy relates to the coming elections only.[70] There is a close cooperation between the C.P. and Labor Party in Durban, but not in Joburg. In Joburg the Labor Party repudiates C.P. support and says that the C.P. can help it best by attacking it publicly.

The C.P.S.A. has gone through the usual "crises." The pendulum has swung to the extreme left—and came a purge—and now to the right—with another purge. [The Party has a] confused and hesitant policy re natives.

[Mofutsanyana] admitted too much emphasis on European workers. At present practically all of Party's activity being devoted to European worker, though there are some small groups at Sophiatown, Vrededorp and Benoni.

The so-called African "intellectuals" are definitely workers.[71] They are only "intellectuals" in the sense that they have had a bit more formal education than the masses. Therefore they could probably be employed and trained as organizers of masses.

He admitted that Party is now suffering from its past mistakes. In past it named every intellectual untrustworthy and a traitor to the cause.

Split in the Party on . . . whether establishment of a Native Republic would be a step toward a worker's and peasant's government. [The issue was] not really understood and often misinterpreted. Some affirmed, others denied. Was this a revolutionary move toward national liberation?

But Comintern stopped discussion on this slogan as abstract, since conditions did not warrant its discussion here: i.e., there was no practical reason for an internal fight in the Party over it. It is now said to be only a "prospective" policy and is being held in abeyance. Present slogan is liberation of all workers—black and white.

The S.A. trade unions are little more than government company unions, with an aristocracy of privileged labor. They almost approximate German and Italian labor corporations.

In both trade unions and the C.P. there seem to be too many "office" and swivel-chair organizers. They are all overcome by the "insuperable obstacles" confronting them.

Native Kaffir-beer bootleggers* depositing £ 8–£ 10 weekly in bank posing as "washer-women." . . . Bank manager naively comments on "how much money can be made washing clothes."

Ray Phillips, American Missionary Board man and doing recrea-

---

*A bootlegger is someone who sells liquor illegally.

tional work among natives for the Chamber of Mines, properly has *The Rotarian* among his periodicals.

Interesting to speculate to what extent natives, socially ignorant, could be used by fascists. There is already a good deal of anti-semitism among natives. In case of a depression and a resultant acute situation developing between white employers and privileged white workers, to what extent could native masses, already justly distrustful of white workers, incipiently nationalistic, restive, and ready for organization, be duped by clever fascist demagogues?

Natives can get around the breach of contract provisions when they are on a day pay (24 hour notice) basis of employment. Those trying to organize them are encouraging them to make all new work contracts on this basis, so that they can legally cease work.

There is no overt publicity on racial lines by African traders—no demand that people "patronize their own race."

Colored and Indians don't allow natives in their sports organizations but natives allow colored in theirs.

Escom House, the twenty-one story "skyscraper," has a separate entrance for Africans, and they use the goods elevator. But Indians go in the main entrance and up the passenger elevator, because they do business there.

December 4

Visit to Orlando—Saturday night. Pitch darkness as we drove through dirt streets with lights off. The natives pay dearly for their amusement—2/6 for this "concert and dance" tonight. The people giving the affair have to pay £3/15 (the manager says £5), for the five piece band, and £2/10 for the hall (the hall rents for £2/10 up to midnight and for £5 till 4 o'clock). On Saturday nights like tonight, they rent the hall till midnight for £2/10 and take a chance on the violation of the Sunday closing ordinance after then. The dance will continue till 4 a.m. They also pay 15s for the rent of the piano.

They sell refreshments and food. The affair is given by the Orlando

Bantu Musical Association, a choir of 17 members, who divide any profits. They are assisted by another local choir. The managers think the hall charges are very exorbitant.

The official admission charge is 1/6, but they charge Joe Hellman 2/6 each for the five of us (Dr. and Mrs. Sachs, Joe, Ellen, and me—this was certainly an injustice to me). When we told the managers about the cleverness of the ticket-seller, they laughed heartily.

Announcement made in three languages—English (by choir leader) and translated into Xhosa and Sesuto. Chairman admonished crowd to be good as there are "white faces present" and also one (me) all the way from America ("the United States of America"). He also announces that he, the choir leader, is of royal blood, and this evoked applause. The leader wears a stiff dress collar, white vest and Tux, and is very fussy.

Before this the manager of the concert placed special seats in front of the audience for us. When we insisted that we wanted to sit on the side, he replied that he "must show us the proper *respect*."

The first choir number was *lousey* [*sic*]. I "bought" several performances for a tickey each and one man bought himself off for 6d.

Not much dancing. The usual few whirling about with weird and fancy steps in solo dances. Music not good and crowd was poor.

December 5

Peter [Dabula] says in old tribal days penalties for illegal children were heavy, on both men and women. But today, in a place like Joburg, these penalties are removed and couples take many more chances and there is considerable illegitimacy.

John looks upon a child as a burden, which "keeps a man from getting ahead," and seems quite unconcerned about the one he casually mentions is to be born to him soon by an unwed mother.

Peter says it is all rot to say that the domestic girls won't live in their mistresses' homes. He claims that mistresses have never wanted them there. Mrs. Hellman claims that the society matrons in their society group discussions allege that the girls simply refuse to live in the house, and demand a separate outside quarter for themselves (though she admits that the mistresses themselves don't want the girls in their houses). A number of fellows live almost entirely off domestic girls.

Peter charges that another factor is the mutual fear of the white masters by both white mistresses and domestics. It is common gossip among the girls that the white "gentlemen" of the homes in which they work make constant "passes" at them. Peter says Ruth has had many such experiences in her work.

Visit to Prospect Township—Sunday noon.[72] The place is being vacated and is now half-demolished, but throngs are everywhere—congregated in front of the squalid shanties, in backyards, on corners, in the roads—all chattering, but not much gayety in evidence. Lots of drinks. The usual piles of rock, barren ground, ugliness and lack of anything suggesting care or beauty.

We were eyed suspiciously by the inhabitants (many of whom are [boot] "leggers" as we cruised about, but John spied a woman he knew who used to be his "sister-in-law"; i.e., he used to sleep with her sister.

She took us to her hut—one in a long connected row of corrugated tin huts—almost lean-to's. There were two parallel rows separated by a dirt causeway of about 20 ft. and the whole thing fenced in with tin. Colored and natives all live together in the tin-hut yard, but the rest of Prospect Township seems predominantly native.

It had a bed and makeshift furniture. This was mainly in a yard mainly colored. She called in all her relatives to meet the "American Doctor" and then went out and brought in three bottles of soda water for us to drink. [All] the while we were sitting there intoxicating ourselves with the smell of the heavy stuff she had cooked away and sold. In the meantime a half-paralyzed drunk stumbled in to recover the hat he had left a short time before.

After a bit of reassurance by John, she became more friendly. She was already a bit "mellow" through sampling her own stock—and reached behind a curtain and brought out a half-pint bottle of brownish-yellow looking stuff, which, without comment, she poured into glasses for us. After that we were all friends and soon another bottle was produced to replace the dead one and we were all good friends. This half-brandy, half whiskey-like concoction she told me is called "sea-water" and can be made very quickly—"much more quickly than American liquor." It was amply powerful.

She apologized because her husband—a colored man from the inevitable wedding photo on the wall, though she is certainly native—was out at work. They were happy for me to take some snaps and posed willingly. All colored but the lady of the hut.

Drunks were all about. A drunken young woman at the yard gate told me that when I got in there they wouldn't let me out again and that she would live with me. She wasn't too bad to look at, at that.

We were invited to return again.

Wemmer Barracks: dormitories for native single men (or men whose wives are not with them) who live in town by special permit. Municipally controlled. 294 rooms, consisting of 10 and 6 men each who sleep on cots. Cost of accommodation is 10/- per month. They must provide their own food.

They have a sports ground and an African in charge of sports with 2 African assistants.

Office has 3 African clerks who check records, entries and discharges, messages, etc. Superintendent is European and 2 European clerks.

This municipal activity competes with the Bantu Sports Club which caters to the mine workers. An African, Dan Twala, is in charge of this club.

After lunch, we went into the Wemmer Barracks, following a small group of costumed Zulu dancers. They belonged to Shoemaker's troupe and we (Vil-Nkomo and I) went into Shoemaker's barracks room (he shares it with 11 others). The fellows refused us permission to take snaps at first, but Vil shot Shoemaker a line about how whites in England and even America had told me about the "great Shoemaker" and he wilted and smiled and ordered his troupe to pose for a picture. I gave him 2 bob. He and his troupe were to dance again at 4:40 p.m. at Salisbury Jubilee Compound.

We drove slowly through the notorious "Malay Location" in Vrededorp.* Teeming masses in the streets—natives, colored and Indian—[and] the usual dreary shacks. Beer sellers out in front on the watch for customers and police. This section is a slum now being "cleared."

As we drove along Portland Avenue—Brixton, we could see Orlando in the distance—off behind a huge mine dump, and looking like a huge assemblage of dog houses with shiny tin roofs.

Next rode through Western Native Township. . . . In Western

---

*Founded in 1896, the Malay Location for Indians and Coloureds in the southwest part of Vrededorp had a similar fate as Prospect Township (see note 72, this section). The Indian location became known as Pageview.

Native Township are to be seen the same squat brick shanties with tin roofs and crowds everywhere in the streets.

There was a guard at the gate, but he didn't stop us as we drove through—nothing like Orlando.

. . . Encountered a Basuto wedding. A young couple were being led about in the middle of the road by a small dancing group; the bride affected the usual shyness and shame, with head bowed and lowered eyelashes. The couple, according to custom, must "follow the leader" and go as the wedding group commands. [I] had to get permission from the mother-in-law to take a picture. They posed under a small white parasol held over them by a young bridesmaid. They were soon whisked away in a big car. Both were well-dressed.

Just across the road we encountered another and more elaborate *Ndunduma.** A more elaborate one than the other, but with the usual burlap sack enclosure and earthen dance floor. The Harmony Kings Jazz Band, consisting of a piano, 2 saxes, drum and banjo was playing while 2 girls danced together and a disconsolate-looking fellow sat watching.† The admission was one shilling, but as Vil-Nkomo knew the people running it, we got in free. John and I had one dance by John coaxing the two shy girls apart and then we left.

In front of the gates of Western Native township, a young comrade was speaking in defense of Dhladhla, who is in jail for contempt of court because of his public comments on the Vereeniging case which is still in court. A small, diffident group stood by, while a stern looking, rain-coated European C.I.D. [Criminal Investigation Department] man stood a few feet away and was the most alert listener. His side-car motorcycle was parked a short distance away.

We drove through Sophiatown next and there teeming thousands gutted the streets, all seemingly strolling aimlessly about. (What else was there for them to do?) Noted a black "golfer" in white flannels coming in from his "golf game" in a nearby field.‡ Plenty of drunks, male and female. The men carrying sticks everywhere. A Zulu war dance troop was putting on its act until it had to duck the sudden, heavy downpour which cleared the streets like magic.

On the way back we went through Fordsburg,[73] where the Euro-

---

Ndunduma was a form of Zulu proletarian concert and dance developed in Johannesburg locations in the 1920s and 1930s. M. Dikobe describes an *ndunduma* in his *Marabi Dance* (1973).

†Led by Jacob Maduse, the Harmony Kings were a prominent Johannesburg band that broke away from the Jazz Maniacs.

‡Because Africans were prohibited from playing on white golf courses, they had to make do with open fields.

pean miners held out in the mine strike of 1922. They were bombarded from the air and by cannon planted on a nearby mine dump by order of General Smuts. Fordsburg is now inhabited by poor whites, colored and Indians.

Passed by a gang of "amalaitas," young native ruffians, who hold spontaneous fighting tournaments which resemble cock-fights, and which are strictly private.[74]

Amalaitas like Cape Town skollies—mostly young kitchen boys who attack and rob people in the streets. They go in gangs of never less than four. Recent tendency for them to attack Europeans. Use knives, knobkerries, sticks and sjamboks as weapons.* "Amalaitas," a Xhosa or Zulu word, means "rogues."

Old Newclare just outside the fence from Western Native township and on the side opposite Sophiatown.† On a Sunday afternoon, is an exciting experience (to put it mildly). It is a private township like Sophiatown and is in terrible shape. The whole town loitered about in streets. The population is African and colored and they live side by side and the children, at least, play together freely. Indians and Malays also there.

Many "blanket" natives were seen strolling about in Newclare— very colorful in their bold-design blankets, rakishly slung about their bodies.‡

We stopped at one roadside meeting and were looked upon with great suspicion by the small group squatting about the young speaker as we approached. We sat down and the speaker immediately stated (in Barolong) that it was too bad, but they were merely assembled to raise money to bury a dead man and that though they didn't know what the strangers expected to hear and were there for, the meeting was ended. It was explained that I was not a C.I.D. man but an American Negro, and then the atmosphere became less hostile and I was invited to speak. I shot the usual line and though there was curiosity and interest, there was no great enthusiasm in this stolid group. I was courteously thanked and gave a shilling for the collection. They agreed to let me take a snap and sat the Paramount chief among them who was present on a bench in front—just next to the speaker.

---

*A sjambok is a thick whip made of hippopotamus or rhinoceros hide.

†Newclare (a name derived from the nearby suburbs of Newlands and Claremont) was originally proclaimed a European area but sales were so poor that plots were sold to Coloureds and Indians. Later Africans moved in, but they were evicted in 1937 and forcibly removed to Meadowlands. The area is currently a Coloured residential area.

‡The wearing of blankets was usually associated with Basotho migrants, but Xhosa migrants also wore blankets.

Just behind (a few feet) the camp stool meeting a native woman was busily engaged in "planting" a bottle of Kaffir beer in the ground—in full daylight.

At the corner, as we drove off, we encountered a personal fracas— one native chasing, throwing rocks at, and threatening with a stick, a younger fellow who was on the run. The roads were cluttered up with drunks in all stages.

Another block and a crowd was assembled about another fight. A woman, bleary-eyed, hovered over a helpless, bleeding and battered, well dressed, young drunk—whose head rolled about as he sat sprawled on the ground. He was bleeding from the mouth and head cuts. Soon his punisher, a squat, heavy-set, powerful looking fellow, came up, pushed the woman roughly away, stooped over and delivered a series of heavy punches straight in the face of the helpless one. The crowd stood idly by and gazed. Blood gushed from the mouth of the victim in a heavy stream. The woman swayed and wailed. The persecutor was vengeful, the victim uttered not a sound. The puncher yelled out that this man had beaten his wife and he showed me the huge lump on his wife's forehead. She sat mournfully nearby. The puncher said call the pick-up van, he did not care. He was terribly incensed.

Further back in the same yard an *Ndunduma*—back-yard "dance hall"—was in progress. A two piece band—piano and a "kazoo"— playing inside a square enclosure of burlap. Dancing was on the ground. An admission charge was demanded, but as there was little activity, we contented ourselves with a peek inside.

Rushed to Croesus cemetery in quest of a funeral, but were informed that the burial was taking place in a private cemetery at Brixton (Croesus is a municipal cemetery)* where the dead girl was being placed in a grave on top of her mother who had been buried some years ago. After the funeral, the mourners were to return to the house for food and drink.

In Croesus cemetery the policy of racial segregation is pursued also. There is an Indian plot on the Newclare side of the road. On the opposite side is first the colored section and then, further in, the native section.

At the cemetery we could hear the incessant cacophony of chatter, song and laughter from Newclare—3/4 of a mile away.

---

*Croesus Cemetery is the Newclare cemetery for blacks situated next to Croesus, a white township.

Had good service at the Langham Hotel on occasion of Gidoomal's dinner. White employees were very courteous. We used checkroom and elevators, though dinner was held in a banquet room. Some . . . 15 or so Indians present (there were 7 or 8 whites; Jack Phillips and I were the only colored). We were served with cocktails, wine, whiskey and champagne—though this was technically against the law for the non-Europeans present, unless we had all held liquor permits.

Ernest [Sigamoney] sort of "uncle tommed" by profuse thanks to whites for attending the dinner. The Indian women were very quiet.

The Indians present were all Hindus, it seems. At the Agent General for India's office, I was told that there is much bad feeling between the Indians here. The Agent General is being ostracized by some groups, because as a Moslem he married a Hindu woman.* This was told me by the paralytic white man who is the Agent General's secretary.

There is a class division among the Indians. The commercial class is well-off and real exploiters (especially of natives) and they have no concern for the Indian workers.

---

*The marriage of the Moslem Indian Agent to a Hindu woman took place in 1936 and led Gujarati-speaking Hindu leaders to resign from the Natal Indian Congress.

Dr. Wulf Sachs and John

Peter Dabula

Jack Phillips

Bantu Sports Ground

Tennis Players, Bantu Men's Social Centre

Bantu Men's Social Centre

Western Native Township Co-operative Store

Wedding scenes, Western Native Township

Wedding scenes, Western Native Township

Wedding scene, Western Native Township

Workers at Van Ryn Deep Mine, Benoni

Alexandra location

Dr. Xuma's house

Gana Makabeni

Zulu dancers

Pretoria

December 6

Opening session of the Native Representative Council.[1] Rainy day. 12 elected national representatives (one still to be elected in Natal). 4—all chiefs—nominated by the government—Paramount Chief of the Zulus,[2] Chief Poto (Pondoland),[3] Chief Makapane (Transvaal),[4] and a chief from Bechuanaland.

Government considered the opening of the Council to be such an important occasion that it invited the leading chiefs of the union to attend as its guests.

[European officials present include] the 5 prin. [principal] native commissioners (European) in the Union. And the Permanent Secy. for Native Affairs is chairman.

The 16 native Councillors are seated in a semi-circle before tables, in front of the hall and facing the Europeans on the platform. (The European members of the Council are on the platform, of course; on either side of the hall seats are reserved for "chiefs.") All natives on first floor;

European spectators in gallery, and I sat there. About 75 natives present on the floor, including chiefs but excluding Councillors.

One of retainers of Paramount chief of Zulus, a tall, gangling, fussy old fellow, was busy exhorting the chiefs and telling them where to sit. The retainer wore a leopard skin coronet and a red feather on his head.

Native police with rakish hats (like the N.W. [Northwest] Mounted Police), navy blue coats, khaki pants, navy blue leggings, brown belts and black shoes, stand at ease in the side aisles at front of hall and on each side of room.

Opening of the session announced in English, Afrikaans and native language. Prayer in English and native language. Smuts, whom Ballinger described as "South Africa's arch hypocrite," spoke. Read from manuscript and began in English. Deputizing for Gen. Hertzog.

Mentions "substantial increase in land for nat. settlement, better conditions in the reserves, nat. reps. in Parliament," etc. as part of Government's scheme for native welfare.

Natives called here to constitutionally participate in the task of their own government "through wisdom and moderation, statesmanlike uses" of powers urged and hoped for.

Smuts traced development of Council system in Cape and Transkei, and the two other states. Mentions prov. [provision] for location advisory boards under Urban Areas Act and says these boards have been of valuable assistance to management of locations.

Says election due to cooperation with and loyalty to officials of Nat. Affairs Dept. Tells Councillors now fully they can trust the able and sincere officials of the Nat. Affairs Dept. He points this out as a step toward improved race relations. Says it is proved that Nat. Affairs Dept. is making a serious effort to meet needs of native welfare.

Formally declares the first session of the Nat. Rep. Council open and wishes it all possible success. Very mild applause at end of speech. The native audience sits very quietly and apparently only mildly attentive.

The speech was then translated into Zulu by a *white* interpreter! As Ballinger says, that's a pretty bad start. The white interpreter's reading of Smut's speech in Zulu sounds very flat and mechanical. A native now interprets the speech in Sesuto.

Minister for Native Affairs . . . now speaks from manuscript—in Afrikaans.

Smit, Secy. for Native Affairs, is presiding.[5] He invited Rev. (Dr.) John Dube "to say a few words" in reply to the previous speeches.[6] Dube spoke in English and was interpreted. Dube says "thank you for the great addresses delivered." He deems it a "great honor" to say "thank you most heartily." Says councillors hope they may justify hopes held in them. Has a suggestion (not advised by his fellow-members) that there may be a photograph taken with Councillors and Europeans on platform so that this historic occasion may be preserved. Gen. Smuts thanked Dube for his remarks and said he hoped his suggestion would be adopted.

Chairman asked if any other member of Council wished to speak. One of Councillors arose (speaking in Sesuto) to second suggestion of Dube's. Thanked speakers for their speeches; assured them that the Councillors, representatives of entire native population of South Africa, will always be loyal to the government. Apologized for Vereeniging— said it was not representative of native attitudes. Expressed shame for it. Said he didn't know how natives would wipe it off, but they could only hope it would not happen again. He appealed that Vereeniging should be forgotten by Europeans and natives alike. (This ass-licking speech was made by Chief Poto).

For the after-tea meeting, the seating was rearranged, and the European members of the Council and other officials sat at an oblong table directly in front of the native councillors. The natives' Parliament representatives sat in the front row.

Chairman, seated, outlines procedures for the Council as laid down by law and outlined also revenue and expenditures provided for natives by law. Revenue exceeds £ 2,000,000, including the £ 1,000,000 set aside by Parliament for acquisition of lands.

Expenditures on native education, first item to be discussed:

£ 68,598—balance—April, 1938
£ 340,000—grant from Parliament
£ 500,000—2/5 of general tax
—————
£ 908,598 available for education.

Government follows policy of keeping about £ 20,000 in reserve, since it is never known what tax returns will be.

Chairman reads off figures of estimates, etc., announces that education directors of provinces are on hand to answer questions, and invites questions. One chief protests that they can't ask intelligent questions as they've had no chance to study the figures. But chairman makes it apparent that he is capable of steam-roller tactics, if necessary, and says there can be no delay.

Chairman says flatly there can be no question of any added expenditures in the estimates because "there is no more money." "I cannot increase."—there can be no increase in estimates for one province without taking money from other provinces.

Before the afternoon session, Godlo[7] protesting against steamroller tactics of Chairman Smit. Says he hadn't anticipated that.

Mrs. Ballinger also protested vs. steam-roller tactics and fact that Chairman Smit was "talking too much." She said they should accept the education estimates only with a reservation, protesting against their meagerness. Sen. Malcomess cautioned her that he had promised the big-wigs to keep her moderate during this meeting.

The Councillors have many questions re education. Smit says re need for increased salaries for native teachers, that increased salaries for native teachers could only be brought about by decreasing the number of teachers or cutting down on the number of schools. Says Council could recommend this if it desires, but he thinks it would be unwise. It all boils down to Smit's constant iteration: "*I have no money.*"

Smit defends himself by saying that for present he must carry on with native education as before. He admits that it is not satisfactory, but until union government decides what it is going to do about native education, there's nothing he can do.

Impossibility of fair and free discussion due to fact the chairman of meeting is head of department which must, of necessity, be under fire.

Subject to a reservation stating the Council's dissatisfaction with the amount provided for native education, Godlo moved a resolution passing the appropriation of £880,000 (some odd). But Jabavu moved an amendment that action on Godlo's motion be suspended until Native Education is discussed later.

Smit reported the government had ordered him to seek the advice of the Council on the following questions: Should native education be transferred to central government from provincial councils? Under what department should it come? Should there be a native education card?

Smit reads excerpts from Welsh and Inter-Departmental Committee on Native Education reports to natives. Says these committees agree that the government should take over native education, but disagree as to how and in what department it should be controlled.

Native education still remains in the hands of the missions. Provincial Councils have no responsibility for education funds. They merely disperse funds provided by the Native Affairs Department.

Jabavu argued for transfer of native education to Union government and that Union government be held responsible for financing that education.

Heaton Nicholls defending Native Affairs Commission's report.[8]

Said education [was] most controversial of all subjects. Said report made no attack on missions and recognizes great importance of missions to native education. But question is now one of method of support of and control of native education. Missions have had to get money from overseas. Says the commission sought advice from "two of the greatest South African authorities on native education," Dr. Loram[9] and Dr. Roberts,[10] formerly principal of Fort Hare.

Loram says native education should be controlled by department responsible for natives, i.e., under union government (Native Affairs Department).

[Nicholls] argues subtly for differentiated education for "you highly civilized, town dwelling people" as against the "great mass of your people" who live in the countryside. So long as state funds private people supporting native education, native education will be starved. Pleads for native education being "under control of this government and under control of Native Affairs Commission."

Thema attacks policy of education designed to help native (he says "Bantu") "develop along his own lines" as impossible under present conditions in South Africa; and then denies whole validity of concept of any race "developing along its own lines."[11] Argued against division of Africans and the danger of "special education" for different nationalities and for black men. Pointed to inevitable change in Africa. A good speech.

Godlo says natives are suspicious of what is behind report of Native Affairs Commission—that education [be] along the lines suggested by Native Affairs Department.

Question as to establishment of Union Advisory Committee for Native Education (to include two native members nominated by Native Rep. Council).

Godlo moved establishment of such an advisory committee, and demanded to know why two of the Provinces had refused consent for only two natives to sit on a body dealing with native education. This body to be created to carry on during the interview stage—while Union government is deciding what to do with native education. Motion passed.

At the reception for the Council at the woe-begone Dougal Hall on the location, the location managers and location superintendent stood and sang (in native lang. [language]) the African National Anthem. Dougal Hall is a barnlike, dirty and dilapidated place—a great contrast with the Council's Town Hall meeting place.

. . . A lot of the European officials were absent and sent no apologies and no one to speak for them. At the reception, the location officials present made flattering speeches and were very "pally" with the chiefs and with me. The native commissioner for the Pretoria District spoke.

Findlay[12] and Simons went with me to Dougal Hall. One of the native ushers tried to put us up front, but I insisted that I wanted to sit in the middle. He insisted that respect must be shown us and we must sit up at the tables in front of the audience. I told him that I had a right to sit with my people, and this rather stumped him, but he said that then the others (Simons, Findlay and Rev. Stowell[13]) must sit up front. But we sat in the audience.

The European officials on the Nat. Rep Council for the most part treat the native councillors as though they are schoolboys and talk to them sometimes patronizingly and sometimes crossly.

Heaton Nicholls said, when questioned as to the way Smit was chairmaning the Council meeting, "Well, we've got to keep them under control."

According to Mrs. Ballinger, Smit, the Chairman, is quoted as saying at the end of the first day's session: "The Council will be all right. One or two of them may try to make trouble, but the others will keep them in order."

Godlo, Jabavu and Thema are said by Mrs. Ballinger to have expressed resentment at Chief Poto's apologetic speech on the first day.

Rev. Stowell is amazed that the meetings are being held in this new City Hall—in the chamber called "Pretorius Hall." There was a clause in the bill providing for the building that it should be used for *Europeans only*.

Rev. Stowell pointed out that real significance of this meeting was in the unparalleled recognition by the government of a political consciousness among natives and of their right to national expression on political matters. He thinks this will ultimately prove fatal to the government here.

I agree with Rev. Stowell that the native police standing or hovering above the native audience are indicative of the control of Europeans.

Conversation with Mrs. Ballinger:

The European representatives of the natives were in Pretoria for the opening of the Native Rep. Council and held a caucus to lay down their strategy and policy on Native questions.

European representatives of natives in Parliament are not parliamentarians and have misgivings about their power in Parliament.

In the European Reps. caucus, when Mrs. Ballinger raised the question of the right to strike for natives, Malcomess and Berman (the government rep. from the Provincial Council and against social equality) held this to be too *dangerous*. Brookes sided with Ballinger but Rheinold [Rheinallt] Jones remained silent.

Mrs. Ballinger says native representatives don't want native issues on boards for coming elections and must not therefore take too radical a stand.

Simons and Findlay: they are opposed to increasing private landholding among natives on ground that it will give them a petty bourgeois psychology more difficult to organize and radicalize.

They also says that it is harmful to build houses and permit private building of houses in the sub-economic housing schemes, for the same reason. They suggest that workers' *flats* are much better, from radical point of view.

George Findlay, advocate, Pretoria, spoke of the immense cost of the poll tax. The cost of collection comes to close to 50% of the gross proceeds—due to cost of prosecution, conviction and imprisonment of evaders. Thus the tax is not a financial measure at all but an instrument of policy re native—to compel him to work.

Findlay says white worker must be convinced of the truth that the natives want a place in industry and the capitalists want them to have it. That therefore, for their own protection, white workers must organize natives.

Findlay also holds to the theory that interbreeding of white and non-white in South Africa leads to a superior type—that skin pigmentation, broad nostrils, etc. make for better adaptation to this climate.

Mr. and Mrs. Findlay both think that Jack Simons is colored.

December 7

Second day's session of Council Meeting . . . , morning chiefly devoted to stock-breeding, dipping, etc. Mainly educative for the Council members. They listened to a Department of Agriculture expert discuss technical questions. They asked many questions. Thema twitted the Chairman Smit a bit.

A number of the black spectators in the audience . . . were asleep by noon. A very small attendance.

The immigration official at the 2d day's session took a "damned nigger" attitude toward the Council. He was very impatient and aloof and seemed ready to explode at any minute. His attitude was in direct contrast to that of the young expert from the Agriculture Dept.

This morning Godlo, Jabavu and Thema were unavoidably late and when they came to take their seats Smit . . . upbraided them as though they were schoolboys. Told them if they couldn't come on time and not interrupt the proceedings he would recommend to the Minister of Native Affairs (Grobler) that a day's pay be deducted. They were nonplussed and said nothing, but a row is brewing. Sen. Malcomess told Jabavu to raise a point of order and to ask if they were to be treated with proper dignity. But Senator Brookes wants them to talk to Smit "on the quiet!"

Jabavu makes a motion, the sense of which is to attempt [to keep] the tribes homogeneous. Thema points out the impracticability of this, but Smit calls for a second and vote on the motion without permitting further discussion.

By end of second day, Smit's strategy became obvious—i.e., to divide the Councillors on provincial lines, and it seems this is relatively easy to do on questions like education, expenditures released land, etc.

At the end of the second day's session, the Council members decided to hold a caucus. It was difficult to get them together, and then Senator Jones talked to them for 15 minutes. When he left I heard the Councillors, led by Jabavu, discussing their pay and the rumor that they were to get £5 for expenses. Jabavu urged that they should request that their pay be given to them before they leave Pretoria; otherwise they won't get it till after Xmas. With that they broke up and I took their pictures.

In the unofficial meeting between the European Parliament representatives and the members of the Council, Rev. Brookes moved that the Council should organize on the basis of "committee" of the whole so that they could elect their own chairman (the secy. for native affairs is the regular chairman). But this motion was opposed by Sen. Welsh and others. Sen. Welsh, ex-Transkei chief magistrate, denied that the Bunga experience could apply here and that the Bunga is successful.[14] Says that the natives are lost without magistrates present.

[Mrs.] Ballinger says session is a farce. Councillors disorganized, no caucus had been held by them, motions pushed through in five minutes, when they are unprepared to discuss them and vote intelligently.

Jabavu said very timidly that he had almost been "offensive" to the

Chairman (Smit) on the afternoon of the second day. But none of them would raise the issue of their dignity since the chairman had reprimanded three of them like domestic servants that morning when they came in late for the session. Even Senator Malcomess had written a note to Jabavu urging him to challenge Smit, who told them that if they came in late and interrupted the sessions again, he would recommend to the Minister [of Native Affairs] that they have a day's pay deducted.

It was ironic that I should be led to the Secretary of the Interior to request an extension of my permit by Senator Malcomess—a cheap politician, who was talking to me on the way about these damned Russian Jew Communists. He said he has the commercial man's point of view on the native question and that he is interested in making the country peaceful for his grandchildren. He said you can't knock 6-1/2 million people continually against a stone wall without something happening. But the Communists ("like Ballinger") would destroy all he and others could do for the natives. Things had to be done gradually. He would chase all the Communists out of the country. Says businessmen are *for* the natives.

One of the councillors at Pretoria told me that Africans were disappointed because American Negroes don't come to help them; he said we feel we are too much better than the African to think about helping him. He was surprised when I told him how hard it is for an American Negro to get into this country.

Pretoria locations survey. There is no local native affairs dept. in Pretoria. The natives there come under the Public Health Dept. on the assumption that the "native is a disease."[15]
[Pretoria locations are] terribly crowded. Government has been promising new accommodations for years but nothing is done. There are the usual colored sections and the usual fitting Asiatic Bazaar. Colored are not supposed to live in town, but they do, as law can't be enforced through inadequate accommodations for them in locations.
Bantule Location [has] municipally built white concrete houses [with] mud floors, tin roofs.[16] Natives dislike concrete as too cold. Rent at 25s per month for two rooms and 30/ for three rooms. Electricity supplied at 5s per month.
Eight water taps for Marabastad[17] and Bantule Locations. . . . Pools of stagnant water even on dry days where washwomen empty their waste water. No drainage; have had street lights for only a couple of years.

Only short stretch of paved road I've seen in a location is in Marabastad, but [it's] because munic. [municipal] lorries have to use it on way to the inevitable sewage disposal works beside the location.

Native trading store in the location sells plenty of Kaffir malt from which Kaffir beer is made. Small sacks all ready for sale at 3d each. The beer is illegal, but the European factory at Benoni and at Pretoria manufacture the Kaffir malt. Before winning a test case, native traders used to be arrested for selling Kaffir malt.

Rev. Stowell runs a "bootleg" high school in his back yard. No school for natives is supposed to be in town, so his school gets no government financial aid and his teachers are all unpaid volunteers from the European community.

Rev. Stowell said two of his male native teachers cried as I spoke this morning. . . . He said they were especially moved when I told them about white teachers serving under black presidents and principals, black judges trying white cases, etc. [in America].

Teachers' complaints about salaries. These fellows in Pretoria say that top salaries for Transvaal teachers are £5.10. They start at £4.10. The heads of schools get a £ or so more, according to number of pupils in the school.

They also complain that they have no definite pay master. There is plenty of shifting the buck on teacher's salaries between the mission officials and the government.

They say the children must pay a fee of 1s per quarter (until recently 1/6—and still 7/6 for Stan. V and VI pupils) and parents must buy books—amounting to about 15s per year for more advanced pupils.

They say transportation costs are very high from the locations. No municipal buses to locations. Natives can't ride on any buses or trains. A bad and expensive private bus service—charging 4d each way for near locations and 6d for the more distant ones.

Mr. Isaac Makau—about forty—teacher in the Anglican School at Sophiatown. An Afrikaner school inspector got rough with him and said to him: "Do you know to whom you are speaking?" and Makau replied: "Yes, a Kaffir speaking to a Dutchman" and the inspector pushed him out of the classroom and he got sacked.

Pretoria has a reputation for its severe race prejudices and intense jim crow—vide [Washington] D.C.

When natives buy shoes, suits, hats, etc., they must go to a special place in back of the store where they can't be seen; in some places they can try on clothing and in some they can't. Can't use lifts at all.

All natives are called "Jim, Jack, or John; Mary, Annie; or girl and boy," when they enter stores.

Pretoria store addressing account to a teacher who has been teaching for twelve years as "Boy Phillip."

Asylum

Asylum

European Native Representatives at Native
Representative Council

African representatives, Native Representative Council

Session of Native Representative Council

John Dube and Father Huss

Johannesburg II

Discussion with Mr. Boardman, jr. partner of Boltons Furniture Co.

In the furniture trade wage rates laid down by Wage Board arrived at in agreement with Furniture Workers Association, composed of employers and employees. Highest rate is 3/4 per hour. Anyone doing 5 years apprenticeship and thus qualifying as a journeyman, *must be* paid this wage.

Idea of [this] country is that native must be paid less than white, and thus native is excluded from the industry, since employers will not pay this wage to a native. But this doesn't imply that natives cannot do the work as well as whites. The same applies to colored workers. Enough white workers (though not good ones) to supply demand.

Even if employer did bring in a native, white workers would not work on equal basis with a native, though he will have a native working for him. This would require parallel shops—one for natives and colored and another for whites.

Native here thought of as a slave.

Government here is interested not in white labor, but in Dutch labor. Dutch labor not as well qualified as the labor of other nationalities; the Dutchman is not as good as the native; government out to protect Dutchmen everywhere—workers and farmers; really a Dutch government.

Up to 2 years ago, there was a differentiation between colored and native labor in furniture industry; but since then position is uncertain. Unskilled labor gets 15–20s per week; skilled labor gets £ 3–£ 4 per week. Too big a gap between skilled and unskilled labor. White labor in unions are beginning to think that the gap should be closed up some.

White worker quite used to working next to colored in Cape, but not so much here. Some industries here are moving toward colored labor. In a lot of factories here, much of the labor is obviously colored and employees prefer to hoodwink themselves into calling this labor "white."

Mr. Boardman was curious to know how I managed to get in the country and said it is even more difficult for an African to get out.

<hr>

■■■■■■ **December 9**

Lynn Saffery,[1] Institute of Race Relations [said] at executive committee meeting of the Joburg Col.-Europ. [Colored-European] Joint Council,[2] attitude of colored was that Indians and natives create the housing problem, and made representations to effect that municipal Native Affairs departments should compel natives to move out of Vrededorp and Newclare. They crit. [criticize] Indians on grounds that Indians were encouraging natives to live in these areas because of high rents paid. The colored said the natives were on a different social and economic level. They objected to having the colored township (Coronation Township), placed adjoining native location because this would lead to the degeneration of the colored population.[3]

No avoidance of wage regulations in Furniture Industry—too many inspectors.

A new type of furniture business growing up where shops manned entirely by natives but financed by white capital. Make cheap furniture. These are virtually sweat-shops and are not listed as factories. But natives earn much more than they could at any other job. Unorganized and uncontrolled and increasing. Goods sold by native hawkers. They sell a stool for 15/ that it costs Boltons 25/ to make.

The union is very strong in the furniture industry—one of best organized unions in country. Not much dispute—they are too well off. Little unemployment and trade is increasing, thus absorbing white workers. But standard of work is not improving and is far below European standards.

[Saffery] knows of no native union in furniture trade and no native member of a white union, though it has been discussed in the union.

[He gave me a] classic description re government support to farmers when government took large numbers of Dutchmen and put them to work on roads at 1s per hour. He drove through one district with one of ministers about a fortnight after work began and every Dutch worker was found sitting under a tree smoking and drinking and natives were doing the work—being paid by the Dutchmen at rate of 6d per hour.

[He pointed out] personal loyalty of native worker, but he's difficult to organize. If he doesn't like his boss, he'll move and move. Very conscientious worker—more so than white. Hasn't got white man's ambition to make money—beyond a certain point he's not interested. Doesn't like overtime, etc.

Educated natives alert to fact that doors are not open. 7 or 8 years ago in Bantu Center and Joint Council meetings, natives used to refer to government as "our father"—but this has now completely disappeared.

He pointed out that lower officials are harsh toward the native and the higher officials are ignorant of his condition. He said that, e.g., they moved the natives out of town to locations without giving any consideration to or making provision for their transportation to town, where their work is indispensable to town's business. He said that for places like Orlando the Joint Council and Rotary Club had to demand that transportation facilities had to be provided, that private native busses should be licensed, etc.

He said the real burden of location life is the transportation cost. His boys pay about 4/6 per week for transportation which amounts to more than 1/5 of their wages.

He said he would be bitterly attacked for saying so outside his office, but the fact is that native labor in South Africa is simply regarded as slave labor.

Admits that government policy is in conflict with business interest—both because of possibility of cheaper labor for industry, increased business as a result of increased consuming power if natives got higher wages.

He thinks progress will be very slow. He admits that a large section of the population kept in poverty holds back the country and leads to the degeneration of the whole population, which will eventually be pulled down to the level of the slave population, but says the stupid Dutch government doesn't know enough about history to realize this vital fact.

The difference between the U.S. and S.A. is that Americans are materialistic and moving up constantly. Thus the Negro has found his chance in the economic world there. But the South African Dutch are not materialistic, nor financiers, nor business men, nor statesmen. They are backward and are constantly moving down instead of up. They are being pressed both from above and below. They are actually menaced and know it, and are determined to keep the native down for their own protection.

Conversation with J. Grey—ex-C.P.er and Party "angel," expelled as a "provocateur" and fervent supporter of Kotane. He emphasizes financial corruption, intellectual dishonesty and stuffy bureaucracy of recent Party leaders here. Says they have had money in the past but have done absolutely nothing. He was expelled for criticizing the handling of expelled leaders.

Says Mafutsanyana and Gaur Radebe are both puppets of the present leadership and are ineffective office workers.[4] Roux is too naive and trusting and was easily duped and robbed by the crooks who wrecked the Party.

He says the change in present leadership must come from the Comintern. Bitter recrimination. He says all best men have been lost to Party.

Interview with Max Gordon, Secretary of African Laundry Workers Union, [who detailed the] African unions in Joburg.[5]

1. African Laundry Workers Union. About 1500 natives in industry and about 1000 in union. Three years old. Industry almost 100% native. In 1932 Wage Board agreement set wage rates at £ 1.2.6 and £ 1.5 per day. Big strike in 1936 . . . during Empire Exhibition . . . closed down industry completely. [Workers] won the strike in one day [and] got 30–40% increase. Wage now varies from £ 1.2.6 but after year employment, wage is £ 1.7.6 and goes to £ 2.

[Union] asked for Wage Board Inquiry three years ago and are only getting it now—to be held probably in February 1938. When Laundry Workers Union went out on strike in 1926, 27 native workers were arrested for breach of contract and public violence. Got release on a technicality—they were charged under wrong section of the Act. [Union made a] threat to employers that if they didn't concede strikers' demands all workers would go to police station on next day and demand to be arrested. Employers conceded.

One laundry employed 100 scabs (from pass office—Nat. Affairs Dept.) but they couldn't do the work from inexperience.

Laundry workers strike in 1934—lasted 9 months. Strike of employees of one laundry. Employer conceded demands, but refused to recognize the union. Strike lost ultimately. Bad strategy. The Trades and Labor Council supported strike to extent of about £160. The Council has generally given financial support to native strikes.

The Secy. of the Union (Euro.) was arrested and charged with inciting to public violence. All Bantu strikers were arrested but discharged. Arrested for illegal absence from work. They put in a counter claim for 2 weeks wages because their employer had failed to give a weeks notice. He had told them if they didn't like conditions they could quit. They won claim in Magistrates Ct. but lost in higher ct. on employers appeal.

2. African Bakers Industrial Union. About six months old. About 900 natives in industry. About 200 Bantu in Bakers Union. In 1927, 99% of skilled workers in industry were Europeans; today there are 5 native bakers to every 2 Europeans. Wage Board gets over equal wage for equal work by fixing a ratio of 5 assistant bakers to 2 bakers. Work is identical for bakers and assistants. Wage for bakers is £5 to £2.10 for assistants; all others (unskilled) get £1.9.3. This is a new agreement going into effect on first of year.

3. African Commercial and Distributive Workers Union. About 4 months old. Membership of about 300 with about 40 also in industry on Rand. Receive average of 17/6 to £1.

4. African Printing Workers Union. About 2 months old and membership of 150. Mostly unskilled. Skilled workers all colored, Indian and European, who are all in one union. Wage covered in a clause in the Industrial Conciliation Act Agreement.

5. South African Clothing Workers Union (Makabeni).

6. Broom and Brush Workers Union. About 200 in industry and about 80% organized. 135 union members.

7. Furniture, Bedding and Mattress Workers Union (J. Mackay, col. [Coloured] secy.).[6] About 2 years old. About 1100 union members out of 1300 workers in industry. About best organized Bantu union. European workers union assisted their organization to extent of about £200.

8. Bag and Trunk Workers Union. About 2 years old. A registered union. They are about 60% colored, but told the government they are 75% colored.

9. African Tin Workers Union. About 1 year old. Also registered. About 65%–70% colored.

10. African Motor Union. About 3 years old. Union about 400 strong. Only native craft union in existence; others are all industrial.

11. African Stone and Cement Workers Union. A paper organization of about 50 or 60 members. Held strike recently of about 100 unskilled workers demanding wage increase to agreement wage. Strike collapsed after 3rd or 4th day. They tried to picket and in trying to prevent importation of scabs, a fracas occurred and employer personally shot one striker through mouth.

Trades and Labor Council supported them financially [and] paid for solicitor fees. Legal case handled badly. About 18 strikers arrested and charged with public violence for throwing stones at police. (They were 24 hour notice workers and were not charged with contract violence.) [It happened] at time of Vereeniging and bail set at £2 at first and increased to £3 each. All convicted (except the wounded one) and sentenced to 6 weeks hard labor.

12. South African Colored Mine Workers Union. Affiliated with Trades and Labor Council on basis of 900 members; must be about 200 strong.

13. South African Railway and Harbor Workers Union (Non-European). Only recently formed here.

14. African Gas and Power Workers' Union. [A union] in name only.

Most of the Bantu unions have colored and Indian members. Only the colored mine workers union excludes Bantu.

Gordon says Boardman is all wet. There are a number of factories in Joburg in which whites and natives work side by side on an equal basis—e.g. in Leather Industry (where there is only one union for all), clothing industry, laundry industry and even in furniture shops—such as Cohens, and Steel and Barnetts.

Gordon contradicted what Boardman had to say about inability of native workers to understand specialization. There is specialization in a [number] of industries, including furniture, clothing, leather and laundry industries and with pay variations.

Organization of native workers brings decrease in wage evasions by employing natives as unskilled workers and giving them skilled work to do. Very little evasion in laundry industry. But still plenty in the construction industry among painters, bricklayers, etc.

European women are not allowed on non-European trams and have been refused admission to them.

Dr. Sachs took me, without prior notice, into Joburg's most posh restaurant—The Criterion—for dinner tonight. We were in prominent seats but nothing happened, though Dr. Sachs was more fidgety and ill-at-ease than I was. I enjoyed a fine dinner (Schnitzel)—at his expense.

South Africa is an *entire* country ridden by race prejudice—unlike U.S. in that there is absolutely no escape at all for these black and colored people.

▬▬▬ December 10

Interview with Superintendent of local jail, "The Fort."[7] [Jack] Simons and I were not permitted to visit the cells. We were told that a new and recent order requires permission to be gotten from Pretoria. This is due to criticisms of jail conditions in the press by people who have visited the jails.

The Superintendent advised us to visit the Pretoria prison, adding that "the Fort is not a show place." It is very old and it is planned to tear it down and build a new jail soon.

European prisoners (only short-term—under a month—Europeans are kept here) are completely separated; but natives, Indian and colored are together.

The diet for the natives consists of mealie meal, mealies and vegetables. They also get nuts, he says. The Europeans get meat and vegetables, bread, etc.

Natives are not allowed to smoke in any South African prison, but whites are. Their "privileges" consist of the right to write letters, to receive visitors and to read. But all books are censored and there is no library for natives.

Much labor is farmed out from South African prisons. Mine labor may be obtained by the mines by a payment of 2s per day to the government (and the government takes care of room and board). Farm labor is farmed out at rate of 6d per day and farmer is responsible for guarding the prisoners.

He [superintendent] said there is relatively little disaffection among native prisoners and very little trouble. He says that when a native does cause trouble it is usually because he "is off in the head."

There are only a few educated natives among the prisoners and these are real trouble makers and slickers. They are usually in for forgery—of passes, etc.

European prisoners get gratuities and clothes upon discharge. But natives do not get these (except for clothing when it has been too far gone to keep for them). A few skilled native workers get a pittance for their work.

Most of the natives are put on unskilled work—road work under armed European guards.

There are some native "assistant guards" in the prison.

There is no provision for teaching natives trades or giving them education, but there is for Europeans.

There are about 1400 non-European prisoners [jailed for such offenses as] assault, rape, liquor and pass offenses. Most of the 200 females are in for liquor law violations.

Interview with Head Interpreter of local Magistrates Court. He has about 16 interpreters under him of whom only 2 are natives. He doesn't favor native interpreters because he claims that they tend to be partial to members of their own tribe in court disputes.

He stresses the vital role which the interpreter plays in the court procedure. Says he must do more than merely interpret, but that they must also understand native custom. E.g., he says many raw natives don't understand the European court procedure. They have a traditional deference for law and authority. In their tribal courts they would not be brought before the chief for trial unless it was known that they are guilty. Thus, when they are brought before a European judge they often plead guilty when they are not at all guilty. Their attitude is that if they are brought into court at all they must be guilty of some violation. The interpreter must question them deeply in order to bring out their real position.

One case was cited of a native being charged with stealing a crate of apples. He pled guilty, and the interpreter accepted the plea without question. The facts of the case were these: At the market a native boy was told to load a crate of apples onto a lorry. He put the crate on the back of the defendant's lorry, this being the wrong one. The defendant didn't notice the apples and drove away to the country, discovering the apples at his destination. On his return to the market he turned the crate over to the Market Superintendent who disposed of them, as he couldn't locate the owner. Later the owner of the apples, finding that they were missing, had his boy point out the lorry onto which he had placed them and defendant's lorry was indicated and he was charged with their theft.

After his conviction the true facts were learned and an appeal on his behalf was allowed and he was released. His plea of "guilty" merely meant that he knew about the apples. The interpreter could have avoided this conviction by understanding native attitude better.

Many of the interpreters they try lose their tempers when a native fails to understand them immediately. They feel that the native makes their language look badly in court. These, he says, are undesirable types.

He says there are many English words that he has never heard any equivalent for in the native languages—e.g. "cruelty," "please."

He says the interpreter is really the natives' public defender.

The interpreters take the attitude that in most cases when a native pleads guilty, he is honest and not guilty; but when he pleads "not guilty," then he is regarded with suspicion, for the natives who are hardened criminals and who have had prior experience with European law will always plead not guilty, no matter how heavily the evidence is weighted against them.

The interpreters are not too well paid—they get up to £500 (for the head interpreter).

In the "yard" where prisoners wait outside on benches for their cases to come up, there is no segregation; whites and non-whites all sit together.

Visit to the Joburg Non-European Government Hospital. There are separate Hindu and Moslem private wards. The necessary alterations were paid for by the respective Indian groups but the government foots the upkeep. These are for paying patients.

There are separate wards for Chinese and Colored and for natives. But in the children's ward all are together.

Matron says natives take to hospitals without difficulty.

The matron says that native patients are extremely fond of vegetables. This is contrary to the mine compounds. [Her] contention that vegetables have to be chopped up with meat and served in stews or the natives won't eat them.

The matron says she believes in feeding her patients well and giving them less drugs.

48 native girls in training. They get a little lecture work but the Matron stresses "practical" training. They get hospital certificates on passing the exam, at end of 4 years. They must take a stiffer exam (after more training which the hospital does not afford) before they can get qualified nurses' certificates. This hospital's training did not yet qualify the native girls for this exam.

There are no native qualified nurses at the hospital. These are all European.

No trouble placing their girls—a great demand for them. Plans on foot to accommodate 72 of them soon. Additions being made to the hospital, which now covers 3 floors.

It is kept very clean. But it is overcrowded—about 370 patients with only 310 beds, so a large number sleep on mattresses placed side by side on the floor. Hospital especially crowded over the week-ends because of large number of assault victims.

There are no colored nurses because they don't want to nurse native patients and don't get along with native nurses.

Several of the European nurses told us the natives are wonderful patients, uncomplaining, dutiful and grateful. They said they would never want to nurse Europeans again. They tell with pride how some of their male patients have brought them flowers after their release.

[Discussion with] Gana Makabeni. The South African Clothing Workers Union (for natives) was organized in 1928 by the C.P. Similarly organized were the Laundry Workers Union, African Mattress and Furniture Workers Union, African Baking Workers Union, the Dairy Workers Union, the Rope Workers Union.

A body called the African Federation of Trade Unions (non-European) was organized out of these unions by the C.P. toward end of 1928.[8] Short-lived and only a paper organization.

Owing to bad management of the unions, they broke up, except for the Clothing and Laundry Workers Union.

As result of Party policy, internal disputes, expulsion of Gana in 1932, etc., unions were weakened. The Clothing Union stuck with Gana. The Clothing and Laundry Unions both left the Party in 1932. Laundry Workers had over 500 [members] and Clothing Workers about 300 in a loose organization at this time.

Clothing Workers had a big strike in 1928 soon after its formation . . . because of victimization of one employee. Strikers demanded reinstatement of worker. The strike in the factory lasted 3 weeks and then a general strike in the industry was called and lasted another 2 weeks. No strike pay. Communal cooking in the C.P. hall.

During the early period of the strike, another clothing workers strike broke out in Germiston over dismissal of 3 European girls and Joburg native workers in industry were asked to assist by pulling out all native workers in industry in Germiston. This was done by natives in Germiston. In one factory there were 6 native scabs and a fight occurred . . . within three days in Germiston.

Then it was decided to call a general strike in Joburg to aid the native strikers there. But European workers refused to come out in aid of native strikers "because of the Industrial Conciliation Act." They gave only meager aid—financial aid for food, etc. No strike pay.

No charges made against native strikers in the 3 week period, but when general strike was called, the strikers were arrested. First, all the ring leaders, including Gana, under provision of Riotous Assemblies Act. Picketing was indulged in which was illegal under Wage Industrial Conciliation Act. A whole procession of native strikers totalling about 200 were arrested and charged with illegal procession.

All of arrested strikers were convicted—some for desertion, some for illegal procession and some for exciting to violence. Gana fined £ 5; some other leaders £ 7.10, down to £ 1. The accused decided not to pay the fines, but the police found some money on some of them and took this to pay the fines. This broke the strike, but the union survived.

Union has had several minor strikes since. In 1931 a strike occurred in a Joburg factory when a native worker thrashed a European girl with his belt, when she hit him with scissors. He was fired and rest of native workers walked out. Strike lasted only a day and through Garment Workers Union the native worker was paid by union until other employment was found for him (over a period of 4 weeks). One white girl walked out with the natives.

Wage determination by Wage Board in May, 1932, as result of evidence given by union (clothing) representative. Advocated then "equal pay for equal work," asked £ 6 for pressers and cutters. Determination fixed £ 3. Before that rate was from 15s to £ 1.50. . . . A large number of natives were dismissed after this, because employers refused to pay natives £ 3. At this time European pressers were getting up to £ 6, but there were very few European pressers. But when natives were fired, Europeans were employed at £ 3—the native wage. A ratio clause in 1932 fixed an obligation on an employer to employ one worker earning £ 3 to every 2 workers earning any other amount.

The Union has had great difficulty in meeting the costs of a headquarters, hall, etc. In March, 1935, when the union had no finance, the Garment Workers Union offered financial support. They were prepared to pay cost of an organizer, provide an office. Funds of Clothing Workers Union are entrusted to the Garment Workers Union. Collection is done by the Clothing Workers. Three or four employers now deduct union dues for the native union. Now the Garment Workers Union gives only an office and secretarial help.

The Clothing Workers Union is the oldest native union still in existence. 300 members in Joburg, 150 in Germiston. About 700 natives—

unskilled and skilled—employed in industry. Union includes unskilled and skilled workers.

There are colored members of the Clothing Workers. The colored members are males. The female colored and a few colored males are in the (European) Garment Workers Union. About 20–25 colored in Gana's Union. The colored are pressers and cutters.

Gana says natives are anxious to be organized in trade unions, but that they are suspicious of whites. It is admitted that the I.C.U. collapse has made organization more difficult.

Lithebe was emoted when I told him about the affair. He is very sensitive. He hates whites and pointed out that though Mrs. Hellman knows him very well she would not shake hands with him at the Ballinger meeting the other night. He says white man is a fool not to believe that the native can think—all men are made in one image, he says. He believes that most European writers of books on natives are exploiting him. He called a European who came in to see him about new photographic proposals for native lang. [languages]. These efforts, he says, are to make it easier for European interpreters in the courts.

In the Political Science courses at the South African universities, they teach the students that the South African government is a democracy; but Jack [Simons] says they devote little attention to the status of the native or to native law. (A "Platomai" democracy).

Non-Europeans can't use public libraries in Joburg—no opportunity for reading.

On Sunday night I saw a native all "dressed up" in a complete Scotch Kiltie outfit, Tam[9] and all. What a sight!

■■■■■■ **December 11**

The Joburg colored go in for some elaborate private affairs at the Ritz Hall. The wedding reception I attended included about 300 invited guests. A six-piece orchestra played for dancing. Fruit salad, tea, soft drinks and cakes were served to all. Most of the guests were "dressed." The bride and groom entered with fan-fare and marched down the long hall between the lines of the guests—led by youngsters in evening clothes. There was a huge wedding cake; large and fancy sugar statues, etc. The bride and groom received the congratulations (and presents) of guests as they filed by. The party cost a tidy sum—and these are working people.

■■■■■■ **December 13**

Peter took me into the [train] station . . . through the non-European entrance—"for non-Europeans only" [or] "for niggers only," as Peter put it.

On the train from Joburg to Bloemfontein I was put into a double compartment in the 1st class coach, with a young Afrikaner, with whom I exchanged not more than a dozen words (and who is lying silently on his bunk across from me now—about an hour from Bloemfontein). I asked Cook's to reserve me a coupe, but they didn't succeed. No incidents.

Bloemfontein

December 14

All African Convention.[1] Second day. Jabavu presiding. Interpreted in Sesuto. About 100 present. Meeting held in barn-like communal hall on the "Batho Location." "Smoking prohibited" signs in English, Afrikaans and three native languages.

Jabavu very enthusiastic about report [of] one check for £ 10 from Max Yergan.

Great attention to subject of the development of business among Africans. Discussion on economic uplift, led by a young fellow named Kumalo, who speaks in English.[2] Has had experience in store-keeping in proclaimed native reserves, but says he has little knowledge of town conditions. Refers to necessity for training African business men in commercial schools—accounting, stenography, etc. After training, young men should be apprenticed to establish African businesses. African commerce today is strictly individual enterprise.

Refers to saying that Africans will not stick together and prefer to

256

patronize other people than their own. Says difficulty is that African business men themselves are not prepared to give best service. "No magic in business." A very pointed speaker.

[Kumalo's speech is] translated in Sesuto (a very lengthy and *free* translation) and Xhosa. There is a lot of time wasted in these translations. Some of the translations take much longer than the original discussion.

Max Jabavu, M.R.C., discussing subject of economic uplift. Says affluence wins respect. . . . Says failure of African business is due to extended credit.

One native trader from Cape says chiefs can't run business because people come and hail the chief and expect things from him for nothing. [He gives] reasons for failures of African businesses—tribal differences and jealousies; dishonesty of directors in cooperative associations; failure of members to pay up their shares and to abide by provision that credit not exceeding £1 should be extended. Appeal to national spirit toward success of African business enterprise.

One speaker stressed that when a man is engaged in business, everything else—his wife, family, politics, religion—must be secondary. Nothing must interfere with business if it is to succeed. (The references to neglect of wife, etc. for business evoked much laughter, and the speech, forcibly delivered, was enthusiastically received.)

One speaker says that difficulty of native business man is not his lack of business knowledge, but his inability, through lack of capital and credit references, securities, etc., to purchase from wholesale dealers. Capital is necessary for business and this must be obtained through cooperative effort.

Procedure [during these discussions] is very informal, much humor and laughter, banter and suggestions to speakers from audience. A surprising amount of *levity* in the convention. Jabavu always leads the laughter. Recitals of native business failures and crooked businessmen evoke *much laughter* among the delegates.

Report by Mr. Msimang on Farm Labor. In some instances [farm workers are paid] no wages at all; others wages are from 10/ to 18/ per month. Usually wages not paid in cash—need to pay off food debts. Workers kept in debt to employer for food. Laborer must build his own house. Must use services of his wife and children. Veiled slavery.

[Msimang made] recommendations for protection of farm workers:

(1) fixed wage scale on yearly basis.

(2) a wage scale based on values of services rendered.

(3) a fixed rate of pay for adult children.

(4) a system of apprenticeships for minor children in accordance with Apprenticeship Act.

(5) no minor children should be employed except under apprenticeship system.

(6) provision for inspectors of farm labor in line with provisions of Industrial Council Act.

(7) fixed rate of hire for oxen of employer or vice versa.

(8) a fixed rate of hire grazing for live and small stock.

(9) a fixed rate for hire of private land.

(10) regulation of hours in accord with rates of pay.

(11) provision of schools for education of laborers' children within a given radius.

(12) provision of housing for laborers by employers at fixed rate of rental in accord with Nat. Urban Areas Act.

(13) on this basis laborer accepting wages in kind will be able to get proper value of his wage on cash basis.

Machinery for obtaining these recs. must be through a "Farm Laborers Association" organized by the African Convention.

Tsotsi's discussion of education for Africans re Native Affairs Department report.[3] Warns re "education to fit native for his place in society." A slave driver would give a slave an education to fit him for his "place" in society.

Opposes Native Affairs Department report suggestion that native education be placed under Native Affairs Department as it has nothing to do with native education. Favors inter-deptal [departmental] commission recommendation that native education be placed under Education Department.

Casts suspicion on "Bantuization" of native education discussed in Native Affairs Department report, as the Department does not concern itself with "Bantuization" of other aspects of native life. Says it may mean differentiation and inferior educational treatment. But if "Bantuization" means replacing of white teachers in Bantu schools by black teachers, then he is for it, as teaching is only broad economic avenue now open for educated Africans.

Criticizes salary differentiation between white and black teachers.

Mission schools must be displaced by public schools, since education is a public function, though moral influence of missionary bodies can be continued in schools.

Evils of missionary schools:

(1) teachers are public servants and should be responsible to government.

(2) appointment of teachers by one man.

(3) denominational influences.

(4) teachers should be appointed on basis of educational merits and qualifications rather than their religious views.

Rajuili—African Youth and Social Evils.[4] Defense of social customs such as that of *ukumetsha* among the Xhosa.[5] Under Xhosa custom, girls were under strict supervision and control (enthusiastic response to this). Socially recognized and sanctioned pre-marital sexual play without actual intercourse. Girls' vaginas examined by mothers against rupture. White man substitutes "filthy" contraceptives for this custom and makes the woman his wife though she doesn't bear children, thus committing *sin*.

More conception among "civilized" native girls than the uncivilized, because the former often haven't become sufficiently sophisticated to use contraceptives.

Increased temptations . . . and illicit love matches . . . among detribalized young men and women town dwellers. Home discipline broken down, due to weakening of tribes and chiefs. Latter are figureheads and puppets of government. Inability of working mothers to properly care for and train children.

White man's education teaches child that his race is inferior and his parents barbarians. History teaching exalts Napoleon, castigates Chaka as a cruel savage.

Recommendations:

(1) must inculcate race consciousness and pride in black children.

(2) must inculcate pride in chiefs; and restore their power.

(3) improvement of economic conditions.

(4) organized recreational facilities. Criticizes Pathfinders and Wayfarers as encouraging children to disobey parents.[6] They make native children obedient "yaas [yes] bosses."

(5) support cooperative and economic uplift movements.

Goulam Gool upbraided Godlo and the Convention for not bringing up on the floor of the last convention meeting the question of support for the Native Rep. Council, instead of boycotting it. He said had the question been submitted to the meeting it would have been voted down. He is convinced that the convention, "a gathering of priests and teachers," is hopeless and innocuous, and that only important work is that of trade union organizations.

Talk by Mrs. Ballinger: what European representatives can do depends on what natives can do and on direction in which native organizations are moving. Impressed by rapid progress of natives evidenced in discussions at Nat. Rep. Council meeting. Praised grasp and understanding of problems and forces by members of N.R.C. [Native Representative Council]. Impressed here by extent to which natives are seeing their problems in economic terms. *Develop. of trading* the *one* advantage which can be gotten out of segregation.

Sen. Malcomess [made an] apology for Sen. Welch's absence. Reps. of native interests will make it a duty to attend every meeting of Nat. Rep. Council. Chairman Smit had to learn lesson of patience. [Council] of high educative value to "Europeans who represent you." Praised high quality of speeches by native councillors. Advised councillors to get together before hand in caucus to avoid disagreement as between the Cape and Natal. [He] also advises councillors to demand agenda beforehand.

Says he knows of farm wages of 5/- per month. Curses malnutrition forced on natives. Whole native race is starving because natives share with each other.

Malcomess telling how they treat farm natives in his (Cape) district. Says they pay them 12/6 per month there, give them enough rations for their families, skim milk and pay their poll tax, and that their workers are *satisfied.*

Suggests that convention *withhold action* on Msimang's report until Government Farm Labor Committee issues its report and then the European reps. of natives and native councillors should be called in conference on the recommendations in the report. *Tactics of delay.*

He says he wants natives for next few months *"to be moderate,"* to keep natives question from being injected into the coming election. Counsels: "have patience." Says Europ. nat. rep. task is to *educate* white people.

Malcomess' suggestion to withhold action put into a motion and carried with only one dissent (Goulam's [Goolam] sister). *European influence strong.* Why were the European reps. invited?

The radicals, [Goolam] Gool and Co., take view that Convention, by accepting the Native Representatives Act, instead of boycotting the elections, has destroyed public interest in the Convention. They point out that the attendance at the Convention is now meager (about 100) and attribute it to public disgust at the Convention's compromises.

Radicals point out weakness of Joint Councils, which are controlled by ministers, who took a liberal attitude on repressive bills and won a large following among natives. But when the bills were made law the

Joint Councils made an about face and took the attitude that natives must make the best of the bills, and thus let natives down.

Mrs. Ballinger points out that the elections (though limited and segregated) have had a beneficial effect in that they have stirred up a new political interest in the native people.

Mrs. Ballinger refers to growing liberalism among certain groups. She says that at present moment there are about a dozen groups (and this is their weakness, of course) trying to organize a party without a color bar.

Mrs. Ballinger says only liberalism this country has had in past has been philanthropy, but points to a new economic liberalism that is growing up. She says industrialism is only twenty years old in South Africa.

She upbraided Miss Gool[7] on boycott attitude because she is not a Bantu and does not represent them and it is the Bantu who have to pay the price of a boycott.

Mrs. Ballinger admits that the seven European reps. for natives are only a stop-gap to keep the election door open for natives. (Gool et al point to these reps. as sops and pol. [political] propaganda.

Mrs. Ballinger says she campaigned on realistic ground that these European representatives can't change the native laws.

Mrs. Ballinger cautioned the Convention about the extreme difficulty of organizing farm workers in their hope for a Farm Laborers Association.

Mafutsanyana [Mofutsanyana] on labor and wages. [He talks about] detribalized people who have no land and are forced to live in industrial areas. Mine wage agreement reducing wages of native mine workers from 3s per shift to from 1s to 2s. Improvement in skill of native mine workers, though not in their wages. 850,000 natives employed in the Union. Out of this number 52% earn from £13 to £30 per annum; 46% earn from £30 to £44 per year. 1/3 to 1/2 of the Africans' earnings go for rent; they pay from 25s up.

He says there will never be any change through a Convention that merely meets periodically "to pass pious resolutions." The only solution must be the organization of the masses of people.

The Convention is known to the people and is their only hope, but it must be organized beyond its present skeletal form. There must be branches in every locality which will deal with the day to day activities of the people.

Cites difficulties of organization: pass laws, Riotous Assemblies Act, etc. In the reserves, if more than ten people wish to meet, permission must be gotten from the magistrate.

Native Laws Amendment, soon to be put into effect, will mean wholesale deportation of natives from locations, etc.

Moses Kotane on labor and wages. Fund. [Fundamental] question is that of wages. White man came to country to enrich himself. He realized that if native should develop too far he would lose his hold on the country and its cheap labor. Wages purposely kept low in order to keep the native down. Culprit is the Chamber of Mines, who are responsible for keeping down native wages.

Says Convention has found a scapegoat today in the European reps. of the natives upon whom all burdens are being placed. But masses of people must be organized. Organization of natives is only remedy. Low wages cause of all native evils in the country.

Z. K. Matthews [on] Native Laws Amendment Act: Act part of general policy of segregation worked out for future of black man in South Africa.[8] Chiefly applies to urban dwellers. Objects of act: (1) to make provision for more effective resid. [residential] segregation of natives in towns. (2) to restrict urban native population. (3) to introduce a new system of dealing with Kaffir beer. Important because of its relation to disaffection with police among native people.

[The act will make the] locations system to be more efficiently administered; to remove natives from white areas in towns; to make locations more particularly the places where natives must stay; to make locations more like compounds . . . fences, gates, etc.—like concentration camps.

Urban population has greatly increased since last census, and dissatisfied whites wished to remove the "redundant" natives from towns. To estimate "redundant" (surplus) natives, a biennial census will be taken and local labor needs estimated. "Foreign" natives to be dealt with first.[9]

Government's own committee reported against any further legislation on this point. Thus the real reason for this legislation is in fact that farm labor is increasingly scarce. It is hoped that more labor will thus be provided for farms. Labor bureaus, "to distribute labor more evenly throughout the country," will be established to send surplus labor where it is most needed.

Entering towns will be more difficult. Natives entering proclaimed areas will have to obtain a special permission to enter, even for a visit. A native under eighteen, unaccompanied by parents, not admitted. A native female must be twenty-one and have two permits—one from magistrate and one from municipal officer in district in which she resides. Casual ("togt" laborers) must wear a special badge.*

Matthews doesn't think act can be put into effect. Natives will run any risks to get better wages offered in town. Whole object of act is [to] control movements and wages of laborers [and] to keep native on farms and at mercy of farmers.

Under provisions of this act, a body like the [All] African Convention could be choked off simply by refusing permission for native delegates to enter an urban area like Bloemfontein.

Matthews said that there is already power invested in the Native Affairs Department to empower Atty. Gen. [Attorney General] (meaning the local authority) to prohibit native meetings.

Goulam [Gool] suggested that the time is ripe for another pass-bearing campaign and it met only with unreserved mirth throughout the audience.

Mrs. Ballinger: in last few years there have been two slight increases in mine wages—one of them being the 1d or 2d per day increase for natives winning First Aid badges.

Mr. Ballinger has worked for payment of railroad fares by mine of natives recruited. (This was fought for by him at Geneva.) Mrs. Ballinger says that no native organization has backed him up in his fight. Mines say this would cost them £ 400,000 per year, but Mrs. Ballinger says this would be made up for in increased consumption.

She says that none of the industrial leg. [legislation] has any specific color bar except for the Industrial Conciliation Act, which excludes pass-bearing natives.

Amendment to Industrial Conciliation Act passed during this session of Parliament provides for Minister of Labor to have power to appoint a rep. of native interests on Industrial Council Board.

Meeting of "Rump Parliament"—Left Wing group meeting after end of regular session on December 14 at eleven o'clock, p.m. Thirty

---

*"Togt" labor is day labor regulated by pass laws.

people, mostly young, on hand, including the Trotskyites and Stalinists. Five women present. Devoted to discussion of what they had expected from the Convention and its short-comings in this respect. Criticism of Convention leadership for lack of initiative.

No full report of the activities of the Convention's Executive Committee. Position of Convention in 1936 meeting had been opposed to any compromise or to any support for Nat. Rep. Bills, as Nat. Rep. Councils were dummy councils or "ventilating chambers." But subsequently the Exec. Com. met and decided to support the Council. Goulam Gool was replaced on the Exec. Com. for his opposition to this action.

Weakness of African organizations stressed and need for Convention to strengthen them. Need for broadening scope of Convention to protect *all* the oppressed peoples of South Africa. Feeling that the Convention today is not really expressing will of masses of African people. Convention lacks an organizer and a consistent policy. [Africans have been] betrayed by Convention . . . in accepting support of Nat. Rep. Act.

An earnest group and orderly meeting.

The National Liberation League of S.A. was started in December, 1935—outcome of Brussels Congress of League Against Imperialism in 1927 to which Le [La] Guma was a delegate. Le Guma was the founder and organizer (he was out of [Communist] Party at that time).

Started in C.T. [Cape Town]. Branches in Pretoria, Port Elizabeth, Naauwport Junction, Riebeck West, Hermon, Ebenezer, Wynberg, Athlone, Kensington. Total membership now about 2,000; 2/3 colored. C.T. organization overwhelmingly colored.

One national conference in C.T. at Easter, 1936—all branches represented. League has recently devoted attention to problem of industrial traders and they have now promised to support the League.

Le Guma says that there seems to be some undercover sabotage going on at the Convention—evidenced in the attitudes expressed by men such as Alex Jabavu on the question of other non-European groups than native [participating], the fight of some to put off the next meeting of the Convention for five years, etc. This he attributes to the Nat. Rep. Councillors and the European Nat. Reps., who fear that the Convention will develop into a native mass organization and get out of hand.

Jabavu pointed out how the Convention has steadily lost ground in public support: there were 700 present at the first Convention, 400 at the second, and only 100 at this one.

Entire afternoon session on third day devoted to approval of the draft constitution. Much wrangling. The Convention voted against employment of an auditor for its accounts on the grounds of "too much expense," and substituted an ad hoc committee for the work.

The Convention seems to degenerate toward the end of the afternoon session—especially [over] the question of whether the Convention is to meet annually, biennially, or every three, four or five years.

Rheinold [Rheinallt-] Jones' greeting to Convention: said he has done 18,000 miles on his work as Senator since election day. Discusses contribution of Bantu Welfare Trust to the Convention (£ 180 up to now). Convention must make sure that it "merits support of the Trust." He as a Trustee of the Trust, says that if Convention does "effective and *useful*" work for the African people it will continue to receive the support of the Trust.

Goulam Gool moved that in draft constitution, other non-European groups along with Bantu, be included. His motion opposed by a young native and Thema. Mafutsanyana, in opposing Gool's motion, made a dumb speech. Mack Jabavu also opposes the motion on grounds of government differentiation of the groups. A terribly narrow and chauvinistic attitude and passive acceptance of government tactics. A definite threat to make the Convention exclusively Bantu. [Jabavu is] a big, dumb, bigoted sycophant.

In answer to a question as to whether the Bantu Welfare Trust contribution is for natives only, Rheinold Jones says, "Yes"; thus implication is that A.A.C. is for natives only if it accepts the contribution and this was clearly defined by one speaker.

Motion carried to leave the provision as it stands—a grave mistake and a victory for bigoted, black chauvinism which plays directly into the hands of the divisive policy of the government.

There was very vigorous discussion and wrangling over this issue.

Mrs. Ballinger says convention could not possibly have carried Gool's motion; that colored themselves are in large part responsible for this attitude, and that the Convention would sell out on this issue for the £ 50 from the Bantu Trust.

After an informal caucus outside, the supporters of Gool's motion went back in and got the principle accepted in the organization clause, which is to state specifically that all non-European organizations shall be admitted to the Convention (and without much opposition.)

The only "strong" language used on the floor during the whole Convention was used by Kadebe [Radebe], [of] the C.P., when he referred to "the bloody five years." Jabavu was so shocked he almost fell out of his seat and choked on his tea-cake, in objecting to the term. Kadebe retracted amid tumultuous laughter.

Mrs. Ballinger commented on the extreme "good humor" of the meeting; there's far too much levity in view of the problems with which the organization is confronted.

The Convention has decided to meet once every three years. The Executive Committee will meet once a year. The new constitution was summarily approved by standing vote.

After constitution was adopted, the Convention, on spur of moment, decided to hold elections, and Jabavu and Xuma (incumbent vice-president) were presidential nominees. Left-wingers canvassed for Xuma. Secret ballot.

Jabavu won re-election by vote of 50 to 14. (Xuma absent in England.)

Jabavu's election was followed by a spontaneous demonstration of applause, lifting him up to the shoulders of several men, the singing of the African National Anthem and three cheers for Jabavu.

Rev. Mahabane, a Methodist minister, was elected vice-president of the Convention—to the disgust of the Left-wingers.[10]

Selby Msimang reelected General Secy. unopposed. A little too high for the task, he then led a discussion on the important subject of the relationship of the Convention to organizations. Convention depends on active cooperation of affiliated organizations. If existing organizations were doing their jobs, there would have been no reason for the Convention to appear. But they exist in name only.

Convention should establish a central organizing and publicity Council under direction of General Secy., with fifteen divisional committee organ., each with an organization and publicity staff. (Despite his liquor, Selby is reading a good paper.) Selby emphasizes need for literature—pamphlets—for use by organizers. Msimang's report approved together with organizational scheme.

Report by Women's section of the Convention—The National Council of African Women—affiliated with the Convention.[11] Has branches in a number of centers. Start in organization of women given by Mrs. Rheinold Jones. Then women came to Convention and decided to go back home and organize the women.

After Jabavu's hasty departure (11 p.m.) to catch a train while the Convention was still in session, Thema criticized Jabavu for not remaining over until tomorrow to extend greetings and good-will to the Congress which opens tomorrow. Says Jabavu's action is certain to be misinterpreted. He says one of the things African leaders lack is how to get on with other people. An indication of how Africans fail as leaders.

Meeting getting disorderly. Mafutsanyana hopped on Thema for not making his statement of criticism when Jabavu was here and announced that he was leaving tonite.

On the subject of a resolution on the Nat. Laws Amendment Act, involving Kaffir beer, the meeting was thrown into complete chaos largely due to several individuals who themselves seemed to have sipped too much Kaffir beer—especially Keable Mote, a politician known as the "lion of the North" in the O.F.S.[12]

A resolution reappointing Yergan as External Affairs Secy. and extending his powers was approved.

The meeting gradually withered away and at 12:15 [a.m.] when policy, a vital question, was being discussed, only a handful of people were left in the hall. Thema came in at end of Convention very "tight." A bare handful were left to sing the African National Anthem at the end.

It was particularly indictable that Jabavu should have left the Convention without any consideration of one of the most vital items on the agenda—that of policy, on which the Exec. Com. had submitted a mimeographed memo. This question was wretchedly dealt with at the midnite end of the Convention, with no one left to consider it. So, in effect, the Convention adjourned until three years hence without having adopted any policy.

Beside Janub Gool, only one women spoke from the floor during the entire Convention, and this one acted like a mild edition of Mrs. Bethune.[13] One other said a few words later.

The delegates to the Convention are dressed well enough, though not too well, but the "back bench" spectators are really tatterdemalion proletarians—in tattered rags and many barefoot.

One delegate walked 400 miles from Dearston (Cape Prov. [Province]) to get to the convention, and a collection was taken up for him.*

---

*Bunche is referring to Rev. J. Marela, who had walked most of 400 miles from Pearston to Bloemfontein. Conference delegates took up a collection to buy him a return ticket.

I didn't learn until after I had contributed 1/6 that he is a *minister*. He is sick.

The A.A.C. is strictly a convention which came spontaneously into existence in December 1935 to fight the Franchise Bills. It won enthusiastic support until its leadership sold out on the Cape Franchise issue.

It lacks effective leadership; Jabavu is hopeless; Jabavu can't conduct a meeting. The Convention has really served its purpose and should go out of existence.

All these African organizations suffer from untrustworthy leadership. Everyone bitterly criticizes Jabavu and Seme, but they hold on to their jobs.

Rheinold Jones, in criticizing the showing of the Nat. Rep. Councillors at Pretoria, stressed their utter lack of preparation, due to the laziness of men like Thema about getting hold of factual data, their failure and reluctance to read—even the Government reports—and their lack of social perspective and understanding.

He stressed their dependence on him and the other European representatives for points of view and facts. He says he never criticized them for fear of the charge of assuming an attitude of racial superiority. Says he had Thema call a caucus meeting of the councillors for the Sunday before the opening session, and Thema himself did not show up.

Jones said that the European Rep. group sent Sen. Welsh to Smit to tell him of the general dissatisfaction with his chairmanship of the first two days and to insist that the Councillors be treated with proper dignity. He says this attitude was wholly endorsed by the Native Commissioners, who are anxious that the Council establish itself as a dignified body, that it have a proper meeting place, formalities and ceremonies, etc. Jones said Smit improved greatly toward the end.

Jones said Dube's soft attitude can be attributed to his advanced age.

Jones expressed dissatisfaction with Jabavu's leadership at the present Convention, but said that the old man has stood up well in earlier years.

Jones referred to the different attitudes of Africans, arising out of their different cultural backgrounds. They have an understandably different attitude toward money and time than whites. When Mrs. Jones invited native women to tea at four, she can be sure that several of them will come for lunch. At Jones' reception for the N.R.C. members on Sunday afternoon, some twenty came (uninvited) for lunch and one came at 7 a.m. Several others, when the reception was over, came to him and asked if he would give them money for their return fares home. When he asked them how they got to his house, they replied simply, "with single tickets."

Jones said he was sorry the question was raised about the Bantu Trust contribution to the Convention because it was the wish of the donor that it be employed exclusively for Bantu, but that he was compelled to speak the truth and answer affirmatively.[14] He said it is embarrassing for the Convention or any organization to have to rely upon someone else for its financial support, and that the Convention can't depend on continued support from the Trust. The money from that source should be regarded as "a gift from Heaven."

Jones was impressed by my suggestion re social orientation education for young educated Africans in preparation for future leadership. Suggested that Institute of Race Relations might institute vocation schools for such purpose.

Jones was very curious about Max Yergan's Committee and was anxious to be in touch with it.[15]

Jones attributes much importance to trad. [traditional] African attitude toward the chief. He says the chief was looked upon as a father and the people came to him expecting him to do things for them. This attitude they carry-over into their modern relationships. Thus, the higher a man is in their esteem the more they expect him to do for and give them. (Compare with Dr. Sachs' "prolonged sucking" theory.)

Jones mentioned the "appallingly low standard of living of even the educated African" and he is right. He also pointed out the great gap between their nutrition and their clothes, etc.

The Bloemfontein location is the best appearing of all the locations I've seen yet, though it has the same pretty bad looking sections. At best, however, these are poor excuses for decent living conditions. The locations at Bultfontein, Hoopstad and Brantford are miserable, squalid looking places. The people are scarcely as well off as their livestock. They [locations] are desolate and dreary looking. Population of [Bloemfontein] location is 30,000.

The municipality affords loans for house builders—for construction materials, including bricks (latter only recently). Municipality charges 5% interest on money loaned for construction—repayable in installments.

There are also two native builders employed by municipality who provide plans and mark out foundations for private builders. Municipal houses built by African contractors and labor, and under native building inspectors.

Stands are 75' x 50'. The 7/ stand rent includes water (35 houses to a tap) and rubbish removal and latrine removal (double pail system).* No gas service. No telephone service for private homes. A lodger's permit of 2/6 per month must be paid for each lodger. No overcrowding is allowed, except in the old location, the condemned area which is being gradually destroyed. The [municipality] built houses on demand and rent at 17/ per month for two room houses.

No houses can be built solely for rental, but tenants can be taken in. If builder moves away he can sell either to the municipality (which is eager to buy the houses and will pay a good price) or to a private buyer. Munic. aiming at 200 munic. built houses; about 120 up now. One municipal bath house in old location (for men only).

The municipality used to try to maintain separate sections in the Bloemfontein location along tribal lines—Masuto [Basotho], Barolong, Xhosa, etc. groups in distinct residential areas. But this policy was successfully fought in the Location Advisory Board.

Grazing ground is provided for location by the municipality—milk cows, limited to two per family, graze free; oxen at 2/5 per month. No private slaughtering is allowed (though much of it is done illegally). Beasts must be sent to municipal abattoir and are slaughtered there at cost of 7/6 for oxen, 2/6 for sheep.

Stalls in the market rent for 1/6 per day and Europeans, though barred, get around this regularly by sending their produce to be sold by native employees.

No trader's licenses for Bantu anywhere on the Bloemfontein locations. The municipality grants hawkers licenses only in order to protect the small European traders in town. There is a good deal of illegal trading going on in fixed places, which have scouts looking for the police.

Lepolesa[16] says that the location's residents asked for the 10 o'clock curfew law in Bloemfontein to help them keep their youngsters out of town and mischief at nite. Before this there was no curfew regulation. Now it applies from 10 p.m. to 4 a.m.

He says the location police are not abusive. Only eight police (two European sergeants and six natives) for whole location.

Lepolesa says the Bloemfontein Location Advisory Board (twelve members elected, three nominated by the government) is innocuous, largely due to poor caliber of elected members. He was a nominated

---

*A pail was placed under a toilet seat in a latrine. When sanitation workers removed a full pail, they replaced it with an empty one. Hence, the "double pail" system.

member and at the end of his year term was dropped by the government as too radical.

The Bloemfontein Municipal Council appointed in September, 1936 a Social Welfare Officer at £ 120 per year, to organize recreational and social activities on the native location. The native appointed, about 45, has no qualifications for the job and is said by Lepolesa to be a complete flop.

The assistant M.O.H. [Medical Officer of Health] is resident on the location and residents pay him 3/6 per visit. Town medical practitioners charge 7/6; yet most of residents, because of their distaste for municipal departments and fear of being sent to isolation hospital ("one-way") in case of contagious diseases, go to the town doctors. A dispensary in location.

Council has just voted £ 20,000 for the erection of five primary schools on location, each school to accommodate 800 children. To replace mission schools.

The missions here have amalgamated in a general body setting up a central body called "The Native Education Advisory Board" for the province. Each school has its committee, elected by popular vote, consisting of a minister from each denomination and two elected members. Denominations represented: Lutherans, Anglicans, Methodists, Dutch Reformed, and A.M.E. (Catholics have been holding out). The school committee is supposed to select the teachers.

Lepolesa told me that the Bantu high school on the location had been staffed by Bantu, including the principal (Lepolesa himself used to be principal). But this year the government has appointed a white principal and three white teachers (there are now three white and four Bantu teachers) and African teachers' organizations are protesting bitterly. The Education Department had promised that a Bantu would be appointed principal. Two Bantu teachers have been given notice that their employment will end in March, 1938. Suggestion that Bloemfontein people withhold their children from the school until European principal is replaced by a Bantu.

The Bantu High School has been run by a committee from two denominations, the Methodists and Dutch Reformed. The municipality built the building. The nat. members of the school committee (who had been elected by the parents—three Europeans and six natives) have resigned over the European prin. [principal].

Lepolesa says that the municipality has refused to provide electric service for private homes on the location, though streets and communal hall are lighted by electricity. But they have promised to extend the service next year.

No pick-up vans or beer raids. Individuals are allowed home brewing at rate of four gallons per family per day; i.e., not supposed to be in possession of more than four gallons at any time. A lot of illicit selling. A lot of drunkenness in old area on Sunday p.m.'s.

Lepolesa favors the lobola, but he thinks it is losing its real significance now that cash is being substituted. Says in Basutoland the cattle were always kept by the parents of the bride to show to the children of the marriage. It was very seldom that cattle had to be returned.

Lepolesa afraid to take an active part in the African Convention for fear of losing his education job.

Lepolesa's house has cost £ 257.

Mapikela, N.R.C., is "head man" of the Bloemfontein location—by appointment of the Municipal Council at salary of £ 12.10 per month.[17] He has held the job for eight years. Is a carpenter by trade and makes fat sums through grabbing juicy municipal contracts for himself, as these must pass through his hands.

By general agreement the East London location is accepted as the very worst, and filthiest in all S.A.[18] (This is Godlo's location.)

Troupes of small children (boys) dressed in skirts composed of lattered strips (like Hula skirts) and with bottle tops around their waists and whistles in the mouths, doing Zulu dances. Each group has its leader. They know how to commercialize their talents, too, for they expect pay from me as I watch them.

December 16

It is Dingaan's Day and the Silver Jubilee of the African National Congress. When first organized in 1912, the Congress was known as the "South African Native National Congress"*—attempt to weld Africans into a unified whole over tribal lines; following example of whites in becoming one national entity to enable black people to survive "in this extreme struggle for existence."

---

*The South African Native National Congress changed its name to the African National Congress in 1923.

[The conference] started out with a procession, led by a band, around the location. Meeting opened with singing of African National Anthem. Then a black preacher announced the program for the day, which is entirely devoid of any serious considerations, but devoted to social celebration of the Silver Jubilee of the Congress. Said time has come when Africans must "repent of their sins" and must get down on their knees and pray for joy that Congress has continued for twenty-five years. Christ is the leader of the African National Congress.

The Congress, though having no money to organize, has slaughtered two oxen for the "Jubilee Feast."

The whole a.m. devoted to religious services, the singing of hymns, sermons and scripture reading. The Bishop of Bloemfontein spoke, pointing out the many good things on earth that are God's work, abjuring complainers and agitators.

A black Anglican priest emphasized the necessity for Africans to repent their sins and understand God.

Seme, the president of the Congress, who, I am told, gets arrested for bad debts every time he comes to the Congress, got up and humbly thanked the Bishop for his "helpful and encouraging thoughts." Seme in frock coat and white spats, a stovepipe hat, morning pants.

The Congress has an official chaplain who presided at the first a.m. session. The chaplain, in mentioning my name, said: "Our people for a long time have believed in the fable that the 'Americans are coming,'" and that many Africans gave money to most anyone to bring the Americans here. When I spoke, I said the slogan should be: "The Americans may come, but the Immigration Officials will meet them."

H. M. Kuschke, Chief Inspector of Nat. Educ. in O.F.S., spoke as though addressing a group of school kids. Told of his grievances, his toothache, etc. Drew abscessed tooth analogy by saying that the "abscess" in S. A. black-white relations was "mutual suspicion." [He said there was a] place for a "harmonious color scheme of white, brown, yellow, and black in S. A."

Cool crowd out for first day's session of Congress because of Dingaan's Day—a holiday. Kekane, as head of the A.A.C. delegation, made plea for a place for young men in the organization.[19] Mafutsanyana, also rep. [representing] the A.A.C., made plea for unity.

Mapikela, who got only five votes as vice-presidential candidate for the A.A.C. last nite, indulged in a lengthy, vicious and demagogic attack on the Convention and its leaders, while praising the Congress and its work. He's very voluble and fiery here, full of all sorts of platform pyrotechnics, but he scarcely opened his damned mouth at Pretoria.

The lone woman speaker criticized the Congress on the extreme attention to festivities.

The Congress shows a complete lack of organization or preparation—a ridiculous waste of time.

Seme says Congress has had no funds during his term of office. Says he has been running Congress out of his own pocket. Congress is a national movement. Its aim "is to unite the African hearts and to teach them the value of unity and action." Tries to create African public opinion—to destroy tribalism and to develop idea that all are Africans who must work together. Not desire of Congress to destroy the Convention; a great possibility of cooperation between the two organizations, if constitutions are drawn up to avoid competition between them. [Seme] appeals for cooperation of African leaders on both sides of ocean.

Seme is a *hesitant* speaker, without force or personality. (Incongruity of Seme addressing this group in his formal clothes and high hat.)

The role of the European reps. is a dangerous one—they are now counselling extreme moderation among the natives so as not to inject the native issue into the coming election, and also so as not to offend the Afrikaners and thus make their task more difficult in Parliament. They can't see that anything they do of significance for the native is bound to offend the reactionaries and that it is impossible to please both sides. They lack the courage to take a strong stand. (Cf. Mrs. Ballinger's letter in *The Friend,* December 16).[20]

At the concert and dance of the Congress on Dingaan's day, because of poor preparation and inadequate entertainment, Mapikela (responsible for poor arrangements) went around begging people to speak. He asked Jack Simons and me, but we refused because that was no place for speeches.

But several others agreed, Thema among them, and he told a "*fable*"—all about how God made a series of inspection observations of the world he had created, and found things going well in Europe and America—everybody working, skyscrapers, subways, steamships, railroads, etc., but was shocked when he viewed Africa, and found it difficult even to find the people he had put there, hidden away as they were in their mud huts at the bases of mountains. And when he did find them, they were not working but only singing, dancing and drinking Kaffir beer. God was angry and resolved to destroy Africa, but saner counsel prevailed and he sent white men down to make use of the valuable mineral resources, etc. to be found there.

Jack and I both revolted at this and asked to be permitted to say a few words. Jack spoke first and refuted Thema's fable by picturing the harsh conditions of life in Africa and pointing out how much was done by Africans despite these conditions; counselling against any acceptance of inferiority status and plea for native leadership

Then I arose and said I wished to complete Thema's dream or fable. That in mine God took another look at South Africa sometime after his earlier decision had been made and saw the black man doing all the work and the white man reaping all the profits—on farms, in mines and industries. Then God exclaimed: "My God, what kind of country *is this!*" (shocked laughter). I pointed out that if God was consistent then S. A. would be returned to the black man forthwith—but that God needn't be so burdened, if black man could only be awakened to the fact that he *actually* had the country back now. Without his labor the farms and mines wouldn't be worth a tuppence. Duty of organizations to make him realize and employ his power.

■ **December 17**

First day [of Congress was] completely wasted. Fiddled around on morning of second day, trying to cook up a program—they even sent a car for me but I refused to speak—until the Mayor of Bloemfontein came at 10:20 (he was due at 10) to address the Congress. Only a handful of people in the audience this morning—not more than 50.

Seme passed the buck and had the former Pres.-Gen. of Congress, Rev. Mahabane, introduce the Mayor.

The Mayor expresses continuing interest in the Bantu people. [He] has always fought for trading rights for Bantu in O.F.S. Hopes this right will ultimately be given as "a right and proper thing." Said Congress has consolidated native public opinion; has developed race consciousness and pride; and has played a very definite part in placing the Rep. of Natives Act on the statute books (this occasioned applause), which has been a big step forward for the Bantu. N.R.C., he says, an opportunity given to natives to express their opinions re native legislation to government as considered opinion of Bantu of the country. Congress can be of great assistance to N.R.C. Counsels "cooperation, moderation and patience"—"for it is only thus that much can be accomplished."

Rev. Calata,[21] in replying to Mayor, said his people had been brought up under chiefs and had learned obedience and loyalty and for this reason accepted the Nat. Rep. Act. But, according to views of native people, the act should have gone much further. No difference between interests of black and white in South Africa and their destiny is one of cooperation. Expresses African desire for full citizenship; expresses confidence in statesmanship of the British Empire. . . . "This is an age of fellowship among nations."

Address by Assistant Location Superintendent. Refers to Congress as "mouthpiece of Bantu people." Emphasizes importance of N.R.C. (Seme leads the applause). Indication of the most generous attitude the government has yet taken. Plea to all for *"moderation* in your speeches"— "let a spirit of calmness prevail in your deliberations."

Seme's presidential address (at long last!) Congress is founder of unity movement in this country; (takes a defense line at outset—against those who would compare Congress with other African organizations—like comparing a tree with its branches or fruits).

The whole tone of the Congress, whenever it has had any at all, has been that of looking back to past achievements—if any.

Seme not too subtly tooting his own horn. (Seme was the founder of the Congress in 1912 and Dr. Dube the first president.)

[Seme says] chief aim of Congress is to teach unity and cooperation to Africans. If unity is achieved, force is unnecessary. Encourages formation of "African Clubs,"[22] shops. Refers to his attendance at 1907 Atlanta Conference of Negro Business League.[23] Thirty-three Negro bankers there. Deduces that therefore black men can do these things.

[He gives] mild encouragement for young leadership. Chiefs watching to see if young educated Africans intend to cooperate in building up of African nation.

[He says] recent nat. legis. [legislation] . . . is fruit of work of Congress. Congress took lead in creation of Location Advisory Boards. Officials of Congress conferred with the Minister on Urban Areas Act.

Nat. Rep. Council doesn't represent "our highest aspirations"— "we accept it as a beginning"; impossible for Councillors to really represent the masses of African; Council only an opening wedge.

Says Councillors are peoples' *only leaders.*

Significance of the three Africans who read newspapers all through the Mayor's speech this morning—indifferent to appearance of white officials as an institutional thing.

Repeated apology of speakers at the Convention, Congress and the Women's Council, when they announce before beginning: "this is an African meeting and I will lose my mother's tongue (or language)."

Distrust of Africans, for each other—hesitancy about making critical statements re government, etc. in presence of other Africans.

The picture of Congress is not complete without mention of the large, old fellow, dressed in a blue sergeant's uniform and wearing a white-topped officer's cap, who acts as Sgt.-at-Arms and has been in this capacity since the inception of the Congress, I hear. He stands in front of the rostrum, salutes when the audience applauds the speaker, stops [people] smoking (as he has me) and makes himself a generally pompous nuisance.

There was always in evidence this *dependence on outsiders* among the Africans. Several told Jack [Simons] and me last night how happy they were that we were helping them. At the Congress they eagerly pounce on any outsider and ask for "an address."

Seme sits up behind the table looking scared as a rabbit. Constantly turning a pencil in his fingers and saying nothing. The secretary runs the meeting. Lepolesa says he has not been himself at all during this meeting and is very jittery due to the presence of an American here.

All blame the lack of organization and preparation of the Congress on Seme, who they say will not be reelected. They say he was surrounded by able men five years ago but that he expelled them all.

Seme, "very oxfordian," telling me of his attendance at B. T.'s [Booker T. Washington's] Negro Business League meeting in Atlanta in 1907, his being at Oxford with A. Locke, etc.[24] A typical "slicker."

Meeting of African Women's National Council. Org[anization]. under the sponsorship of Mrs. R. [Rheinallt] Jones (who is referred to by the members as "our mother") at Kimberley about five years ago. Mrs. Nikiwe (Port Elizabeth) chairwoman—very nattily and well dressed—sporty hat, short fur coat, pretty dress.

The forty or fifty women present are quite well dressed in best European manner. On the whole, they make a better appearance and speak more intelligently than the men at the Congress.

Concerned with organizational problems, and formation of a national organization from the existing branches. Question as to whether this Council would be responsible to the African Convention. Mrs. Jones says there is no obligation for them to be responsible to the Convention unless they want to. Doesn't offer much encouragement for affiliation with National Council of Women (European),[25] but endorses their "dream" of affiliation ultimately with international Council of Women. They all arose when Mrs. Jones left.

The same tendency as in men's organ. to lean heavily on advice of Europeans. (To what extent is this a deliberate effort to draw women away from the established African organizations, thus weakening them?) Ma and Pa Jones working hand in glove on moderation and splitting tactics.*

The name agreed upon is: *The National Council of African Women* (this is the temporary name for one year). One speaker from Cape makes appeal for keeping doors open to all non-European women and is glad term African instead of Bantu was adopted in name of organization.

Mrs. B. [Ballinger] makes plea for support of women. Raises question as to rapidity with which name of organization was accepted, since suggested name is not an African name.

Mrs. B., Mrs. Jones and Mrs. Marquard were invited as advisors (intimation that Mrs. B. and Mrs. Marquard on the one hand and Mrs. Jones on the other, don't quite see eye to eye on aspects of the Council). Mrs. B. suggests selection of a beautiful African name rather than imitation of a European one.

Hopes for gradual merging with European [women's] organization, but cautions that this can't come for a long time. Points out confusion re "National Council of Women" (European) and "National Council of African Women."

Mrs. Ballinger states that Mrs. Marquard states that Mrs. Jones has already wrecked two native organizations with this very tactic of encouraging them in the false hope of early affiliation with European organizations.

Mrs. Ballinger says the Council hasn't yet discussed question of affiliating with the Convention "and won't—at least not at present."

Visited "H and H" ("Heaven and Hell"), a large house just around the corner from Lepolesa's, run by a Masuto witch-doctor, who has everyone scared of him. Also a canteen for Kaffir beer. He used to run a

---

*Ma and Pa Jones refers to Mr. and Mrs. Rheinallt Jones.

religious service in front and sell beer and do witch-doctoring in the rear. Now he has dispensed with the religious services.

We entered a large room in the rear. Several women sitting about on the floor and about 10 men sitting on a bench along a wall—each with a large tin of beer before him. Lepolesa and I greeted them—one yelled out "Kaffir beer, that keeps us free of disease."

Then we went through a door to the front of the house, where we met the first wife of the "doctor." He is away in Joburg "on business"—and later the younger second wife, and the daughter of the eldest son. She ranks high in the household and the senior wife takes no decisions without first consulting her. They were very congenial. The daughter-in-law was busy sewing on a Singer portable machine.

The old lady—a typical Basuto with the customary straight-line facial marks*—brought me a small bucket of K.B. [Kaffir beer] (which retails for a tickey) and also brought out a bottle of yellow brownish fluid for me "to take back to America." This was ginger beer, I later learned. The K.B. was a sort of foamy stuff about the color of malted milk, and had a slightly sour, chalky, and slightly butter-milkish taste— not particularly unpleasant. Not much apparent kick and it couldn't have had an alcoholic content of more than 5%. I was warned by Lepolesa not to drink too much of it as it is very loosening for the bowels, and I did feel a slight kick from only one glass of it some time later.

There was a huge square tin of "working" beer sitting in a shallow box on the floor, and foaming over—directly beneath a large picture of Christ and the disciples hanging from the wall. The senior wife says she makes the beer out of ground Kaffir corn, water and yeast.

Many pictures on the wall—of both European and natives. Plenty of chinaware in the two cupboards. Particularly conspicuous were the two rows of large white mugs with "Mother," "Father," "Grandfather," etc. painted in large black letters on them.

From "H and H," we strolled across the tracks to De Erf, all that is left of the old locations. The other two locations, Waaihoek (no. 1 and the big old location) and Bethanie (no. 2 old location) have been cleared out.

There are only about 70 mud huts left in De Erf, and all of these have now been purchased by the municipality in this condemned area. They are rented temporarily at the rate of 7/ per month per room. They are in bad shape, with no yards and rarely ever with glass windows. Great ruts and pools of water in the roads. The place is in violent contrast with the

---

*Medicine was rubbed into light incisions on various parts of the face and body in order to ward off witchcraft.

appearance of the rest of the location, and the inhabitants seem very poor. It is here that Lepolesa says many fights occur over the weekends. The rest of the location looks down on the inhabitants of De Erf.

Along the back edge of De Erf, looking across the demolished mud huts, can be seen the fine-looking brick houses erected by the municipality under its sub-economic housing project for poor whites (apparently it is desirable to get these as far out of town as possible, too).

On the subject of distinctions, Lepolesa told us last night that the city couldn't get any of the local men to do the sanitation disposal work. For this work, "raw" natives are imported from the Transkei and these are housed some distance from the location in a municipal compound. The men are fairly well paid and say as long as they can get this sort of work they will never go to the mines.

Lepolesa says the local urbanized men will not consider going to the mines unless they are very hard up for money. The more urbanized and sophisticated natives become, the more difficult it will be to get them down into the mines. He says also that the location natives look down upon the sanitation disposal men and will have nothing to do with them socially.

Second night meeting [of Congress] held in small magistrate's court next to the Communal Hall—a bioscope was on there.

[Bunche's notes include a listing of resolutions passed by convention.]

On the second night the Congress split wide open over the issue of the report on the three-sided factional dispute in the Cape Province.[26] The meeting got out of hand and chaos reigned for one half hour. Things got so bad that Elias (a worker) yelled out for the "court martial"—meaning the Sgt. at Arms. Finally, after consulting with Jack [Simons], I decided to try my hand at restoring order and succeeded, by pointing out that white men pass oppressive laws in orderly bodies and that black men can only overcome these by themselves conducting orderly and calm bodies. My words were received carefully and seriously, amid deep quiet and applause at the end. I apologized for barging in on the basis of my deep interest in their work. The chairman impressed upon them the importance of my advice and later came and asked me to please remain in the meeting to help keep order by my presence.

Jack left after hearing that the location sergeant had been making inquiries as to whether he had been sleeping in the location. Mpinda had him spirited off the location in a native cab just before they came for him.

Jack made a good point when he pointed out that there would never be such disorder in a *tribal meeting*—the effect of detribalization, increasing the difficulty of organization.

It was finally voted that [factional] issue be discussed until 11 p.m. when the vote for officers would take place.

Seme arose and suggested that since the chairman was involved, that the chief—the old noble-looking Patriarch who had previously arisen and tried vainly to restore order by upbraiding them for acting like children—take the chair. (The chief (Chief Songo Kama of Middledrift) is Governor of the "Upper House" of the Congress—an institution created by Seme, which has no known function or usefulness.) This caused a storm of protest on the grounds that the chief had the personal respect of the body and should not be put in the chair on a controversial question which would cause him to lose that respect. Seme then withdrew his motion and Rev. Mahabane was put in the chair.

The Cape dispute, involving Prof. Tyler [Thaele],[27] Mr. Oliphant[28] and Rev. Calata, et al., has to do with money matters, property, and a deficit of some £ 300. Apparently some one has gotten away with some dough. Rev. Calata, Prof. Tyler and Mr. Oliphant made lengthy statements, clearing up nothing.

It develops now that the Congress had suspended Thaele last year, but he was demanding the right to vote for his delegation. Bedlam broke loose on this issue and finally my old bearded chief friend arose and walked out, shaking his head in sad and quizzical humor. He was apparently saying this could never happen in a chief's court in the good old days.

A chief called me outside and through an interpreter told me that he didn't understand anything that was going on inside, that they paid no attention to their chief and leader and that this was all incomprehensible to him. With all of that I agreed.

Seme is trying to delay the election of officers, apparently sensing that he faces defeat, and either hoping that some supporters of his will arrive tomorrow or that some opposing delegates will depart. He has begun to raise constitutional difficulties re voting. It is now 11:30 p.m.

After great difficulty the presidential election was finally brought off—with Seme and Mahabane as rival candidates. Rev. Mahabane won by 26 to 9, with one spoiled vote. Seme then asked permission to withdraw his name in order to give Mahabane a unanimous vote, but was told it was "too late."

Later, Seme talked with me outside and told me he was glad he had found the "right man" to succeed him—that Mahabane is the best leader because he is sane and "*moderate.*" (The Rev. had served a term of three years in the office before.) Seme was glad a "radical and fire-eater" had not been put in office, because a man like Mahabane will appeal to the whites, "who can do much for us."

There was applause and the singing of the African National Anthem on the announcement of Mahabane's election. Even the Tyler faction (pro-Seme group) shook hands—but nothing like the demonstration that had been accorded Jabavu at the Convention.

After the presidential election the meeting soon dispersed—at about 1 a.m.

Why do so many of the leaders of these African organizations carry on their deliberations in broken English, when they speak their own languages so much more fluently.

Just note Seme, in stating his objections to the elections, started out by saying that he would speak in Zulu "because there are *chiefs* here." But on protest (from Tyler and others) he shifted to English, with Sesuto and Xhosa interpreters.

▰▰▰▰ December 18

Up at 7 preparing for my departure for Durban at 8:20. I rode to the station from the location in a native cab and was politely shown into an unreserved first class coupe (unreserved coach) by the cheery ticket examiner.

Later on, while I was busy writing up my notes, the ticket examiner knocked and informed me that a "couple of laddies" wanted to see Dr. Bunche. They were two Congress members—one a "big shot" politician from Cape Town. They had greeted me as I had passed them on the platform earlier, heading towards the ticket examiner to get my reservation, and the "politician" had then informed me that the "reserved coach" was "back the other way."

The train from C.T. was over an hour late and we will have to wait at the station here until it comes in—we'll be well over an hour late in starting.

Uneventful trip—ate lunch and dinner in the dining car, read and slept all day, until about 10:30 when I gave up from fatigue and went to bed. Was too tired even to write Ruth. The road-bed was far too rough to attempt writing anyway. The week on the location had done me in. I was tired, dirty and hungry. The train food—tho not very good—tasted delicious to me after location diet.

Wycliffe Tsotsi

T. M. Mapikela

Goolam Gool (third from right) and Jane Gool (far right)

Goolam Gool, Cissie Gool, Z. R. Mahabane

S. M. Lepolesa

ANC Procession

Bloemfontein location scene

Pixley Seme

Durban

Durban a little India. Tropical, with thick vegetation on surrounding rolling hills—banana, pineapple trees, endless fields of sugar cane. Temples and domes sticking up all over town—truly oriental, Indians all over the streets.

Went out some 30 miles to Umkomaas Sunday—drove right through sugar cane area. Caught my first glimpses of the Indian Ocean.

Umkomaas is an Indian peasant area. They own (freehold) plots of from 5 to 15 acres of good land on the rolling hills. Their best paying crop now is bananas. They also grow pineapples, sugar cane and vegetables.

Most of the old Indian men came to South Africa many years ago as indentured labor, served out their five yr. terms and remained.[1] Many of the Indian men in this area work on the large sugar estates or as waiters at the nearby beaches.

Boys begin work on the sugar plantations at about 14 and receive from 13/- to 15/- per month. Men (women don't work in this area) receive from £ 1.10 to £ 2 per month and food. Grub consists of rice and mealie meal.

Two Indian schools within a radius of two miles. One, with 270 pupils, is [government] aided. The other, with 80 pupils, is not.

The young, dark Indian principal of the school we visited was very eloquent, but nervous. Referred to "the deep debt of ingratitude" he owed us for coming so far. The ceremony ended with the singing of "God Save the King" in the worst rendition I've ever heard. No free education for natives or Indians, though there is for colored (but not compulsory).

Up to 1899 Indians went to Europ. schools. There are 4 standards in the educ. system—European, colored, Indian and native. Colored teachers treated better than Indian and native [teachers]. Mauritians and St. Helenans, unless they are fair enough to slip into the white schools, attend the colored schools.[2] Formerly the Roman Catholics were chiefly responsible for what little education the colored children rec'd [received], but now there are govt. schools for colored.

The colored have devoted their week-ends mostly to booze and dance. No business among them. First colored business now being started. No colored press here.

Indian traders prohibited in Zululand.

███████ **December 20**

[I talked with] Champion, second to Kadale [Kadalie].[3] In 1927, [at] a Natal conference it was decided to send Kadale overseas to study labor conditions and to attend the Geneva Labor Conf. Before Kadale's departure, a Natal I.C.U. native pub. [published] a pamphlet accusing Champion of misplacing funds. This annoyed Kadale and Champion and [they] decided to sue, and lost the action, because the I.C.U. books were unaudited. White newspapers pounced on this.

Real cause of I.C.U. collapse: When Kadale was overseas, his friends told him that if he stayed longer he would not be permitted to return, as Champion was working hand in hand with govt. to keep Kadale out. These were govt. provocateurs, trying to break up I.C.U. This caused Kadale to cancel his trip to U.S. and return. Took diff. [different] attitude toward Champion then, as he believed the rumors. Had taken up drink during his approximately 6 mos. stay abroad. He returned in Nov., 1927.

On his return, he called a special I.C.U. conference in which it was decided to have the I.C.U. books audited. During Kadale's absence, Champion had had one I.C.U. officer (Provincial Secy. for Natal)—a colored man—arrested for the theft of £ 800 of organization money.[4] Convicted and sentenced to 12 months. A personal friend of Kadale.

On his return, Kadale got thru a resol. [resolution] in the governing body for audit of books. He engaged the auditors himself. Books audited in Champion's absence, though Champion was the Ass't Nat'l Secy. of the I.C.U., in charge of all the branch offices and had taken Kadale's place in his absence.

The audit showed a deficit of about £ 800. The auditors said they could give no certificate because of this.

Kadale blamed Champion and asked for his suspension—this was done by a vote, the Natal branches not voting. This pleased the Natal branches which had been vs. [against] the centralization of funds. After the suspension vote (at May, 1928 conference in Bloemfontein) all of the Natal branches walked out. This was the first and most fatal split in the I.C.U.

The Natal branches proceeded to hold their own conference in Durban, on May 31, 1928. These branches contributed most of funds of the I.C.U. The Natal branches asked Champion to be the genl. secy. of the I.C.U. of Natal. After a month's delay, during which Kadale accepted Champion's invitation to come to Natal for a conference, Champion accepted.

Kadale had advised Champion not to accept the Natal invitation. He had first treated the secession with contempt. Told Champion his suspension was merely camouflage for govt's consumption and would soon be lifted. It was lifted, but because he was "fed up" with Kadale, Champion refused to come back into the fold. He thought Kadale was not sincere, and that tho he did not steal any money, he was extravagant.

From time of Natal secession, the National I.C.U. steadily lost strength, but the Natal I.C.U. grew in power. The Natal membership approximated 50,000, registering men and women alike.

The Natal I.C.U. paid over £ 1000 per month for clerks and secretaries, and £ 50 per month rent for Durban office (117 Prince Edward Street). Natal I.C.U. ran a clothing factory, "The African Workers Clothing Factory," with a European in charge (an American—Beatty [Batty]).[5]

In 1929, the Natal I.C.U. boycotted the municipally brewed Kaffir beer for 11 months, and boycotted and picketed all the European-owned Kaffir eating houses, closing them. They closed one shop owned by an Indian by boycott.

Champion doesn't believe in calling strikes unless the organ. is in a position to feed the strikers.

There was one strike of rickshaw pullers called in 1930.[6] Strike lasted 14 days. The rickshaw pullers used to pay 10/- per week to owners (Europ.) of rickshaws. The strike demanded a reduc. [reduction] to 6/- of this rental. For 14 days there was not a rickshaw in the street. Strikers fought to stop strike-breakers. The companies complained that they were losing money and strike was not won. But in a month or so later, the rental fee was reduced to 6/- and the minim. [minimum] tariff was upped from 3d to 6d.

Champion was banished in Sept. 1930 by the Min. of Justice, Pirow. [Champion] must leave Natal for a period of 12 mos. and this was subsequently extended for 2 more years. [Ban imposed] conditions under which he might visit his family—report to police, no speeches, attend no meetings, no press interviews.

Champion says Natal I.C.U. is not yet dead and that natives still have a deep affection for it.

Irony of *Champion*, the big shot among black "reds" and Kadale's right-hand man in the I.C.U., now advocating the development of African business as the solution to the oppression of Africans.[7] Refusing to consider my allegation that this is a blind alley, and my pointed reference to American Negro experience.

There are no municipal residential restrictions, but there are property covenants. There is no proposed colored township as in Joburg. There is no great fear of colored here—the problem is the Indian.

In tram cars, the three rear seats upstairs are reserved for non-Europeans. On "unreserved" trams anybody can sit anywhere, but on trains "reserved" coaches are for non-Europeans. Tram car signs say that all seats except the last three upstairs are reserved for persons of European descent.

Durban, too, has censorship in the movies. When certain types of pictures are being shown at the two non-European houses, signs are put out stating that children and natives will not be admitted.

The Commissioner for Native Affairs told me there is a usual charge of £5 for a permit to enter the locations. But he waived it in my case. His girl secy., after making out two passes for me, told me that if I entered the location alone, I wouldn't need any pass at all—only if I was accompanied by someone would it be necessary. She said that most of the local natives live in town, but that under new law they were being ejected, but no new locations had been established for them yet, "the poor blighters."

[Discussion with M. Gamiet.] In the early days, Malay was real skilled worker in Cape wood-work, carpentry, musicians, tailors, etc. Were small shopkeepers, too, until Indians pre-empted this in the 1890's. During the time of the Transvaal under Paul Kruger,[8] . . . Malays were required to carry passes (metal discs) in their pockets, but the colored had to wear theirs on their sleeves. Later on, the colored were required to carry passes in order to go out at night, but the Malays did not. As a result, many coloreds used to wear fezzes at night in order to pass as Malays.

The Cape Malay Association was organized in 1912 and was recognized by the government as recognizing the Malay community. The reason for organizing it was that after the Boer war there was differentiation between the Malay and Cape Colored in the Transvaal in 1905, '06, and '07. Colored could pass borders freely, but Malays were required to carry permits. There was an attempt to treat Malays as Asiatics. This lasted about 2 or 3 years, and led to the group consciousness of Malays.

This organization is the first non-European political organization to acquire property.

M. A. Gamiet was the founder and the first and only president. He fought for the cooperation of all the non-European organizations and for cooperation with natives.[9] The association attained a membership in Cape Town alone of between 4000 and 5000 about 1920–24. Gamiet was the first colored man on the Executive Committee of the Cape Federation of Labor Unions in 1916. He always stood for the industrial organizations of non-Europeans. The Malay organization is still nominally in existence, but it has been non-active since Gamiet left Cape Town six months ago.

Says Australians introduced the econ. color bar in S.A. They came to help Eng. in the Boer War—remained as workers, refusing to work beside non-Europeans. Says Dutch would not refuse to work with non-Europeans, though they were opposed to anything suggestive of social equality. Says hope of non-European lies with the native.

Gamiet says Smuts is the dirtiest politician in the world, but he is a supporter of Hertzog!

"For European" and "Non-European" signs are all over the town. Separate counters at the P.O. Even some of the rickshas bear signs reading "For Europeans Only."

<h2>December 22</h2>

Talks with Kajee: definite lines between Mauritians and St. Helenans and rest of non-European community here.[10]

There are still some 800 Indians in Natal who retain the municipal franchise since the 1924 muni. [municipal] disfranchisement act didn't apply to those who already exercised it. Kajee says that these 800 are still able to control elections in some wards.

The disfranchisement in general elections came in 1896. There are a couple of Ind. [Indians] who still have the broad franchise right.

There is a strong faction in the Ind. community receiving support from such official Indian sources as the Agent-General and the Ind. govt., which is hoping and working for a modified Indian franchise—even if only along the lines of that extended to the natives in the Nat. Represen. Bills. Kajee [is] strongly opposed to this kind of sop.

The So. African Indian Congress is apparently a one-man show, and Kajee admits that it has no mass support.[11] Indian businessmen are its chief financial backers. But Kajee contends that its leadership since Gandhi has largely come from the masses—and Hindu masses at that.

Kajee explains the emphasis on the educated and trading class of Indians by Gandhi and the Ind. govt. by fact that the restrictions against Indians began in 1887 against the merchant and artisan Indian, i.e., the "free immigrant." The indentured Indian labor was not stopped until 1911, and therefore the "better classes" were the first to need protection.

Kajee discussed the traditional fear of the Indian popul.—a fear which had roots in the Indian religion and which was encouraged and exploited by the Brahmins. The breakdown of this fear complex is Gandhi's greatest service to the Indian people.

Kajee on Gandhi: Admits that economically he [Gandhi] is a reactionary. Says he has a disastrous tendency to compromise and bend at crucial moments. He likes the flattery and the ceremonious obedience and humility shown toward him by his lieutenants.[12] He came to S. Africa to undertake legal work for 2 wealthy Indian families here and was catered to by rich Indian merchants.

In the S.A. general strike which he called and the march of 300 Indians across the Transvaal border to break the immigration laws there, Gandhi was spirited away at night by two C.I.D. men and imprisoned.[13] The march continued and Smuts was respon. for shooting some of the marchers. When Gandhi was released from jail he called the strike off, on the ground that blood was being shed and he couldn't take unfair advantage of his foe. He did get an agreement from Smuts to modify the immigration law. He had gotten the mass movement going because of the £ 3 tax.

In the India proposed general strike of 1922, when Kajee claims India could have broken away from Britain, all plans were well-laid and the country was ready. Gandhi was imprisoned and during his incarceration the popul. of a small Ind. town in the north broke loose prematurely, burned the jail and killed 17 police. This caused Gandhi to call off the strike, saying India was not yet ready for it.

In another instance, one of Gandhi's sons fell in love with one of Goulam Gool's sisters—a Moslem. The girl wrote to Gandhi telling him of their love and asking him for his approval of this union of a Hindu and a Moslem as a fine demonstration of the breaking down of the religious barriers between the groups, which he had advocated. (The son was in S. Afr.) Gandhi refused and published a letter about marriage and carnal sex. But two weeks later he recalled his son and married him to a *Hindu* girl.

The Colonial Born Settlers Indian Association.[14] Formed in 1933 by Christopher.[15] Christopher had been active in Congress and became dissatisfied with it.

Under old Ind. indenture system, Indians serving out their tenure had 2 alternatives: they could have their fare paid back to India or stay here and receive Crown lands. [Under the] repatriation scheme, Union govt. paid fare of Indians and families back to India and £ 20 additional on the condition that they could not return within the first year, but must return before the expiration of 3 years or not at all. If they returned, they had to reimburse the govt. The colonialization scheme [was an] attempt to get S.A. govt. enrolled in a scheme to aid India find a "colony" for her surplus popul. This issue broke the Indian Congress into factions.

This agreement was made by the Indians and Malan, who was then Min. of the Interior. When Hofmeyr succeeded Malan, he started a movement to ascertain how many S.A. Indians would support the colonization scheme. This issue split the Congress and led to the formation of the Colonial Born Assoc.

The Assoc. takes attitude that native born Indians are South Africans and must take their proper place in S.A. [They] recognize an identity of interest with other non-European groups on basis of identity of econ. (working–class) interests. Assoc. has taken an active part in the support and formation of non-European unions.

Christopher maintains the new industrial legislation and the civilized labor policy, while causing some hardship to non-European workers, has meant a considerable wage improvement for them. Indian traders, however, are fearful of the Association's stand for industrial legislation.

Christopher says the government is now more disposed to give natives trading rights in the reserves and locations. They say coloreds are also beginning to believe that the solution of their problem is in the development of business.

The policy of the government is not to employ any more Indians on the railways. Only about 500 are left.

Talk with Capell—Engineer's Union. Said most of labor men I met in Joburg are communists—Kulk, Wolfson, etc. Said labor people want to organize natives, but their efforts are hampered by the insincere efforts of "reds" and irresponsible "agitators" who are misleading and robbing the natives. Said honest labor organizers can't compete with wild promises, equality, etc. advanced by the "reds."

Says natives can be organized with whites, but not so long as the "reds" are misleading them.

Advanced the usual theory that natives can't be accepted on same plane as whites because latter have the advantage of "thousands of years of civilization" behind them and natives are "*raw*." Natives not so skillful but they are good *helpers* for skilled white workers.

Advanced a biological theory re mine blasting. He said that no matter how much training is given them, natives simply can't learn to do mine blasting properly and 9 out of 10 accidents from this in the mines result from white miners permitting natives to do blasting.

Says natives are fundamentally different from American Negroes, and that we are superior.

Don M'timkulu affirmed that many natives have found it impossible to obtain passports when they wish to go abroad to study. He had great difficulty himself, and had to enroll aid of local European officials and undergo a long delay before he finally got it. When it was first issued, it was marked "for 12 months only"—though ordinarily passports here are good for 5 years. He asked for a longer period out of country and it was a long time before he could get it.

Don told how one of his friends had tried to get a passport in order to go abroad to study and had been continually unsuccessful. Then he learned that one was being issued to a blind native who was being sent to England to learn methods of teaching the blind. He went to the office with this native posed as his attendant, and was issued the passport.

Rev. M'timkulu[16] says Natal has not supported the African Convention because of the feeling that the Convention is attempting to usurp the position of existing organizations such as the I.C.U., which is still strong and active in Natal. He points out that the Convention developed around the Cape franchise and the Native Rep. Bills, and that Zulus are not interested in the franchise because it is foreign to their experience; their thinking is entirely in terms of *land* and *more land*. They think that if they can get more land their problems will be solved. But they aren't interested in buying any land—they think it must be *given* to them because they say the land belonged to their fathers and they wish it to be given back to them.

Rev. M'timkulu said that very definitely the chiefs are mere puppets of the government. The people cannot expect support from them.

Don M'timkulu thinks that though the Nat. Rep. Council is merely a sop to the natives, still, insofar as Zululand is concerned, it has a definite value, in that it is giving the Zulu the first—though very first experience—he has had with the franchise. Thus it is of important educational value. From this first step he feels that the govt. will be forced to go further.

Don spoke at the Rotary Club, of which he is proud, and had lunch with its members, and told them that the so-called "racial" problem here is not racial at all, but economic.

Example of "Indian privilege"—an Indian legislator, visiting S.A., had an appt. [appointment] with Hofmeyr, but when he went to the gov't bldg. to keep the appt., he was refused permission to use the lift by the European operator. Hofmeyr's secretary came down and finally had to take the Indian up by operating the lift himself.

The liquor situation here is curious. There are Indian bars which sell any sort of liquor, hard or soft. But no Indian may purchase bottled liquor for "off" consumption unless he has a special permit.

Kajee told me that he tried to get first-class accommodations for the four young Indians sailing on the Taswan with me, and was told by the company that they could give them 1st class accommodations but the difficulty concerned the dining room—they couldn't serve them in the dining room.

December 23

[Visited] native men's barracks . . . established in 1915. . . . Housing accommodation for 3000 men. Drab cement buildings—army barracks atmosphere. Eating and cooking rooms—large barren halls with great open hearths lining the sides. Men can cook here on open fires.

Several open-air, cold-water shower sheds.

The latrines in the latrine sheds are equipped with running water, but no stools ("squat" toilets). They were reasonably clean and free of odor.

In the rooms furnishing accommodation at 5s per month, there are from 10 to 20 beds. In one room I visited there were 11 beds, close together, in room approx. 15′ x 30′. At this rental the men must furnish their own bedding. The "beds" are metal cots over which wooden planking serves as "springs" and "mattress."

The barrack population is reasonably stable, but there are special accommodations for transients at 6d per night—on plank beds.

There are also rooms providing accommodation at 10s per month. In these small rooms, about 6′ x 12′, are three beds—the same plank models—but for these bedding is provided.

Under construction is a new block of about 24 single rooms—these to rent for 15s per mo., for those who can afford to pay a higher price for privacy. In these, wash bowls, boards and electric plates will be provided. They are about 6′ x 12′ each. Beds, but no bedding will be furnished. They are all taken up even before completion.

One "refinement" is a married men's service—the "women's block." Here are 22 rooms in which the married men may obtain private accommodations for periods of five days (with a 3 day extension when the wives come from great distances) for their families and themselves—sort of a "procreation" accommodation. During this period the married man leaves his regular room, and at no extra cost, moves in with his family. There is a long waiting list, of course. There is a large kitchen shed with open hearths for the women to use.

One young Zulu woman with 2 small children was there—one, 10 mos. old at her breast—[she] had come from 70 miles up country to visit her husband.

There is a Native Welfare Officer (Europ.) employed by the Municipality to supervise recreational and social activities for the hostels, compounds and locations. There are football and cricket teams.

Barren recreation hall—barn-like with rows of backless wooden benches. Free bioscopes shown here once per week.

There are 4 Bantu clerks and 40 ordinary Bantu workers under the European supervisor of the barracks.

The officials, both European and native, are all quite willing to point out that the Durban Municipal Native Affairs Dept. has plenty of money for native affairs because of the handsome revenue it obtains from the Municipal Monopoly of the brewing and distribution of Kaffir beer.

Nearby are several other barracks and locations—the munic. quarters for married natives; that for Indians, the barracks for Indian railway employees; and the native sports ground.

There are free accommodations provided for Indian govt. employees and their families. These are separated from the married natives location by a wire fence which has been recently erected. Our native woman informant says this fence was erected in response to requests by both Indians and natives . . . [because] native and Indian children were always fighting and that the Indians are dirty and would empty all their rubbish on the native side.

The native married quarters—rows of brick, tile-roofed houses—are not too bad. They are 2 room houses, solidly constructed and not like the Orlando "dog houses." They are all party wall places, however, and have only a very small patch of ground in front. The backyards are cemented.

They rent for £1 per month and are equipped with electricity (no extra cost), which is provided from about 4 p.m. till early the following morning; piped water in each house; outside latrine sheds equipped with flush toilets and shower bath pipes; and a small storage shed.

There are 120 such houses—some of which have only recently been built. The rooms are of good size. Cement floors are included. The windows are well constructed and finished, but the ceilings are unfinished, though not unsightly. The residents have grown nice flower patches in the small bits of ground in front of their homes.

There are restrictions on lodgers, etc. Only one family can reside in each house unless, because the family is small, special permission is given to take in lodgers.

The usual restrictions re entry-permission required. The place is well policed—there being 7 day and 5 night guards.

The rubbish is removed by the Indian municipal employees.

The roads are well paved and lighted.

Location about a mile from town—no bus transportation. People use rickshas at 6d each way. Taxis charge 2s each way.

Conversation with Mr. Chandley, the chief clerk in Native Affairs Dept. Office.[17] Said there are 5 "eating" houses, municipally controlled, for beer distribution. Food concessions rented out to private individuals.

He said the married quarters location is definitely uneconomic at the rental of £1 per mo., but that beer revenue makes this possible. He says the native here is "supporting himself" thru the permission given him to continue his beer custom.

There are 4 Durban locations. There are about 9000 natives living in municipal locations. There are about 15,000 domestics living on the premises of their mistresses or masters.

(Don M'timkulu says the Zulu does very little work other than domestic work in Natal. The Zulu, he says, looks down on work on the sugar plantations, and this is monopolized by Indians. Even where natives are employed in agriculture or industry, he says, they are chiefly imported Pondos.)[18]

About 10,000 natives live in private barracks and compounds. They are maintained by employers who wish their employees to be in close proximity to their work.

The Durban municipality has recently instituted a system of licensing houses in which natives may live in town. The municipality approves the site and type of dwelling in which natives may rent town quarters.

There are very few natives owning their own homes in town—only 60 were on the list consulted by Chandley. About 15,000 natives live in temporary quarters in town now, and these are mostly slum areas.

Chandley says there are no Asiatic bazaars or exploitation of native renters by Indian landlords. This is controlled by a licensing system which has been instituted during the past two years in response to the danger of European and Indian exploitation of native renters. The municipality approves the site and type of dwelling in which natives may rent town quarters. Licensed houses will eventually deal with about 20,000 natives in town.

Chandley says location advisory boards serve as an outlet for the expression of native opinion as a group. There are open elections by natives. There are three elected seats and two nominated Council members. They serve one year terms.

[Municipal] Brewery occupies 4 stories just beside the Native Affairs Dept. offices. Has a capacity of 2000 gal. [gallons] per day and turns out capacity daily. Beer retails at 1/6 per gal.

30 employees. A typical, bloated, purple faced European brewer was in charge.

Under Native Beer Act of 1908, Durban was first municipality to engage in Kaffir beer brewing, which began in 1910. The profits are paid into a native admin. fund—all go for native welfare.

The beer has an alcoholic content of between 2% and 3%. The European brewer says the content could be much higher (and *is higher* in the native home brew) but that it is purposely kept low. He stresses the nutrition and medicinal value of K.B. [Kaffir beer]. Says it accounts for fact that natives, who drink it by the gallons, are free of many ailments that Europeans suffer from.

The sale hours are restricted. It is distributed thru 5 "eating" houses—which are run by the Municipality and are open from 10 to 2 and 3 to 6, "so as not to conflict too much with native working hours," says the chief clerk in the Native Affairs Dept.

The brewing is a relatively simple process. The Kaffir corn* of selected quality, usually from the O.F.S. or Transvaal, and purchased at an average price of 17/6 per bag on contract, is placed in a huge wooden vat and water is added. Then, after about 24 hours, it is spread out in the open and allowed to germinate. Then it is rotated in a huge, heated metal vat (reaching max. temp. of 120 degrees). Then it is ground, cooked (with steam) in huge, wooden vats to cool, strained and put in large wooden barrels.

The beer deteriorates quickly and must be provided for day to day consumption. It continues to ferment or "work" and cannot be bottled. It has a chalky, muddy color, but is not pungent to the taste. The natives like it to be a bit sour in taste and scorn "sweet" beer.

At the eating houses, natives line up in queues, pass a Europ. at a

---

*Kaffir corn is a species of sorghum.

counter, where they purchase 3d and 6d tickets and then go to a table loaded with tin cans of two sizes where a native in perpetual motion dips the beer up for them out of the barrel. I saw plenty of natives in the "eating" houses drinking, but none eating. The eating is done at private concessions outside of the wired enclosure that is the "Victoria" Munic. eating house in the native market on Grey St.

There is no limit on how much beer the natives wish to buy and drink, but it must be consumed on the premises. The place, despite the crowd, isn't particularly noisy for a "bar." The men sit on benches at long wooden tables and drink out of the large tins—there's no foam to blow off.

Native attendants move about picking up the emptied tins and casually dip them in a barrel of murky water for "cleaning."

Meeting at Gandhi Library to welcome Seth Govin [Govind] Das, M.L.A.[19]

Das, a son of a rich Indian, and disowned by his Rajah father, who had been warned against his Nationalist "radical" son by the British, is a fervent Indian Nationalist. He is also interested in an Indian film company which is to produce "patriotic" Indian films and is selling shares on this East and South African tour. Has sold about £5000 worth on this trip.

Plenty of chauvinism and Indian Nationalism at the meeting— appeals to Mother India. References to "grievances particularly affecting the Indian population."

Seth Govin Das emphasized Hindustani language chauvinism—"language slavery." Gave his [introduction] in English, then switched to Hindustani—a jerky, unpleasant sounding tongue. Says Indian disability laws of S.A. cannot remain on statute books whenever India gains her independence—a bold and foolish threat. Says India is surely moving toward indep. [independence].

Maurice Webb of the local Institute of Race Relations spoke.[20] Says basis upon which the white, brown and black peoples will work out the pattern of South Africa society is "equity, understanding, personal goodwill and friendship."

The South African Indians have been relatively free of communalism and religious division in the past but with increasing prosperity among South African Indian merchants it has been menacing lately with the invasion of Indian pundits and priests. Govin Das warned against this.

There is not much to see out at Lamont.*[21] A small cluster of cream-colored buildings about 1/2 mile off the road. A tennis court, administration building and a communal hall under construction. It is surrounded by rolling, green hills.

It is about 8 miles from Durban. Lamont will be a combination location and village. The land is owned by the municipality.

It is looking toward the future in an effort to provide space for a possible future expanding native population. 425 acres are now available. Lamont location has 1/2 acre sites. On these sites, the land is rented from the municipality at an annual rental which will amount to about £ 13. This part of the project is not in operation yet. He said roadways, lights, sewerage and water are to be provided.

The municipality will set building standards. A minimum of £ 25 for building materials will probably be set. There are now about 100 municipally built houses there and it is planned to build about 400 more. The municipally built houses cost about £ 120 each for the building only. They will rent for about £ 1 per month.

Single men's hostels will also be built at Lamont. It is planned to house an ultimate population of between 3500 and 4000.

"Unreserved" trams are for natives. On the regular trams non-Europeans, including natives, ride upstairs and fill up from the rear.

Gandhi—passsive resistance and vague hope for the solution of their problems through a free India, are the dominant influences in the thinking of South African Indians on their problems.

Gool thinks that the Ind. Congress in South Africa is top-heavy, with no roots in the masses of Indians, representative only of the merchant classes, and pro-imperialistic.

On Xmas eve, Goulam, Bull, Nick and I strolled about on West St., watching the revellers perform. The colored troops were predominant—string bands of colored youth, good looking mulatto girls, kids, all

---

*Bunche was visiting Lamont with Goolam Gool and Nick, an unidentified Indian, as part of his tour of African living areas.

thronged in the town's main street, playing, singing, yelling and fighting all along West Street.

Native S.A.P.'s [South African Police] were prominent—taking illegal dimensioned sticks away from native boys. There were fights—mostly between whites, but one big inter-racial row between colored and whites. The Indians and natives were relatively sedate and orderly, but the whites and colored were very rowdy and many of them were drunk. Saw one fight between colored and native girls, and several rows between whites. No vehicles allowed in West Street that night.

Bull and I went into a non-European bar—Tattersalls, at corner of Dowdy and West Sts. There were plenty of Europeans (presumably illegally) there. Immediately adjoining is an *Indian* bar run by the same management. In this one, *Cave Spirits*—looking like gin—is the most popular and cheapest drink. Also much dirtier and dingier than the non-European bar—though some Indians were in evidence in the latter.

Went to Peter's Cafe—a non-European cafe run by an Indian. Plenty of drunks, Indian and colored, in evidence. One fellow was flashing a knife as he staggered about challenging everyone in sight, including me. But he soon became contrite and maudlin and began to berate himself for not being as good as his brothers.

One's impression of the colored population here is inevitably one of a derelict population, addicted to drink, no serious purpose and completely at sea.

There is obvious resentment by the coloreds of Indians and natives.

In this town the coloreds think themselves superior not only to the natives but also to Indians—though the Indians are much further advanced economically.

■■■■■ **December 26**

Conversation with Dr. Northcutt [Notcutt] of Natal University.[22] [He said] parallel classes for non-Europeans are given at Sastri College (an Indian secondary school).[23] There are about 25 to 30 students in these classes—6 natives, 1 colored and rest Indians. This arrangement was begun about 2 years ago. It was agreed to by the Natal Univ. Council only on proviso that it pays its own way. There is a very small "parallel" library, too. Only a few courses are offered and many courses cannot be taken unless the student is able to pay for indiv. tuition. Northcutt says that University of C.T. and "Wits" [Witwatersrand University] are the only 2 other colleges admitting non-Europeans under any arrangement.

He told about the Natal meeting of Burnsides' Socialist Party last year[24]—when he (Northcutt) raised question of membership of non-Europeans. There was an attempt to evade the issue and some members got up and said that the most important things was to keep Burnsides' seat and that though they were good Socialists, they wouldn't want to sit next to a non-European in a meeting.

Luncheon at Orient Club. Luxurious place, large grounds, covered with beautiful foliage, flowers, tropical fruit trees. Long verandah. Tennis courts, ping pong tables, billiards room. Many big cars owned by Indian merchant big-wigs.

Seth Govin Das, M.L.A., advising rich merchant Indians to avoid communalism, which will break up unity. Kajee pled for unity in the Orient Club, which is now chiefly Moslem and has few Hindu members. Kajee and Gamiet also pled for unity of Indians with other non-European groups. But Indian unity was the keynote of the meeting.

I sat next to a local Swami (Hindu priest) at the luncheon and he told me about the prohibition movement in India, sponsored by the Congress which he says is to protect the peasantry. Others maintained that the real purpose of the regulation is to drive the British out of India by depriving them of drink.

Two of Gandhi's four sons are present: Monilal, editor of the *Indian Opinion* and a supporter of Christopher's Foreign and Colonial Born Indian Association, and Randas, who is visiting South Africa for his health.[25]

▬▬▬ December 27

Albert Park, a municipal "garden" where Goulam's Cape Town cricket team played the local Indian team, is open to all races—no segregation. The playing fields there are better than anything [Washington,] D.C. offers to the Negro.

Trip to Umbumbulu with M'timkulu. Passed three beautiful farming regions, rolling, green hills. Sugar cane principal crop. Section dominated by the Ilbowo Sugar Mills.

Rode through Umlazi Reserve. Natives in reserve lands growing mealies now, since slump in sugar market. A quota has been set on sugar production.

Zulu huts are thatched and round. They are not grouped together in villages but are separated from each other by some distance. Don says this has always been the Zulu custom, though in old days there would be 8 or 9 huts in a family kraal.

In Natal there are *mission reserves* in which land had been early given to the missions. In some of these, natives still own land by freehold right. The idea was originally that this land would be held by the missions until they could instruct the native in the customs of private landholding, and then be turned over to the natives. When some natives were sufficiently developed to obtain freehold rights thus, the govt. cracked down and suspended this mission privilege.

On the land of the mission reserves, some natives still pay quit rent. This now goes to the govt. which turns over 50% of the rent to the mission to be used for improvements on the reserve. The govt. now runs the mission reserves.

Adams Mission reserve and school controlled by the American Board Mission.[26] The station is over 100 years old and the school about 70. There is a high school and a small junior college or teachers' training school. There are about 400 pupils of whom 70 are girls. Girls and boys eat together in a common dining hall. The teaching staff is about 3 to 2 Bantu to white.

There are separate and superior living accommodations for the white staff. Some of the latter live in very posh bungalows.

The students pay £ 11 per year only for tuition, board and room.

No smoking is allowed on the campus, which covers a large area, and is thickly vegetated. Much of the surrounding land belongs to the school which derives revenue from raising sugar cane.

Broughton), assistant editor of the *Daily News,* [says] the condition of the coal miners in Northern Natal is worse than that of the Rand gold miners.[27] They especially suffer from the "token" system of wage payment which is so manipulated that the native remains always in debt to the company store and never gets much of his wages in cash.

Broughton says that a good study should be made of *hours of work* engaged in by workers. He says also that conditions are changing. But it is the common thing for workers to work 16 hour shifts still.

Broughton says Afrikander is opposed to including black men in the armed military forces here because:

1. The Afrikander himself dislikes the whole military idea and is reluctant to undergo the compulsory military training, many openly balking.

2. He is afraid the native's process of detribalization would be speeded up by military service, and this is contrary to the present policy of returning natives to the tribal life.

3. He is afraid the native will learn the lesson of organization in military service and apply it to other fields.

4. Broughton says there is a reluctance to give native soldiers arms but no great fear that in event of a war, natives will be recruited in labor battalions.[28]

He says there is tacit but effective press censorship by the papers themselves. Discussions of native wages, hours of work, etc. are taboo, as is any attack on the Dutch or English people. He says the Chamber of Mines is dominated by English and Jews and is very jittery. (Northcutt says that Govt. has undoubtedly been dominated by the Afrikander farmer.)

Broughton thinks that in the event of the collapse of the gold boom and the Rand mines, there will be a return to the "Kaffir and Mealies" period—the agricultural-pastoral level of existence in the country.

Broughton says that in final analysis, if the Afrikander has to choose between econ. progress and less segregation, he will always prefer a policy moulded on the old tradition of segregation and "Kaffir and Mealies."

Indian traders are not supposed to be able to rent land for stores in the native mission reserves, but they are able to do so by leasing land from native free-holders in the mission reserves.

Took my shoes in to a repair shop in Mercury Lane—opposite Cook's and told European clerk that I wanted a good job; as the soles put on in Cape Town were just paper and let the water right through.

The clerk informed me that while Malay and Indians were employed here, too, in his shop, only Europeans are employed and I could be sure of a good job.

Took picture of the "king" of the rickshaw pullers on the Marine

Drive—immense headgear, painted feet and shanks (white), with small Union Jack at peak of his headgear. He was thoroughly commercial—required pay for the pose and took off his headgear and hid behind it, when a white woman tried to snap him while I was getting ready.

The Zulu rickshaw boys [wear] feathered plumes, leglets and anklets. Most of them can't speak English. They are cheap enough—a minimum charge of 6d.

No J.C. [Jim Crow] in any of the Durban Parks, nor on the benches in them.

Witnessed . . . native police taking a stick of illegal dimensions from a native house boy on Moore Road. They took his two sticks and broke them up, and when he made some Zulu smart crack, they chased after him, one of the police threatening to throw his knobkerrie at the fugitive as they ran. I ran behind them and the chase led up a winding staircase to the second floor of an old bldg. When I got there the victim was cowering on the floor as the 3 policemen threatened him. I think they would have beaten him if I hadn't been there. Soon a European officer (off duty) came up and yelled at the top of his voice at the now defiant but quiet native and turned to me, saying: "There's too much of this stick fighting going on and we've got to stop it."

The Zulu women look very chic and seductive in their short skirts and cloths tightly wound about their breasts. They are plump, happy faced women.

The short skirts worn by the Zulu women, which are very attractive, are the traditional garb and are made of severely washed skin.

There is no municipal segregation in Durban—on Bredenkamp Street, e.g., colored and white live side by side. Similarly, in Kajee's district, colored, Mauritians and St. Helenans and white all live side by side.

There is definite segregation on the Durban beaches—some sections for whites and some for non-whites.

Walked into a branch Post Office and there were separate entrances marked for "Europeans" and "non-Europeans." I walked into the European entrance and bumped into Northcutt—he flushed but was very cordial.

Also noticed special windows marked for "non-Europeans" at Barclays Bank and its branches this morning.

But at the main P.O. [Post Office], though there is a separate counter marked "non-Europeans," plenty of natives are seen at the other counters—presumably on business for white employers, but the colored and Indians go to the non-European counter.

M'timkulu says the morals of the local Indian youth are being endangered by the colored girls. The Indian girls are kept so close that the boys turn to the colored girls, but must keep pace with the "faster" colored fellows in order to make time—so therefore they cut loose, which they can do better than the colored fellows, since they have more money, cars, etc.

December 30

Trip to Pietermaritzburg.

Non-cooperation attitude taken by some South African Indians toward Natal Ind. Congress when it refused to take attitude of hostility toward the S. Af. Agent-General for India when he, a Moslem, married a Hindu woman. A harmful split in the Congress. Some even refuse to attend meetings.

Naidoo of Pietermaritzburg, one of the non-cooperators, emphasizes the franchise as the solution to the Indian's problems in So. Afr.

Seth Govin Das advises a policy of watchful waiting for So. Afr. Ind. Congress until it is seen what attitude the Ind. Cong. takes in India. Das himself opposed participation in the new coast elections, but still supports the Congress.

Among the S. Afr. Indian leaders there seems to be a definite expectation that at the next coming Indian-S. Afr. Round Table Conference (which is tentatively scheduled for next Xmas, the union govt. will offer Indians a sop like the N.R.C. given the natives.[29] The attitude of the Indian leaders is dead-set opposition to the acceptance of any such compromise.

Das boasted that if India were free today the restrictions on the Indian in So. Afr., which he claims are the greatest suffered by Indians anywhere in the world, would not exist. (Very naive.) Says first thing Indians should get here is the right to vote. They have a just claim to it because they are civilized, educated and about 85% native born, many in business, and even white women vote.

Das said the Indians should be given the general franchise—not what the natives were given. Indians should accept nothing less; in fact, Indians should be represented in Parlia. [Parliament] by Indians, and if it is not possible now, it will be when India gains her freedom.

He then turned to a plea for revival of Indian culture here. He said the Indian lang. should be made the second language in the schools. "You are not to forget that you are Indians." He added that Indians must also fight for the just demands of other non-Europeans—the natives especially.

The mayor, in replying to Kajee's tender of thanks, and also obviously replying to Das' dumb appeal to the Indians to remain Indians, . . . very forcefully pointed out that So. Afr. "is a white man's country," and that white man and white ways are dominant here. Therefore any group wishing to rise must make itself worthy of it, i.e. by adopting the white man's ways.

Das, very foolishly, had laid a trap for himself . . . by demanding full rights for S.A. Indians, most of whom were born in South Africa, and at the same time advising S.A. Indians to be Indians first and S. Africans second.

The Chief Native Commissioner for Natal spoke and pled for patience and tolerance in re Indian problem. Said it must not be forgotten that there is a white problem too—which is just being ironed out—i.e. conflict bet. Eng. and Dutch elements. He added that the most formidable problem, i.e. the native problem, is showing signs of improvement, due to the solution of the English-Dutch problem. But "toleration, cooperation and good-will" are essential if these problems are to be solved.

At dinner at home of an old 76 year old Indian—who was born here one year after Indians were first brought to South Africa. He has 3 wives, all living, is the father of 33 children, 21 of whom are living. His first born is now 63 years old. He has 76 grandchildren and 7 great grandchildren.

We all (about 30 of us) sat at a very long table—and were served with over a dozen different dishes. No cutlery—we ate with fingers and the flat Indian pan cakes like Mexican tortilla[s]. After this we were asked to step out for a while and then ushered back in to eat the sweets courses—pudding, rich cakes, etc. Everything was highly seasoned, many very hot dishes, etc. But no meat—as Seth Govin Das is a vegetarian.

At end of meal, we all lined up outside while one man poured water out of a pitcher for us to wash our hands and mouths and another held a towel.

The women did nothing but work in the kitchen and wait on the table. There was not a single woman at the meeting either.

December 30

Don M'timkulu [took me to visit Johannes] Shembe, a Zulu prophet, about fifteen miles from Durban. The current "prophet" is the son (about 35) of the former prophet [Isaiah] who died about 1934.[30] The son is a Fort Hare product. The movement has been on about 15 years.

The old man who was working as a farmer in the Free State and had no connection with any church claimed to see a "vision" calling him to come and preach to his people in Natal.

A church bldg., only in which to keep the sacred vessels, but most of the worship is done outside. Their Sabbath is on Saturday as per Old Testament.

The prophet is regarded as God's representative and his followers give everything to him a la Father Divine.[31]

A big yard for dancing—always in African dress.

About 1000 people in his one village—*Ekupakemeni* (meaning "the high place"). A rural village, and all their property is incorporated. They live communally. Papers credit him with a total following of about 20,000 with prop. [property] in farms throughout Zululand. Many Indians and even whites now numbered among the group.

Emphasis is strongly on side of native custom—more anti-missionary teaching rather than broadly anti-white.

There's no pretension about the "prophets" [by] neither the old man or his son; they seek no publicity and indulge in no ostentation.

December 31

Just listening to New Year's Eve broadcast at 6:30 p.m. The Indian broadcast is just completed—and the announcer wishes everyone of "whatever race, color or creed," "Happy New Year."

After last night's "orgy" I slept until 8:30. I woke up feeling weak in the stomach and with a slight "head." I took some salts and then got down to the job of packing. I enjoyed my last bowl of Kajee's Kaffir corn porridge. Don M'timkulu phoned and then came by. Goulam said goodbye and went to play cricket. Bull seems ready to be sad about my leaving—he says the house will be so strange and quiet with me gone. Bull's a sincere, honest, loyal and likeable guy—he's regular. Don took me and the boys to the pier in his Reo. Kajee, Bull and Dr. Goovar came along. Northcutt and Coblanz were on board waiting to see me off when I boarded the ship half an hour before sailing time. Also Gamiet, Shaik and Suleiman. I have a 3 berth stateroom all to myself. I collected my refund from the Immigration Officer on board. In the dining room I'm at a table for 3—the Chief Engineer and a young Dutch girl en route to Beira. The engineer didn't show up at either meal today. I read and wrote a letter to Ruth to start the new year right. To bed at 11 p.m.

Rickshaw puller with Don M'timkulu

Seth Govind Das, Kajee, Gandhi, Durban

Indian school, Umkomaas

Epilogue

By the time Bunche left South Africa on 2 January 1938, his research experiences so excited him that he left reluctantly. "One can do 'placer' field-work here," he enthusiastically reported to Herskovits, "just run a bit of water over the surface and the material pops out at you."[1] He even had his permit extended to allow him to stay until 30 April so he could put in several more months of research. But at the urging of Schapera and Simons, he kept to his schedule and headed on to East Africa. He was mindful that his grant was for "research training," not research.

Despite his brief stay, he was satisfied that he had fulfilled his goals. "All in all," he summed up in his quarterly report to the SSRC, "I consider my visit to South Africa to have been an exceptionally profitable if not always pleasant one. . . . It is a land terribly ridden with race prejudice, but I found this to be no great handicap to my work, even in tackling the scores of officials with whom I had to have contact. I have had no really unpleasant experiences, though some that might be described as humorous or ludicrous." And perhaps to counter the reservations of Malinowski and others about the ability of African-American researchers to carry out field research in Africa, he added: "I am reasonably convinced that an American Negro, endowed with a reasonable amount of common sense, tact and a fair sense of humor, can do effective fieldwork, even in South Africa, once he gains admission to the country, of course."[2] Indeed, he concluded his color had been an asset in his research. He related to Herskovits: "I have found that my Negro ancestry is something that can be exploited here."[3]

Bunche spent the next five months in East Africa before heading on to Indonesia and finally returning to the United States in late 1938. Even before he left South Africa, Herskovits had begun encouraging him to write a book based on his South African experiences. At first, Bunche hesitated to put his findings in print because he wanted to return to South Africa and worried that a critical publication would put him on the South African government's "*black* list."[4] But he also understood that publishing was essential if he wanted to carve out a reputation for himself as an academic. Moreover, it served as a convenient excuse for sidestepping another stint of university administration. Mordecai Johnson had indirectly sounded him out about taking the deanship of the College of Liberal Arts or the Graduate School of Arts and Sciences when he returned. However, he adamantly resisted taking on another administrative position (or "university wet-nursing" as he disdainfully put it) until "I prove to myself (and the public, maybe) that I can't do scholarship, and I'd be sorry that such a day will ever transpire."[5]

On his return, he decided to move ahead with his plans to write a book about South Africa. In early 1939, the SSRC awarded him the $500 John Anisfield grant to write up his proposed topic—"An Analysis of the Political, Economic and Social Status of the Non-European Peoples in South Africa." Bunche proposed the following chapters in his outline: a historical survey, the South African government and its color policy, labor problems, social controls, significant forces in white South Africa, what European and "non-European" South Africans think, "non-European" political and protest organizations, and a comparison and contrast of the American and South African experiences in race relations.[6]

Bunche took up the latter theme in a speech on race relations in the United States and South Africa that he delivered at Howard University and Northwestern University. He pointed out some obvious similarities between the racial attitudes and stereotypes that whites manufactured in both countries: that blacks were "happy, child-like primitive[s]" and that as "hewers of wood and drawers of water," they must carry the white man's economic burden, whether in the cotton fields of the American South or the gold mines of South Africa. He also recognized a parallel between the antagonisms between whites—whether "Yankees vs. Southerners" or "Boers vs. English." He commented on the parallels between informal and formal labor, social, and residential controls at work in both countries. And he noted the impact racial discrimination had in creating an "escape psychology," as reflected in the fixations some African-Americans and South African Coloureds had with differentiating skin color within their own groups, passing for whites, creating a black business community, and succumbing to the racial appeals of black leaders.[7]

However, he also understood a basic difference: that while African-Americans were a "numerical and racial minority—a 'black menace' in the eyes of the South, to be sure, but still less than one-tenth of the total population of the nation," Africans were a distinct majority in South Africa. While he saw very little hope for Coloured and Indian South Africans, he thought the Africans' numbers and economic power gave them hope for the future. On the other hand, he believed South African whites were not about to loosen their controls because their obsession with their minority status had contributed to "a group 'fear psychosis' almost approaching hysteria, and which manifests itself in a vigorous determination to keep the threatening non-European groups in their respective 'places'—places carefully demarcated for them by white policy."[8]

Burdened by his teaching and administrative responsibilities as chair of the Political Science Department, Bunche did not make headway on his South Africa monograph in 1939. In addition, Gunnar Myrdal, a Swedish economist, whom the Carnegie Corporation appointed to direct a study on the American Negro, recruited him (and other members of the Howard faculty) to serve on his staff. Their research eventually appeared as *An American Dilemma,* a massive work that set the tone for race relations research for the next several decades. By mid-1939, Donald Young was encouraging Bunche to postpone his South Africa work and devote his time to the Myrdal study. Bunche was reluctant to do this, although carrying out an American study had long been a priority for him. Eventually he relented and became a key assistant to Myrdal, accompanying him on trips around the American South and drafting memoranda which still retain a reputation as the most outstanding analysis of African-American political and economic movements of that era.[9]

From that point on, Bunche never returned to his South African notes, although from time to time he exchanged letters with South African acquaintances such as Cissie Gool, Christian Zierfogel, Abe Desmore, Gana Makabeni, A. B. Xuma, Julius Lewin, who came to New York in 1947 to work with him for a year in the United Nations Trusteeship Council, and Z. K. Matthews, who renewed his friendship with Bunche when he was visiting professor at Union Theological Seminary in 1952–53.

Bunche's research for the Myrdal study, his disillusionment with the National Negro Congress and the outbreak of the Second World

War led him to reappraise his independent radicalism and shift toward a more pragmatic stance. Although he still questioned whether African-Americans were ever destined to achieve full rights and equality in a capitalist system, he moderated his views on the New Deal. He contended that while the New Deal did not go far enough, it had at least brought in black advisers, offered more jobs to black workers, and set in place some useful programs such as Social Security, minimum wage and hour legislation, and the AAA-sponsored cotton control program. He also conceded that organizations such as the NAACP that advanced black voting rights through court challenges made a positive contribution to breaking down walls of segregation and discrimination. And he even went so far as to advocate financial aid to black small businessmen.[10]

The outbreak of the Second World War alarmed Bunche and many other black leaders. They understood that if a totalitarian ideology such as Nazism was victorious, it would erase even the minor gains they had achieved. In analyzing the implications of the war for black people, Bunche showed that he had not strayed from his anti-colonial stance by arguing that Africa principally figured in the war as a convenient battleground for European nations. "The Black men of Africa . . . are the innocent pawns in the disgusting spectacle of the so-called civilized nations and their rulers fighting each other to death, destroying their manhood and property to determine which nation will be dominant, which nation will receive the lion's share of African and other spoils."[11] Therefore, he had no illusions about the common plight of black people in Africa and the United States: "We are not permitted to share in the full fruits of democracy, but we are given some of the peelings from the fruit."[12]

As he assessed the competing forces in the global conflict, he concluded that the choice for blacks lay between "what is less bad as against something much worse."[13] The victory of Hitler's master race philosophy and a brutally efficient Nazi machine bent on "totalitarian, fascist imperialism" would inevitably lead to "abject, hopeless slavery" for African Americans and Africans. Nazism was a far greater threat than the "democratic imperialism" of France and Britain or a flawed American system that allowed for some possibility of extending democratic values and improving the status of blacks.[14] To Bunche, there was no question of which side blacks should back, and he threw his support behind an anticipated American entry into the war. As he disclosed to Julius Lewin, "For my part, I am inclined to be all for it, and rather selfishly so. Conditions here are such that a Hitler victory would inevitably result in an American fascism. That would, of course, mean the end of me and my people."[15]

In 1941, Bunche entered a new phase of his life by accepting an offer from William Donovan of the Office of the Coordinator (later the Office of Strategic Services (OSS)) to become a senior social science analyst with responsibility for colonial peoples in Africa and the Near East. He remained in that position until January 1944 when the Department of State appointed him divisional assistant in its Division of Political Studies. A year later, he became associate chief in the Office of Special Political Affairs with responsibility for trusteeship affairs. As the U.S. delegation's technical expert on trusteeship issues at the conference organizing the United Nations in 1945, he forcefully advocated advancing colonial territories to independence.[16]

After the Department of State loaned him to the United Nations as Director of the Trusteeship Division in May 1946, Bunche joined the United Nations in 1947 as a permanent civil servant. One of his first assignments was assisting with mediation in the Middle East, but when Jewish terrorists assassinated the chief negotiator, Count Bernadotte, in 1948, he assumed the count's place and brokered an armistice between Israel and four Arab states. For his achievement, the Nobel committee awarded him its peace prize in 1950.

Winning the Nobel Peace Prize catapulted Bunche into the international limelight, and he was accorded celebrity status, especially in the black world. News of the Nobel prize quickly spread throughout South Africa and generated a variety of reactions from the black community. For instance, it did not set well with *The Torch* (19 December 1950), a radical Cape Town newspaper, which labeled Bunche a "Negro Quisling" for settling the Palestinian issue at the expense of Arabs and for having sided with "imperialist" forces in other conflict situations.[17] In contrast, ANC president Dr. Xuma congratulated Bunche on his accomplishments as a Middle East mediator: "We wish . . . to let you know that the non-white world and reasonable whites think very highly of your achievement. They appreciate the object lesson that men of your type and training should be in this struggle for freedom of opportunity."[18] Word of the Nobel award even filtered down to small towns. When a young African in Kroonstad in the Orange Free State heard about it, he seized on the example of a black man trying to help out Jewish people in the Middle East as a comeback to Jewish kids he was scrapping with.[19]

Bunche's Middle East negotiating was the first in a number of mediation efforts he carried out through the United Nations. In 1955, Secretary General Dag Hammarskjold appointed him Undersecretary General for Political Affairs at the United Nations. In that post he was the architect of United Nations' peacekeeping activities and oversaw its involvement in Yemen, Congo, Cyprus, and the Middle East. He remained an active presence in the United Nations until illness forced his retirement shortly before his death in 1971.

In looking back on Bunche's life, his distinguished career as a public official will undoubtedly overshadow his earlier contributions as an academic. But as his South African research notes demonstrate, his pioneering work on Africa deserves renewed recognition. His notes are not only a testament to his instincts and skills as a researcher, but his findings illuminate a dimension and an era in South Africa's past that others will profitably mine for years to come.

NOTES

1. Bunche to Herskovits, 30 Nov. 1937, MJH Papers.
2. "Quarterly Progress Report of Ralph Bunche for SSRC, submitted 1 December 1937," RJB Papers, Box 126.
3. Bunche to Herskovits, 30 November 1937, MJH Papers.
4. Emphasis in original. Bunche to Herskovits, 10 January 1938, MJH Papers.
5. Bunche to Herskovits, 30 November 1937, MJH Papers.
6. "SSRC John Anisfield grant for race relations study during 1939," RJB Papers, Box 126. His grant proposal included taking a trip through the American South to reacquaint himself and improve his understanding of the region.
7. See the detailed notes for a talk on "Race Relations—African and American" that Bunche gave to the wives of Howard faculty on 17 February 1937. RJB Papers, Box 43.
8. "SSRC John Anisfield grant."
9. Assessments of the Myrdal study include: David Southern, *The Use and Abuse of an American Dilemma, 1944–1960* (Baton Rouge: Louisiana State University, 1987); John H. Stanfield, *Philanthropy and Jim Crow in American Social Science* (Westport, Conn.: Greenwood Press, 1985); Walter A. Jackson, "The Making of a Social Science Classic: Gunnar Myrdal's An American Dilemma," *Perspectives in American History*, n.s., vol. 2 (1985): 221–49; and Walter A. Jackson, *Gunnar Myrdal and America's Conscience: Social Engineering and Racial Liberalism, 1938–1987* (Chapel Hill: University of North Carolina Press, 1990).
10. Ralph Bunche, "The Programs of Organizations Devoted to the Improvement of the Status of the American Negro," *Journal of Negro Education* 8 (1939): 539–50.

11. Ralph Bunche, "Africa and the Current World Conflict," *Negro History Bulletin* 4 (October 1940): 11. See also Bunche's "The Role of the University in the Political Orientation of Negro Youth," *Journal of Negro Education* 9 (1940): 571–9; and "The Negro's Stake in the World Crisis," a speech delivered at State Teachers College, Montgomery, Alabama in December 1940; and "World Problems and the Negro," a speech delivered at Lincoln University in February 1941. (RJB Papers, Box 43.)

12. Bunche, "Africa and the Current World Conflict," 13.

13. Kirby, "Ralph J. Bunche and Black Radical Thought," 135.

14. Bunche, "Africa and the Current World Conflict," 14.

15. Bunche to Julius Lewin, 17 October 1940, RJB Papers, Box. 1. The issue of whether to participate in the war also sparked an intense debate among black South Africans. Some professed loyalty to the government, but many were indifferent or openly hostile to South African government appeals for their support, reasoning that Nazi domination could be no worse than white South African rule. Like Bunche, some black South African intellectuals weighed the alternative of Nazi rule and opted to support Britain. A. P. Mda, an Orlando schoolteacher and later president of the ANC Youth League, wrote that with democracy at stake, Africans "are siding, as we have always sided, with that power which has always defended and upheld the rights of small nations—the indomitable Britain," (*Imvo Zabantsundu,* 3 August 1940.)

16. See Robert Harris, "Ralph Bunche," for details on Bunche's involvement in decolonization.

17. Jack Simons also questioned Bunche's association with the United Nations. Reflecting on his contacts with Bunche a half-century earlier, he described Bunche as a 'radical liberal' and "was surprised when he joined the UN bureaucracy because I considered it to be a somewhat conservative honeypot for careerists, rather than genuine radicals. (Letter from Jack Simons to Robert Edgar, 18 May 1986.)

18. A. B. Xuma to Bunche, 18 May 1949, RJB Papers, Box 3.

19. Conversation with Nana Mahomo, Washington, D.C., July 1990.

Notes to the Travel Diary

■■■■■■■ **Cape Town**

1. Abe Desmore went to the United States on a Carnegie grant to study juvenile affairs and social work and received an M.A. in Education from Columbia University in 1935. He met Bunche at a conference that Howard University's Social Science Division sponsored in May 1936 on "The Crisis of Modern Imperialism in Africa and the Far East." During the mid-1930s he was secretary of the Cape Peninsula Coloured-European Joint Council, and he was editor of the *Sun* for a time. He was principal of Trafalgar Junior High School. He eventually emigrated to England and died there. He wrote *With the Second Cape Corps thro' Central Africa* (1920), *Torch Bearers in Darkest America: A Study of Jeanes Supervision in Some Southern States of the United States of America* (1937), and *Elements of Vocational Guidance* (1939).

2. Harry Snitcher (1910–) is a Cape Town advocate. In the late 1930s and 1940s, he served as chairman of the Cape Town district committee of the Communist Party. Active in the New Era Fellowship, a debating society, and the Hands Off Abyssinia Committee, he ran unsuccessfully as a National Liberation League candidate for the Cape Town City Council in 1940 and as a Communist Party candidate in 1946.

3. Zairunissa "Cissie" Gool (1900–1963) was the daughter of Dr. Abdurahman and his Scottish first wife, Helen Potter James. She married Dr. A. H. Gool in 1919. After graduating from the University of Cape Town with an M.A. in psychology, she engaged herself in politics and became the first president of the National Liberation League in 1935. In 1938 she was elected to the Cape Town City Council and continued to be reelected, even when listed as a

member of the Communist Party in 1950. She led a passive resistance campaign in 1946. She obtained an LL.B. from the University of Cape Town in 1962.

4. Originally used as a site for military drills, the Grand Parade was the Hyde Park corner of South Africa. Most speaking took place on the steps below a statue of King Edward VII. The Parade itself was an open space which was the scene of political rallies, government ceremonies, and anti-government protests. In 1963, invoking the Riotous Assemblies Act, the government prohibited all anti-government demonstrations on the Parade, but in February 1990 it became the site for Nelson Mandela's first rally after being released from prison.

5. Isaac Schapera (1905–), one of the best known anthropologists of the 1930s, was born in South Africa and studied under A. R. Radcliffe-Brown at the University of Cape Town before going on to the London School of Economics (LSE) in 1926 to do his Ph.D. studies under C. G. Seligman and B. Malinowski. He took up a teaching post in 1930 at Witwatersrand University and assumed the chair of anthropology at the University of Cape Town in 1935. In 1950, he returned to LSE to take up the chair of anthropology, a position he retained until his retirement in 1969. He began his research on Tswana peoples in 1928 and almost all his best known writings are in that area: *Married Life in an African Tribe* (1940), *Migrant Labour and Tribal Life* (1947), and *Tribal Innovators: Tswana Chiefs and Social Change, 1795–1940* (1970).

6. Born in Cape Town, Sam Kahn (1911–1987) earned his law degree from the University of Cape Town. He practiced in Cape Town and was active in political cases, especially after 1948. He was active in the Socialist Party while in university and later became active in the Communist Party. A close friend of Cissie Gool, he was a founding member of the National Liberation League and the Non-European Unity Movement. He served as a Cape Town City Councillor from a predominantly Coloured area from 1943 to 1952. Elected to Parliament in 1948 as a representative of Western Cape Africans, he was expelled in 1952 for being a communist. He was served with a banning order in 1955 but it was overturned on appeal. He left South Africa in 1960 to England, where he remained active in political affairs, including advocacy of Palestinian rights.

7. "Jim Crow" was a term first used in the American North in the 1830s as the title for a minstrel song and dance show, but by the 1840s, it was applied to the use of separate railway cars for blacks in Massachusetts. Later the term came to refer more broadly to all discriminatory and segregationist laws and practices, especially those that regulated contacts between the races in public places. The classic study of Jim Crow is C. Vann Woodward's *The Strange Career of Jim Crow* (1957). See also Stetson Kennedy, *Jim Crow Guide to the U.S.A.* (1959).

8. Arthur McKinley, a Jamaican resident of Cape Town, was agent for the *Bantu World* and became treasurer of the Cape Town branch of Garvey's UNIA in July 1938. He died in April 1939. See the *Black Man* (4 June 1939, p. 19) for Garvey's obituary of McKinley.

9. In 1912 African leaders from around South Africa met in Bloemfontein to establish the South African Native National Congress (later the African National Congress (ANC)). In the coming decades, the ANC was largely dominated by educated Africans—lawyers, ministers, teachers, doctors, journalists—

who steered the organization along a moderate course, challenging discriminatory laws and policies and promoting equal rights for all racial groups, but stressing nonviolent tactics such as petitions and deputations and, with a few exceptions, eschewing militant protest until the 1940s. The ANC's influence has waxed and waned over the decades, but it remains the leading organization for the political and economic advancement of Africans. Detailed accounts of its history are provided by Peter Walshe, *The Rise of African Nationalism in South Africa* (1971); Thomas Karis and Gwendolyn Carter, *From Protest to Challenge: A Documentary History of African Politics in South Africa, 1882–1964* (1972–1977), 4 vols.; and Francis Meli, *South Africa Belongs to Us: History of the ANC* (1988).

10. The ideas of Marcus Garvey exploded on the South African scene after World War I. Garvey's UNIA had a strong presence in Cape Town and chapters were scattered about the rest of South Africa, but his ideas—especially "Africa for the Africans"—had a profound influence on black South Africans on many levels throughout the country. The Garvey movement is given extensive treatment in Robert Hill and Gregory Pirio, " 'Africa for the Africans': The Garvey Movement in South Africa, 1920–1940."

11. At the beginning of the Second World War, a number of black South Africans reacted positively to the news of Japanese armies rolling back European colonial armies in Southeast Asia. A South African military intelligence report compiled by Major P. J. Pretorius related: "The natives say 'We are Sons of Ham. The Japanese is not a white man, he belongs to our race. He is the liberator of the black and yellow races; he will free them all and assemble them as blood brothers and will find for all of them conditions superior to those existing today. Wages will be better and higher for all native races; living conditions will be improved and the whites will go under,' and they say quite bluntly and candidly that when the Japanese reach Africa the natives will help them against the White race" (28 May 1942, NTS 9629 511/400, State Archives, Pretoria). For additional comments, see Edward Roux, *Time Longer than Rope: A History of the Black Man's Struggle for Freedom in South Africa* (1964), 306–7.

12. As boxing's world heavyweight champion, Joe Louis had a massive following in the black world. South Africa's African press followed his fights closely. Z. K. Matthew recollected: "When Joe Louis was going to fight, Africans would get up early in the morning so that they could hear it over the short wave radio" (*New York Amsterdam News*, 23 May 1953).

13. Started in Johannesburg in 1932 by R. F. Paver, a white businessman, the *Bantu World* was the first attempt at creating a mass newspaper for Africans. R. V. Selope-Thema edited the newspaper until he retired in 1952. See Les Switzer, "*Bantu World* and the Origins of a Captive African Commercial Press in South Africa" *Journal of Southern African Studies* 14 (April 1988): 351–70.

14. Edited by Robert Vann, the *Pittsburgh Courier* was one of the most popular Afro-American newspapers of the 1930s, claiming a circulation of a quarter of a million in 1938. Vann gave extensive coverage to the Italo-Ethiopian war, going so far as to send a correspondent, J. A. Rogers, to cover the war firsthand. See Andrew Buni's *Robert L. Vann of the Pittsburgh Courier: Politics and Black Journalism* (1974).

15. In the late nineteenth century, a lack of new land for Europeans as well as droughts, poor farming, inheritance laws, and the devastation of the South African war (1899–1902) combined to throw large numbers of whites off

farms and into poverty. Largely unskilled and uneducated, these "poor whites" lived marginal existences in rural and urban areas and found it difficult to compete with African workers for jobs. The Carnegie Corporation's commission on poor whites reported in 1931 that 300,000 whites (90% of whom were Afrikaners) could be classified as "poor whites" out of a total European population of 1,800,000. The government's "civilized labor" policy (see page 162) was one program adopted to address the "poor white" crisis.

16. The South African poll tax was a tax levied on all African adult males to force them to work in the European wage economy. This is in contrast to the American poll tax levied on voters at polling booths in Southern states to discourage blacks from voting in elections. Liquor laws were aimed at preventing liquor sales to Africans or allowing them to brew their own beer in the urban areas. Pass laws controlled the right of Africans to move, live, or qualify for jobs in specifically defined areas.

17. Edward Roux (1903–1966) was a Cambridge-trained botanist. He joined the Communist Party in 1923 and was an active member, helping to edit the Party newspaper, *Umsebenzi*. In 1935 he was removed from the Party's politburo, and in 1936 he left the Party. He took up a teaching post at Witwatersrand University after the Second World War. He is well known for his account of African resistance and protest, *Time Longer than Rope* (1948) and his autobiography (written with his wife Win Roux), *Rebel Pity: The Life of Eddie Roux* (1970).

18. Formed in 1908, the South African Labour Party was closely aligned with white working-class interests. Its high point came in the 1924 election when it allied itself with Hertzog's National Party and became part of the governing Pact coalition. The party split in 1927 and never again played an important role in white politics on a national level.

19. In response to attacks by police raids looking for illegal visitors and beer brewing, black residents of the Vereeniging location protested on 18 and 19 September 1937. Two white and one African policemen were killed in fighting. In retaliation, the police fired on demonstrators, wounding many; they arrested 450. See Edward Roux, *Time Longer than Rope*, 282–86 and Baruch Hirson, *Yours for the Union: Class and Community Struggles in South Africa* (1989), 63–73.

20. For comments on passing, see Graham Watson, *Passing for White: A Study of Racial Assimilation in a South African School* (1970); Sheila Patterson, *Colour and Culture in South Africa* (1953); H. F. Dickie-Clark, *The Marginal Situation: A Sociological Study of a Coloured Group* (1966); and Beryl Unterhalter, "Changing Attitudes to 'Passing for White' in an Urban Coloured Community," *Social Dynamics* 1 (1) (1975): 53–62.

21. Cape Africans had had to carry a "work permit" which was tantamount to a pass. However, a 1937 amendment to the Native Urban Areas Act that gave Africans coming to urban areas only fourteen days in which to find work was not rigidly applied in the Cape until a later period, and it had little impact on the growing number of Africans in Cape Town. Government censuses enumerated 13,583 Africans in Cape Town in 1936 and 31,258 in 1946. Those figures likely did not include African squatter communities, which mushroomed around Cape Town.

22. A Muslim, Dr. Abdullah Abdurahman (1872–1940) was a grandson of

freed slaves and the leading mixed race politician of his era. He took his medical degree at the University of Glasgow in 1893. In 1903 he joined the African Political Association (APO), became its president in 1905, and dominated it until his death. Between 1904 and 1940 (with the exception of 1913–1915) he was elected to the Cape town City Council and from 1914 on to the Cape Provincial Council. An assessment of his political career is found in Gavin Lewis, *Between the Wire and the Wall,* esp. 198–204 and Richard van der Ross, *The Founding of the African People's Organization in Cape Town in 1903 and the Role of Dr. Abdurahman* (1975) and *The Rise and Decline of Apartheid* (1986).

23. The *Cape Standard* editor, George Manuel, who wrote as "Gemel," described Hanover Street: "This street is the favourite of the Coloured man in Cape Town. It is the busiest part of District Six. Each day endless strings of hooting vehicles glide along the thronged thoroughfares. People of all types come and go in colourful succession. they buy and bargain, idle and gossip, hurry and toil. . . . It is a street of Coloured people, beloved by Coloured folk." (*Cape Standard,* 31 August 1936) See George Manuel and Denis Hatfield, *District Six* (1967) for additional descriptions.

24. U Street was the center of black social and business life in the segregated Washington, D.C., of the 1930s. It was Washington's "black Broadway," a mecca for top black entertainers, who performed at dance halls, cafes, jazz spots, cabarets and supper clubs. For discussions on U Street's prominence, see Juan Williams, "Once Upon a Time, 14th and U Was the Center of Black Culture in Washington, D.C. Can It Become That Again?" *Washington Post Sunday Magazine,* 21 February 1988, 22–31; and Sandra Fitzpatrick and Maria Goodwin, *The Guide to Black Washington* (1990), 205–30.

25. Founded in 1932 by C. L. Stewart, a printer, and A. S. Hayes, a journalist, the *Sun* was a journal of conservative Coloured opinion. From 1936 on, the newspaper was owned by Samuel Griffiths, a white businessman, and it gave editorial support to segregationist ideas. The *Standard* was started up by an Indian firm in 1936 to rival the *Sun.* It gave sympathetic coverage to anti-government movements and became an outlet for young black writers.

26. Moviegoing at the Star and other cinemas is given an imaginative treatment in Bill Nasson, " 'She Preferred Living in a Cave with Harry the Snake-Catcher': Towards an Oral History of Popular Leisure and Class Expression in District Six, Cape Town c. 1920–1950," in Philip Bonner et al., eds., *Holding Their Ground: Class, Locality and Culture in 19th and 20th Century South Africa* (1989), 286–94.

27. Established in 1935 as a rival to the APO, the National Liberation League (NLL) aimed at appealing to the African community and stressed working class unity. Under its president, Cissie Gool, the NLL advocated militant tactics, but in practice, it followed APO tradition and participated in city council and parliamentary elections. For details, see Gavin Lewis, *Between the Wire and the Wall,* 184–98.

28. Born in Bloemfontein of French and Malagasy parents, James LaGuma (1894–1961) joined the Communist Party in 1924 and was on its national executive when it dissolved in 1950. He was a labor organizer who became secretary of the Port Elizabeth branch of the ICU and then General Secretary in Cape Town until Kadalie's purge of Communist members in 1926. He was a delegate to the Congress of Colonial Peoples in Belgium in 1927 and went on to visit the

USSR. He was expelled from the Communist Party in the late 1920s, but was readmitted in 1931. In 1928 he went to Johannesburg to serve as secretary of the South African Federation of Non-European Trade Unions; in 1933 he helped organize the Garment Workers Union. During World War II, he served in the Cape Corps in Egypt and Ethiopia. He was one of the founders and secretary of the National Liberation League, but was expelled from it in 1939 for advocating that whites should be barred from holding office in the organization. He was chairman of the national executive of the Coloured Peoples Congress.

29. Jan Smuts was prime minister of South Africa 1919–1924 and 1939–1948. In 1933 he entered into a coalition government with Hertzog in which they merged their parties to form the United Party.

30. The Malays were descendants of individuals brought over by the Dutch East India Company in the late seventeenth century as slaves or political exiles. Over the years, as a result of intermixing with Europeans, Arabs, Indians, Chinese, Ceylonese, and Africans, they became a mixed race group. What bound them together is their Muslim faith. For details, see I. D. DuPlessis, *The Cape Malays* (1972), 1–5.

31. Gerard Paul Lestrade (1897–1962) was born in Amsterdam. After earning a B.A. from the University of Cape Town and M.A.s from Harvard University and the University of London, he was appointed Chief Ethnologist for the Department of Native Affairs in Pretoria. In 1935 he took up the chair of Bantu languages at the University of Cape Town, a post he held until his death.

32. D. D. T. Jabavu (1885–1959) was the son of John Tengo Jabavu, editor of *Imvo Zabantsundu,* a major Eastern Cape African newspaper. He was educated at Lovedale before going on to the University of London, where he graduated with a B.A. with Honours in English in 1912. He was appointed to the faculty of Fort Hare in 1915 and taught there until his retirement in 1945. He was the key figure in the establishment of the All African Convention. Strongly influenced by the ideas of Booker T. Washington, he was able to make a short visit to Tuskegee Institute in 1913. He wrote an account of a 1931 visit to the United States, *E-Amerika* (Lovedale Press, 1932).

33. A. B. Xuma (1893–1962) was in England and the United States while Bunche was touring South Africa. Xuma had received his higher education at Tuskegee, the University of Minnesota and Northwestern University, where he completed his medical degree. He opened up a medical practice in Johannesburg and also became active in political organizations. In 1936, he was elected vice president of the All African Convention and, in 1940, he was elected president of the ANC, a position he held until 1949. For Xuma's American connections, see Richard Ralston, "American Episodes in the Making of an African Leader: A Case Study of Alfred B. Xuma," *International Journal of African Historical Studies* 6 (1973): 72–93.

34. Bishop Richard R. Wright (1878–1967) was a long-time force in the AME church. A graduate of Georgia St. College and the University of Chicago, he taught classics at Wilberforce College. Eventually he completed a Ph.D. on "The Negro in Pennsylvania" in sociology at the University of Pennsylvania. He also rose in the ranks of the AME church, serving as editor of the church magazine, the *Christian Recorder* (1909–1936), and as president of Wilberforce College (1932–1936). He was elected Bishop of New York in 1936 and

then served as Bishop of South Africa (1936–1940). He had a special interest in Wilberforce Institute and founded the R. R. Wright School of Religion there. For his analysis of South Africa, see his "South Africa Has Its Own Color Lines" *Opportunity* (May, 1939): 138–41. His wife, Charlotte Crogman Wright, wrote a book on their stay in South Africa, *Beneath the Southern Cross: The Story of an American Bishop's Wife in South Africa* (1955). Detailed accounts of the AME church in South Africa are contained in J. Mutero Chirenje, *Ethiopianism and Afro-Americans in Southern Africa 1883–1916* (1987) and Carol Page, "Black America in White South Africa: Church and State Reaction to the A.M.E. Church in Cape Colony and Transvaal, 1896–1910" (Ph.D. dissertation, Edinburgh University, 1978).

35. Born in 1889, Professor Amos White received a B.A. in 1906 from Harvard University and an M.A. in 1937 from Ohio State University. He was professor of Greek language and literature at Wiley University from 1908–1912 before becoming professor of French at Wilberforce College in Ohio in 1912. He remained in that post until he came out to South Africa to become principal at Wilberforce Institute in early 1937. He and his wife, Luella, who had been a domestic science teacher at Wilberforce College, later wrote an account of their experiences in *Southern Africa: Dawn in Bantuland: An African Experiment* (1953).

36. Wilberforce Institute was an AME school founded in 1908 at Evaton, Transvaal by former African students of Wilberforce College in Ohio. See J. M. Nhlapo, *Wilberforce Institute* (1949); R. R. Wright, "Wilberforce in South Africa," *Opportunity* (October 1937), 306–10; and James Campbell, "Our Fathers, Our Children: The African Methodist Episcopal Church in the United States and South Africa" (Ph.D. dissertation, Stanford University, 1990), chap. 6.

37. Rev. Henry Francis Gow (1887–1968) was born of an African-American mother and a West Indian father, Rev. Francis M. Gow, who had moved to Cape Town in the 1880s. Henry left South Africa about 1905 to receive his education in the United States at Wilberforce College and Miami University and teach music at Tuskegee Institute until his return to South Africa to become principal at Wilberforce Institute in 1925. He served in the American army in France during the First World War. He obtained a D.D. from Morris Brown University. He later became pastor of the Bethel AME church in Cape Town, was appointed General Superintendent of the AME church in South Africa in 1945, and eventually was made a Bishop in 1955, the first South African to achieve that position in the AME church. He gained a reputation as a choir conductor and founded the Coleridge-Taylor Musical Society. He succeeded Stephen Reagon as president of the APO (1942–1944) and served as chairman of the Coloured Advisory Council, 1943–1945. He served on the Cape Town School Board and he ran for the Cape Town City Council in 1944, but was soundly defeated by Cissie Gool.

38. J. B. M. Hertzog (1866–1942) was a founder of the National Party and Prime Minister from 1924–1939.

39. Johnny Gomas (1901–1979) was born in Abbotsdale, near Kimberley. He spent most of his life in District Six and participated in a number of political and trade union organizations. He was Cape Provincial secretary of the ICU when he was purged in 1926 for being a member of the Communist Party. In 1933 he was dropped from the Communist Party over the controversy of

whether the Party should relate to non-Communist groups. A tailor by trade, he later helped to organize the Laundry Workers and Dyers' Union. He was a leading participant in the Western Cape ANC (he was jailed for three months in 1928 under the Native Administration Act). He was a major figure in the National Liberation League. In 1959 he broke from the ANC and joined the newly formed Pan Africanist Congress. See Doreen Musson's biography, *Johnny Gomas, Voice of the Working Class: A Political Biography* (1989).

40. Moses Kotane (1905–1978) joined the Communist Party in 1929 and involved himself in trade union organizing. In the early 1930s he studied at the Lenin School in Moscow. Because of a dispute with Party leaders, he was removed from the politburo in the mid-1930s. He left for Cape Town and became one of the key figures in rebuilding the Party. In 1939, he was chosen secretary-general of the Party, a position he held until his death. Details on his life are found in Brian Bunting, *Moses Kotane: South African Revolutionary* (1975).

41. For detailed accounts of the ICU, see P. L. Wickins, *The Industrial and Commercial Workers' Union of Africa* (1978) and Helen Bradford, *A Taste of Freedom: The ICU in Rural South Africa, 1924–1930* (1987).

42. George Golding (1906–1967) was headmaster for a decade at the AME Bethel Primary School before being appointed in 1939 principal of Ashley Street Boys' Primary School, a position he held until his death. He attended the Berlin Mission School and Zonnebloem College. He married Frances Singh in 1934. He was editor of the journal of the Teachers League of South Africa, *Educational Journal*. He served as chairman of the Coloured Advisory Council in 1943 and was a founder and president of the collaborationist Coloured People's National Union, founded in 1944. He also served for a time as editor of the *Sun*. An avid tennis player, he won a number of championships and was a founder of the South African Coloured Tennis Board. His curriculum vitae stressed his relations with American blacks, including hosting people like Bunche, Mrs. Paul Robeson, Max Yergan, and AME dignitaries as well as attending to the entertainment of African-American troops whose ships stopped at Cape Town during the Second World War.

43. Dr. Julius Friedlander (1910–1961) received his medical training at the University of Cape Town. He left Cape Town for Durban, where he assisted in studies on tuberculosis at King George V hospital and contributed to a volume, *A South African Team Looks at Tuberculosis*.

44. For discussions of tuberculosis, see Randall Packard's publications: "Industrialization, Rural Poverty and Tuberculosis in southern Africa, 1850–1960," in S. Feierman and J. Janzen, *Health and Society in Africa;* "Tuberculosis and the Development of Industrial Health Policies on the Witwatersrand, 1902–1932," *Journal of Southern African Studies* 13 (2) (1987): 187–209; and *White Plague, Black Labour* (1989).

45. Named after a local bird, a large green and yellow bushshrike, Bokmakierie is a housing complex started up in 1930 for low-income Coloureds in the Athlone area. Part of a voluntary segregation program, its establishment followed the pattern of other separate areas for Coloureds in Cape Town: Maitland Garden Village in 1921, Athlone in 1925, and Sunnyside in 1929.

46. Born in Nyasaland (Malawi), Clements Kadalie (1896–1951) made his way to South Africa, where he found employment in Cape Town and helped to start up a trade union for African dockworkers. From that base he created the

ICU. Following the ICU's collapse in the late 1920s, he moved to East London where he kept up a branch of the ICU, but he was never again a major force in national political life. See his autobiography, *My Life and the ICU* (1970).

47. The Native Administration Act (1927) gave the government sweeping powers over Africans throughout the country, including the right to appoint native administrators, chiefs, and headmen; to remove African "tribes" "from any place to any other place within the Union," to legislate by proclamation for the African reserve areas, and to punish "any person who utters any words or does any other act or thing whatever with intent to promote any feeling of hostility between Natives and Europeans." The latter provision was used repeatedly to disrupt African politicians from organizing in African areas by banishing them.

48. The Riots and Assemblies Act of 1914 was passed in the aftermath of a major white labor strike in 1913. Aimed at undercutting labor militancy, the act prohibited trade unions from recruiting members by force, banned violent picketing, permitted magistrates to ban meetings thought likely to endanger public safety, and greatly increased police powers to arrest people. The act was amended in 1930 (and many times since) to give the minister of justice sweeping powers to prevent public meetings, banish persons from living in specified areas, and ban publications.

49. Samuel Masabalala was an ICU organizer in Port Elizabeth. He was tried for inciting a riot after the October 1920 disturbances, but was acquitted. Several years later, he was briefly appointed ICU organizer-in-chief. He was also active in the Cape ANC, served on the national executive of the ANC in the late 1920s and worked on the ANC newspaper, *Abantu Batho*.

50. Selby Msimang (1886–1982) was present at the launching of the ANC in 1912 and was one of its stalwarts over the decades. In 1920 he was elected president of the ICU, but stepped aside for Clements Kadalie to avoid an internal fight. Educated at Edendale Training Institution and Healdtown Institution, he became an interpreter, a mine clerk, a solicitor's clerk (in Pixley Seme's office), and a journalist for *Umteteli wa Bantu*. In 1935 he became secretary of the All African Convention and was a member of the delegation that met with Hertzog to discuss his "Native" bills. He was provincial secretary of the Natal ANC 1942–1956 and on the executive committee of the Liberal Party (1956–1968).

51. Pixley ka I. Seme (1881–1951) was president of the ANC from 1930 to 1937. He earned a B.A. from Columbia University in 1906 and then completed his law studies at Oxford University. On his return to South Africa, he established a law firm with Alfred Mangena and was one of the founding members of the ANC. He joined with D. D. T. Jabavu in convening the All African Convention, but later turned against it. See Craig Charney, "Pixley Seme '06: Father of the African National Congress" *Columbia College Today* (Spring/Summer 1987): 15–17.

52. The Natives Land Act of 1913 has been a cornerstone of segregated South Africa. The law froze the unequal land division between blacks and whites by stating that Africans could not buy European land and vice versa. It also attacked sharecropping arrangements that made it possible for some blacks to maintain a base on the land by restricting the number of black heads of household who worked on European farms and stipulating that blacks could

only rent white farm land with labor service. The act set off a flurry of expulsions of black sharecroppers, especially in the Orange Free State, but it took a number of years before sharecropping was a spent institution. Solomon Plaatje's *Native Life in South Africa* (1916) remains a classic account of the impact of the law on Africans.

53. For an analysis of this period of ANC militancy, see Philip Bonner, "The Transvaal Native Congress, 1917–1920: The Radicalisation of the Black Petty Bourgeoisie on the Rand," in Shula Marks and Richard Rathbone, eds., *Industrialisation and Social Change in South Africa* (1982).

54. Kotane had been to the Soviet Union on two trips, from 1931 to 1933 to study at the Lenin School and in 1935–1936 to resolve an intraparty feud over whether the Communist Party should have relations with non-Communist groups. Kotane advocated that it should. He was opposed in Moscow by Lazar Bach and Maurice Richter, who were executed by the Soviet government.

55. John David Rheinallt-Jones (1884–1953) was born in Wales and came out to Cape Town in 1905. He moved to Johannesburg in 1919 where, although he did not have a university education, he took up the post of secretary to the Witwatersrand Council of Education. He later became assistant registrar at Witwatersrand University and a lecturer in race relations. He was one of the founders of the Joint Council system in the 1920s and the Institute of Race Relations in 1929, which he served as secretary. He was very active in the Pathfinders. From 1937 to 1942, he was elected senator, representing Africans in the Orange Free State and Transvaal in Parliament. In 1947 he left the Institute to join the Anglo American Corporation as an adviser on "native affairs." He married Edith Barton Jones in 1910. She received an M.Sc. from the University of Leeds, immigrated to South Africa in 1905, and taught in high schools in Cape Town and Basutoland. The founder of the Wayfarers' movement for African girls in the Transvaal, she was also "native affairs" adviser to the South African National Council of Women. She lectured in Shona at Witwatersrand University. She died in 1944. For details on their lives, see Edgar Brookes, *R.J.: In Appreciation of the Life of John David Rheinallt Jones* (1953).

56. *The African Defender* (*Umvikeli-Thebe*) started in 1936 in Johannesburg as an organ of *Ikaka Labesebenzi* (Workers' Shield). Edited by Moses Kotane and Edward Roux, it emphasized educational themes, political consciousness raising, and the Italo-Ethiopian War, which was closely followed in the African community.

57. Bunche is probably referring to M. J. Adams, a builder, Cape Town city councillor, and vice chairman of the Reform Party. He was the first chairman of the Cape Town Coloured-European Council established in 1931 to promote better housing, higher wages, education, and self-upliftment in the Coloured community. He was forced to resign his office in the Reform Party due to his outspoken views favoring segregation. In a city council election held while Bunche was there, Adams defeated an independent candidate, J. A. Cunningham, 1110 to 516 votes. He was appointed chairman of the Streets and Drainage committee, replacing Dr. Abdurahman, who was pushed off the committee.

58. Born in 1889, David Henry Sims completed B.A.s at Georgia State University (1905) and Oberlin College (1909), finished a course at Oberlin Theological Seminary (1912), and an M.A. at the University of Chicago (1916).

He was Professor of German and Education at Morris Brown College (1912–1917), and was dean (1918–1923) and president (1924–1932) of Allen University in South Carolina until he was chosen AME bishop in South Africa in 1932. He served in that capacity until 1936. A photograph of Sims is in *Who's Who in Colored America 1938–1940*, 470.

59. Sidney Bunting (1873–1936) was a London-born leader of the Communist Party in South Africa. An Oxford graduate, he came to South Africa after the South African War and established a law practice. In 1921 he became secretary of the Communist Party and steered the Party toward recruiting African members. He opposed the "Native Republic" slogan, and in the ensuing Party turmoil he was expelled from the Party in 1931. See Edward Roux's *S. P. Bunting: A Political Biography* (1944).

60. In order to appeal to growing black nationalist sentiment in the late 1920s, the Communist Party advocated establishing a black–led republic as stage one in the creation of a republic of workers and peasants. The aim was to make possible alliances with "reformist" and black nationalist organizations, but the policy also caused bitter splits within the Party. A controversy still exists over whether the "native republic" idea was originated by the South African Party or whether it was a directive from the Comintern. See Martin Legassick, *Class and Nationalism in South African Protest* (1973) and Sheridan Johns, "The Comintern, South Africa and the Black Diaspora," *Review of Politics* 37 (1975): 200–34.

61. The League of African Rights was founded in late 1929 under the auspices of the Communist Party, which was trying to create a rival to an ANC turned conservative and an ICU in disarray. The league's focus was on expanding the franchise to more Africans and free education for all races. It popularized the song "Mayibuy' iAfrica," sung to the tune of "O My Darling Clementine." After a promising beginning, the league was disbanded a short time later on the directive of the Comintern for taking a "reformist" line.

62. Born in Wales and educated at the University of Wales, E. A. Ball came out to South Africa in 1925 to become the headmaster at Healdtown Institution in Fort Beaufort. He took over as principal of Zonnebloem College in 1934 and principal at Wesley Training College in 1937.

63. P. M. Heneke was principal of Trafalgar High School and president of the Teachers' League of South Africa in 1935. Later he served on the Coloured Affairs Council (1943–1945). For details on the Teachers' League, see M. Adhikari, *The Teachers' League of South Africa, 1913–1940* (M.A. thesis, University of Cape Town, 1986).

64. Harold Cressy (1889–1916) was the first "coloured" graduate of the University of Cape Town in 1911. He taught at several schools in Cape Town before he was appointed the first principal of Trafalgar High School, established in 1912. He was also editor of the *Educational Journal* and an assistant secretary of the Cape Town APO branch. He died in 1916. A Cape Town high school is named after him. See Dr. Goolam Gool's tribute to him in *Torch*, 19 May 1947.

65. Born of a Sierra Leonean father and an English mother, Samuel Coleridge-Taylor (1875–1912) was named after the English poet. A composer, Coleridge-Taylor wrote choral, chamber, and orchestral music as well as ope-

ras. He is best known for his composition "Song of Hiawatha." See William Tortolano's *Samuel Coleridge-Taylor: Anglo-Black Composer, 1875–1912* (1977).

66. Bunche's talk was reported in the *Cape Standard,* 25 October 1937.

67. Descended from a St. Helenan family, Stephen Reagon (1884–1942) was educated at Woodstock Public School. He was vice president of the APO and, when Abdurahman died in 1940, succeeded him as president. He was also secretary of the APO Building Society and manager of the APO Burial Society. He represented the Cape Flats in the Cape Provincial Council (1930–1933) and Ward 7 in the Cape Town City Council until he resigned in 1928. He was a nominated member of the Cape Town School Board and was active in sports administration, especially soccer.

68. Sidney George Maurice (d. 1967) received a B.A. from the University of South Africa in 1922. He worked as a secretary and a teacher and served as principal of several schools, including Trafalgar High School. He was a founder of the New Era Fellowship, a left-leaning debate and discussion group in Cape Town, and he was a leader of the Teachers League of South Africa. In 1943 he made a dramatic political shift by agreeing to participate in the Coloured Advisory Council, but resigned from it in 1949.

69. J. W. Kay, a builder and contractor, was a senior vice president of the APO. On Reagon's death in 1942, he took his place on the Cape Town School Board.

70. Founded in 1902, the African Political Organization (APO) was open to all races, but was actually dominated by mixed-race leaders like Dr. Abdurahman. It was moderate in tone and tactics and sought political change through constitutional means—deputations, petitions, and participating in elections. For details, see Gavin Lewis, *Between the Wire and the Wall,* chaps. 1–3 and Richard Van der Ross, *The Founding of the African People's Organization in Cape Town in 1903 and the role of Dr. Abdurahman* (1975).

71. A Round Table conference in February 1927 between the Union of South Africa and the government of India created an Indian-appointed Agent General to represent the political and economic interests of South Africans of Indian descent in South Africa. For details, see Uma Mesthrie, "From Sastri to Desmukh: a Study of the Role of the Government of India's Representatives in South Africa, 1927–1946" (1986).

72. Sharkey Effendi came from a Muslim family who came from Turkey. His father, Ahmed Effendi, unsuccessfully contested a seat in the Cape Parliament in 1893, the only non-European to have done so.

73. Ernest Gustaf Nyman (1880–1947) was deputy mayor of Cape Town when Bunche visited and became mayor from 1943 to 1945. Born in Sweden, he came to South Africa as a young man and started a firm of road machinery importers in Maitland. He served in the Cape Town City Council for several decades and represented the Maitland district, which had a large Coloured vote, in the Provincial Council.

74. Bunche is probably referring to Bishop James Limba's Church of Christ, which was established in Cape Town in 1910. For details about the church, see L. Mqotsi and N. Mkele, "A Separatist Church: Ibandla Lika-Krestu" *African Studies* 5 (2) (1946): 106–125.

75. Eight miles from the Cape Town city center, Langa is an African loca-

tion built by the Cape Town City Council. The first occupants took up residence in 1927. In the mid-1930s, it had a population of about 3,700 people. For a view of Langa in a much later period, see Monica Wilson and Archie Mafeje, *Langa: A Study of Social Groups in an African Township* (1963).

76. A graduate of Fisk University, James W. Ford served in the Signal Corps during the First World War. He joined the Chicago Postal Workers Union and the Communist Party in 1926. He became one of the Party's key black leaders, being appointed head of the International Trade Union Committee of Negro Workers in 1929. In that capacity, he wrote articles on South Africa. See his articles in the *Liberator*, April–June 1931, and a series on "International Trade Union Unity and South African Labour," which appeared in a South African Communist publication, *Inkululeko*, May–July 1946. In 1932, 1936, and 1940, he was the Party's vice presidential candidate on its presidential ticket. For details, see Mark Naison, *Communists in Harlem during the Depression* (1984).

77. The Dutch Reformed Church or Nederduitse Gereformeerde Kerk (NGK), is the oldest and most popular church among Afrikaners. Since 1857 the church had a strict policy of segregating its churches on a racial basis. In the twentieth century it went to the extent of founding separate daughter churches for Coloureds, Asians, and Africans. The Coloured church is called the Nederduitse Gereformeerde Sendingkerk.

78. Anna "Sister Nannie" Tempo (1867–1946) lived on Jordaan Street on the slopes of Signal Hill in Upper Cape Town. Born in Worcester, the daughter of William and Magavi Tempo, former slaves from Mozambique, she traveled with her employer, Miss H. Schreiner, to Australia, England, and the United States. When Miss Schreiner married into the Stakesby-Lewis family, Sister Nannie became the matron in 1914 of the Stakesby-Lewis hostels for "respectable" African and Coloured visitors to Cape Town on Harrington St., but she gravitated toward work among female prostitutes and unmarried mothers. A warm, generous, outgoing person, she opened a home, Sister Nannie's House, in 1922 with the help of the Dutch Reformed Church where she cared for those mothers and their children. She received the King George's Coronation Medal in 1937. Her work is remembered through Die Nannie Huis ("Nannie's House"), a government-subsidized home for unmarried mothers in Eland Street, Athlone, a Coloured suburb of Cape Town.

79. Emmett Scott (1873–1957) was Booker T. Washington's long-serving private secretary (1897–1915) and part of the Tuskegee machine. He later became secretary and secretary-treasurer of Howard University and was very active in the National Business League. See Maceo C. Dailey, "Emmett Jay Scott: The Career of a Secondary Black Leader" (Ph.D. dissertation, Howard University, 1983).

80. The life of Christian Zierfogel (1903–1957), the "self-made Professor of District Six," exemplifies the classic story of a man who came from humble origins and worked his way up the ladder. Eventually he became manager of J. Milner & Son before deciding to work for the "upliftment of his people." He opened a library with his own 3,000-volume collection and was later appointed librarian at the Hyman Liberman Institute in 1933. He accepted the idea of complete, not piecemeal, segregation: "In this manner the coloured people could become farmers instead of farm labourers, as they will come in posses-

sion of a certain amount of land instead of being landless under the present system" (*Cape Standard,* 5 July 1937). He was very active in intellectual, sporting, and social welfare associations around Cape Town. He also published several books, including *The Coloured People and the Race Problem* (1936), *Brown South Africa* (1938), and *The Rise of Colour Bars in South Africa.* See accounts on him in the *Christian Science Monitor,* 6 June 1934 and *Cape Standard,* 14 February 1939.

81. Located in Muir Street, the Hyman Liberman Institute was established in 1934 by the Cape Town City Council with a bequest from Hyman Liberman, a nineteenth-century Polish immigrant who became a merchant and mayor of Cape Town (1904–1907). Patterned on London's Toynbee Hall, the institute was set up as a "reading room for the poorer people of Cape Town," but it also served as a community center and included a nursery school, sporting and scout clubs, and a community education center.

82. Bunche spoke with James Orr Denby, who had been in the Foreign Service since 1921 and had served in Japan, Greece, Philippines, China, and Ireland before being posted to Cape Town in late 1936. He was born in 1896 in China and educated at Princeton University and George Washington University.

83. Despite preaching a segregationist line, the National Party in the 1920s aimed at attracting the Coloured vote by offering them advantages being offered to white workers and exempting them from restrictive laws applied to Africans. Some Coloured leaders were taken in by this deceptive line. However, when the franchise was extended to more white voters in 1929, the policy lost its appeal. See Gavin Lewis, *Between the Wire and the Wall: A History of South Africa "Coloured" Politics* (1987), 119–39.

84. Izak David Du Plessis (1900–1981) is best known for his works on the Malay community, *The Malay Quarter and Its People* (1953), a book commissioned for the Race Relations series of the Department of Coloured Affairs of the Ministry of Interior, and for *The Cape Malays* (1972). He was educated at the University of Cape Town and taught at Stellenbosch University and University of Cape Town. From 1953 to 1963 he served as a commissioner and subsequently as Secretary and Adviser for Coloured Affairs in the government. He became first chancellor of the University of the Western Cape. A well-known Afrikaans poet, he published many volumes of poetry and short stories and translated the works of Omar Kayyam into Afrikaans.

85. George (1900–1981) and Betty (Radford) (1906–1973) Sacks were long-time activists in leftist circles in Cape Town. Born in Surrey, England the daughter of a chaplain in the army, Betty Radford came out to South Africa in 1933 to visit an aunt. In 1934 she took a trip to the Soviet Union. In 1937 she started the *Guardian,* which over the next eleven years was to become an independent newspaper of the left. She also edited the women's page for the *Cape Times.* In 1943 she was elected to the Cape Town City Council as a member of the Communist Party. In 1946 she was charged with sedition in the Mine Workers Strike but was acquitted. In 1934 she married George Sacks, a surgeon who lectured at the University of Cape Town Medical School from 1934 to 1961, acquiring a reputation for his training of physicians at Groote Schuur Hospital. The Sackses joined the Communist Party in 1941, but about 1948 they drifted away from it. In 1943 George ran unsuccessfully for Parliament in the Salt River constituency. In the post-Sharpeville era the Sackses left South Africa for England in 1961, where Dr. Sacks worked for about five years as an

assistant editor for the medical journal *The Lancet.* He authored *The Intelligent Man's Guide to Jewbaiting,* a satire on anti-Semitism.

86. Dr. Abdul Hamid Gool (1886–1973) was the husband of Cissie Gool. The son of Malay and Indian parents, he was sent to Khedive College in Cairo at the age of 7; when he was sixteen he moved to London for his medical training. He became the second black doctor to practice in Cape Town. Although not as politically prominent as his wife or his brother Dr. Goolam Gool, he was active in the APO and the National Liberation League.

87. Groenekloof was the second mission established by the Moravians. Its early history is detailed in Bernhard Kruger, *The Pear Tree Blossoms: A History of the Moravian Mission Stations in South Africa, 1737–1869* (1966).

88. D. van der Ross was among the first Coloured students to graduate from the University of Cape Town. He became principal of Battswood Secondary school in Wynberg in the late 1920s and principal of a training school for teachers in the mid-1940s. He was secretary of the Teachers League of South Africa, an association formed in 1913 to promote the interests of Coloured teachers. The organization split over the issue of whether teachers should involve themselves in the political arena, and van der Ross joined a moderate splinter group, the Teachers' Educational and Professional Association. When S. G. Maurice resigned as vice chairman of the Coloured Affairs Council in 1949, van der Ross replaced him, but also later resigned from the council over his refusal to go along with apartheid policies.

89. Elder Solomon Lightfoot Michaux (1885–1968) was founder of the Church of God. A charismatic evangelist, he had a strong base in Washington, D.C., but used radio broadcasts to reach a much wider audience. See Lillian A. Webb, *About My Father's Business: The Life of Elder Michaux* (1981).

90. An Anglican school, Zonnebloem was founded in 1858 by Bishop Robert Grey "for the education of the children of African Chiefs and of pupils of all races of South Africa." The school had a reputation for educating the sons of African chiefs. Fewer Africans attended Zonnebloem as new schools for Africans opened up in the rest of South Africa; whites were prevented from attending by a 1913 law, thus making the school almost exclusively "Coloured." See Janet Hodgson, "A History of Zonnebloem College, 1858–1870," 2 vols. (M.A. thesis University of Cape Town, 1975).

91. Chief Yeta III, king of the Lozi in Zambia from 1916 until he stepped down because of ill health in 1945, was on his way to London to attend the coronation of George VI in 1938. His father, Lewanika, had started the tradition of sending members of the royal family for higher education at South African schools such as Lovedale and Zonnebloem. For Yeta's reign, see Gerald Caplan, *The Elites of Barotseland, 1878–1969* (1970), 119–61.

92. Jack Simons (1907–) was born in Riversdale in the Cape. He earned a Ph.D. at the London School of Economics. From 1937 to 1964 he taught African law and administration at the University of Cape Town. He was also a member of the Communist Party and served on its national executive. In 1965 he left South Africa and taught sociology at the University of Zambia until his retirement. Among his writings are *African Women: Their Legal Status in South Africa* (1968) and, with his wife, Ray Alexander Simons, *Class and Colour in South Africa* (1969).

93. Born in England, Hector Monteith Robertson completed a Cambridge

Ph.D. that critiqued Weberian economics, then went to South Africa to take up a post as senior lecturer in economics at the University of Cape Town. He later became Jagger Professor of Economics. His writings include *South Africa: Economic and Political Aspects* (1957) and "150 Years of Economic Contact between Black and White: A Preliminary Survey" *South African Journal of Economics* 2 (December 1934): 403–25 and 3 (March 1935): 3–25.

94. A graduate of Zurich University, Dr. Frederick Bodmer was a lecturer in German at the University of Cape Town. He arrived in South Africa in 1927 and left in 1939. With Lancelot Hogben, he co-authored *The Loom of Language* (1943).

95. Abdurahman's first wife was Helen Potter James, whom he met when he was a student in Glasgow. He had two daughters, including Cissie and Rosie, a medical doctor, by her. As a Muslim, Abdurahman was permitted to marry additional wives. He married his second wife, Margaret May Stansfield, before he and Helen James were divorced in 1925 and had two daughters and a son by her. He kept separate homes for each family.

96. For a discussion of black travelers on South African railways, see Ronald Ellsworth, "The Simplicity of the Native mind: Black Passengers on the South African Railways in the Early Twentieth Century," in Tom Lodge, *Resistance and Ideology in Settler Societies* (1986), 74–95. Jack Santino assesses the experiences of black porters on American trains in his *Miles of Smiles, Years of Struggle: Stories of Black Pullman Porters* (1989); see also Bernard Mergen, "The Pullman Porter: From 'George' to Brotherhood," *South Atlantic Quarterly* 73 (2) (1974): 224–35.

Basutoland

1. Studies on Basutoland's colonial political economy include Colin Murray, "From Granary to Labour Reserve," *South African Labour Bulletin* 6 (4) (1980): 3–20; Robert Edgar, *Prophets with Honour: A Documentary History of Lekhotla la Bafo* (1987); John E. Bardill and James H. Cobbe, *Lesotho: Dilemmas of Dependence in Southern Africa* (1985), 22–38; and Judy Kimball, " 'Clinging to the Chiefs': Some Contradictions of Colonial Rule in Basutoland, c. 1890–1930," in Henry Bernstein and Bonnie Campbell, eds., *Contradictions of Accumulation in Africa* (1983), 25–70.

2. The "conquered territory" is the land taken from the Kingdom of Lesotho following the wars with the Orange Free State Afrikaners during the 1850s and 1860s. The land lost in the Treaty of Thaba Bosiu (1866) included land in the triangle between the Caledon and Orange Rivers in the Orange Free State. Recovering the conquered territory has been a rallying cry for Basotho politicians ever since.

3. Russel William Thornton was Director of agriculture in Basutoland from 1934 to 1941. Educated at Stellenbosch College, he had worked in the Cape and Union of South Africa's departments of agriculture, eventually becoming Director of agriculture from 1928 to 1934. He authored an article on "The Origin and History of the Basuto Pony" (1936).

4. Capt. Matthew Blyth (1836–1889) was the British agent for Fingoland in the Transkei (1869–1876), chief magistrate of Griqualand East (1876–1883), British agent in Basutoland (1883–1884), and chief magistrate of the Transkei.

5. Cecil Rhodes (1853–1902) is most celebrated for making his fortune at the Kimberley diamond fields and, through the vehicle of his British South Africa Company, colonizing the territory that took his name, Rhodesia. He also had a political career in the Cape Parliament, becoming prime minister in 1890 and serving until he had to resign following his involvement in the disastrous Jameson Raid in 1895. Among the many biographies of Rhodes are John Flint, *Cecil Rhodes* (1974); J. G. Lockhart and C. M. Woodhouse, *Cecil Rhodes: The Colossus of Southern Africa* (1963), and Robert I. Rotberg, *The Founder: Cecil Rhodes and the Pursuit of Power* (1988).

6. The Glen Grey Act of 1894 was intended to force African males living in reserve areas to go out to work by transferring land to private ownership and imposing a tax on every adult male African "who . . . is fit for and capable of labour" unless they could prove they had worked for wages for three months in the past year.

7. A discussion of Basotho land tenure is contained in Hugh Ashton, *The Basuto* (Oxford University Press, 1952), 144–57.

8. Edmund Charles Richards (1889–1955) started out as a colonial official in the East African Protectorate; served in the King's African Rifles in the East African campaign in the First World War; and then resumed his career in colonial administration in Tanganyika, rising through the ranks to deputy chief secretary before receiving an appointment as resident commissioner of Basutoland (1935–1942). From 1942 to 1948, he served as governor of Nyasaland. He retired to Griqualand East in South Africa.

9. Margery Perham (1895–1982) was a well-known writer and educator on African affairs. Her *Native Administration in Africa* became a classic work on indirect rule in Africa. In 1937 she published *Native Administration in Nigeria.* She was a major figure in establishing a school of colonial studies at Oxford, where she was a fellow at Nuffield College. She visited Basutoland in 1929 (see her account in her travel memoir, *African Apprenticeship* (1974)) and published (with Lionel Curtis) *The Protectorates of South Africa* (1935).

10. Donald Cameron (1872–1948) was British colonial governor of Tanganyika (1924–1931) and Nigeria (1931–1935). See Harry Gailey, *Sir Donald Cameron Colonial Governor* (1974).

11. The son of King Lerotholi and brother of King Letsie II, Griffith Lerotholi (ca. 1871–1939) was asked to serve as regent for Letsie's son, Tau, until he came of age. Griffith disagreed, stating he wanted to sit on the throne "with both buttocks." Upon Tau's death, the controversy died down and Griffith reigned as Paramount Chief from 1913 to 1939.

12. Moshesh or Moshoeshoe (ca. 1786–1870) was the king who forged the Basotho kingdom during the 1820's and who made it one of the leading African states of his era. He is most noted for his diplomatic skills and his understanding of changing political currents. See Peter Sanders, *Moshoeshoe: Chief of the Sotho* (1975) and Leonard Thompson, *Survival in Two Worlds: Moshoeshoe of Lesotho, 1786–1870* (1975).

13. Born in Ireland, Alan Pim (1871–1958) was educated at Leipzig University and Trinity College, Dublin. After joining the Indian Civil Service, he

rose to high-level positions until his retirement in 1930. He then gained recognition for leading a series of investigative commissions on administration and finances on Zanzibar, Kenya, British Honduras, Swaziland (1932), Bechuanaland (1933), and Basutoland (1935). His report on Basutoland came after a trip in 1934 that followed a prolonged drought. It recommended the implementation of soil erosion measures, an improved court system, and a reduction in the number of chiefs. He was appointed financial and economic commissioner for Northern Rhodesia in 1937.

14. A graduate of Cambridge University, Oswin Bull (1882–1971) was sent out to South Africa from England in 1907 by the YMCA. He served for twenty years as the traveling secretary of the Student Christian Associations in South Africa. He had a hand in bringing Max Yergan to South Africa in 1922. After a stint as principal of the Lerotholi Training Institute in Maseru, he served as director of education in Basutoland from 1935 to 1945, when he retired. He was coeditor of the *South African Outlook*, 1946–1956.

15. In 1843 Moshoeshoe staked out a public position against killing people accused of witchcraft. In 1853 he issued a law declaring, "When anyone is killed in a case of witchcraft, the murderer will be most severely judged, and sentenced to death."

16. The 1909 South Africa Act included a clause stipulating that the British could hand over the High Commission Territories (Bechuanaland, Swaziland, and Basutoland) to the Union of South Africa, but only after the British consulted African opinion in those territories. This became a focal point for rallying African opposition to incorporation. For details, see Ronald Hyam, *The Failure of South African Expansion, 1908–1948* (1972).

17. The Chamber of Mines set up the Native Recruiting Corporation to recruit labor in the Union of South Africa and throughout the British Protectorates of Bechuanaland (Botswana), Swaziland, and Basutoland (Lesotho). For more details, see Alan Jeeves, *Migrant Labour in South Africa's Mining Economy: The Struggle for the Gold Mines' Labour Supply 1890–1920* (1985).

18. On Basotho women migrating to South Africa, see Phil Bonner, " 'Desirable or Undesirable Basotho Women?' Liquor, Prostitution and the Migration of Basotho Women to the Rand, 1920–1945," in Cherryl Walker, *Women and Gender in Southern Africa to 1945* (1990).

19. Donald and Douglas Fraser, two brothers from England, founded Frasers trading firm in 1877 near Mafeteng, Basutoland. Later the firm established branches throughout Lesotho and in the Orange Free State. A history of Frasers is James Walton's *Father of Kindness and Father of Horses: Ramosa le Ralipere; the Story of Frasers, Ltd.* (Wepener, 1958) and Christopher Danziger's *A Trader's Century: The Fortunes of Frasers* (1979). For trading relationships, see Tim Keegan, "Trade, Accumulation and Impoverishment: Mercantile Capital and the Economic Transformation of Lesotho and the Conquered Territory," *Journal of Southern African Studies* 12 (2) (1986): 196–216 and Bridget Selwyn, *A Survey of the Role of White Traders in Lesotho from the Times of Moshoeshoe to the 1950s* (B.A. thesis, National University of Lesotho, 1980).

20. Cyril Collier (1889–1942) was the son of Sydney Collier, who came out to Basutoland as a bugler for the Cape Mounted Rifles during the Gun War in the 1880s. He set up trading stations in Mafeteng and Tsita's Nek. The father's trading stores were linked with Frasers, and Frasers employed Cyril be-

fore he opened up stores at Teyateyaneng in 1916 and Maseru in 1925, where he established a partnership with Willie Yeats.

21. A French missionary, Francois Coillard composed Lesotho's national song, "Lesotho, Lefatse La Rona (Lesotho Our Land)," which was sung to a tune by the Swiss composer Ferdinand-Samuel Laur. For details on the song's evolution, see Albert Brutsch, "From Work Song to National Anthem" *Lesotho Notes and Records* 9 (1970–71): 5–12. The Xhosa national song is Nkosi Sikelel'i Afrika. For details, see note 9, Thaba 'Nchu section.

22. Educated at Morija Training College and Ft. Hare, where he received a diploma in commerce, Edgar Thamae assisted Max Yergan in the Student Christian Association from 1924 to 1936. He then worked as a clerk-typist at Fort Cox Agriculture School before returning to Basutoland, where the Department of Education employed him.

23. Max Yergan (1892–1975) was educated at Shaw College and Springfield College before joining the YMCA staff. In 1915 the YMCA sent him to East Africa to organize YMCA groups among African regiments in the British army. Later in the war he served as a chaplain in France. The YMCA made him its representative in Alice, South Africa, in 1922. By the end of his stay in 1936, his experience had radicalized him, and he moved to the left. On his return to the U.S., he was one of the founders and leaders of the Council on African Affairs in 1937 and president of the National Negro Congress (NNC) from 1940 on. However, he veered sharply to the right, leaving the NNC in 1947 and the council in 1948. He achieved notoriety as an anticommunist crusader and an apologist for the apartheid regime in the 1950s and 1960s. His main publication on South Africa is *Gold and Poverty in South Africa* (1938). For details on his South African experience, see David Anthony, "Max Yergan in South Africa: From Evangelical Pan Africanist to Revolutionary Socialist," *African Studies Review* 34 (2) (1991).

24. Henry Jankie (1876–1950) was educated at Morija Training Institution and ordained as a Paris Evangelical Mission Society minister in 1926. He served at Phamong, Maseru (1937 to 1946), and Maphutseng (1946 to 1950). He contributed to E. Jacottet's *Practical Method to Learn SeSotho*. For more details on Jankie, see Dan Mohapeloa's *Letlole la Lithoko tsa Sesotho* (1950), 27–29.

25. Opened in 1916 as the South African Native College, Fort Hare became the primary institution of higher learning for "non-whites" in South Africa. The college also attracted many students from southern, central and East Africa. Its graduates are a who's who of southern African leaders in the twentieth century. See Alexander Kerr, *Fort Hare, 1915–48: The Evolution of an African College* (1968).

26. In 1937 the British administration issued Proclamation 61, which aimed to pare down the number of chiefs by recognizing the Paramount Chief as principal "native authority" and listing 1,330 chiefs recognized by the government. Proclamation 62 undercut a major source of revenues for many chiefs by stipulating that only "gazetted" or recognized chiefs could hold courts and levy fines. It also created a national treasury, which paid out salaries to government-recognized chiefs.

27. An analysis of Basotho courts is found in E. H. Ashton, *The Basuto* (1952), 220–48.

28. The son of Josefa Molapo, who was disqualified from succeeding his

father on the grounds of insanity, Motsoene was chosen by his uncle, Jonathan Molapo, as his successor. He became chief following Jonathan's death in 1928. He died on 5 December 1937.

29. Mrs. Susie Wiseman Yergan (1893–1971) was born in Savannah, Georgia, and graduated with a B.A. from Shaw University in 1916. She taught for several years in Raleigh, North Carolina, high schools before marrying Max Yergan in 1920. She accompanied him to South Africa. She was active in securing scholarships for women to attend Lovedale and Fort Hare and organizing women into Home Improvement and Zenzele Women's Clubs, which still exist today. She and Max Yergan divorced in 1945. See her article "Africa-Our Challenge," *Crisis,* (June 1930).

30. The British colonial administration set up the Council of Chiefs in 1903 to allow for discussion and advice on issues. The Council had 100 members, 5 selected by the British Resident Commissioner and the rest by the Paramount Chief. Most of the council members were chiefs, although a few outspoken commoners did manage to participate. For a discussion of the Council, see L.B.B.J. Machobane, *Government and Change in Lesotho, 1800–1966* (1990).

31. Leo Marquard (1897–1974) was born in Winburg, Orange Free State. He completed a B.A. and M.A. at Oxford University as a Rhodes Scholar. He taught history at Grey College School in Bloemfontein. During the Second World War he taught in the Military College and assisted in army education. From 1946 to 1962 he was editorial manager of Oxford University Press in Cape Town. He was a founder of the National Union of South African Students in 1924 and the Joint Council in Bloemfontein in 1927. He was a leading figure in the South African Institute of Race Relations and its president in 1957, 1958 and 1969. He was a founder of the Liberal Party in the 1950s. Marquard wrote *The Black Man's Burden* (1943) (under the pseudonym John Burger) and *The Peoples and Policies of South Africa* (1952). Mrs. Nellie Jean Marquard (d. 1980) was a graduate of Grey College in Bloemfontein and earned a M.A. from Oxford University in English literature. During the Second World War she taught English at Stellenbosch University. She was active in the South African Institute of Race Relations, the Liberal Party, and the Women's Defence of the Constitution League (known also as the Black Sash).

▬▬▬ Eastern Cape

1. Born in Scotland, Alexander Kerr (1885–1970) was principal at Fort Hare from 1915 to 1948. He had visited black colleges in the American East and South in 1922 on a Phelps-Stokes grant. He also served on the Kerr Commission on education in Southern Rhodesia and the Carr-Saunders Commission on Higher Education in Central Africa. See his *Fort Hare 1915–48: The Evolution of an African College* (1968).

2. Educated at Lovedale, Z. K. Matthews (1901–1968) became the first African graduate of Fort Hare in 1923, the first African headmaster at Adams College in 1925, and the first African law graduate of the University of South Africa in 1930. He received an M.A. at Yale University in 1933 (he met Bunche at Howard University on a study tour of the American South organized by Prof. Charles Loram) and went on for additional graduate studies in social an-

thropology under Malinowski at the London School of Economics in 1934. He taught native law and social anthropology at Fort Hare until he resigned in 1959, when the college came under the administration of the Department of Bantu Education. Matthews was active in ANC politics and served as Cape provincial president; in 1956, he was one of the treason trialists. He also served on the Native Representative Council. He left South Africa in 1961 to work for the World Council of Churches in Geneva and ended his career as Botswana's ambassador to the United Nations (1966–68). He had direct contact with Bunche again in 1952–53, when he was visiting professor at Union Theological Seminary and was active on South African issues at the United Nations. See his autobiography, *Freedom for My People* (1981).

3. Called Fingoes by Europeans, the Mfengu were refugees who fled the wars of the Mfecane and sought sanctuary among Xhosa groups in the 1820s. They took their name from the phrase—*siyamfenguza* ("we are hungry and seeking shelter)—they used when asking for protection and sustenance. Gcaleka Xhosa gave them cattle so that they could start anew, but in the war of 1834–35 with the British, many Mfengu turned on their benefactors and sided with the British. Thousands moved to the Ciskei, where the British gave them land as a buffer between white settlers and the Xhosa. Many Mfengu actively assisted the British against Xhosa groups in later wars. Many also converted to Christianity and were among the first to acquire education through the mission schools. See Richard Moyer, "A History of the Mfengu of the Eastern Cape, 1815–1865" (Ph.D. dissertation, University of London, 1976).

4. Roseberry Tandwefika Bokwe (1900–1963) was the son of Rev. John Knox Bokwe, a noted minister and music composer. Educated at Lovedale and Fort Hare, he taught and became headmaster at John Dube's school, Ohlange Institute. He left in 1928 to study medicine at Edinburgh University; he also spent time at the University of Dublin. After receiving his medical degree in 1933, he returned to South Africa in 1934 and set up a private practice in Middledrift. He was appointed assistant district surgeon in 1937 and district surgeon in 1945. He served as Treasurer of the Cape African National Congress and on the national executive of the African National Congress in the 1940s. (*Umteteli wa Bantu,* 7 April 1934 and Alfred Xuma, "Dr. Rosebery Bokwe," *Drum* August 1954)).

5. The great grandson of Chief Moroka, Dr. J. S. Moroka (1892–1985) attended Lovedale before going on for his medical degree at the University of Edinburgh, graduating in 1918. Baptized into politics through the All African Convention, he became its treasurer in 1936. He was elected to the Native Representative Council in 1942, and although he started denouncing it in 1946, he did not resign from his position until late 1950. Although not a card-carrying member of the ANC, he unseated Dr. Xuma as its president-general in 1949, but was replaced by Albert Luthuli in 1952.

6. Born in 1910 in Ladysmith, Donald Guy Sydney M'timkulu grew up in Cape Town, where his father was a Methodist minister. He received his education at Lovedale Institution, Adams College, and Fort Hare, where he completed his B.A. in 1927. He completed an M.A. at Ft. Hare/Rhodes University in English the following year. He taught at Adams and Healdtown until 1934, when Carnegie awarded him a grant to study social anthropology at Yale. He completed an M.A. and passed his comprehensives for the Ph.D. (he eventually

completed his degree in 1955 with a thesis on the social and economic development of mission reserves in Natal). He then won a scholarship at LSE, where he studied education and anthropology under Malinowski. He toured the American South in 1936 and published a series of articles in *The Teachers' Vision IV* (1937) on his impressions. Upon his return to South Africa he succeeded Z. K. Matthews as headmaster at Adams in 1938 and Dr. Dube in 1947 as principal at Ohlange Institute until 1955. From 1955 to 1958 he was senior lecturer in the Department of Education at Ft. Hare. He resigned in protest over the segregation of the universities. He later worked for the International Missionary Council and the World Council of Churches and held lectureships at universities in the United States and Canada, where he presently lives. See Henry Nxumalo, "He Was Always First" *Drum* (August 1955): 39; "Don Mtimkulu," *Zonk* (September 1949): 39; interview, Don M'timkulu, 13 December 1989.

7. Born in 1870 in Keiskamma Hoek, H. M. Taberer was a leading figure in recruiting African labor for the South African mines. Appointed director of the Government Native Labour Bureau in 1907, he later became a key official in the Witwatersrand Native Labor Association and the Native Recruiting Corporation.

8. In 1927, 16,480 Cape Africans (about 8% of all Cape voters) had the vote (in addition Coloured voters comprised about 12% of the electorate), but then the Hertzog administration began whittling away at African voting strength by rigorously examining African voter qualifications and diluting the African vote by extending the franchise to European women in 1930 and to *all* European men in the Cape and Natal (who previously had to meet property and education standards). The 1936 law divided the Cape province into three districts from which African voters elected European representatives to Parliament. See Govan Mbeki, *South Africa: The Peasant's Revolt* (1964), 23–31 and C. M. Tatz, *Shadow and Substance in South Africa: A Study in Land and Franchise Policies Affecting Africans, 1910–1960* (1962).

9. Mission schools were under heavy attack by African teachers for missionary paternalism, poor teacher salaries and conditions of service, being underfinanced, and having a shortage of classrooms. However, when the Nationalist Party passed the Bantu Education Act of 1953, bringing black education under state control, and began promoting inferior education for black students, African nationalists redirected their protests at the government.

10. Born in the Netherlands, George Frank Dingemans (ca. 1879–1954) was graduated from Edinburgh University with an M.A. in Classics in 1899. He had gone out to South Africa in 1904 to take up an appointment with St. Andrew's College in Grahamstown, but stepped down a short time later to become one of the first teachers at Rhodes, where he occupied the chair of Afrikaans and Netherlands until his retirement in 1943. A speaker at Fort Hare's first graduation, he served on its council from 1918 to 1943 and was its president from 1933 to 1944. Although not Jewish, he was a fervent Zionist and played an active role in combatting anti-Semitism in South Africa. See Dolly Elias, "In Memoriam: G. F. Dingemans: A Fighter in the Battle for Righteousness," *Jewish Affairs* 9 (3) (March 1954): 22–26.

11. Named after John Love, secretary of the Glasgow Missionary Society, Lovedale Institute was established in 1826 for training teachers and clergy— later it added a technical school. The Free Church of Scotland took it over

later. The school was open to all races and produced some well-known European graduates, but it is best known as one of the premier schools for Africans in southern Africa. Lovedale's printing press was also widely known. See R. H. W. Shepherd, *Lovedale* (1940).

12. Born in Port Elizabeth, Margaret Ballinger (1894–1980) was educated in history at Oxford University and taught history at Rhodes University and Witwatersrand University before marrying William Ballinger. She ran for one of the four "native" seats in 1937 and retained it until Native Representatives were done away with in 1960. She was one of the founders of the Liberal Party in 1953. Her autobiography is *From Union to Apartheid: A Trek to Isolation* (1969).

13. J. H. Hofmeyr (1894–1948) was minister of education (1933–1948) and finance (1939–1948) under the United Party government. See Alan Paton's biography *South African Tragedy: The Life and Times of Jan Hofmeyr* (1965).

14. Born in Glasgow, William Ballinger (1894–1974) had been involved in Scottish municipal affairs and the British Independent Labour Party before coming out to South Africa in 1928 as an adviser to the ICU. His controversial association with the ICU is documented in Peter Wickins, *The Industrial and Commercial Workers Union of Africa* (1978). Ballinger wrote *Race and Economics in South Africa* (1934). Married to Margaret Ballinger (see note 12), he was a Native Senator from 1948 to 1960.

15. Born in 1873, Carl Malcomess farmed in the East London and Berlin districts in the Eastern Cape. He served the King William's Town district in the Cape Provincial Council from 1933 to 1937, when he was elected "native" senator for the Cape Province. He served in this position until his death in 1950.

16. The product of marriages between Xhosa men and Khoi women, the Gqunukhwebe created a chiefdom in the eighteenth century between the Bushman and Fish Rivers. See Gerrit Harinck, "Interaction between Xhosa and Khoi: Emphasis on the Period 1620–1750," in Leonard Thompson, ed., *African Societies in Southern Africa* (1969).

17. Kama (ca. 1798–1875) was a Gqunukhwebe Xhosa chief who took a loyalist stance during the 1850 war and received land around Middledrift as his reward. A devout Wesleyan Methodist, he strongly opposed the cattle killing in 1856–57, but afterward was treated poorly by British officials. See Drusilla Sizwe Yekela, "The Life and Times of Kama Chungwa, 1798–1875," (M.A. thesis, Rhodes University, 1989).

18. Educated at Healdtown, Morija, and Lovedale, Alexander Macauley ("Mac") Jabavu (1889–1946) taught in Kimberley before becoming the editor of *Imvo Zabantsundu* following the death of his father, John Tengo Jabavu, in 1921. He was elected vice president of the ICU in 1926. A founder and chairman of the Location and Advisory Board Congress in 1928 and a treasurer of the Cape Native Voters' Convention, he also served on the executive committee of the AAC. He was secretary to the Ciskei Bunga. He was elected to the Native Representative Council for the rural areas of the Cape Province from 1937 to 1942.

19. *Imvo Zabantsundu* ("African Opinion") was established in King William's Town in 1884 and became the leading newspaper for Africans. Floated by liberal white backers, *Imvo* was edited by John Tengo Jabavu, who used the newspaper to champion various African causes and to articulate his personal views on a range of issues. After John Tengo's death in 1921, *Imvo* remained in

the hands of his sons, D.D.T. and Alexander, before it was bought out by the Bantu Press. See Les Switzer's articles, "The African Christian Community and its Press in Victorian South Africa," *Cahiers d'Etudes Africaines* 24 (96) (1984): 455–76 and "The Ambiguities of Protest in South Africa: Rural Politics and the Press during the 1920's," *International Journal of African Historical Studies* 23 (1) (1990): 87–108.

20. Dr. Neil McVicar (1871–1949) was the medical officer at Fort Hare College and Superintendent of Victoria Hospital, Lovedale. Born in Scotland, he obtained his M.D. from Edinburgh University and served as a medical missionary at the Blantyre Mission in Nyasaland for the Church of Scotland before coming to Lovedale in 1902. He took charge of the Victoria Hospital. He had been a promoter of the Fort Hare College idea and served on its governing council from 1916 to 1937, when he retired. He founded the Native Health Association. He wrote extensively, including *Tuberculosis Among the South African Natives* based on his thesis for his M.D. See R. H. W. Shepherd, *A South African Medical Pioneer: The Life of Neil McVicar* (1952).

21. The Representation of Natives Act of 1936 provided for Africans in the Cape Province to elect three members (who had to be "British subjects of European descent") to the House of Assembly. The vote was restricted to any male who owned property worth £75 or earned a salary of at least £50 per year, who was at least 21 years old, who was able to sign his name, address, and occupation, and whose name had previously appeared on the voters' roll.

22. Set up with the backing of Winifred Holtby, the Society of Friends of Africa assisted William Ballinger's work when he was sent out to advise the ICU. When the ICU collapsed, Ballinger continued to represent Friends of Africa in areas such as advising African trade unions and cooperative societies and submitting memoranda to Wage Boards. For more details on the group's background, see Vera Brittain, *Testament of Friendship: The Story of Winifred Holtby* (1930).

23. Donald Molteno (1908–1972) studied law at Cambridge and practiced law in South Africa from 1932 until 1964 when the University of Cape Town appointed him senior lecturer in Roman Dutch law. He was a Native Representative from 1937 to 1948. He was active in the Institute of Race Relations from 1938 on and served as its president from 1958 to 1960. A founder of the Liberal Party in 1953, he chaired its constitutional committee. A short biography is David Scher, *Donald Molteno: "Dilizintaba" He-Who-Removes-Mountains* (1979).

24. Led by Colonel C. F. Stallard, the Dominion Party broke away from the South African Party when it merged with the National Party in 1934. Largely popular among English-speaking voters in Natal, the party aimed at preserving the connection with Britain. It was also anti-Indian and promoted the Pegging Bill in 1943 to halt Indian movement into white residential and business areas. At the beginning of the Second World War, the party sided with Smuts over the issue of supporting the British. As a reward, Col. Stallard was given a post in the Smuts cabinet. Following the war he dropped out of the cabinet, and the Dominion Party did not play a significant role in white politics thereafter.

25. An Umtata lawyer, Gordon Hemming served in the Bambatha Rebellion in 1906 and in the First World War. Elected to the House of Assembly re-

presenting the Transkei, he served from 1937 until his death in 1947. See B. B. Mdledle's tribute to Hemmings in *South African Outlook* 1 May 1947: 79–80.

26. Educated at Lovedale and Dale College, King William's Town, William Thomson Welsh (1873–1954) was Chief Magistrate of the Transkeian Territories from 1920–1933. Following his father, who had been a magistrate, he started his career in the law department of the Cape Civil Service and served in a number of posts in the Cape. In 1908, he was posted to the Transkei and served as magistrate at Libode, Mqanduli, and Kokstad before becoming Chief Magistrate. He was also chairman of the Transkeian Territories General Council (Bunga). He served in the Cape Provincial Council from 1933 before being nominated to the Senate as a Native Senator.

27. Edgar Brookes (1897–1979) was a founding member of the Institute of Race Relations and its president in 1930–32 and 1948–50. He was a Senator representing Africans in Natal and Zululand in Parliament from 1937 to 1952. He taught at the Transvaal University College before serving as principal of Adams College from 1933 to 1945. In 1952 he became professor of history and political science at the University of Natal. After joining the Liberal Party in 1962, he became its national chairman in 1964. See his autobiography, *A South African Pilgrimage* (1977).

28. A "Buchmanite" is a follower of Frank Buchman, the founder of the Moral Rearmament Association. For its initial South African connection, see Garth Lean, *Frank Buchman: a Life* (1985), 140–43.

29. In 1924 Edgar Brookes published *The History of Native Policy in South Africa* in 1924. According to him, a trip to the United States under the sponsorship of the Phelps-Stokes fund in 1927 changed his views on segregation. He recanted his former position at a Fort Hare conference of African and European students in 1930.

30. After the First World War, a popular belief spread in the African community that American blacks were coming to liberate South Africa from European oppression. This idea had its most concrete expression in the Wellington movement in the Transkei during the 1920s. Inspired by Marcus Garvey's movement, Wellington Butelezi, a Zulu, claimed he was an African-American doctor and began preaching the imminent appearance of African-American liberators in airplanes. The expectations reached such a fever peak around 1926 and 1927 that the government sent a squadron of airplanes in 1927 to impress its power upon people, but some people mistakenly took the planes as scouts for the American liberators. For details, see Robert Edgar, "Garveyism in Africa: Dr. Wellington and the American Movement in the Transkei," *Ufahamu* 6 (1976): 31–57; William Beinart and Colin Bundy, *Hidden Struggles in Rural South Africa 1890–1930* (1987), chap. 7; and Helen Bradford, *A Taste of Freedom* (1987), chap. 7.

31. A confidant of Hertzog and his minister of justice after 1929, Oswald Pirow, an advocate, eventually became minister of defense. During the Second World War his openly pro-Nazi sympathies led him to organize the New Order (*Nuwe Orde*) Group. Eventually he was forced to leave the Nationalist Party in Parliament, although he never seceded from the party.

32. The Cape African Teachers Association (CATA), founded in 1920, was the educational lobby for Cape African teachers. For more details on its

history, see R. L. Peteni, *Towards Tomorrow: The Story of the African Teachers' Associations of South Africa* (1979), 30–47.

33. Jabavu had recently returned from attending a Quaker conference in Philadelphia. In late 1931, Jabavu had also gone to Philadelphia to address a conference on Foreign Missions. He published a colorful account of his visit, *E-Amerika U-welo Luka* (1932).

34. George Haynes (1880–1960) was a well-known African American sociologist. The first black person to receive a Ph.D. from Columbia University (1912), he taught at Fisk University, worked for the International YMCA and the National Urban League, and served as secretary of the Commission on Church and Race Relations of the Federal Council of the Churches of Christ (1922–1947). In 1930 he conducted a survey of YMCA work in South Africa and visited there again in 1947 on another YMCA study tour. See his *Africa: Continent of the Future* (1950) and his articles on South Africa in the *Amsterdam News* (June through September, 1952). See also Daniel J. Perlman, "Stirring the White Conscience: The Life of George Edmund Haynes" (1972).

35. When Jesse Owens, a sprinter and long jumper, won four gold medals at the 1936 Berlin Olympics, the black South African press lionized him. A typical commentary appeared in the *South African Worker* (23 August 1936): ". . . that the German Nazi's are the 'supermen' over all nations and more particularly that the Negro people were a 'barbaric horde' who are incapable of assimilating the white man's civilisation has certainly been disproved by Jesse Owens right in the face of the Nazi chiefs Hitler, Goering and Goebbels. . . . Jesse Owens' achievements must be a very impossible pill to swallow for the Nazi supermen and for our 'pure white' South Africans, too."

▪ Thaba 'Nchu and Mafeking

1. Thaba 'Nchu was the mountain where Moroka's Seleka Barolong settled in 1833. In 1884 it was annexed to the Orange Free State. The town of Thaba 'Nchu was established in 1893. For an overview of Thaba 'Nchu history, see Colin Murray, "Land, Power and Class in the Thaba 'Nchu District, Orange Free State, 1884–1983" *Review of African Political Economy* 29 (1984), 30–48.

2. Paul Olifant Mosaka (1907–1963) was born in Pimville, an African location outside Johannesburg. He went to Healdtown, a Wesleyan Methodist school, and majored in psychology and ethics at Fort Hare. He was the first Transvaal African to receive his B.A. there. He started teaching at Healdtown and then was invited to Thaba 'Nchu by a Fort Hare classmate, Jacob Nhlapo. He was prominent in the Cape African Teachers' Association and edited its journal. Later he moved to Johannesburg to run a general dealer's business in Orlando owned by Dr. Moroka. He also ran a funeral home and an insurance company. A founder of the African Chamber of Commerce, he served as its president. An excellent public speaker and debater, he was elected to the Native Representative Council and was a founder of the African Democratic Party in 1943.

3. Born in 1904, Jacob Nhlapo was educated at Bensonvale Institution and Lovedale. After teaching at Healdtown, he moved on to Moroka High School in 1930 and became its principal in 1934. He became vice president of the South African Native Teachers Association. He received a B.A. from the University of South Africa in 1937 and a Ph.D. from McKinley Roosevelt University in Chicago for his dissertation on "Intelligence Tests and the Educability of the South African Bantu." The principal of Wilberforce Institute from 1940 to 1947, he authored *Wilberforce Institute* (1949). In 1952 he became the editor of the *Bantu World*.

4. Walton Zacharias Fenyang (1877–1957) was a key figure in Barolong political circles and a stalwart Wesleyan Methodist. A large landholder, he had to settle some large debts by selling off most of his farm in the 1930s to the South African Native Trust and private individuals. The son of Chief Tshipinare's daughter in the chief's first house, Fenyang was not a chief, but a power behind the throne. An adversary of the Barolong Progressive Association, he was active in the Orange Free State ANC; he was treasurer of the parent ANC at one point. He was also a delegate to the government sponsored "native" conferences in the 1920s. A friend of Sol Plaatje, he was part of the Thaba 'Nchu group that helped fund Plaatje's newspapers.

5. The advocate the association hired on was Bram Fischer (1908–1975), grandson of the first prime minister of the Orange River Colony. A member of the Communist Party, he was sentenced to life imprisonment in 1966 for his antigovernment activities.

6. Moroka's account of the land issue at Thaba 'Nchu favors his interest. For a detailed accounting of the complexities of the land bargaining, see Colin Murray's chapter, "Trust and Anti-Trust: The Struggle Over Land," in *Black Mountain: Land, Power and Class in the Eastern Orange Free State, 1880s to 1980s* (1991).

7. John Phetogane Moroka, the second son in the fifth house of Chief Tshipinare, was the chief of Thaba 'Nchu appointed by the Native Affairs Department. He died in 1940. He was a heavy drinker. In the late 1930s, the Barolong Progressive Association challenged his chieftainship.

8. Chief Moroka II (ca. 1795–1880) of the Seleka Rolong led his people to Thaba 'Nchu after Moshoeshoe granted them land in 1833. Moroka attracted many Griqua and Sotho refugees in his domain. He became an ally of Afrikaners against the Ndebele and Basotho. Orange Free State leaders allowed Thaba 'Nchu to keep its autonomy, but in 1884, the Free State annexed Thaba 'Nchu.

9. *Nkosi Sikelel'i Afrika* was composed in 1897 by Enoch Sontonga, a schoolteacher in a Wesleyan Methodist school in Nancefield, west of Johannesburg. Later the song was adopted as a closing anthem at meetings of the African National Congress. Over the years, it has been accepted as the national anthem for the African community in South Africa and many other southern African countries.

10. For an overview of the issue of syphilis, see Karen Jochelson, "Tracking Down the Treponema: Patterns of Syphilis in South Africa, 1880–1940," paper presented to the conference on "Structure and Experience in the Making of Apartheid," Witwatersrand University, 6–10 February 1990.

11. According to the biographers of Moshoeshoe, Moroka presented Mo-

shoeshoe with a gift of cattle so he could reside on the land around Thaba 'Nchu. Moshoeshoe was not selling the land, but giving Moroka's people permission to stay in the area. Moshoeshoe also signed a document in 1833 with Wesleyan Methodist missionaries selling them land around Thaba 'Nchu in exchange for animals. There is a dispute, however, whether Moshoeshoe understood he was selling the land as opposed to giving missionaries the right to stay on the land. See Peter Sanders, *Moshoeshoe* (1975), 63–65 and Leonard Thompson, *Survival in Two Worlds* (1975), 126–31.

12. *Witchdoctor* is one of those unfortunate European terms which has only a remote resemblance to African religious practitioners and perpetuates a stereotype that Africans are irrational and superstitious. People who doctor witches do not exist, but there are individuals who dispense medicinal and herbal remedies and some who are witch finders. Moroka is likely referring to one of the latter. A useful discussion is Andrew Spiegel and Emile Boonzaier's, "Promoting Tradition: Images of the South African Past," in Emile Boonzaier and John Sharp, eds., *South African Keywords: The Uses and Abuses of Political Concepts* (1988), 43–45.

13. Dr. Goolam Husain Gool (1905–1962) was sent to Aligargh College in India, a well-known Muslim college, at the age of 9, but returned to South Africa when the passive resistance campaign in India of 1919–21 shut down the college. He completed his medical training at Guys Hospital in London. When he returned to South Africa, he set up a practice in Clermont. He was a founding member of the All African Convention in 1935 and president of the National Liberation League in 1937–38 before being expelled in 1939. A Trotskyite, he was a founding member and chairman of the Anti-CAD and vice chairman of the Non-European Unity Movement from 1945 until his death in 1962.

14. Dr. S. M. Molema (1891–1965) was educated at Healdtown and went on to the University of Glasgow in 1914 for a medical degree, which he completed in 1919. Returning home in 1921, he set up practice in Mafeking. He also started a nursing home in Mafeking for black and white patients, but closed it after an outcry from the white community. He served as treasurer of the African National Congress from 1949 until 1953 and as secretary to Chief Montsioa. He authored *Bantu Past and Present* (1920), *Montshiwa, 1815–1896* (1966), and *Chief Moroka* (1951).

15. This is likely William Mears, A British-born leader of the Wesleyan Methodist Church who came out to South Africa in 1901 and took up residence in 1907 at Shawbury mission station in the Transkci. He was elected president of the Methodist conference in 1933. After his wife died in 1937, he lived in Umtata until his death in 1945.

16. Mafiking, meaning "among the stones," was originally a Tshidi Barolong village established around 1854 for defensive purposes by Molema, brother of chief Montshiwa. It became a center for Barolong Christians and eventually in 1881 the capital of the Tshidi Barolong under Chief Montshiwa. In 1885, when the British annexed Bechuanaland, they sited their administrative capital about a mile from Montshiwa's court and named it Mafeking. The two were separated by a railway line. The Barolong's Mafiking also became known as the *stadt* or *stad* (Dutch for "town"). When Bunche visited, the stadt had a population of about 14,000.

17. Chief Lotlamoreng Montshioa, or Montshiwa (1896–1954) received his primary education at Lovedale. He was chief of the Ratshidi Barolong from 1919 until his death in 1954. Contrary to Bunche's perception of him, he had a reputation as a progressive leader, sponsoring the building of schools and dams and establishing a tribal treasury.

18. Settled in the Mafeking region, the Ratshidi Barolong are part of the Rolong, a Tswana group, which split into four groups in the latter part of the eighteenth century. When Boers moved into their area, the Barolong appealed for British protection in 1884, but in 1895, the British handed over part of the Ratshidi area to the Cape and later the Union of South Africa.

▬▬ Johannesburg I

1. Two of the best accounts of Johannesburg history are Nigel Mandy, *A City Divided: Johannesburg and Soweto* (1984) and Charles Van Onselen, *New Babylon, New Ninevah: Studies in the Social and Economic History of the Witwatersrand* (1982), Volumes I and II. According to the 1936 government census, Johannesburg had a population of 519,268 (257,530 Europeans and 261,738 Non-Europeans).

2. I. B. S. Masole was chairman of the Non-European Reading Circle at Witwatersrand University.

3. Born in Oudtshoorn in the Cape Province, Julius Lewin (1907–1984) majored in English literature and law at the University of Cape Town. He went to London in the 1930s to work for an LL.B. at the London School of Economics, where he taught briefly, and worked for the Labour Party Committee on African Affairs and the Fabian Colonial Bureau. After returning to Witwatersrand University in 1939, he taught native (later African) law and administration. During 1947–48 he accepted an invitation from Bunche to work in the UN Trusteeship Department and then resumed his lectureship at Witwatersrand University. After retiring to London in 1967, he took up appointments at several American and British universities. He authored *Africans and the Police* (1944), *Politics and the Law in South Africa* (1963), and *Studies in African Native Law* (1947) and edited *The Struggle for Racial Equality* (1967).

4. One of six Cape Town districts, District Six contained a diverse community until the government's Group Area's scheme destroyed it in the 1960s. See George Manuel and Denis Hatfield, *District Six* (1967) and Don Pinnock, *The Brotherhoods: Street Gangs and State Control in Cape Town* (1984), chap. 2.

5. Bunche was likely speaking to Dr. Francis William Fox, a London University-trained biochemist who came out to South Africa in 1925 to work at the South African Institute for Medical Research. He wrote *Can South Africa Feed Herself?* (1945) and *Food from the Veld: Edible Wild Plants of Southern Africa* (1982). With Douglas Back, he wrote *A Preliminary Survey of the Agricultural and Nutritional Problems of the Ciskei and Transkei Territories,* a report for the Chamber of Mines (1938).

6. Founded in 1889 by the major gold mining houses, the Chamber of Mines coordinated policy on issues vital to the profitability of the gold mines such as wages and the recruitment of African labor. The chamber created a

monopolistic recruiting organization, the Witwatersrand Native Labour Association, so the mining houses would not have to compete with each other and pay higher wages to black workers.

7. See note 44, Cape Town.

8. Joe Hellman was a lawyer who died in the early 1940s. His wife, Ellen Hellman (1908–1982) was a social anthropologist trained at Witwatersrand University and the first woman to receive a doctorate from there. A prominent figure in the South African Institute of Race Relations, she served as its president from 1954 to 1956. For a time, she chaired the Johannesburg Joint Council and was on the executive council of the South African Jewish Board of Deputies. Her publications include *Rooiyard: A Sociological Survey of an Urban Native Slum Yard* (1946), *Problems of Urban Bantu Youth* (1941), and the *Handbook on Race Relations in South Africa* (1949) (which she edited).

9. Born in Illoki, Russia, Wulf Sachs (1893–1949) received his education at the Neurological Institute in St. Petersburg, where he was a student of Ivan Petrovich Pavlov; the University of Cologne, where he received his medical degree; and the University of London. He came to South Africa in 1922 as a general practitioner. He was attracted to psychoanalysis and went to Europe in 1930 for further training. A disciple of Sigmund Freud, he was the only psychoanalyst in South Africa for some years and established a Psychoanalytical Training Institute in Johannesburg. He devoted time to the Non-European Mental Hospital in Pretoria and in black locations around Johannesburg such as Rooiyard and Doornfontein, where he met John, the subject of his book, *Black Hamlet*. Active in the Zionist Socialist Party, he was on the executive of the South African Zionist Federation before he left the Zionist movement in 1943. He edited the independent journal *The Democrat* from 1944 until 1947. Among his other writings are *Psychoanalysis: Its Meaning and Application* (1934), and *The Vegetative Nervous System: A Clinical Study* (1936), and a play, *Escape From the Past*. At his death, he was finishing a manuscript on the psychology of suffering.

10. Named after Johannesburg city councillor Edwin Orlando Leake, a former Johannesburg mayor and chairman of the Non-European Affairs Committee, Orlando Township, situated about eleven miles southwest of Johannesburg, was started up in 1932 and was supposed to be a showplace living area for Africans. Because of the large influx of black people into the urban areas during the Second World War, overcrowding reached crisis proportions and led to a squatting problem. Orlando Township had a population of around 18,000 in 1936. It was later incorporated in Soweto. See W. J. P. Carr, *Soweto and African Administration* (1991).

11. Educated at Dale College in King William's Town and Witwatersrand University, Llewellyn I. Venables had been a civil servant in the Justice Department before becoming an official in the Johannesburg Department of Native Administration in 1931. Appointed head of the renamed Non-European Affairs Department from 1944 to 1951, he resigned in 1951 over a dispute with the city council. Later he worked as an estates manager and as a magistrate in Kliptown.

12. Named after Howard Pim and located 12 miles southwest of Johannesburg, Pimville was set up initially for refugees from the plague as Johannesburg's first African location in 1904. Africans built their own homes there on

land leased by the Johannesburg municipality. In 1938 about 12,500 residents lived in Pimville.

13. Many independent African churches incorporated the name *Zion* in their titles. Zionist churches usually emphasize divine healing and prophecy. For details, see Bengt Sundkler, *Zulu Zion and Some Swazi Zionists* (1976).

14. Competitive bidding for songs was commonly practiced at African concerts. For other examples, see David B. Coplan, *In Township Tonight! South Africa's Black City Music and Theatre* (1985), 76–78.

15. In 1919 Rev. F. B. Bridgman of the American Board mission founded the Bantu Men's Social Centre (BMSC), situated in Eloff St. Extension, to provide cultural and recreational facilities in a Christian setting for African men in and around the Johannesburg area. Peter Abrahams's *Tell Freedom: Memories of Africa* (1954) contains a description of the BMSC.

16. After arriving in South Africa in 1936, John Gray (1903–1947) became professor of sociology and head of the Department of Social Sciences.

17. For a discussion of Witwatersrand University's internal debate over admitting black students, see Bruce Murray, "Wits as an 'Open' University 1939–1959: Black Admissions to the University of Witwatersrand," *Journal of Southern African Studies* 16 (4) (1990): 649–77.

18. A graduate of Carleton College (1914) and Yale Divinity School (1917), Ray Phillips (1889–1967) was an American Board missionary in South Africa from 1918 to 1958. He was in charge of social work in Johannesburg and served as secretary at the Bantu Men's Social Centre. He was one of the leading lights in the Institute of Race Relations. He founded and was director (1940–57) of the Jan Hofmeyr School of Social Work at Witwatersrand University.

19. The two principal Johannesburg newspapers aimed at a black readership were the *Bantu World* (see note 13, Cape Town section) and *Umteteli wa Bantu* (Mouthpiece of the People) (see note 30), founded in 1920 by the Native Recruiting Corporation.

20. A. S. Vil-Nkomo worked at the Bantu Men's Social Centre and was a leader of the Order of Elks and the Gamma Sigma Club, a debating society. He became the first African sanitary inspector for the Benoni location in 1938.

21. Dr. C. C. P. Anning (d. 1951) came to South Africa from England in the early 1930s. He was Medical Officer of Health (MOH) for Pietermaritzburg before studying tuberculosis and health in the U.S. When he returned, he was appointed MOH for Benoni. During World War II, he was director of Medical Services for the Sixth South African Division in Italy. After the war, he became Medical Adviser to the Social Services Department of the Chamber of Mines.

22. When Bunche visited, the African press was intensely debating the issue of whether to use the word *native* or *African* or *Bantu*. Eventually politically-minded people chose *African* as the preferred word because it connoted the fact that they were the indigenous inhabitants of the continent. The South African government later substituted *Bantu* for *native,* thinking it would not do to call black people African since Afrikaners had already appropriated the name *Afrikaner* for themselves. An interesting discussion of the naming controversy is L. B. Mehlomakulu's "African, Bantu, Native or Kafir?" *Cape Standard,* 20 March 1945.

23. Born in Kimberley, Peter Dabula was brought to Johannesburg when he was young. He later worked in the Non-European Affairs Department in Benoni.

24. Jack Phillips claimed to have been an entertainer in various countries when he arrived from Australia in the early 1920s, but some believed he hailed from South Africa. He ran the first Inchcape Hall from around 1922 at Eloff Street Extension until it was demolished; he then moved the club to City and Suburban streets, an area with a sizable black community about a mile east of the city center. Although he renamed his club the Ritz, Africans still called it the Inchcape.

25. A gift from Howard Pim and John Hardy, the Bantu Sports Club was built for African recreational purposes on twelve acres of abandoned mining property in the center of Johannesburg. The property included two football fields, tennis courts and a clubhouse. Dan Twala was its organizing secretary.

26. John Henry Lewis was world light heavyweight champion from 1935 to 1938. In early 1939 he fought Joe Louis for the heavyweight championship, but lost in a first-round technical knockout. Henry Armstrong was world champion as a featherweight (1937–38), lightweight (1938–39), and welterweight (1938–40).

27. Johannesburg celebrated its fiftieth anniversary by holding the Empire Exhibition from 15 September 1936 to 15 January 1937 at the Milner Park showgrounds, now part of Witwatersrand University.

28. The second son of a minister, Dan Twala (1906–1983) was born at Barberton. After receiving his early education at Witbank and Lovedale, he completed his matriculation at Fort Hare. He aspired to become a medical doctor, but he settled in Germiston as a shop assistant. Active in community affairs and sporting clubs, he served as president of the Johannesburg African Football Association and secretary and manager of the Bantu Sports Club in 1936. He was a radio sports commentator, secretary of the Bantu Dramatic Society (1932–1940), an actor (in films like "The Two Brothers," "They Built a Nation," and "Jim Comes to Johannesburg") and a founder and drummer in the Rhythm Kings band. See a portrait of him in *Zonk* (July 1951).

29. Dingaan's Day or the Day of the Covenant (as it came to be known in 1952) celebrates the 16 December 1838 victory of an Afrikaner commando over King Dingane's Zulu army at Blood River in Natal. To Afrikaner nationalists, the day symbolized their divine destiny to remain in Africa. Sometime after the Second World War, the African community began celebrating 16 December as Heroes' Day to commemorate the heroic resistance of African leaders to European conquest. For an examination of Afrikaner historical mythology and the Day of the Covenant, see Leonard Thompson, *The Political Mythology of Apartheid* (1985), esp. 144–188.

30. *Umteteli wa Bantu* (Mouthpiece of the People) was established in Johannesburg in 1920 by the Native Recruiting Corporation on behalf of the Chamber of Mines. Although the paper was not intended to be a force for radical change, it provided a forum for a number of black writers, including Solomon Plaatje, H. I. E. Dhlomo, Selope-Thema, Richard and Selby Msimang, Simon Phamotse, Alan K. Soga, and H. Tyamzashe, and is an essential source of news about the black community.

31. The "Native Printer" in Maseru refers to the African-owned press, which produced the newspaper, *Naledi*. For more on the Tlale family which ran the press, see Robert Edgar, *Prophets with Honour: A Documentary History of Lekhotla la Bafo* (1987), 238–39.

32. See note 66 in this section for information on the National Industrial Councils.

33. Named after the wife of Herman Tobiansky, who, in 1899, had bought 237 acres of land four and a half miles west of Johannesburg, Sophiatown became a unique living area for black people because Indians, Coloureds, and Africans could buy and own land there and because there was no European superintendent. Sophiatown became celebrated in 1957 when the government removed its inhabitants to Meadowlands. Eventually the area was transformed into a white residential area. See Pippa Stein and Ruth Jacobsen, eds., *Sophiatown Speaks* (1986); Don Mattera, *Memory is the Weapon* (1987); Tom Lodge, *Black Politics in South Africa since 1945* (1983), 91–113; and Andre Proctor, "Class Struggle, Segregation and the City: A History of Sophiatown, 1905–1940," in Belinda Bozzoli, ed., *Labour, Townships and Protest* (1979), 49–89.

34. In 1931 Xuma married Priscilla Mason of Liberia. Three years later she died giving birth to their second child. In 1940 he married Madie Beatrice Hall of North Carolina in Cape Town.

35. Black newspapers regularly featured advertisements of American hair-straightening and hair care products. And African-American visitors encouraged their use, particularly since they were symbols of westernization. At Wilberforce Institute, female students took their cue from American magazines and styled their hair so that, as Mrs. Charlotte Wright (wife of R. R.) observed, "no girl at Wilberforce Institute had short hair, and in appearance they looked very like their American cousins." See Charlotte Wright, *Beneath the Southern Cross,* 47–50 and Amos and Luella White, *Dawn in Bantuland,* 69, 79, 154, 198–99.

36. Lying between Sophiatown and Newclare, Western Native Township was set out in 1918 by the Johannesburg municipality for Africans employed in Johannesburg. In the late 1950s, the area was proclaimed a Coloured area and Africans were evicted. The Coloured suburb of Westbury was built on the old location.

37. With financial assistance from Howard Pim, the Western Native Township Cooperative Society started the Africa Co-Op Store in 1932. The society managed to earn a profit in its first few years of life, but then bad management and a small membership created problems and the society went out of existence by the mid-1940s.

38. Named after the wife of King Edward VII, Alexandra was set aside for white workers in 1905, nine miles from the city center. When transport and housing costs proved too high, the municipality offered plots to Africans and Coloureds with freehold rights. In 1934 the location's population was 15,000, but it had increased to 50,000 in 1939 and mushroomed to over 100,000 during the Second World War. Alexandra was the focal point for a series of celebrated bus boycotts in 1940, 1944, and 1957. For descriptions, see Tom Lodge, *Black Politics in South Africa since 1945* (1983), 153–188; Baruch Hirson, *Yours for the Union* (1989), 136–147; and *Alexandra I Love You: A Record of Seventy Years* (1983).

39. A successful Alexandra real estate agent and bus company owner, Richard Baloyi (d. 1962) was active in civic and political affairs. He served as treasurer-general of the ANC from 1938 to 1949 and was a member of the Native Representative Council from 1937 to 1942. He was associated with Selope Thema's Nationalist Minded Bloc in the early 1950s.

40. Born in Bristol, England, Clement M. Doke (1894–1980) came to South Africa with his family from New Zealand in 1903. He earned a B.A. degree at Transvaal University College in Pretoria in 1911. From 1914 to 1921 he was a Baptist missionary in Zambia and compiled *The Grammar of the Lamba Language,* submitted for an M.A. degree in 1919 at the University of South Africa. He earned a doctorate at Witwatersrand University in 1924 for *The Phonetics of the Zulu Language.* Appointed lecturer in Bantu languages at Witwatersrand University in 1923, he became professor of Bantu studies in 1931 and remained in that position until his retirement in 1953. He published *A Textbook of Zulu Grammar* (1927) and the *Zulu-English Dictionary* (1948) in collaboration with Dr. B. W. Vilakazi. He was also editor of the journal *Bantu Studies* (1ater *African Studies*) for 23 years.

41. The contest for control of Tswana orthography was not a new one, and the noted African journalist and politician Sol Plaatje had been at the center of it. See the chapter, "Language and Literature: Preserving a Culture," in Brian Willan's *Sol Plaatje: A Biography* (1984), 324–48.

42. He is likely referring to Job Richard Rathebe. Educated at Kilnerton Training Institution, he was the first secretary of the Bantu Men's Social Centre (1919–1940). He was an avid sportsman and participated in the YMCA and the Pathfinders as well as the Institute of Race Relations and the Joint Councils. He visited the United States and England in 1938 on a grant from the Carnegie Foundation.

43. A Dutch Reformed minister, Daniel F. Malan (1874–1959) became a leading figure in Hertzog's National Party and a cabinet minister in 1924. After Hertzog joined with Smuts to form the United Party in 1933, Malan broke away to establish the *Gesiwerde Nasionale Party* (Purified National Party), which attracted extreme Afrikaner nationalists to its fold. He became prime minister when his Nationalist Party won the election of 1948.

44. Morris Alexander (1877–1946) was a leading Cape Town criminal lawyer. He served in the Cape Town City Council (1905–1913) and the Cape and Union Parliaments from 1908 to 1946 (excluding 1929–1931). He represented Cape Town's Castle district, an area where the Coloured vote was strong. A well-known liberal on race issues, he was a member of the pro-British Unionist Party. When he could not bring himself to join the South Africa Party, he resigned the Unionist Party in 1920 and founded the Constitutional Democrat Party. He was its sole member in the House of Assembly and was a founder of the Jewish Board of Deputies. See Enid Alexander's biography, *Morris Alexander: A Biography* (1953) and Gustav Saron, *Morris Alexander, Parliamentarian and Jewish Leader* (1966). His nephew was Julius Lewin, who knew Bunche in London.

45. Issy Diamond had received a one year jail term in 1931 for "incitement to violence" for organizing a demonstration of black and white workers over wages and jobs. The demonstration had proceeded to the Johannesburg City Hall and then to the Rand Club, where police broke it up. The government

banished Diamond from the Witwatersrand under the Riotous Assemblies Act, but a court overturned that order on appeal. He was suspended from the Communist Party in 1935 for associating with anti-Party elements. A barber by profession, Diamond also participated in the founding of the Hairdressers' Union.

46. Born in Lithuania, Emil Solomon "Solly" Sachs (1901–1976) came to South Africa as a child. In 1928 he was studying law at Witwatersrand University when he was elected general secretary of the Garment Workers Union. In 1952 the government ordered him to resign as secretary of his union and prohibited him from attending all meetings. He defied the ban and was sentenced to six months' imprisonment. An Appeals Court suspended his sentence, but he left for Great Britain in 1953 and took up research posts at Manchester University and the London School of Economics. His books include *The Choice Before South Africa* (1952), *Rebels Daughters* (1957), *The Anatomy of Apartheid* (1965), and, with Lionel Forman, *The South African Treason Trial* (1958).

47. Gana Makabeni (d. 1955) was one of the first Africans to join the Communist Party in the mid-1920s. He was closely associated with S. P. Bunting and was expelled from the Party with him in 1932. His primary activity was in trade union organizing. Between 1928 and 1955, he was secretary of the African Clothing Workers' Union and general secretary of the Co-ordinating Committee of African Trade Unions, comprised of ten unions claiming a combined membership of 4,000 in 1939. He was also one of the founders of the Council of Non-European Trade Unions and was its president from 1941 to 1944. He served on the ANC National Executive in the 1940s and briefly was acting treasurer-general in 1948–1949.

48. Managed by Jonathan Kopie "Kappie" Masoleng, the Darktown Strutters were a vaudeville troupe with a nationwide following. By the late 1930s, they had broken apart, but they became the nucleus of another vaudeville group, De Pitch Black Follies, led by Griffiths Motsieloa. They were celebrated for their tap dancing routines and performing the music of Layton and Johnstone.

49. Americans John Turner Layton, Jr., and Clarence Johnstone formed a vaudeville team in the early 1920s. They moved to London in 1924 and were a popular team in theaters. The partnership broke up in 1935.

50. From the late nineteenth century, African-American culture inspired and influenced African culture. This was expressed through minstrelsy and vaudeville, dance, and vocal and music styles such as dixieland, spirituals, ragtime, and jazz. A commentary on this interaction is provided in David B. Coplan, *In Township Tonight!* (1985).

51. An African-American jazz pianist and composer, Fats Waller (1904–1943) was a popular entertainer in night clubs and show revues. His song "Ain't Misbehavin' " has become a classic.

52. The Mills Brothers—Donald, Harry, John, and Herbert—began singing professionally in 1922. They achieved national recognition in the 1930s on stage and through radio, records, and film and remained popular through the 1940s and 1950s. Their best known songs include "Glow Worm," "Goodbye Blues," "Lazy River," "Paper Doll," and "You Always Hurt the One You Love." Of the four brothers, only Donald survives.

53. Bernard Lazarus Emmanuel Sigamoney (1889–1963) was a Durban

schoolteacher and secretary of the Workers Industrial Union before he went to England in 1922 to study for the Anglican ministry. He returned to South Africa in 1927 to start up an Indian mission in Vrededorp. He was ordained as a priest in 1928. He also served as principal of an Indian school housed in the African Congregational Church in Doornfontein. He participated in the Transvaal Indian Congress and he was prominent in sporting circles. At the time of his death, he was chairman of the South African Non-Racial Olympic Committee.

54. An excellent analysis of the Garment Workers Union is Iris Berger's "Solidarity Fragmented: Garment Workers of the Transvaal, 1930–1960," in Shula Marks and Stanley Trapido, eds., *The Politics of Race, Class and Nationalism in Twentieth-Century South Africa* (1987), 124–55.

55. Through the Native Urban Areas Act (1923), the government tried to bring order to African urbanization by setting up African locations separate from European residential areas, creating advisory boards to encourage a limited form of African participation in governing, and instituting controls on trading, beer brewing, and vagrancy. See T. R. Davenport, "African Townsmen? South African Natives (Urban Areas) Legislation through the Years," *African Affairs* 68 (271) (1969): 95–109.

56. Passed in 1856 in the Cape Colony, the Masters and Servants Act's main intent was to bind servants to masters by making it an offense for a servant to break a contract (which included desertion, insubordination, and insulting behavior). The law remained in effect until its repeal in 1974, when Alabama dock workers and miners decided not to offload South African coal based on an American law that prohibited the importation of goods produced by forced labor. By then, the Masters and Servants Act had been superseded by other laws controlling black employees, and it no longer served a twentieth-century purpose. See Colin Bundy, "The Abolition of the Masters and Servants Act," *South African Labour Bulletin* 2 (May–June 1975): 37–46.

57. The Savoy Ballroom was located on Lenox Avenue between 140th and 141st in Harlem. Opened in 1926, it was the premier dance joint and could hold up to 4,000 people. See David Lewis, *When Harlem Was in Vogue* (1981).

58. Studies on Benoni include D. Humphriss and D. G. Thomas, *Benoni, Son of My Sorrow: The Social, Political and Economic History of a South African Gold Mining Town* (1968) and J. B. Whitehouse, *History of Benoni* (1939).

59. Studies on the Ku Klux Klan, the notorious American white supremacist organization, include David M. Chalmers, *Hooded Americanism* (1965) and Wyn Craig Wade, *The Fiery Cross: The Ku Klux Klan in America* (1987).

60. A Nazi-inspired imitation, the Greyshirts were headed by L. T. Weichardt, a South African of German descent. The National Party absorbed the Greyshirts in 1939. Later, Weichardt revived the Greyshirts as the South African National Socialist Bond. The government interned him during the Second World War. For details, see William Vatcher, *White Laager: The Rise of Afrikaner Nationalism* (1965) and Patrick Furlong, *Between Crown and Swastika: The Impact of the Radical Right on the Afrikaner Nationalist Movement in the Fascist Era* (1991).

61. Bunche is referring to Ray Phillips's *The Bantu are Coming* (1930), based on his Yale Ph.D. dissertation. In 1938 Phillips published a sequel, *The Bantu in the City*. For Ray Phillips's use of film as pacifier, see *The Bantu Are Coming*, 147–50.

62. Issy Wolfson (1906–1980) was born in Luipaardevlei (now part of

Krugersdorp). On the death of his father, he left school at the age of twelve to support his family. He eventually matriculated at night school. After joining the Communist Party as a young man, he became involved in trade union organizing. He helped establish the Witwatersrand Tailoring Workers Union in 1934 and was its secretary until his banning in 1952. He was also an executive member of the Trade and Labour Council. During the Second World War he served as an airraid warden. After receiving a banning order, he was employed in the private sector. During the state of emergency declared after the Sharpeville Massacre, the government jailed him for close to three months. His banning order was lifted shortly before his death.

63. The son of a German Social Democrat, William Karl Frederick Kalk (1900–1989) had been a member of the Young Communist League in the early 1920s and backed S. P. Bunting in moving the Communist Party toward recruiting Africans. He trained at the Lenin School in Moscow in 1930. He was a member of the Party executive in the 1930s. Trained as a cabinetmaker, he served as secretary organizer of the Transvaal Leather and Allied Trades Industrial Union from 1931 until 1953. In that year the government banned him under the Suppression of Communism Act and prohibited him from holding a trade union office.

64. Willie de Vries was secretary of the Pretoria Trades Hall Committee and general secretary of the South African Trades and Labour Council from 1937 to 1947. He served as a delegate to the International Labour Organization (1941–1947). After the Second World War, he was chair of the Witwatersrand Central Juvenile Affairs Board.

65. The Wage Act of 1925 provided for the creation of a Wage Board, whose function it was to lay down minimum wage rates in industry. The original act did not cover Africans, but provided for them in a 1937 amendment.

66. Passed in 1924, the Industrial Conciliation Act established industrial councils, made up of representatives of employers and registered trade unions, to regulate wages and conditions of service in most sectors of the economy. The legislation aimed to bureaucratize trade unions and curb their activism, but it did not prevent several militant unions from carrying on through the 1930s. The act excluded Africans from its definition of *employee,* and thus did not cover them. For an analysis of the act, see Robert Davies, "The Class Character of South Africa's Industrial Conciliation Legislation," *South African Labour Bulletin* 2 (6) (1976).

67. The Mines and Works Act of 1911 entrenched the color bar on the mines; eventually, thirty-two occupations were reserved for European workers. The Mines and Works Amendment Act of 1926 (or "Color Bar" Act) provided for the government to restrict certain skilled occupations on the mines, such as operating machines to Europeans and Coloureds.

68. Born into a staunch Afrikaner nationalist family in the Western Transvaal, Johanna Cornelius (1912–1974) came to Johannesburg in 1930. She joined the Garment Workers' Union and was its president from 1934 to 1937. In 1938 she founded the Tobacco Workers' Union, later known as the National Union of Cigarette and Tobacco Workers. In 1952, when E. S. Sachs was banned from serving as an official in the Garment Workers' Union, she was elected its general secretary, a post she held until her death. See the portraits of her in E. S. Sachs, *The Choice before South Africa* (1952) and *Rebels' Daughters* (1957).

69. Edwin Mofutsanyana (1899–) was one of the first Africans to join the Communist Party (1927). He was an organizer in Johannesburg and Potchefstroom before the Party sent him to the Soviet Union in the early 1930s to attend Party schools. Upon his return he was appointed secretary-general of the Party for several years, but was succeeded by Moses Kotane, when the Party reestablished itself in Cape Town in the late 1930s. From the mid-1930s to the late 1940s, he was a leading African political figure, serving on the executives of the All African Convention, the African National Congress, and the Communist Party of South Africa. He was also an editor of the Communist newspaper *Inkululeko*. He ran unsuccessfully for the Native Representatives Council on several occasions and served on the Orlando Advisory Board. He was less active in the 1950s, and left South Africa in 1959 for Lesotho. He lived there until 1991, when he returned to his birthplace, Witzieshoek.

70. The Seventh Congress of the Communist International meeting in Moscow in 1935 had promoted the idea of Communist Parties allying themselves in Popular Fronts with antifascist groups. This set off an intense debate within the Communist Party in South Africa over whether to work toward a nonracial front or to work separately with black and white groups, even white groups like the South African Labour Party, which traditionally supported segregation. In 1937 provincial elections the Communist Party stated it would back Labour Party candidates, but the Labour Party did not welcome its support and refused to go along with a People's Front.

71. This issue was linked to a discussion over whether a class of African capitalists existed in South Africa and whether it supported or retarded the liberation struggle. See the debate waged in the columns of the Communist newspaper *Umsebenzi*, between Mofutsanyana, Roux, and Gilbert Coka (13, 20, 27 April and 4 May 1935).

72. Located about 2½ miles from the center of town, Prospect Township consisted of stands (privately owned, mainly by whites and some Indians and Chinese) rented out on a monthly basis to Africans, who were packed into small rooms. The Johannesburg City Council demolished it in 1938 as part of a slum clearance scheme and relocated its approximately 7,000 inhabitants to Orlando. The city council handed over the site to the South African Railways and it eventually became a large goods yard.

73. Named after Lewis Peter Ford, a British mining magnate, Fordsburg (also known as Veldschoendorp) was founded in 1887. It became a white working-class area and was a key center of the 1922 white workers' strike. Indians settled in Fordsburg, but they could not own property there. Fordsburg was also the scene of many rallies of the Congress Alliance in the 1950s at Freedom Square, the Hyde Park corner of Johannesburg. The government unsuccessfully tried to move Indians out in the 1970s under the Group Areas Act.

74. *Amalaita* were African gangs that first appeared at the beginning of this century. Peter Delius has identified one *amalaita* group as young Pedi migrants, many of them domestic servants, to the cities (Peter Delius, "Sebatakgomo: Migrant Organization, the ANC and the Sekhukuneland Revolt," *Journal of Southern African Studies* 15 (3) (1989): 581–616). It is thought the name *amalaita* comes from the word *olaita* which referred to the gangs' pressing victims to pay money or "light" the way so they could pass unharmed. More descriptions of *amalaita* exploits are provided in Charles Van Onselen, *New Babylon, New Ninevah:*

Studies in the Social and Economic History of the Witwatersrand, vol. 2 (1982), 54–60; Paul La Hausse, " 'The Cows of Nongoloza': Youth, Crime and Amalaita Gangs in Durban 1900–1936," *Journal of Southern African Studies* 16 (1) (1990): 79–111; and Modikwe Dikobe, *The Marabi Dance* (1973).

Pretoria

1. The Representation of Natives Act of 1936 made provision for an advisory body, the Natives Representative Council (NRC), which met for the first time in 1937. It was composed of 22 members: the chairman (Secretary for Natives Affairs), five appointed white "native" commissioners, four appointed Africans, and twelve indirectly elected African representatives (3 from the urban areas, 9 from the rural areas). The body could deliberate and give advice on legislation in the European Parliament affecting Africans and it could recommend legislation on African matters. The council was hampered from the outset. As its ineffectiveness became clear, it attracted strong opposition from within the African community, who viewed the council as a talk shop and a means to control African opposition. Finally, African representatives in the council boycotted it, and it was disbanded in 1951, when the government shifted its "native policy." See C. M. Tatz, *Shadow and Substance in South Africa: A Study in Land and Franchise Policies Affecting Africans, 1910–1960* (1962), 92–122. Margaret Ballinger gives a bland account of the first session of the NRC in her *From Union to Apartheid: A Trek to Isolation* (1969), 141–55.

2. Prince Arthur Edward Mshiyeni was the second eldest son of the Zulu King, Dinizulu. Educated at Lovedale, he was schooled as an Englishman and he embraced Western culture and modern ideas. Following the death of his brother, King Solomon, in 1933, he served as regent and acting paramount chief until 1948 when Solomon's son Cyprian came of age. Mshiyeni, however, had supported another son of Solomon's to succeed him. A flashy dresser, Mshiyeni was a favorite of white administrators for his support of the status quo.

3. Victor Poto (1898–1974) was educated at Buntingville Institution, Healdtown, and Clarkebury and started studies at Fort Hare when he had to return to Mpondoland to assume the paramountcy of the Mpondo on the death of his father. He served in the Bunga as well as the Native Representative Council from 1937 until its demise in 1951. In 1963 his Democratic Party contested Kaiser Matanzima's Transkei National Independence Party for elections to a legislative assembly. Poto's party overwhelmingly won the popular vote, but did not win a majority in the assembly because the government had the power to appoint a large number of chiefs, who were government supporters. He stepped down as party leader in 1966.

4. Appointed chief in 1934, Mokopane (Makapane is the Afrikaans spelling) was head of a small Ndebele-Pedi-Tsonga location near Potgietersrus.

5. Douglas Laing Smit (1885–1961) started his career in the Cape Civil Service in 1903 and served in the posts as magistrate in Port Elizabeth and East London. In 1933 he was appointed under–secretary for justice and, the following year, secretary for Native Affairs, a post he held until his retirement in 1945. He was part of the South African delegation to the United Nations con-

ference in 1945 and a member of the Native Affairs Commission (1945–1950). Later he was the United Party M.P. for East London from 1948 to 1961.

6. John Dube (1871–1946) was born at the Inanda mission station in Natal. Educated at Inanda and Amanzimtoti Training College, he went to the United States in 1887 and studied at Oberlin College. He returned to South Africa in 1892 as a teacher and became superintendent of Incwadi Christian Industrial Mission. He had a second sojourn in the U.S., studying theology from 1897 to 1899 at Union Missionary Seminary in Brooklyn. Ordained a Congregational minister, he was attracted to Booker T. Washington's ideas on industrial education and, in 1904, founded his own school, Ohlange Institute, patterned on Washington's ideals. He started a newspaper, *Ilanga lase Natal,* in 1903 and was its editor until 1915. He was also active in politics, working in the Natal Native Congress and serving as the first president of the South African Native National Congress, from 1912 until 1917. A conservative figure, he opposed radicalizing influences in the ANC. See Hunt Davis, "John L. Dube: A South African Exponent of Booker T. Washington," *Journal of African Studies* 2 (1975–76): 497–528; Manning Marable, "John L. Dube and the Politics of Segregated Education in South Africa," in A. Mugomba, *Independence without Freedom,* (1980): 113–128; "Pages from History: John Langalibalele Dube," *Sechaba* (January 1982): 18–23; and Shula Marks, *The Ambiguities of Dependence in South Africa: Class, Nationalism, and the State in Twentieth-Century Natal* (1986), 42–73.

7. Richard Hobbs Godlo (1899–1972) was a journalist, reporting for the *East London Daily Dispatch* and serving as editor of *Umlindi we Nyanga.* A founder and long-time president of the South African Congress of Advisory Boards, he represented the Cape Province (urban) in the Native Representative Council representing the Cape Province (urban) from 1937 to 1941. In 1937 he was chairman of the Joint Council of European and Bantu in East London and a member of the Native Advisory Board in the East Bank Location. In the 1940s he was a member of the ANC National Executive.

8. Heaton Nicholls (1876–1959) served in the British army in campaigns in North India, Ceylon, and Burma before coming to South Africa after the South African War. He served as a police officer and a colonial official in Northern Rhodesia. He moved to Australia and was a sugar farmer before returning to South Africa after 1910 to take up sugar farming in the Umfolozi Valley in Natal. He headed the Zululand Planters Association and the South African Planters Association. He was first elected to Parliament in 1920 from Zululand and represented planters' interests. He was a member of the Native Affairs Commission. He was appointed South Africa's High Commissioner to London in 1944 and served in the Senate from 1947 to 1954. He authored *Bayete* (1923) and *South Africa in My Time* (1961).

9. Dr. Charles T. Loram (1879–1940) was born in Pietermaritzburg and educated at the University of Cape of Good Hope, Cambridge University, and Columbia University. His Columbia Ph.D. dissertation was entitled "The Education of the South African Native." He served on the Phelps-Stokes Commissions investigating African education. In 1920 he was appointed a member of the South African Native Affairs Commission. He was also chief inspector of native education in Natal. In the late 1920s he broke with the South African government on African education policies and moved to Yale University as Sterling Professor of Education. He had close ties with the Carnegie Founda-

tion and promoted the idea of industrial education for Africans and the need to retain European intellectual control over Africans. For an examination of Loram's views, see Richard Heyman, "C. T. Loram: A South African Liberal in Race Relations," *The International Journal of African Historical Studies* 5 (1) (1972): 41–50.

10. Born in Scotland, Dr. Alex Roberts (1857–1938) was educated at Edinburgh University and taught at Lovedale from 1883 to 1920 (and served as its principal, 1899–1901 and 1902–4). He was a member of the Native Affairs Commission from 1920 to 1935 and was nominated as a senator representing African interests from 1920 to 1930.

11. R. V. Selope-Thema (1880–1955) was a graduate of Lovedale. He was secretary of the ANC delegation that went to the Paris peace conference in 1919. He was a founding member of the Johannesburg Joint Councils and the first secretary of the Bantu Men's Social Centre. He edited the ANC newspaper *Abantu Batho* and later edited the *Bantu World* for twenty years. He served as a member of the Native Representative Council from 1937 to 1950.

12. George Schreiner Findlay (W. P. and Olive Schreiner were his uncle and aunt) (1897–1978) was a Pretoria lawyer who joined the Communist Party in the late 1930s. He was also on the Central Committee of the Johannesburg Communist Party's District Committee, but later drifted away from the Party. He wrote a pamphlet, *Miscegenation: A Study of the Biological Sources of Inheritance of the South African European Population* (1936).

13. Rev. Donald F. Stowell did his theological training at Oxford and Wells Theological College. Ordained as a priest in 1925, he came out to southern Africa and served in various parishes, including Sophiatown (1931–33) before moving to Pretoria (1933–38). He took charge of St. Faith's Mission in Rusape (Mashonaland), Rhodesia, in the late 1940s.

14. A model for the NRC, the Bunga ("Council"), or United Transkeian Territories General Council, was established in 1932 as an advisory body comprised of European officials and traditional African leaders. For discussions of the Bunga's operations, see Roger J. Southall, *South Africa's Transkei: The Political Economy of an "Independent" Bantustan* (1982) and Gwendolyn M. Carter, Thomas Karis and Newell M. Stultz, *South Africa's Transkei: The Politics of Domestic Colonialism* (1967).

15. At the beginning of the twentieth century, European officials predicated urban policy on the idea that Africans were disease carriers who had to be segregated by themselves. See M. W. Swanson, "The Sanitary Syndrome: Bubonic Plague and Urban Native Policy in the Cape," *Journal of African History* 18 (3) (1977). Other African locations situated next to sewage plants included Ndabeni and Langa in Cape Town as well as Klipspruit, Sophiatown, Martindale, Newclare, and Western Native Township on the Witwatersrand.

16. Established in the early twentieth century, Bantule Location was situated in northwest Pretoria. It primarily served as a living area for Pretoria municipal workers and consisted of two divisions—one in which Africans could build their own homes and another in which the municipality built homes for rent. The location is no longer in existence.

17. Marabastad is in the Apies Valley and, beginning in the 1880s, was the living area for African servants in Pretoria. Eventually, the authorities proclaimed it an African location, but they moved its residents to Atteridgeville

after starting it up in 1939. Vivid descriptions of life in Marabastad are found in Ezekiel Mphahlele's *Down Second Avenue* (1959) and Naboth Mokgatle's *Autobiography of an Unknown South African* (1971).

Johannesburg II

1. The assistant director of the South African Institute of Race Relations, Lynn Saffery (1910–1979) specialized in industrial relations. Born in Humansdorp, he studied at the University of Cape Town. He left the institute in 1942 after an internal dispute to take up a post as labor officer in Northern Rhodesia. After returning to South Africa, he went into business as a supplier of building materials and, on retirement, took up farming in the Transvaal.

2. The Joint Councils trace their origins to the visit of the Phelps-Stokes Commission in 1921. The councils brought together liberal whites and educated Africans in the larger towns. They sponsored research projects and published pamphlets on "race issues, labour conditions, proposed legislation, and on industrial relations, the liquor laws, problems of delinquency."

3. Proclaimed a "Coloured" area, Coronationville was conceived in 1936 and had its first houses built in 1939. It was adjacent to Newclare, about 6 miles west of the city center. Vrededorp was a mixed residential area—with Indian, Coloured and white residents—when the government declared it a white area in 1962. Peter Abrahams relates his life growing up in Vrededorp in *Tell Freedom* (1954).

4. Gaur Radebe (1906–1983) was active in the Communist Party before it expelled him in 1942. In 1937 he was secretary of the African Cement, Stone, and Building Workers' Union. He also participated in the Transvaal ANC and was elected to the ANC's national executive in 1949. He was linked to Selope Thema's African National Bloc in the early 1950s. He joined the Pan Africanist Congress in 1959 and served as an official in their offices in Accra, Dar es Salaam, and Zambia.

5. A member of the Workers' Party, a Trotskyist group, Max Gordon (1923–1977) moved to Johannesburg from Cape Town in 1935 and eventually took over the leadership of the laundry workers' union. His union offices were a center for unemployed workers and a night school for workers. He received a subsidy from the Institute of Race Relations to organize unions—he set up six—and was very successful in attracting new union members through winning higher wages for unskilled workers through the Wage Board. He organized and served as secretary of the Joint Committee of African Trade Unions, which claimed a membership of 15,700 in 1939. During the Second World War he was interned; upon his release, he was harassed by the police to such an extent that he was later driven from involvement in politics and trade union organizing. For more details on Gordon's efforts, see Baruch Hirson's *Yours for the Union: Class and Community Struggles in South Africa* (1989).

6. J. F. Mackay was treasurer of the first black furniture union, the Furniture Workers' Union, which broke up in the early 1930s. With Simon Ndabulla, he started up the Non-European Furniture, Mattress and Bedding

Workers' Industrial Union for black workers in the industry. He also helped to organize workers in the box and trunk industry.

7. Situated on Hospital Hill, the Fort was originally built in 1893 as a prison for black and white prisoners, but it was enlarged in 1896 to become a fortress against British invasion. After the South African War, it reverted to its function as a prison and housed prisoners from the 1914 rebellion, the 1922 mine workers' strike, and succeeding generations of political prisoners. A women's section was added on in 1937. In 1983 the Fort shut down as a prison, but it remains a historical monument.

8. Established in March 1928 under Communist Party sponsorship, the Federation of Non-European Trade Unions was formed to fill the void left as the Industrial and Commercial Workers' Union began to break up. With Ben Weinbren as chairman, T. W. Thibedi as chief organizer, and James La Guma as secretary, the federation concentrated on building up African industrial unions: the Native Bakers' Union, the Native Laundry Workers' Union, the Native Clothing Workers' Union, and the Native Mattress and Furniture Workers' Union. The Federation broke apart in the early 1930s because of internecine Communist Party squabbles and because it repeatedly called workers out on strike. See Jon Lewis, *Industrialisation and Trade Union Organisation in South Africa, 1924–55* (1984), chap. 4.

9. Tam is short for tam-o'-shanter, a Scottish cap with a round, flat top.

▬▬ Bloemfontein

1. This was the third meeting of the All African Convention (AAC). It was first convened in Bloemfontein in December 1935 to galvanize African opinion against the Hertzog bills in Parliament, which proposed to remove Cape Africans from the common voters' roll. An official account (representing Jabavu's slant) of the 1937 meeting was published as *Minutes of the All African Convention, December 1937*.

2. Martin Kumalo was an agricultural instructor at Adams College. Upon the death of his father, he moved to Inanda to work as managing director of his family's Kumalo Stores. He was a member of the AAC executive committee.

3. Born in the Tsomo District of Transkei, Wycliffe Mlungisi Tsotsi (1914–) studied at Lovedale and Fort Hare, where he graduated in 1936. He taught at Blythswood Institution and practiced law in Lady Frere. He was president of the AAC from 1948 to 1959. He left South Africa in the early 1960s and has lived in Zambia and Lesotho, where he presently lives. In 1936 his essay, "How Can Youth Develop Co-operative and Harmonious Relations among the Races of the Earth," won first prize in an essay contest sponsored by the New History Society in New York City (*Race Relations* 4 (2) (May 1937): 42–47).

4. S. S. Rajuili, who worked in the teacher–training department at Lovedale, was the editor of *The Teacher's Vision*, the journal of the Cape African Teacher's Association (CATA). His complete address to the convention is found in *Minutes of the All African Convention, December 1937*, 55–58.

5. For a disapproving view of *uMetsho,* see J. H. Soga, *The Ama-Xosa: Life and Customs* (1932), 131–36.

6. The Pathfinders were created as a separate body for "non-European" boys within the Boy Scouts of South Africa in 1922; in 1937 the Pathfinders were made an independent body with its own constitution. Founded in 1925, the Wayfarers was the counterpart for girls. Rheinallt Jones was Chief Pathfinder for South Africa and Mrs. Jones was superintendent for the Wayfarers in the Transvaal. See Deborah Gaitskell, "Upward All and Play the Game: The Girl Wayfarers' Association in the Transvaal 1925–1975," in Peter Kallaway, ed., *Apartheid and Education: The Education of Black South Africans* (1984), 222–64.

7. Sister of Abdul Hamid and Goolam, Jane Gool (1902–) was one of the founders of the Non-European Unity Movement. She received her B.A. degree at Ft. Hare College, and she was active in the All African Convention. In 1961 she was banned from attending any political gatherings for five years. In 1963 she left South Africa for Tanzania with her husband, I. B. Tabata, also serving a banning order. In 1965 they moved to Zambia and in 1980, to Zimbabwe. Tabata died in 1990.

8. The Native Laws Amendment Act (1937) aimed at controlling the influx of blacks into urban areas by providing for biennial industrial censuses in municipalities. The government intended to remove "surplus" blacks from the urban areas and generally prohibit Africans from owning land in the urban areas, thus bringing urban policy in line with the 1913 Natives Land Act. See *Race Relations,* vol. 7 (4): 59.

9. Although an oxymoron, *foreign natives* was a malleable term mining companies used to set apart "foreign" workers recruited from territories such as Mozambique, Nyasaland, Northern and Southern Rhodesia, and Tangyanika. At the beginning of this century, mining companies defined workers from the High Commission Territories as "non–foreign," but reclassified them as "foreign" in 1963. Later workers from the independent Bantustans were designated "foreign" workers in line with the South African government's ultimate objective of making black South Africans foreigners in their own land. See Martin Legassick and Francine de Clerq, "Capitalism and Migrant Labour in Southern Africa: The Origins and Nature of the System," in Shula Marks and Peter Richardson, eds., *International Labour Migration: Historical Perspectives* (1984), 141–65.

10. Zaccheus Richard Mahabane (1881–1970) was a Methodist minister. Elected president of the Cape African Congress in 1919, he also served as president of the African National Congress (1924–1927, 1937–1940). He was a founding member of the AAC and its vice president in 1937.

11. The National Council of African Women was holding its first national meeting in 1937. Its first elected president was Charlotte Manye Maxeke and its first general secretary was Mina Soga. A description of this meeting appears in Ellen Kuzwayo's *Call Me Woman* (1985), 101–3.

12. Keable 'Mote was born in 1898 in Lesotho. Educated at Grace Dieu Institution in Pietersburg, South Africa, he was a teacher before joining the ICU in Bloemfontein in 1924 and serving as its provincial secretary in the Orange Free State. He was known as the "Lion of the Free State" for his ferocious attacks on the government. After leaving the ICU, he took up a teaching position at a Catholic school in Kroonstad.

13. Mary Jane McLeod Bethune (1875–1955) was a founder and president of Bethune-Cookman College in Florida and a founder of the National Council of Negro Women in 1935. She also served as director of the Division of Minority Affairs of the New Deal National Youth Administration.

14. The Bantu Welfare Trust was a fund established by a Johannesburg businessman, Lt. Col. Donaldson, a Scottish immigrant, who made his fortune in the mining industry. The trust contained about £50,000 and was administered by a committee at the South African Institute of Race Relations.

15. Max Yergan was the secretary for External Affairs for the AAC. His committee was called the International Committee on Africa when it was first established in 1937. Later its name changed to American Council on African Affairs. On his return to the United States, Bunche joined its executive board for a period of time. See Hollis Lynch, *Black American Radicals and the Liberation of Africa: The Council on African Affairs, 1937–1955* (Cornell University, Africana Studies and Research Center Monograph Series no. 5 (1978)).

16. Born in Lesotho, S. Mac Lepolesa attended Lovedale and became a teacher and trader. He was general secretary of the All African Convention in 1937 and 1940. He later served as deputy speaker of the ANC. He left South Africa in the 1950s and settled in Basutoland, where he opened a cafe. He served in the Legislative Council before Lesotho's independence and as chairman of the Public Service Commission in the 1970s.

17. Nicknamed "Map of Africa," Thomas Mtobi Mapikela (1869–1945) was born in the Cape. He had training as a carpenter and made his living as a builder and contractor in Bloemfontein locations such as Waaihoek and Batho, where Africans were permitted to build their own homes. He was part of the delegation of Africans who went to London in 1909 and was a founding member of the ANC. He was the speaker at ANC conferences and arranged for accommodation of ANC delegates at Bloemfontein meetings. He participated in the Joint Councils movement and was a treasurer of the Location Advisory Boards Congress. He served in the Native Representative Council (1937–1942). He also participated in the 1942 ANC delegation to the Minister of Native Affairs, Denys Reitz. He was active in sports. In Bloemfontein headmen were elected to preside over location wards; he was elected headman for his ward as well as being appointed headman of all the Bloemfontein locations.

18. The East London locations' notoriety was well deserved. For a description, see A. D. Dodd, "The East London Locations," *The South African Outlook,* 1 November 1937.

19. H. L. Segie Kekane was a delegate from Cape Town.

20. Mrs. Ballinger wrote to the *Bloemfontein Friend* (16 December 1937) to correct its reporting on the first day of the All African Convention. Her letter read in part: "I cannot claim to have initiated a discussion on the problem of the economic uplift of the Native. The Parliamentary representatives of the Native people who, last week, attended the meetings of the official Native representatives of the people in Pretoria as listeners, are this week attending, as their other duties permit, the discussions of the unofficial representatives of the people gathered together in annual conference here in Bloemfontein. Their attendance is by invitation and their participation in the proceedings of the conference has been confined to greetings except where special invitation to speak

has been extended. In offering my personal greetings, I took occasion to re-mark, in regard to a proposal from a sub-committee of the convention to em-bark on the organization of farm labour that it would be well to realize that the organizing of farm labour has never been successfully achieved anywhere, and that they should not be discouraged (that is, in regard to efforts to other directions) if they do not succeed where others have failed.

Your report goes on to state that 'The convention resolved that the ques-tion of farm labour organizations should be taken in hand by members of the Parliament and of the Representative Council, and that they should wait until the present Farm Labour Commission had made its report; and thereafter that a special session of the convention should be convened to consider the matter carefully.' Again this departs just sufficiently from the exact fact as somewhat to misrepresent the actual decision arrived at. The conference decided to hold over consideration of the report of its sub-committee on farm labour until such time as the Farm Labour Commission should have reported and thereafter to consult with the Parliamentary representatives of the members of the Native Representative Council as to what line of action should be pursued."

21. An Anglican priest, Rev. James Calata (1895–1983) joined the African National Congress in 1930 and was elected president of the Cape ANC, a posi-tion he held until 1949. He assisted in replacing Dube with Z. R. Mahabane as president of the ANC in 1937 and helped to revive the ANC. He also served as secretary-general from 1936 until 1949, when he stepped down in favor of Wal-ter Sisulu. By that point, Calata's moderate politics were out of favor (he was not comfortable with the Programme of Action) but he remained on the ANC National Executive and continued as senior chaplain of the ANC. Dur-ing the Defiance Campaign in 1952, he was served with a banning order and he was one of the Treason Trialists. See "Hamba Kahle, Canon Calata," *Sechaba* (April 1983): 30–32.

22. African Clubs were Pixley ka Seme's proposal for building up advanc-ing African economic business interests and keeping African money circulating in their own community. The idea was to create clubs generated by ANC funds, which would start up businesses and shops offering goods and services at a cheaper price than European businesses and would generate jobs for Afri-cans. At the same time, Seme thought it was important to have Europeans manage the ANC's business enterprises and "to satisfy the Minister for Native Affairs of our good intentions" since he was "the father appointed over our in-terests as well as our progress." See Seme's articles on the clubs in *Umteteli wa Bantu,* October and November 1934.

23. Seme admired Booker T. Washington, whom he had witnessed address the Negro Business League of America in 1907 in Atlanta, Georgia. Washing-ton founded the National Negro Business League in 1900. Funded by philan-thropist Andrew Carnegie, the league preached that the best way to overcome racial prejudice was through economic advancement—promoting values such as self-sacrifice and self-help and encouraging black consumers to patronize black businesses. Because black businessmen did not have white consumers and could not get loans from white lending agencies, they had to appeal to their own community. See Louis Harlan, "Booker T. Washington and the National Negro Business League," in *Seven on Black Reflections on the Negro Experience in America* (1969), 73–91.

24. Alain Locke (1885–1954) was a leading African-American educator and philosopher. The first black to win a Rhodes scholarship, he was a classmate of Pixley ka Seme at Oxford. He came to teach at Howard in 1912. His most famous publication is *The New Negro* (1925). His influence on the South African writer Herbert Dhlomo is noted in Tim Couzens, *The New African: A Study of the Life and Works of H. I. E. Dhlomo* (1985), 111–12. Locke's philosophy is examined in Leonard Harris, ed., *The Philosophy of Alain Locke: Harlem Renaissance and Beyond* (1989).

25. The National Council of Women was founded in 1909 and is part of an international network of councils. Its motto is the Golden Rule and it addresses such women-related issues such as community welfare, legal disabilities, culture, nursery schools, health care, and nutrition. It also lobbies Parliament on issues of concern.

26. The dispute within the Western Cape ANC was over the 1936 election for the presidency. Despite being defeated by A.V. Coto, Thaele continued to pose as president and collect money to pay off his personal debts. The 1937 ANC conference appointed an arbitration board that in February 1938 ruled that the 1936 election was valid.

27. Nicknamed the "Professor," James Thaele (1888–1948) was born in Basutoland, attended school at Lovedale and then left for the U.S. in 1913. He obtained a B.A. from Lincoln University in Pennsylvania in 1921. On his return to South Africa, he set up a night school in Cape Town for Africans studying for junior certificates and matriculation. He became president of the Western Cape ANC in 1922, but was defeated for reelection in 1936. An avid disciple of Marcus Garvey, he edited the newspaper *African World* in Cape Town.

28. The ANC president, Dr. Xuma, suspended Stephen Oliphant, secretary of the Western Cape ANC, in 1941 for siding with a faction defying ANC policy in an intra-Cape fight. For a while, Oliphant edited *Inkokeli,* a monthly Xhosa-English magazine in Cape Town.

Durban

1. The first Indian indentured servants arrived in Natal in 1860 to work the sugar plantations. A small group of Indian merchant immigrants began arriving between the 1870s and 1890s. See Surendra Bhana and Joy Brain, *Setting Down Roots: Indian Migrants in South Africa 1860–1911* (1989).

2. The first batch of about fifty Mauritians arrived in Natal in 1850 to work in the sugar plantations; the St. Helenans also came in small numbers amd were mainly employed as domestic servants. Both groups were Westernized and had the same legal status as Europeans and allowed to vote (even after Indians lost the right to vote in 1893) on the European voters' list. H. F. Dickie-Clark estimates that in 1936 the numbers of St. Helenans and Mauritians around Durban were about 1,000 and 6,000 respectively. For further details on Durban's coloured community, see H. F. Dickie-Clark, *The Marginal Situation: A Sociological Study of a Coloured Group* (1966).

3. A. W. G. Champion (1893–1975) had worked at various jobs in the mines before joining the ICU in 1925 as its Transvaal secretary. That same year

he was delegated to Natal as secretary of the union. While Kadalie was overseas in 1927, Champion took over, but on Kadalie's return, Champion was charged with financial misdealings. After he was suspended as I.C.U. secretary, Champion broke away to form his own I.C.U. yase Natal. In 1929 the government expelled him from Natal after riots in Durban, but allowed him to return in 1933. At various points he was a leading figure in the national ANC. In the Natal ANC he was a dominant figure, serving as provincial president from 1945 to 1951, when Albert Luthuli ousted him. Later he was a conservative figure in advisory board politics in Chesterville near Durban.

4. Bunche is likely referring to William Smith, I.C.U. secretary for northern Natal in 1927 before moving to Johannesburg to become I.C.U. financial secretary in early 1928. Smith joined Champion when he broke with the parent I.C.U. in 1928 and took I.C.U. money with him.

5. Albert Batty (d. 1930) ran a cutlery business in Cape Town. A socialist, he founded an Industrial and Commercial Union in 1918 which catered to dock workers. After a chance meeting with Clements Kadalie, he helped Kadalie found the Industrial and Commercial Workers Union in 1919. In the later 1920s, he moved to Durban and worked for A. W. G. Champion. He managed the African Cooperative Society, which tried to start up manufacturing enterprises, but the society went bankrupt in 1930 after the Durban beer riots.

6. Ricksha pullers went on strike in 1918 and 1930. See Paul La Hausse's M.A. thesis, "The Struggle for the City: Alcohol, the Ematsheni and Popular Culture in Durban, 1902–1936" (1984), chaps. 1 and 5.

7. Although white officials perceived Champion as a radical, his actions in the I.C.U. and later on were anything but. In 1926 he supported Kadalie's purge of communists from the union executive. He advocated the I.C.U. buying property and he advanced the notion of African advancement through business.

8. Paul Kruger was president of the Transvaal Republic from 1883 to 1902.

9. A rival of Abdurahman's, M. A. Gamiet was a tailor and a founding member of the Cape Malay Association (CMA) and its president from 1925 to 1943. An accommodationist group, the CMA supported the Pact government in the 1924 elections. The CMA expected that the Nationalists were going to enhance the status of Malays politically and economically and protect their religion since many of them were Muslim. Gamiet opposed legislation based on race. The Hertzog bills disillusioned him, and he supported the radical National Liberation League against segregation in 1937. He was a managing director of Protea Trading Company.

10. Born in Bombay, India, Abdullah Ismail Kajee (ca. 1894–1948) was brought to South Africa as an infant. He became a broker in 1920 and started his own business firm, A. I. Kajee (Pty.), Ltd. He was the moderate head of the Natal Indian Congress, supporting Indian business and property interests, from the mid-1930s to 1945, when more radical members ousted him. Biographies of Kajee include G. H. Calpin's, *A. I. Kajee: His Work for the South African Indian Community* (1946) and B. D. Sannyasi's *Abdulla Ismail Kajee* (1941).

11. Mahatma Gandhi founded the South African Indian Congress in 1894 to protest the disenfranchisement of Natal's Indians. For an analysis of Con-

gress politics, see Maureen Swan, "Ideology in Organised Indian Politics, 1891–1948," in Shula Marks and Stanley Trapido, eds., *The Politics of Race, Class and Nationalism in Twentieth-Century South Africa* (1987), 182–208.

12. This analysis of Gandhi's class leanings is taken up in Maureen Swan's *Gandhi: The South African Experience* (1985). Another assessment of Gandhi's South African years is Robert Huttenback, *Gandhi in South Africa: British Imperialism and the Indian Question, 1860–1914* (1971).

13. A detailed account of the general strike is found in Maureen Swan's "The 1913 Natal Indian Strike," *Journal of Southern African Studies* 10 (2) (1984): 245–69.

14. The Foreign and Colonial Born Association was founded in 1933 to protest a move by the South African government to establish a commission to seek other areas for Indians to migrate to. It largely represented the emerging Indian Hindu middle class (clerks, teachers, etc.) who were born in Natal. The organization rivaled the merchant-dominated Natal Indian Congress. In 1943 the two organizations merged, although unity was short-lived because of personality clashes between leaders.

15. An advocate trained at Lincoln's Inn, London, Albert Christopher was a founder of the Foreign and Colonial Born Association in 1933. He assisted Gandhi during Gandhi's passive resistance campaigns in the early part of the century. During the First World War, Christopher served as a noncommissioned officer in East Africa. A strong supporter of Hindu workers, he opposed the dominant Indian merchant class in Natal. He was a member of the Indian delegation to the United Nations in 1946.

16. Trained first as a teacher before he joined the ministry, Rev. Abner M'timkulu (ca. 1875–1954), Don's father, attended a Methodist seminary in England. He was a minister in Cape Town until moving to Durban in early 1930s. In the early 1940s, he was retired against his will and he accepted an invitation to become president of the independent Bantu Methodist Church. He was Dube's deputy in the Natal ANC, but Champion defeated him for the presidency. During Xuma's presidency, M'timkulu was senior chaplain of the national ANC. He served on the AAC executive committee in 1937, but not enthusiastically.

17. Known as *Mahlalemsamo,* "the one who stays in the inner hut (the administrative office)," Philip E. Chandley later became principal clerk in the Department of Bantu Administration in Durban. He was on the executive of the Durban Joint Council of Europeans and Natives in the late 1920s.

18. For a discussion of Mpondo migrant workers in the Natal sugar industry, see William Beinart, "Transkeian Migrant Workers and Youth Labour on the Natal Sugar Estates, 1918–1940" (History Workshop, University of the Witwatersrand, February 1990).

19. Seth Govind Das was a Congress member of the Central Legislative Assembly in India. In December 1937 he visited South Africa to investigate the Indian Agent-General's role in South Africa and to improve India's links with South Africa.

20. Born in London, Maurice Webb (1889–1966) was a member of the Fabian Society and the Society of Friends, a conscientious objector during the First World War, and secretary of the London Vegetarian Society. He came out to Durban in 1921 to work in a publishing firm. He started participating in

the Durban Joint Council in 1926 and was a founding member and served as long-time regional director of the South African Institute of Race Relations. He was also elected the institute's president. After touring the United States on a Carnegie grant in 1933, he established the Maurice Webb African and Negro Library. Webb chaired the Natal branch of the South African Institute of International Affairs and authored a range of pamphlets and books, including *In Quest of South Africa* (1945), *The Durban Riots and After* (with Kenneth Kirkwood) (1949), *Indian Citizen or Subject* (with Sirkari Naidoo), and *Race Relations East and West* (1953).

21. Lamont Township was named after Rev. Archibald Lamont (1864–1933), a Scottish-born Presbyterian minister who had served on the Durban Town Council and as Durban mayor (1929–1932). For a study of Lamont, see Anne Louise Torr, *The Social History of an Urban African Community, ca. 1930–1960* (M.A. thesis, University of Natal, Durban, 1985).

22. Appointed in 1935, Dr. Bernard Notcutt (1910–1953) was the first lecturer in the Department of Psychology at the University of Natal, Pietermaritzburg, and later was Professor in the University of Natal, Durban (1947–1953). Educated at Stellenbosch University and Magdalen College, Oxford, he held fellowships at Harvard University and the University of California.

23. Founded around 1930, Sastri College was named after Srinivaster Sastri, the first Indian agent of the government of India in South Africa from 1927 to 1929. Sastri had lobbied the Indian community in Durban to establish the high school bearing his name. At the time, it was the only secondary school for Indians in Natal; it remained the premier high school for Indians in Natal. Around 1980 it became a technical college.

24. Born in Glasgow, Scotland, in 1899, Duncan Burnsides came to South Africa as a child in 1903, but left again in 1904. He returned to Johannesburg in 1922 and settled in Durban in 1935. He was a member of parliament for the Umlilo constituency in Durban; later he represented the Fordsburg constituency. He edited a newspaper, *Burnsides' Weekly*. He was a member of the South African Labour Party and secretary of the garment workers' union in Durban. He broke with the Labour Party over its policy of segregation and founded the Socialist Party in early 1937. His new party opposed racial discrimination and fascism and supported a redistribution of wealth and the creation of a socialist society (*Cape Standard*, 8 February 1937; 10 May 1937).

25. Mahatma Gandhi's second son, Monilal (1892–1956) was born in India and came to South Africa with his father. He settled in Phoenix, the Natal Indian community his father founded in 1901. He was an editor of *Indian Opinion* and was active, though not a major figure, in anti-apartheid causes. He led passive resisters into Transvaal and Orange Free State to protest laws preventing Natal Indians entering those provinces; he demonstrated against the Group Areas Act and petty apartheid regulations; and he served a 38-day prison sentence in 1953 for refusing to pay a fine for participating in a Defiance campaign protest. Randas Gandhi (1896–1969) was Mahatma's third son.

26. First named Amanzimtoti Training Institute, Adams College was founded in 1853 by the American Board of Commissioners for Foreign Missions for the education of Africans. Renamed after Dr. Newton Adams, a medical missionary who died at Amanzimtoti mission station in 1847, the school was patterned after other elite African educational institutions. A description of the

school's curriculum in the 1920s is contained in Tim Couzens, *The New African: A Study of the Life and Work of H. I. E. Dhlomo* (1985), 47–54.

27. Morris Broughton (1901–1978) was born in Lancashire, England and educated at the universities of London, Manchester, and Liverpool. He came to South Africa in 1922. While assistant editor of the *Daily News,* he was a radio broadcaster on international affairs. In 1946 he took over as editor of the *Daily News* and, in 1950, the *Cape Argus,* a position he held until his retirement in 1960. He published *Press and Politics of South Africa* in 1961.

28. During the First World War, Africans served in labor battalions in France. During the Second World War the South African government drew on this experience, creating a Native Military Corps in which Africans again served as laborers. The army did not issue them weapons, aside from knobkerries and assegais, to defend themselves. For a discussion, see Louis Grundlingh, "The Recruitment of South African Blacks for Participation in the Second World War," in D. Killingray and R. Rathbone, eds., *Africa and the Second World War* (1986).

29. Government representatives from India and South Africa held a Round Table conference on Indians in South Africa in Cape Town from December 1926 to January 1927. The meeting led to a five-year agreement on issues such as trading, citizenship and residential rights, the entry into South Africa of the wives and children of Indians, and the assisted emigration of South African Indians. The two countries held a second Round Table in 1932. For details, see Bridglal Pachai, *The International Aspects of the South African Indian Question, 1860–1971* (1971), chaps. 3–4.

30. Born in the Harrismith district of the Orange Free State, Isaiah Shembe (ca. 1867–1935) was a farm laborer when he had a vision that brought him into religious work. He assisted William Leshega and his African Native Baptist Church on the Rand before founding his own Church of the Nazarites in 1911. In 1914 he established his religious center, *Ekuphakameni,* "the elated place," near Ohlange. His son, Johannes Galilee Shembe (1904–1976), was educated at Ft. Hare and taught at Adams College before taking over the reins of his father's church on his death. See Bengt Sundkler, *Zulu Zion and Some Swazi Zionists* (1976), 161–295.

31. Born George Baker, Father Divine (ca. 1880–1965) was an African-American prophet whose Peace Mission stressed self–help and black advance. Father Divine amassed considerable wealth through his endeavors. See Kenneth E. Burnham, *God Comes to America: Father Divine and the Peace Mission Movement* (1979) and Robert Weisbrot, *Father Divine and the Struggle for Racial Equality* (1983).

Bibliography

Abrahams, Peter. *Tell Freedom: Memories of Africa.* London: Faber and Faber, 1954.

Alexander, Enid Baumberg. *Morris Alexander: A Biography.* Cape Town: Juta, 1953.

Adhikari, M. "The Teachers' League of South Africa, 1913–1940." Master's thesis, University of Cape Town, 1986.

Alexandra I Love You: A Record of Seventy Years. Johannesburg: Alexandra Liaison Committee, 1983.

Anderson, James. "Philanthropic Control over Private Black Higher Education." In *Philanthropy and Cultural Imperialism: The Foundations at Home and Abroad,* edited by Robert F. Arnove, 147–78. Boston: G. K. Hall, 1980.

Anthony, David. "Max Yergan in South Africa: From Evangelical Pan Africanist to Revolutionary Socialist." *African Studies Review* 34, no. 2 (1991): 27–56.

Ashton, E. H. *The Basuto.* London: Oxford University Press, 1952.

Ballinger, Margaret. *From Union to Apartheid: A Trek to Isolation.* Cape Town: Juta, 1969.

Ballinger, W. G. *Race and Economics in South Africa.* London: Hogarth Press, 1934.

Bardill, John E. and James H. Cobbe. *Lesotho: Dilemmas of Dependence in Southern Africa.* Boulder: Westview Press, 1985.

Barnes, Leonard. *Caliban in Africa: An Impression of Colour-madness.* London: Gollancz, 1930.

———. *The Duty of Empire.* London: Gollancz, 1935.

———. *The New Boer War.* London: Hogarth Press, 1932.

————. *Zulu Paraclete: A Sentimental Record.* London: P. Davies, 1935.

Beinart, William. "Transkeian Migrant Workers and Youth Labour on the Natal Sugar Estates, 1918–1940." Paper presented at History Workshop, Witwatersrand University, 6–10 February 1990.

Beinart, William, Peter Delius, and Stanley Trapido, eds. *Putting a Plough to the Ground: Accumulation and Dispossession in Rural South Africa, 1850–1930.* Johannesburg: Ravan Press, 1986.

Beinart, William, and Colin Bundy. *Hidden Struggles in Rural South Africa: Politics and Popular Movements in the Transkei and Eastern Cape, 1890–1930.* Berkeley: University of California Press, 1987.

Berger, Iris. "Solidarity Fragmented: Garment Workers of the Transvaal, 1930–1960." In *The Politics of Race, Class and Nationalism in Twentieth-Century South Africa,* edited by Shula Marks and Stanley Trapido, 124–55. New York: Longman, 1987.

Bhana, Surendra, and Joy Brain. *Setting Down Roots: Indian Migrants in South Africa, 1860–1911.* Johannesburg: Witwatersrand University Press, 1989.

Blackwell, James, and Morris Janowitz, eds. *Black Sociologists: Historical and Contemporary Perspectives.* Chicago: University of Chicago Press, 1974.

Bodmer, Frederick. *The Loom of Language: A Guide to Foreign Languages for the Home Students.* Edited by Lancelot Hogben. London: G. Allen and Unwin, 1943.

Bonner, Philip. " 'Desirable or Undesirable Basotho Women?' Liquor, Prostitution and the Migration of Basotho Women to the Rand, 1920–1945." In *Women and Gender in Southern Africa to 1945,* edited by Cherryl Walker. Cape Town: David Philip, 1990.

————. "The Transvaal Native Congress, 1917–1920: The Radicalisation of the Black Petty Bourgeoisie on the Rand." In *Industrialisation and Social Change in South Africa,* edited by Shula Marks and Richard Rathbone. London: Longman, 1982.

Bradford, Helen. *A Taste of Freedom: The ICU in Rural South Africa, 1924–1930.* New Haven: Yale University Press, 1987.

Branford, Jean. *A Dictionary of South African English.* 3d Edition. Cape Town: Oxford University Press, 1987.

Brittain, Vera. *Testament of Friendship: The Story of Winifred Holtby.* New York: MacMillan, 1930.

Brookes, Edgar Harry. *The History of Native Policy in South Africa from 1830 to the Present Day.* Pretoria: J. L. van Schaik, 1924.

————. *R. J. : In Appreciation of the Life of John David Rheinallt Jones and His Work for the Betterment of Race Relations in Southern Africa.* Johannesburg: South African Institute of Race Relations, 1953.

————. *A South African Pilgrimage.* Johannesburg: Ravan Press, 1977.

Broughton, Morris. *Press and Politics of South Africa.* Cape Town: Purnell, 1961.

Brutsch, Albert. "From Work Song to National Anthem." *Lesotho Notes and Records* 9 (1970–71): 5–12.

Bunche, Ralph. "Africa and the Current World Conflict." *Negro History Bulletin* 4 (October 1940): 11–14.

————. "A Critique of New Deal Social Planning." *Journal of Negro Education* 5 (1) (1936): 59–65.

————. "Education in Black and White." *Journal of Negro Education* 5 (3) (1936): 356.

————. "French and British Imperialism in West Africa." *Journal of Negro History* 21 (1) (1936): 31–46.

————. "French Educational Policy in Togo and Dahomey." *Journal of Negro Education* 3 (1) (1934): 69–97.

————. "The Programs of Organizations Devoted to the Improvement of the Status of the American Negro." *Journal of Negro Education* 8 (3) (1939): 539–50.

————. "The Role of the University in the Political Orientation of Negro Youth." *Journal of Negro Education* 9 (4) (1940): 571–79.

————. "Triumph? or Fiasco?" *Race* 1 (Summer 1936): 93–96.

————. *A World View of Race*. Washington, D. C. : Associates in Negro Folk Education, 1936.

Bundy, Colin. "The Abolition of the Masters and Servants Act." *South African Labour Bulletin* 2 (1) (May–June 1975): 37–46.

————. *The Rise and Fall of the South African Peasantry*. Berkeley: University of California Press, 1979.

Buni, Andrew. *Robert L. Vann of the Pittsburgh Courier: Politics and Black Journalism*. Pittsburgh: University of Pittsburgh Press, 1974.

Bunting, Brian. *Moses Kotane: South African Revolutionary*. London: Inkululeko Publications, 1975.

Burnham, Kenneth E. *God Comes to America: Father Divine and the Peace Mission Movement*. Boston: Lambeth Press, 1979.

Butler, J. , Richard Elphick, and David Welsh, eds. *Democratic Liberalism in South Africa: Its History and Prospect*. Middletown, Ct. : Wesleyan University Press, 1987.

Calpin, George Herold, ed. *A. I. Kajee: His Work for the South-African Indian Community*. Durban: Iqbal Study Group, 1946

Campbell, James Tierney. "Our Fathers, Our Children: The African Methodist Episcopal Church in the United States and South Africa." Ph. D. dissertation, Stanford University, 1990.

Caplan, Gerald L. *The Elites of Barotseland, 1878–1969: A Political History of Zambia's Western Province*. Berkeley: University of California Press, 1970.

Carr, W. J. P. *Soweto: Its Creation, Life, and Decline*. Johannesburg: South African Institute of Race Relations, 1991.

Carter, Gwendolyn M., Thomas Karis, and Newell M. Stultz. *South Africa's Transkei: The Politics of Domestic Colonialism*. Evanston: Northwestern University Press, 1967.

Cell, John Whitson. *The Highest Stage of White Supremacy: The Origins of Segregation in South Africa and the American South*. New York: Cambridge University Press, 1982.

Chalmers, David M. *Hooded Americanism: The First Century of the Ku Klux Klan, 1865–1965*. Garden City, N.J. : Doubleday, 1965.

Charney, Craig. "Pixley Seme '06: Father of the African National Congress." *Columbia College Today* (Spring/Summer 1987): 15–17.

Chirenje, J. Mutero. *Ethiopianism and Afro-Americans in Southern Africa 1883–1916*. Baton Rouge: Louisiana State University Press, 1987.

Cobley, Alan. *Class and Consciousness: The Black Petty Bourgeoisie in South Africa, 1924 to 1950.* New York: Greenwood Press, 1990.

Coplan, David B. *In Township Tonight! South Africa's Black City Music and Theatre.* Johannesburg: Ravan Press, 1985.

Cornell, Jean Gay. *Ralph Bunche, Champion of Peace.* Champaign, Ill.: Garrard Publishing Co., 1976.

Couzens, Tim. *The New African: A Study of the Life and Work of H. I. E. Dhlomo.* Johannesburg: Ravan Press, 1985.

Dailey, Maceo C. "Emmett Jay Scott: The Career of a Secondary Black Leader." Ph. D. dissertation, Howard University, 1983.

Danziger, Christopher. *A Trader's Century: The Story of Frasers.* Cape Town: Purnell, 1979.

Darity, William, Jr., ed. *Race, Radicalism, and Reform: Selected Papers Abram L. Harris.* New Brunswick: Transaction Publishers, 1989.

Davenport, T. R. "African Townsmen? South African Natives (Urban Areas) Legislation through the Years." *African Affairs* 68 (271) (1969): 95–109.

Davies, Robert. "The Class Character of South Africa's Industrial Conciliation Legislation." *South African Labour Bulletin* 2 (6) (1976).

Davis, R. Hunt. "The Black American Educational Component in African Responses to Colonialism in South Africa." *Journal of Southern African Affairs* 3 (1) (1978): 69–84.

———. "Charles T. Loram and the American Model for African Education in South Africa." *African Studies Review* 19 (2) (1976): 87–100.

———. "John Dube: A South African Exponent of Booker T. Washington." *Journal of African Studies* 2 (1975–76): 497–528.

De Kiewiet, C. W. *A History of South Africa: Social and Economic.* New York: Oxford University Press, 1941.

Delius, Peter. "Sebatakgomo: Migrant Organization, the ANC and the Sekhukuneland Revolt." *Journal of Southern African Studies* 15 (3) (1989): 581–616.

Desmore, Abe. *Torch Bearers in Darkest America: A Study of Jeanes Supervision in Some Southern States of the United States of America.* Pretoria: Carnegie Corporation, 1937.

———. *With 2nd Cape Corps thro' Central Africa.* Cape Town: Citadel Press, 1920.

Dickie-Clark, H. F. *The Marginal Situation: A Sociological Study of a Coloured Group.* London: Routledge and Kegan Paul, 1966.

Dikobe, Modikwe. *The Marabi Dance.* London: Heinemann, 1973.

Dodd, A. D. "The East London Locations." *The South African Outlook* (1 November 1937).

Doke, Clement. *A Textbook of Zulu Grammar.* Johannesburg: Witwatersrand University Press, 1927.

——— (in collaboration with B. W. Vilakazi). *Zulu-English Dictionary.* Johannesburg: Witwatersrand University Press, 1948.

Dubow, Saul. *Racial Segregation and the Origins of Apartheid in South Africa, 1919–36.* New York: St. Martin's Press, 1989.

DuPlessis, I. D. *The Cape Malays: History, Religion, Traditions, Folk Tales, the Malay Quarter.* Cape Town: A. A. Balkema, 1972.

DuPlessis, I. D. and C. A. Luckhoff. *The Malay Quarter and Its People.* Cape Town: A. A. Balkema, 1953.

Edgar, Robert. "Garveyism in Africa: Dr. Wellington and the American Movement in the Transkei." *Ufahamu* 6 (1) (1976): 31–57.

―――. *Prophets with Honour: A Documentary History of Lekhotla la Bafo.* Johannesburg: Ravan Press, 1987.

Elias, Dolly. "In Memoriam: G. F. Dingemans, A Fighter in the Battle for Righteousness." *Jewish Affairs* 9 (3) (March 1954): 22–26.

Ellsworth, Ronald. "The Simplicity of the Native Mind: Black Passengers on the South African Railways in the Early Twentieth Century." In *Resistance and Ideology in Settler Societies,* edited by Tom Lodge, 74–95. Johannesburg: Ravan Press, 1986.

Elphick, Richard. *Kraal and Castle: Khoikhoi and the Founding of White South Africa.* New Haven: Yale University Press, 1977.

Erlmann, Veit. "'A Feeling of Prejudice', Orpheus M. McAdoo and the Virginia Jubilee Singers in South Africa, 1890–98." *Journal of Southern African Studies* 14 (3) (1988): 331–50.

Feuerlicht, Roberta. *In Search of Peace.* New York: J. Messner, 1970.

Findlay, George. *Miscegenation: A Study of the Biological Sources of Inheritance of the South African European Population.* Pretoria: Pretoria News and Printing Works, 1936.

Fitzpatrick, Sandra, and Maria Goodwin. *The Guide to Black Washington: Places and Events of Historical and Cultural Significance in the Nation's Capital.* New York: Hippocrene Books, 1990.

Flint, John. *Cecil Rhodes.* Boston: Little, Brown, 1974.

Fluornoy, Beulah. "The Relationship of the AME Church to Its South African Mentors." *Journal of African Studies* 2 (1975–76): 529–45.

Fox, Francis William. *Can South Africa Feed Herself.* 1945.

―――. *Food From the Veld: Edible Wild Plants of Southern Africa.* Johannesburg: Delta Books, 1982.

Fox, Francis William, and D. Back. *A Preliminary Survey of the Agricultural and Nutritional Problems of the Ciskei and Transkei Territories.* Johannesburg: Chamber of Mines, 1938.

Franklin, John Hope. *George Washington Williams: A Biography.* Chicago: University of Chicago Press, 1985.

Fredrickson, George M. *White Supremacy: A Comparative Study in American and South African History.* New York: Oxford University Press, 1981.

Furlong, Patrick J. *Between Crown and Swastika: The Impact of the Radical Right on the Afrikaner Nationalist Movement in the Fascist Era.* Middletown, Conn.: Wesleyan University Press, 1991.

Gailey, Harry. *Sir Donald Cameron: Colonial Governor.* Stanford, Cal.: Hoover Institution Press, 1974.

Gaitskell, Debbie. "Upward All and Play the Game: The Girl Wayfarers' Association in the Transvaal 1925–1975." In *Apartheid and Education: The Education of Black South Africans,* edited by Peter Kallaway, 222–64. Johannesburg: Ravan Press, 1984.

Gatewood, Willard. "Black Americans and the Boer War, 1899–1902." *South Atlantic Quarterly* 75 (2) (1976): 226–44.

Geiss, Imanuel. *The Pan-African Movement: A History of Pan-Africanism in America, Europe, and Africa.* Translated by Ann Keep. New York: Africana Publishing Corp., 1974.

Gerhart, Gail M. *Black Power in South Africa: The Evolution of an Ideology.* Berkeley: University of California Press, 1978.

Goldin, Ian. *Making Race: The Politics and Economics of Coloured Identity in South Africa* (Cape Town: Maskew Miller Longman, 1987.

Grundlingh, Louis. "The Recruitment of South African Blacks for Participation in the Second World War." In *Africa and the Second World War,* edited by David Killingray and Richard Rathbone. New York: St. Martin's Press, 1986.

Halila, Souad. "The Intellectual Development and Diplomatic Career of Ralph J. Bunche." Ph.D. dissertation, University of Southern California, 1988.

"Hamba Kahle, Canon Calata." *Sechaba* (April 1983): 30–32.

Harinck, Gerrit. "Interaction between Xhosa and Khoi: emphasis on the Period 1620–1750." In *African Societies in Southern Africa,* edited by Leonard Thompson, 145–70. New York: Praeger, 1969.

Harlan, Louis. "Booker T. Washington and the National Negro Business League." In *Seven on Black: Reflections on the Negro Experience in America,* edited by William Shade and C. Herrenkohl, 73–91. Philadelphia: Lippincott, 1969.

Harris, Abram Lincoln. *The Negro as Capitalist: A Study of Banking and Business among American Negroes.* College Park, Md.: McGrath Publishing Co., 1936.

Harris, Joseph. "Race and Misperception in the Origins of United States-Ethiopian Relations." *TransAfrica Forum* 3 (Winter 1986): 9–23.

Harris, Leonard, ed. *The Philosophy of Alain Locke: Harlem Renaissance and Beyond.* Philadelphia: Temple University Press, 1989.

Harris, Robert. "Ralph Bunche and Afro-American Participation in Decolonization." In *Pan-African Biography,* edited by Robert Hill, 119–36. Los Angeles: Crossroads Press, 1987.

———. "Segregation and Scholarship: The American Council of Learned Societies' Committee on Negro Studies, 1941–1950." *Journal of Black Studies* 12 (March 1982): 315–31.

Haskins, James. *Ralph Bunche: A Most Reluctant Hero.* New York: Hawthorn Books, 1974.

Haynes, George Edmund. *Africa: Continent of the Future.* New York: Association Press, 1950.

Hellman, Ellen. *Problems of Urban Bantu Youth.* Johannesburg: South African Institute of Race Relations, 1941.

———. *Rooiyard: a Sociological Survey of an Urban Native Slum Yard.* Cape Town: Oxford University Press, 1946.

———, ed. *Handbook on Race Relations in South Africa.* New York: Oxford University Press, 1949.

Henry, Charles P. "Civil Rights and National Security: The Case of Ralph Bunche." In *Ralph Bunche: The Man and His Times,* edited by Benjamin Rivlin. New York: Holmes and Meier, 1990.

Heyman, Richard. "C. T. Loram: A South African Liberal in Race Relations." *The International Journal of African Historical Studies* 5 (1) (1972): 41–50.

Hill, Robert, and Greg Pirio. "'Africa for the Africans': The Garvey Movement in South Africa, 1920–1940." In *The Politics of Race, Class, and Na-*

tionalism in Twentieth-Century South Africa, edited by Shula Marks and Stanley Trapido, 209–53. London: Longman, 1987.

Hirson, Baruch. *Yours for the Union: Class and Community Struggles in South Africa, 1930–1947.* London: Zed Books, 1989.

Hodgson, Janet. "A History of Zonnebloem College, 1858–1870." 2 vols. Master's thesis, University of Cape Town, 1975.

Huggins, Nathan. "Black Biography: Reflections of a Historian," *CAAS Newsletter* 9 (1) (1985): 1, 6–7.

———. "Ralph Bunche the Africanist." In *Ralph Bunche: The Man and His Times,* edited by Benjamin Rivlin, 69–82. New York: Holmes and Meier, 1990.

———. "Uses of the Self: Afro-American Autobiography." In *Historical Judgments Reconsidered,* edited by Genna Rae McNeil and Michael Winston, 171–80. Washington, D.C.: Howard University Press, 1988.

Humphriss, D., and D. G. Thomas. *Benoni, Son of My Sorrow: The Social, Political and Economic History of a South African Gold Mining Town.* Benoni: Benoni Town Council, 1968.

Huttenback, Robert A. *Gandhi in South Africa: British Imperialism and the Indian Question, 1860–1914.* Ithaca: Cornell University Press, 1971.

Hyam, Ronald. *The Failure of South African Expansion, 1908–1948.* New York: Africana Publishing, 1972.

Jabavu, D. D. T. *E-Amerika U-welo Luka.* Lovedale: Lovedale Press, 1932.

Jackson, Walter A. *Gunnar Myrdal and America's Conscience: Social Engineering and Racial Liberalism, 1938–1987.* Chapel Hill: University of North Carolina Press, 1990.

———. "The Making of a Social Science Classic: Gunnar Myrdal's *An American Dilemma.*" *Perspectives in American History,* n.s. , 2 (1985): 221–49.

———. "Melville Herskovits and the Search for Afro-American Culture." In *Malinowski, Rivers, Benedict, and Others: Essays on Culture and Personality,* edited by George W. Stocking, Jr. Madison: University of Wisconsin Press, 1986.

Jeeves, Alan. *Migrant Labour in South Africa's Mining Economy: The Struggle for the Gold Mines' Labour Supply, 1890–1920.* Kingston, Ont.: McGill-Queen's University Press, 1985.

Jochelson, Karen, "Tracking Down the Treponema: Patterns of Syphilis in South Africa, 1880–1940." Paper presented at History Workshop, Witwatersrand University, 6–10 February 1990.

Johns, Sheridan. "The Comintern, South Africa and the Black Diaspora." *Review of Politics* 37 (2) (1975): 200–34.

Johnson, Ann D. *The Value of Responsibility: The Story of Ralph Bunche.* La Jolla, Cal.: Value Communications, 1978.

Kadalie, Clements. *My Life and the ICU.* New York: Humanities Press, 1970.

Karis, Thomas and Gwendolyn M. Carter. *From Protest to Challenge: A Documentary History of African Politics in South Africa, 1882–1964.* Vol. 2. Stanford, Cal.: Hoover Institution Press, 1973.

Keegan, Timothy J. *Rural Transformations in Industrializing South Africa: The Southern Highveld to 1914.* London: Macmillan, 1987.

———. "Trade, Accumulation and Impoverishment: Mercantile Capital and the Economic Transformation of Lesotho and the Conquered Territory." *Journal of Southern African Studies* 12 (2) (1986): 196–216.

Kennedy, Stetson. *Jim Crow Guide to the U.S.A.: The Laws, Customs and Etiquette Governing the Conduct of the Nonwhites and other Minorities as Second-Class Citizens.* Westport, Conn. : Greenwood Press, 1973.

Kerr, Alexander. *Fort Hare, 1915–48: The Evolution of an African College.* New York: Humanities Press, 1968.

Keto, Clement. "Black Americans and South Africa, 1890–1910." *Current Bibliography of African Affairs* 5 (1972): 483–506.

Kilson, Martin. "Ralph Bunche's Analytical Perspective on African Development." In *Ralph Bunche: The Man and His Times,* edited by Benjamin Rivlin, 83–95. New York: Holmes and Meier, 1990.

Kimball, Judy. "'Clinging to the Chiefs': Some Contradictions of Colonial Rule in Basutoland, c. 1890–1930." In *Contradictions of Accumulation in Africa: Studies in Economy and State,* edited by Henry Bernstein and Bonnie Campbell, 25–70. Beverly Hills: Sage Publications, 1985.

Kirby, John B. *Black Americans in the Roosevelt Era: Liberalism and Race.* Knoxville: University of Tennessee Press, 1980.

———. "Ralph J. Bunche and Black Radical Thought in the 1930s." *Phylon* 35 (2) (1974): 129–42.

Kruger, Bernhard. *The Pear Tree Blossoms: A History of the Moravian Mission Stations in South Africa, 1737–1869.* Genadendal: Moravian Book Depot, 1966.

Kugelmass, J. Alvin. *Ralph J. Bunche: Fighter for Peace.* New York: J. Messner, 1962.

Kuper, Adam. *Anthropologists and Anthropology: The British School, 1922–1972.* New York: Pica Press, 1973.

Kuper, Hilda. "Function, History, Biography: Reflections on Fifty Years in the British Anthropology Tradition." In *Functionalism Historicized: Essays on British Social Anthropology,* edited by George W. Stocking, Jr., 192–213. Madison: University of Wisconsin Press, 1984.

Kuzwayo, Ellen. *Call Me Woman.* Johannesburg: Ravan Press, 1985.

La Hausse, Paul. "'The Cows of Nongoloza': Youth, Crime and Amalaita Gangs in Durban 1900–1936." *Journal of Southern African Studies,* 16 (1) (1990): 79–111.

———. "The Struggle for the City: Alcohol, the Ematsheni and Popular Culture in Durban, 1902–1936." Master's thesis, University of Cape Town, 1984.

Langley, J. A. *Pan-Africanism and Nationalism in West Africa, 1900–1945: A Study in Ideology and Social Classes.* Oxford: Clarendon Press, 1973.

Lean, Garth. *Frank Buchman: A Life.* London: Constable, 1985.

Legassick, Martin. *Class and Nationalism in South African Protest.* Syracuse: Program of Eastern African Studies, 1973.

Legassick, Martin, and Francine de Clerq. "Capitalism and Migrant Labour in Southern Africa: The Origins and Nature of the System." In *International Labour Migration: Historical Perspectives,* edited by Shula Marks and Peter Richardson, 141–65. Hounslow, Middlesex: M. Temple Smith, 1984.

Lewin, Julius. *Africans and the Police.* Johannesburg: South African Institute of Race Relations, 1944.

_____. _Politics and Law in South Africa: Essays on Race Relations._ New York: Monthly Review Press, 1963.

_____. _Studies in African Native Law._ Philadelphia: University of Pennsylvania Press, 1947.

_____, ed. _The Struggle for Racial Equality._ London: Longman, 1967.

Lewis, David L. _When Harlem Was in Vogue._ New York: Alfred A. Knopf, 1981.

Lewis, Ethelreda. _Wild Deer._ Cape Town: David Philip, 1984.

Lewis, Gavin. _Between the Wire and the Wall: A History of South African "Coloured" Politics._ New York: St. Martin's Press, 1987.

Lewis, Jon. _Industrialisation and Trade Union Organisation in South Africa, 1924–55._ New York: Cambridge University Press, 1984.

Linnemann, Russell J., ed. _Alain Locke: Reflections on a Modern Renaissance Man._ Baton Rouge: Louisiana State University Press, 1982.

Locke, Alain. _The New Negro._ New York: A. and C. Boni, 1925.

Lockhart, J. G., and C. M. Woodhouse. _Cecil Rhodes: The Colossus of Southern Africa._ New York: Macmillan, 1963.

Lodge, Tom. _Black Politics in South Africa since 1945._ London: Longman, 1983.

Lynch, Hollis Ralph. _Black American Radicals and the Liberation of Africa: The Council on African Affairs, 1937–1955._ Cornell University, Africana Studies and Research Center Monograph Series no. 5, 1978.

Machobane, L. L. B. J. _Government and Change in Lesotho, 1800–1966: A Study of Political Institutions._ New York: St. Martin's Press, 1990.

McKissack, Patricia. _Ralph J. Bunche._ Hillside, N.J.: Enslow Publishers, 1991.

McVicar, Neil. "Tuberculosis among the South African Natives." _South African Medical Journal_ 6 (1908).

Mandy, Nigel. _A City Divided: Johannesburg and Soweto._ New York: St. Martin's Press, 1984.

Mann, Peggy. _Ralph Bunche, UN Peacemaker._ New York: Coward, McCann and Geoghegan, 1975.

Manning, Kenneth R. _Black Apollo of Science: The Life of Ernest Everett Just._ New York: Oxford University Press, 1983.

Manuel, George, and Denis Hatfield. _District Six._ Illustrated by Bruce Franck. Cape Town: Longman, 1967.

Marable, Manning. "John L. Dube and the Politics of Segregated Education in South Africa." In _Independence without Freedom: The Political Economy of Colonial Education in Southern Africa,_ edited by Agripah Mugomba and Mougo Nyaggah, 113–28. Santa Barbara, Ca.: ABC-Clio, 1980.

Marks, Shula. _The Ambiguities of Dependence in South Africa: Class, Nationalism, and the State in Twentieth-Century Natal._ Baltimore: Johns Hopkins Press, 1986.

Marquard, Leopold [Burger, John]. _The Black Man's Burden._ London: Victor Gollancz, 1943.

_____. _The Peoples and Policies of South Africa._ London: Oxford University Press, 1952.

Mattera, Don. _Memory Is the Weapon._ Johannesburg: Ravan Press, 1987.

Matthews, Z. K. _Freedom for My People: The Autobiography of Z. K. Matthews._ Cape Town: David Philip, 1981.

Maylam, Paul. _A History of the African People of South Africa: From the Early Iron Age to the 1970s._ Cape Town: David Philip, 1986.

————. "The Rise and Decline of Urban Apartheid in South Africa." *African Affairs* 89 (354) (1990): 57–84.

Mbeki, Govan. *South Africa: The Peasants' Revolt.* Baltimore: Penguin Books, 1964.

Meli, Francis. *South Africa Belongs to Us: A History of the ANC.* Bloomington: Indiana University Press, 1989.

Mergen, Bernard. "The Pullman Porter: From 'George' to Brotherhood." *South Atlantic Quarterly* 73 (2) (1974): 224–35.

Mesthrie, Uma. "From Sastri to Desmukh: A Study of the Role of the Government of India's Representatives in South Africa, 1927–1946." Ph.D. dissertation, University of Natal, 1986.

Mohapeloa, Dan. *Letlole la Lithoko tsa Sesotho.* Johannesburg: Afrikaanse Pers-Boekhandel, 1950.

Mokgatle, Naboth. *The Autobiography of an Unknown South African.* Berkeley: University of California Press, 1971.

Molema, S. M. *Bantu Past and Present: An Ethnographical and Historical Study of the Native Races of South Africa.* Edinburgh: W. Green and Son, 1920.

————. *Chief Moroka: His Life, His Times, His Country and His People.* Cape Town: Methodist Publishing House, 1951.

————. *Montshiwa 1815–1896: Barolong Chief and Patriot.* Cape Town: C. Struik, 1966.

Moyer, Richard. "A History of the Mfengu of the Eastern Cape, 1815–1865." Ph.D. dissertation, University of London, 1976.

Mphahlele, Ezekiel. *Down Second Avenue.* London: Faber and Faber, 1959.

Mqotsi, L. and N. Mkele. "A Separatist Church: Ibandla Lika-Krestu." *African Studies* 5 (2) (1946): 106–25.

Murray, Bruce. "Wits as an 'Open' University 1939–1959: Black Admissions to the University of Witwatersrand." *Journal of Southern African Studies* 16 (4) (1990): 649–77.

Murray, Colin. *Black Mountain: Land, Power and Class in the Eastern Orange Free State, 1880s to 1980s.* Edinburgh: Edinburgh University Press, 1991.

————. "From Granary to Labour Reserve." *South African Labour Bulletin* 6 (4) (1980): 3–20.

————. "Land, Power and Class in the Thaba 'Nchu District, Orange Free State, 1884–1983." *Review of African Political Economy* 29 (1984): 30–48.

Murray-Brown, Jeremy. *Kenyatta.* London: Fontana/Collins, 1972.

Musson, Doreen. *Johnny Gomas, Voice of the Working Class: A Political Biography.* Cape Town: Buchu Books, 1989.

Naison, Mark. *Communists in Harlem during the Depression.* Urbana: University of Illinois Press, 1983.

Nasson, Bill. " 'She Preferred Living in a Cave with Harry the Snake-catcher': Towards an Oral History of Popular Leisure and Class Expression in District Six, Cape Town c. 1920–1950." In *Holding Their Ground: Class, Locality and Culture in 19th and 20th Century South Africa,* edited by Philip Bonner et al., 286–94. Johannesburg: Ravan Press, 1989.

Nhlapo, J. M. *Wilberforce Institute.* 1949.

Nicholls, G. Heaton. *Bayete: "Hail to the King!".* London: Allen and Unwin, 1923.

_____. *South Africa in My Time.* London: Allen and Unwin, 1961.

Noer, Thomas J. *Briton, Boer, and Yankee: The United States and South Africa, 1870–1914.* Kent, Ohio: Kent State University Press, 1978.

Nxumalo, Henry. "He was Always First." *Drum* (August 1955): 39.

Pachai, Bridglal. *The International Aspects of the South African Indian Question, 1860–1941.* Cape Town: C. Struik, 1971.

Packard, Randall. "Industrialization, Rural Poverty and Tuberculosis in Southern Africa, 1850–1960." In *Health and Society in Africa: A Working Bibliography,* edited by Steven Feierman and J. Janzen. Waltham, Mass.: Crossroads Press, 1979.

_____. "Tuberculosis and the Development of Industrial Health Policies on the Witwatersrand, 1902–1932." *Journal of Southern African Studies* 13 (2) (1987): 187–209.

_____. *White Plague, Black Labor: Tuberculosis and the Political Economy of Health and Disease in South Africa.* Berkeley: University of California Press, 1989.

Page, Carol. "Black America in White South Africa: Church and State Reaction to the A.M.E. Church in Cape Colony and Transvaal, 1896–1910." Ph.D. dissertation, Edinburgh University, 1978.

"Pages from History: John Langalibalele Dube." *Sechaba* (January 1982): 18–23.

Paton, Alan. *South African Tragedy: The Life and Times of Jan Hofmeyr.* New York: Scribner, 1965.

Patterson, Sheila. *Colour and Culture in South Africa: A Study of the Status of the Cape Coloured People within the Social Structure of the Union of South Africa.* London: Routledge and Paul, 1953.

Perham, Margery Freda. *African Apprenticeship: An Autobiographical Journey in Southern Africa, 1929.* New York: Africana Publishing Co. , 1974.

_____. *Native Administration in Nigeria.* New York: Oxford University Press, 1937.

Perham, Margery Freda, and Lionel Curtis. *The Protectorates of South Africa: The Question of their Transfer to the Union.* London: Oxford University Press, 1935.

Perlman, Daniel J. "Stirring the White Conscience: The Life of George Edmund Haynes." Ph.D. dissertation, New York University, 1972.

Peteni, R. L. *Towards Tomorrow: The Story of the African Teachers' Associations of South Africa.* Algonac, Mich.: Reference Publications, 1979.

Phillips, Ray E. *The Bantu Are Coming: Phases of South Africa's Race Problem.* London: Student Christian Movement Press, 1930.

_____. *The Bantu in the City: A Study of Cultural Adjustment on the Witwatersrand.* Lovedale: Lovedale Press, 1938.

Pinnock, Don. *The Brotherhoods: Street Gangs and State Control in Cape Town.* Cape Town: David Philip, 1984.

Plaatje, Solomon T. *Native Life in South Africa: Before and Since the European War and the Boer Rebellion.* London: P. S. King and Son, 1916.

Proctor, Andre. "Class Struggle, Segregation and the City: A History of Sophiatown, 1905–1940." In *Labour, Townships and Protest: Studies in the Social History of the Witwatersrand,* edited by Belinda Bozzoli. Johannesburg: Ravan Press, 1979.

Ralston, Richard. "American Episodes in the Making of an African Leader: A

Case Study of Alfred B. Xuma." *International Journal of African Historical Studies* 6 (1) (1973): 72–93.

Rich, Paul. *White Power and the Liberal Conscience: Racial Segregation and South African Liberalism, 1921–1960.* Johannesburg: Ravan Press, 1984.

Rivlin, Benjamin, ed. *Ralph Bunche: The Man and His Times.* New York: Holmes and Meier, 1990.

Robertson, H. C. "150 Years of Economic Contact between Black and White: a Preliminary Survey." *South African Journal of Economics* 2 (December 1934): 403–25 and 3 (March 1935): 3–25.

————. *South Africa: Economic and Political Aspects.* Durham: Duke University Press, 1957.

Robeson, Eslanda Goode. *African Journey.* Westport, Conn.: Greenwood Press, 1972.

Rotberg, Robert I. *The Founder: Cecil Rhodes and the Pursuit of Power.* New York: Oxford University Press, 1988.

Roux, Edward, and Win Roux. *Rebel Pity: The Life of Eddie Roux.* London: Rex Collings, 1970.

————. *S. P. Bunting: A Political Biography.* Cape Town: African Bookman, 1944.

————. *Time Longer than Rope: A History of the Black Man's Struggle for Freedom in South Africa.* Madison: University of Wisconsin Press, 1964.

Sachs, E. S. *The Anatomy of Apartheid.* London: Collet's, 1965.

————. *The Choice before South Africa.* London: Turnstile Press, 1952.

————. *Rebels Daughters.* London: MacGibbon and Kee, 1957.

Sachs, E. S., and Lionel Forman. *The South African Treason Trial.* New York: Monthly Review Press, 1958.

Sachs, Wulf. *Black Anger.* Boston: Little, Brown and Co., 1947.

————. *Black Hamlet: The Mind of an African Negro Revealed by Psychoanalysis.* London: G. Bles, 1937.

Sanders, Peter. *Moshoeshoe: Chief of the Sotho.* London: Heinemann, 1975.

Sannyasi, B. D. *Abdulla Ismail Kajee.* Ajmer, India: Pravasi Bhawan, 1941.

Santino, Jack. *Miles of Smiles, Years of Struggle: Stories of Black Pullman Porters.* Urbana: University of Illinois Press, 1989.

Saron, Gustav. *Morris Alexander, Parliamentarian and Jewish Leader.* Johannesburg: South African Jewish Board of Deputies, 1966.

Schapera, Isaac. *Married Life in an African Tribe.* New York: Sheridan House, 1940.

————. *Migrant Labour and Tribal Life: A Study of Conditions in the Bechuanaland Protectorate.* London: Oxford University Press, 1947.

————. *Tribal Innovators: Tswana Chiefs and Social Change, 1795–1940.* New York: Humanities Press, 1970.

Scher, David. *Donald Molteno: "Dilizintaba," He-Who-Removes-Mountains.* Johannesburg: South African Institute of Race Relations, 1979.

Scott, William R. *The Sons of Sheba's Race: African-Americans and the Italo-Ethiopian War, 1935–1941.* Bloomington: Indiana University Press, forthcoming.

Selwyn, Bridget. "A Survey of the Role of White Traders in Lesotho from the Times of Moshoeshoe to the 1950s." B.A. Thesis, National University of Lesotho, 1980.

Shack, William. "Ethiopia and Afro-Americans: Some Historical Notes, 1920–1970." *Phylon* 35: 142–55.

Shepherd, Robert H. W. *Lovedale, South Africa, 1824–1955*. Alice: Lovedale Press, 1940.

———. *A South African Medical Pioneer: The Life of Neil McVicar*. Alice: Lovedale Press, 1952.

Simons, H. J. *African Women: Their Legal Status in South Africa*. Evanston: Northwestern University Press, 1968.

Simons, H. J. and R. E. Simons. *Class and Colour in South Africa, 1850–1950*. Harmondsworth: Penguin, 1969.

Simons, Mary. "Organised Coloured Political Movements." In *Occupational and Social Change among Coloured People in South Africa*, edited by Hendrik Van der Merwe and C. J. Groenewald, 202–37. Cape Town: Juta Co., 1976.

Soga, John Henderson. *The Ama-Xosa: Life and Customs*. Lovedale: Lovedale Press, 1932.

Solomon, Mark. "Black Critics of Colonialism and the Cold War." In *Cold War Critics: Alternatives to American Foreign Policy in the Truman Years*, edited by Thomas G. Paterson, 205–39. Chicago: Quadrangle Books, 1971.

Southall, Roger J. *South Africa's Transkei: The Political Economy of an 'Independent' Bantustan*. New York: Monthly Review Press, 1982.

Southern, David. *Gunnar Myrdal and Black-White Relations: The Use and Abuse of An American Dilemma, 1944–1969*. Baton Rouge: Louisiana State University Press, 1987.

Spiegel, Andrew, and Emile Boonzaier. "Promoting Tradition: Images of the South African Past." In *South African Keywords: The Uses and Abuses of Political Concepts*, edited by Emile Boonzaier and John Sharp, 40–57. Cape Town: David Philip, 1988.

Stanfield, John H. *Philanthropy and Jim Crow in American Social Science*. Westport, Conn.: Greenwood Press, 1985.

Stein, Pippa, and Ruth Jacobsen, eds. *Sophiatown Speaks*. Johannesburg: Junction Avenue Press, 1986.

Sundkler, Bengt. *Zulu Zion and Some Swazi Zionists*. London: Oxford University Press, 1976.

Swan, Maureen. *Gandhi: The South African Experience*. Johannesburg: Ravan Press, 1985.

———. "Ideology in Organised Indian Politics, 1891–1948." In *The Politics of Race, Class and Nationalism in Twentieth-Century South Africa*, edited by Shula Marks and Stanley Trapido, 182–208. London: Longman, 1987.

———. "The 1913 Natal Indian Strike." *Journal of Southern African Studies* 10 (2) (1984): 245–69.

Swanson, M. W. "The Sanitary Syndrome: Bubonic Plague and Urban Native Policy in the Cape." *Journal of African History* 18 (3) (1977): 387–410.

Switzer, Les. "The African Christian Community and its Press in Victorian South Africa." *Cahiers d'etudes africaines* 24 (96) (1984): 455–76.

———. "The Ambiguities of Protest in South Africa: Rural Politics and the Press during the 1920's." *International Journal of African Historical Studies* 23 (1) (1990): 87–108.

———. "*Bantu World* and the Origins of a Captive African Commercial Press in South Africa." *Journal of Southern African Studies* 14 (April 1988): 351–70.

Tatz, C. M. *Shadow and Substance in South Africa: A Study in Land and Franchise Policies Affecting Africans, 1910–1960.* Pietermaritzburg: University of Natal Press, 1962.

Thompson, Leonard. *The Political Mythology of Apartheid.* New Haven: Yale University Press, 1985.

———. *Survival in Two Worlds: Moshoeshoe of Lesotho, 1786–1870.* Oxford: Clarendon Press, 1975.

Torr, Anne Louise. "The Social History of an Urban African Community, ca. 1930–1960." Master's thesis, University of Natal, Durban, 1985.

Tortolano, William. *Samuel Coleridge-Taylor: Anglo-Black Composer, 1875–1912.* Metuchen, N.J.: Scarecrow Press, 1977.

Unterhalter, Beryl. "Changing Attitudes to 'Passing for White' in an Urban Coloured Community." *Social Dynamics* 1 (1) (1975): 53–62.

Van der Ross, Richard. *The Founding of the African People's Organization in Cape Town in 1903 and the Role of Dr. Abdurahman.* Pasadena: Munger Africana Library, 1975.

———. *The Rise and Decline of Apartheid: A Study of Political Movements among the Coloured People of South Africa, 1880–1985.* Cape Town: Tafelberg, 1986.

Van Onselen, Charles. *New Babylon New Ninevah: Studies in the Social and Economic History of the Witwatersrand.* 2 vols. London: Longman, 1982.

Vatcher, William Henry. *White Laager: The Rise of Afrikaner Nationalism.* New York: Praeger, 1965.

Wade, Wyn Craig. *The Fiery Cross: The Ku Klux Klan in America.* New York: Simon and Schuster, 1987.

Walshe, A. P. "Black American Thought and African Political Attitudes in South Africa." *Review of Politics* 32 (1970): 51–77.

———. *The Rise of African Nationalism in South Africa: The African National Congress, 1912–1952.* Berkeley: University of California Press, 1971.

Walton, James. *Father of Kindness and Father of Horses: Ramosa le Ralipere; the Story of Frasers Ltd.* Wepener, 1958.

Watson, Graham. *Passing for White: A Study of Racial Assimilation in a South African School.* New York: Tavistock Publications, 1970.

Webb, Lillian A. *About My Father's Business: The Life of Elder Michaux.* Westport, Conn.: Greenwood Press, 1981.

Webb, Maurice. In *Quest of South Africa.* Johannesburg: South African Institute of Race Relations, 1945.

———. *Race Relations East and West.* Johannesburg: South African Institute of Race Relations, 1953.

Webb, Maurice, and Kenneth Kirkwood. *The Durban Riots and After.* Johannesburg: South African Institute of Race Relations, 1949.

Weisbrot, Robert. *Father Divine and the Struggle for Racial Equality.* Urbana: University of Illinois Press, 1983.

White, Amos, and Luella White. *Southern Africa, Dawn in Bantuland: An African Experiment.* Boston: Christopher Publishing House, 1953.

Whitehouse, J. B. *History of Benoni.* Benoni: Benoni Town Council, 1939.

Wickins, P. L. *The Industrial and Commercial Workers' Union of Africa.* New York: Oxford University Press, 1978.

Willan, Brian. *Sol Plaatje: South African Nationalist, 1870–1932.* Berkeley: University of California Press, 1984.

William, Juan, "Once upon a Time, 14th and U was the Center of Black Culture in Washington, D.C. Can It Become That Again?" *Washington Post Sunday Magazine,* 21 February 1988.

Williamson, Joel. *New People: Miscegenation and Mulattoes in the United States.* New York: Free Press, 1980.

Wilson, Monica, and Archie Mafeje. *Langa: A Study of Social Groups in an African Township.* Cape Town: Oxford University Press, 1963.

Wilson, Monica, and Leonard Thompson, eds. *Oxford History of South Africa.* Vol. 2. New York: Oxford University Press, 1971.

Winston, Michael. "Through the Back Door: Academic Racism and the Negro Scholar in Historical Perspective." *Daedalus* 100 (1971): 679–719.

Wittner, Lawrence. "The National Negro Congress: A Reassessment." *American Quarterly* 22 (Winter 1970): 883–901.

Wolters, Raymond. *Negroes and the Great Depression: The Problem of Economic Recovery.* Westport, Conn. : Greenwood Publishing Corp., 1970.

Woodward, C. Vann. *The Strange Career of Jim Crow.* New York: Oxford University Press, 1957.

Wright, Charlotte Crogman. *Beneath the Southern Cross: The Story of an American Bishop's Wife in South Africa.* New York: Exposition Press, 1955.

Wright, R. R. "South Africa Has Its Own Color Lines." *Opportunity* (May 1939): 138–41.

————. "Wilberforce in South Africa." *Opportunity* (October 1937): 306–10.

Xuma, Alfred. "Dr. Rosebery Bokwe." *Drum* (August 1954).

Yekela, Drusilla Sizwe. "The Life and Times of Kama Chungwa, 1798–1875." Master's thesis, Rhodes University, 1989.

Yergan, Max. *Gold and Poverty in South Africa: A Study of Economic Organization and Standards of Living.* New York: International Industrial Relations Institute, 1938.

Yergan, Susie Wiseman. "Africa—Our Challenge." *Crisis* (June 1930): 193–95, 212–13.

Young, James O. *Black Writers of the Thirties.* Baton Rouge: Louisiana State University Press, 1973.

Zierfogel, C. *Brown South Africa.* Cape Town: M. Miller, 1938.

————. *The Coloured People and the Race Problem.* Ceres: Weber, 1936.

————. *Who Are the Coloured People?* Cape Town: African Bookman, 1944.

Index

391 Index

Moravian mission, 87
Moroka II, Chief, 146, 150–51, 346–47
Moroka, Dr. James, 22, 127, 137, 143,
    145–46, 148–57, 170, 340, 345
Moroka, John P., 146, 346
Moroka Mission Institution, 148–49
Mosaka, Paul, 143, 146, 148, 153–54, 345
Moshoeshoe, Chief, 107–08, 117, 150,
    336–37, 346–47
'Mote, Keable, 267, 363
Moton, Robert, 24
Motsieloa, Griffiths, 354
Moudell, Mr., 114
Mount Nelson Hotel, 14
Mowbray, 55, 67
Mpondo, 298, 358, 368
Mshiyeni, A. E., 230–31, 358
Msimang, Selby, 69, 257, 260, 266, 328,
    351
M'timkulu, Abner, 295, 368
M'timkulu, Donald, 14, 22, 38, 39–40,
    127, 295, 298, 304, 307, 309–10, 340
Murray, A. C., 18
music and entertainment, 75, 165–66,
    174–75, 180, 186–87, 190–92, 198,
    200–01, 207, 212–13, 216, 218,
    254–55, 350, 354
Muslims, 28, 82–83, 96, 251, 303, 307, 323,
    331, 367
Myrdal, Gunnar, 23, 315

Naidoo, Mr., 307
Naransamy, , 192
Natal, 152, 193, 195–96, 229, 260,
    287–310, 366–70
Natal Indian Congress, 219, 307, 367–68
Natal University, 302
National Association for the
    Advancement of Colored People
    (NAACP), 7–9, 316
National Baptist Convention, 3
National Council of Women, 278, 366
National Council of African Women,
    266, 277–78, 329, 363
National Liberation League (NLL), 60,
    65, 89, 264, 320–21, 324–25, 327, 334,
    347, 367
National Negro Congress (NNC), 8, 36,
    315, 338
National Party, 93, 200, 323, 326, 333,
    343–44, 353, 355, 367
Nationalist Party, 27, 353
National Urban League, 7

Native Recruiting Corporation, 176, 337,
    341, 350–51
Native Representative Council, 29–33,
    132, 179, 189, 229–37, 257, 259–60,
    264, 268, 272, 275–76, 295, 307, 340,
    342, 345, 357–60, 364
Native Representatives, 30, 32, 33,
    131–34, 189, 231, 234–36, 259–62,
    264–5, 268–9, 274
Native Republic, 72, 211, 330
Naauwpoort, 121–22
ndunduma, 216, 218
Nederduitse Gereformeerde Kerk, 332
Nederduitse Gereformeerde
    Sendingkerk, 332
Negro Business League, 276–77, 332, 365
Neugebauer, Frieda, 14
New Deal, 7, 10, 316
New Era Fellowship, 320, 331
New York City, 6, 129, 315
Nhlapo, Jacob, 144, 154, 345–46
Nicholls, Heaton, 232–34, 359
Nikiwe, Mrs., 277
Nkosi Sikelel'i Afrika, 111, 149, 233, 282,
    346
Nobel peace prize, 1, 317
Northwestern University, 11–12, 314
Norwich, Dr., 94
Notcutt, Bernard, 302, 305–06, 310, 369
Nyasaland, 91
Nyman, Ernest, 76, 331

Office of Strategic Studies (OSS), 317
Ohlange Institute, 3, 340–41
Oliphant, Stephen, 281, 366
Orange Free State, 24, 104, 110–11, 119,
    146, 151–52, 194, 267, 273, 275, 299,
    309, 317, 329, 335, 337, 345–47, 369
Orient Club, 303
Orlando Bantu Musical Association,
    212–13
Owens, Jesse, 20, 23, 39, 136, 345

Padmore, George, 14–15
Pan Africanism, 14–15, 38
Pan Africanist Congress, 327, 361
passes, 56, 58, 69, 113, 173–74, 188,
    193–94, 199, 204, 207, 249, 262, 323
passing 29, 58, 63–64, 81–82, 88, 92,
    94–96, 169, 193, 264–65, 291, 323
Pathfinders, 259, 353, 363
Paver, R. F., 176, 322
peco, 156

A Note About the Author

Robert R. Edgar is Associate Professor of African Studies at Howard University. He has also taught at Georgetown University and the University of Virginia and, as a Fulbright lecturer, at the National University of Lesotho. His publications include *Prophets With Honour: A Documentary History of Lekhotla la Bafo* (1987), *Because They Chose the Plan of God: The Story of the Bullhoek Massacre* (1988), and *Sanctioning Apartheid* (1990). He is currently researching African political movements in South Africa in the 1930s and 1940s.